6 October 1972, general conference. Elder Bruce R. McConkie stands with
members of the Council of Twelve in solemn assembly, during which he was sustained one of the Twelve.

BRUCE R. McCONKIE

HIGHLIGHTS
from his
LIFE
and
TEACHINGS

BRUCE R. McCONKIE

HIGHLIGHTS
from his
LIFE
and
TEACHINGS

Dennis B. Horne

2000

Eborn Books

Roy, Utah

First Edition, August 2000

Library of Congress Catalog Card Number: 00-105813

ISBN 1-890718-01-7

Eborn Books
Box 559
Roy, Utah, 84067
ebornbk@doitnow.com
www.ebornbooks.com

Printed in the United States of America

To those who love true doctrine.

Contents

SECTION TWO

Preface

Elder Bruce R. McConkie was one of the most remarkable individuals ever to serve in the kingdom of God in this dispensation

For years I had quietly hoped that someone would write a biography of Elder Bruce Redd McConkie, for whom I have felt a great admiration and special affinity. One day as I pondered the fact that one had not been written, the thought came to me that I might make the attempt. I examined my files and found that I had already collected an abundance of information on his life. It seemed a promising start.

Then followed many pleasant and fulfilling hours researching and organizing information into a rough manuscript. It has been a labor of love and profound learning.

Though the title of this book speaks of a portrayal of life and teachings of Elder Bruce R. McConkie—and that is fundamentally what it is—it should be understood that a fair and honest record of his life and teachings is larger than can be embraced by a single volume. Nor can this author, or perhaps any other, capture the unusual dynamics of such a man. I believe, as was properly observed by Elder McConkie's close friend and fellow General Authority Elder S. Dilworth Young, that, "No man can be portrayed accurately by another."[1] The natural course of events associated with my research for this book dictated an emphasis on his public ministry over that of his private life.

An interesting limitation automatically came with this research: Elder McConkie did not keep a journal. His son Joseph Fielding McConkie observed, "Many things he wouldn't have discussed or recorded anyway, because they were too private and spiritual for even family to hear. Dad became a very, very, private man."[2] Despite this intense privacy, from the collected material there has emerged more about Elder McConkie and his spiritual experiences than I could have supposed at the outset.

Without a journal as a primary source, it is nearly impossible to prepare a detailed chronological recounting of Elder McConkie's life. That which is presented here is extracted from sources covering many years, with some precious recorded insights here and there. The story here presented is therefore of necessity incomplete.

Among the treasures found within this book are some choice statements made by Elder McConkie, his family, and his associates. This has helped to lend it an autobiographical flavor, and gives the reader a more accurate understanding of a great man and his work.

Section 2 of this book is a compilation of selected teachings from Elder McConkie, almost all of which are *not* found in previous book publications. Some of his teachings have been used in a limited sense in section 1 to help illuminate his life. Hence the sections are not entirely exclusive, for how could his life be understood without his teachings or his teachings be isolated from his life?

As it happens, Elder McConkie left us his own definition of a biography: "A biography is but the projection through the eyes of a penman of what the writer *believes* were the acts and what he *feels* were the thoughts and emotions of another man who had like feelings with his own."[3]

Only two short chapters are devoted to covering Bruce's life from the time of his birth until his call as a General Authority. One reason for such brevity is that I have had little information available from his early life; another reason is that Bruce was called to be a General Authority at such an early age.

There was little business or professional career to chronicle. Most of his adult life was spent serving as a General Authority. Consequently, the majority of this book centers on his accomplishments in that capacity.

One of the hallmarks of Elder McConkie's great success was his superb self-discipline. Because of such self-mastery, he was able to overcome the world and become a worthy tabernacle for the Spirit of the Lord. His motto was formulated while serving as a mission president: "Seek the Spirit." This seemed to be his goal throughout life. Once a person has been born again and become a new creature by the power of the Holy Ghost, all other good things of life and salvation flow unto him. This he commendably exemplified.

Elder McConkie was probably best known for two things: his mastery of the scriptures and his gospel knowledge. To have one is in large measure to have the other. He was superbly qualified in both. His wife, Amelia, said:

> I know two people who [did these things] from the time they were just boys. They read the scriptures many times over and over, and they loved them. Time and again I have seen them reading from one of the standard works and stop and say, "Now, isn't that interesting. As many times as I have read this, I haven't noticed that before." Then, they would tell you

something that they had learned that was new to them and to us and would be very enlightening and very helpful. I have seen them both pick up the scriptures and open them right to the very passage that they needed or maybe just a few pages one way or the other. They could do this because they had studied them so well that they could just put their finger at about the part in the edges of the pages where the passage was and open it up, and there it would be. Naturally, you know I'm talking about my husband and my father.[4]

This impressive mastery of the scriptures was won through hard work and study. Bruce McConkie constantly studied the scriptures, as is illustrated in a story once told by Truman Madsen, a BYU professor, author, and accomplished gospel scholar himself: "I was so impressed with Bruce's mastery of the scriptures, that I wanted to know how he had done it. So I called his secretary and made an appointment and told her I needed half an hour to ask him how he had mastered the scriptures. So, I got the appointment. I came up, brought my notebook, all ready to hunker down and go to work. I asked, 'How do you master the scriptures?' The answer came very tersely, 'Read them.'"[5]

That was Elder McConkie's secret to success. He read the scriptures diligently all his life. The rewards were plain for all to see, and because of his knowledge of them, he played a major role in preparing the Church's landmark new editions of the standard works.

His son Joseph said: "If there ever was a man on the face of the earth who had good Church discipline, it was Bruce McConkie. He took care of his own stewardship and didn't worry about how others were taking care of theirs. He was incredibly forgiving. Even when he was criticized for his doctrine, which was often, he refused to hold a grudge. He didn't ask for favors. Bruce McConkie ate, drank and slept the gospel of Jesus Christ. Nothing asked was too much."[6]

No one will fully comprehend Bruce R. McConkie by reading this book. The real man was not always the one which we saw at the pulpit—though that was the most familiar manifestation of him. Those who knew him best said that his personality sparkled, with a quick, dry wit and a genuine warmth. They aver that he did not talk much, and he did study quite a bit (though he did not quote scripture in his normal conversation, as he was sometimes accused of doing).[7]

I have long admired and respected Elder McConkie. Many years ago I read a beginning chapter in his book *A New Witness for the Articles of Faith*, which chapter dealt with the Prophet Joseph Smith. It was then that I received a confirming witness of the Spirit that Joseph was indeed a prophet of God.

The Church and the world are better because of the life and teachings of Elder Bruce R. McConkie. It is my earnest desire that this book may help many to better know him. His prominence in the kingdom made him a marked man: one who had the eyes of the public upon him and who was constantly before the membership of the Church. This inescapable reality alone insists that his story be told. I should also make it clear that this book is a result of my own efforts. I alone am responsible for the views and opinions expressed herein. The book is not an official publication of The Church of Jesus Christ of Latter-day Saints or the McConkie family.

A life such as his has sacred rooms we should not enter. He had experiences which he could not relate to others without betraying a sacred trust. His deepest feelings and lofty experiences were not for public consumption. Concerning Elder McConkie, a friend and colleague once observed, "Nothing can interfere with his search to find out about God. Like Nephi of old, his thirst is to receive the vision of his tree of life and to live to pierce the veil himself."[8]

His testimony has been given to the world. Let his critics be silent and stand in reverent awe of a man whose words they cannot comprehend—who has now been in the spirit world for fifteen years, preaching the gospel with apostolic power to those who have yet to hear it.

How precious it is to have men like Elder McConkie to lead and guide the Church. Though he has now passed to another sphere of service, the caravan moves on and others heed the call, receive the keys, and take their places in leading the kingdom forward. The First Presidency and Quorum of the Twelve today continue to lead the Church the way the Lord wants it led. For that assurance I am deeply grateful.

Notes

1. S. Dilworth Young, "Elder Bruce R. McConkie of the Council of the Twelve," *Ensign*, Jan. 1973, p. 11.

2. Sheri L. Dew, "Bruce R. McConkie: A Family Portrait," *This People,* Dec. 85/Jan. 86, p. 52. Hereafter cited as Dew.

3. *The Mortal Messiah*, book 1, p. xvi. Italics added.

4. Amelia S. McConkie, "Aim for the Sun," Salt Lake Institute of Religion Devotional Address, Jan. 17, 1986, pp. 4-5.

5. Story about Truman Madsen related to author by Elder John K. Carmack, who heard the story from Truman Madsen when he gave a lecture in Los Angeles. Cited in a typescript of a taped interview with Elder John K. Carmack, 19 March

1997, p. 4. Quotation has been changed from second to first person by this author.

6. Dew, p. 61.

7. Dew, p. 50.

8. Young, pp. 10-11.

Acknowledgments

I am grateful to have had the privilege of studying and writing about the life of a truly great Apostle. Elder Bruce R. McConkie taught that Joseph Smith was one of the dozen or so greatest men to ever live on the earth in any dispensation. I believe Elder McConkie was one of the dozen or so greatest men to live in *our* dispensation. This thought alone made the project an extraordinary challenge, but one which I loved.

I wish to express gratititude to several people whose help and encouragement was deeply appreciated. My mother and father, Byron and Linda Horne, always showed great interest in the project and became valuable evaluators of ideas. My wife, Celia, was with me the entire way and lent support during the toughest times.

Certain members of the McConkie family read and critiqued the manuscript and seemed pleased with the overall effort. Though I received both compliments and assistance from them, this book has not been commissioned by the McConkie family and they are not responsible for its contents.

Special thanks is due Amelia Smith McConkie (daughter of President Joseph Fielding Smith and wife of Elder McConkie) for allowing me to publish the manuscript and giving permission to use photographs in the Church's possession. My gratitude also goes to F. Briton McConkie (a brother) for encouragement and permission to use certain photographs; and to Joseph Fielding McConkie (a son) for some helpful assistance. Thanks also to Robert J. Matthews for reviewing the chapter on the Scriptures Publications Committee.

Others who were of particular help include Bill Slaughter of the Church's Historical Department; Dan Hogan, an excellent editor; Stephanie Hall, a thorough proofreader; and Bret Eborn, for taking a special personal interest in publishing the book. Bill Moss read the manuscript and gave valuable suggestions about sensitive materials. Elder John K. Carmack of the Seventy consented to what became a very enjoyable and useful interview. Jerry Baker's constructive criticism and thoughtful advice was appreciated.

I owe the most to David H. Garner, my teacher, mentor, and friend. He skillfully edited the rough draft, gave profound counsel about doctrinal and spiritual content, and encouraged me all the way through. Though I alone am responsible for the final product, his help was invaluable. In him we find one of the Lord's finest disciples and an ardent admirer of Elder McConkie. His gracious foreword speaks for itself.

Lastly, I express my deepest gratitude to Elder Bruce R. McConkie. I have benefited more from his teachings than any other man. Upon him rested the Spirit of inspiration, and he taught the gospel of Jesus Christ with power and authority from God. He was a true Apostle and disciple of Christ.

Dennis B. Horne

Foreword

Once in a while, in mortality, walks a man who mingles with his fellows with such an influence for good that they are never quite the same thereafter. Among the ranks of members of The Church of Jesus Christ of Latter-day Saints, Bruce Redd McConkie was such a man. Few have had such an impact in the clarification and understanding of gospel principles for members of the Church, as did this dedicated doctrinarian. His life-long single-mindedness toward scriptural and doctrinal pursuits is legendary. He compiled and wrote more books on doctrinal teachings of the earthly Kingdom of God than any of his peers; including such works as *Doctrines of Salvation* (a collection of sermons and writings of Joseph Fielding Smith), *Mormon Doctrine, Doctrinal New Testament Commentary, The Promised Messiah*, the four-volume set of *The Mortal Messiah, The Millennial Messiah*, and *A New Witness for the Articles of Faith*. These, taken with his numerous other writings and speeches, are a legacy for the worldwide members of the Church.

Elder McConkie's public message was certain, but he never claimed that he spoke for the Lord; rather he was a special witness, and let the Lord speak for Himself. He was so familiar with the recorded words of the Lord that he skillfully wove them into the fabric of his message as part of his own natural expression. Presiding at a stake conference in Rexburg, Idaho in 1955, he spoke for about an hour, with clarity and power. During the early part of his message, President Joseph Fielding Smith of the Quorum of the Twelve came in and took his place on the stand, having just completed his own assignment at a more northern stake conference. Following Elder McConkie's address, President Smith was invited to say a word. As nearly as I can recall he said, "Brothers and Sisters, you have been taught by Brother McConkie for an hour. You may not be aware that nearly every word he has spoken was quoted from the scriptures, by memory. I have followed him in my scriptures as he spoke."

The scriptural language of the Lord became his own. He was personally acquainted with it. When he determined to know what the

Lord said on a subject, it was frequently his practice to study the standard works of the Church with that particular doctrine in mind, taking copius notes, only to repeat the process again for a different doctrine or principle.

Those who knew him best respected the power and brilliance of his mind, were attracted to his tender and loving nature, and appreciated his quick and ready wit. Like his father-in-law, Joseph Fielding Smith, Elder McConkie's public word was unwavering and clear, and at times was accompanied by rebuke or correction. Such firmness occasionally gave the listener the false impression that he was stern, aloof, and unfeeling. However, like his father-in-law, he was gentle and kind and was ever considerate of the needs and feelings of others, so long as those feelings did not compromise his own standards or those of the Church. His love for the Lord and His holy work came first. Elder McConkie was a private man, but, as is always the case, something of the man is revealed in his work.

This compilation contains a few precious insights into the teachings and nature of Elder Bruce Redd McConkie, Apostle and disciple of the Lord. The thoughtful reader of this work will gain added appreciation for this remarkable servant of the Lord and will rejoice in his messages, some of which are not readily available to the public elsewhere. Such an adventure is ever renewing, for the doctrinal insights of prophets provide a safe beacon for mortals to use in their own quest for understanding the things of God, and inspires them with a glimpse of the heights to which one may rise.

David H. Garner

Section One

Bruce R. McConkie

Highlights From His Life

Oscar W. McConkie.

Chapter One

A Noble Father

Oscar W. McConkie's ancestors originated in Scotland, emigrating to America around the time of the Revolutionary War. They pursued such vocations as teacher, doctor, lawyer, and minister; a heritage that has continued in the family. Oscar's father, George Wilson McConkie, was born in Mansfield, Ohio, 28 October 1846. In 1874, while traveling to California, he stopped in Salt Lake City, where he was taught the gospel and was baptized (2 April). There he remained. Little is known about his first wife, Susan Smith.

George entered into the practice of plural marriage by marrying Emma Sommerville on 7 April 1881 in the Salt Lake Endowment House. She bore him five children, one of which was stillborn. George later married a third wife, but suffered a premature death 9 December 1890. He was survived by all three of his wives. Oscar W., Emma's fifth child, was only three years old when his father passed away.[1]

Oscar was born 9 May 1887 in Moab, Utah.[2] Since his father had died when he was so young, it was naturally his mother who became the dominant influence in his life. When he was a little boy, he asked his mother for something to read. She took a copy of the Book of Mormon down from the shelf and handed it to him. Oscar later recorded that as she did so, "there came over her, when she handed it to me, a glorious feeling that she never forgot, such as to give her all over again a testimony that she had acted wisely and that the book was from the Lord. The Holy Ghost seemed to burn her whole soul as with fire, a fire that soothed and sweetened her mind and body."[3]

While living in Moab, Emma had a sacred experience that taught her the value of service and that had a lasting effect on her family and descendants. Her grandson Bruce told the story in this way:

I shall read to you...from the journal of my father in which he speaks of his mother and of my grandmother. My grandmother, Emma Sommerville McConkie, was a ward Relief Society president in Moab, Utah, many years ago. At the time of this experience, she was a widow. My Father writes this:

Mother was president of the Moab Relief Society. J__ B__ (a nonmember who opposed the Church) had married a Mormon girl. They had several children; now they had a new baby. They were very poor and Mother was going day by day to care for the child and to take them baskets of food, etc. Mother herself was ill, and more than once was hardly able to get home after doing the work at the J__ B__ home.

One day she returned home especially tired and weary. She slept in her chair. She dreamed she was bathing a baby which she discovered was the Christ Child. She thought, Oh, what a great honor to thus serve the very Christ! As she held the baby in her lap, she was all but overcome. She thought, who else has actually held the Christ Child? Unspeakable joy filled her whole being. She was aflame with the glory of the Lord. It seemed that the very marrow in her bones would melt. Her joy was so great it awakened her. As she woke, these words were spoken to her, "Inasmuch as ye have done it unto one of the least of these my brethren, ye have done it unto me."

Now, I think that the Lord first tried her faith. When she had proved worthy by manifesting that charity which never faileth, he gave her a glimpse within the veil.[4]

Many years later, as a young man, Oscar McConkie Jr, (Bruce's brother and another of Oscar's sons), read the above account from his father's journal and rehearsed the story to his father to be sure he understood it, saying, "And my grandmother seemed to hear a voice." When his father heard him use the word *seem* he sat up and said, "She didn't *seem* to hear a voice. *She heard a voice.*"[5]

Emma was a highly refined and spiritual woman who lived righteously and obeyed the commandments. Naturally she raised her son Oscar up to the Lord, teaching him those things he needed to know to fulfill his important mission in life and instilling in him a strong sense of faith. When he grew older, his mother told him that once when he was a baby, he had become very ill and looked as though he might die. He said, "A light gathered over my bed as I lay in the dark corner of the room, and they...took it to be a sign that I would recover and discussed it at the time. All who were there saw it, so they all told me."[6]

As he grew up, Oscar was put to work doing chores. He carried milk (which he once spilled and was promptly spanked by his mother), rode derrick horses, and did odd jobs and janitorial work. He cut and hauled wood for the church building and for widows and missionaries' wives.[7]

In his patriarchal blessing, Oscar was told that he would dream dreams and see visions. A grandson would later write:

> On a number of occasions, it was made known to him in dreams that someone was going to die. On each occasion, he would relate his experience to his mother. The people about whom he dreamed always passed away within three days of the time he had the dream. When he was twenty-one years old, he dreamed that he had a terrible tussle with a great snake which was longer than he was tall. In this dream, he became all but exhausted, then summoning all of his strength and exerting his full powers, he killed the snake. Afterwards, the dream was fulfilled—he battled a severe case of typhoid.[8]

While still young, Oscar witnessed the rough life of a frontier town (Moab, Utah), where outlaws and robbers shot up the town, murdered each other, got drunk, and committed various crimes. He watched his brother George risk his life taking a knife away from one man who was about to cut the throat of another man. He was at a dance when the town marshal shot and killed an outlaw, and he later watched as other outlaws searched for the marshal so they could lynch him.[9] These scenes served to teach Oscar the distinction between good and evil in a way he never forgot.

He graduated from Grand County High School in 1906, and then went to Brigham Young University in Provo, Utah. He later studied at the Utah State Agricultural College (Logan) and the University of Utah (Salt Lake City).

While at the agricultural school Oscar courted his future wife. On 13 September 1913, he married Margaret Vivian Redd. Soon after, they moved to Ann Arbor, Michigan, where Oscar studied law at the University of Michigan. Here their first child, Bruce, was born, during the same year that Oscar graduated with his law degree in 1915.[10]

The family moved back to Utah, settling in Monticello, where Oscar began practicing law. He also became very active in politics, running for various county offices. He once said, "I ran for a number of offices in San Juan [County], and in each instance the Lord told me the outcome."[11] He even ran for governor as a Democrat in 1940, but lost.

Along with his law practice, Oscar opened the first county newspaper (*The San Juan Record*), served as city and county attorney, sat as a juvenile judge (1922-25), and organized the first bank in the town. Oscar began his primary occupation in 1928 when he was elected a judge in the third district court. He served in that capacity for twelve years, until he made his unsuccessful bid for governor in 1940. He then moved to Salt Lake City and became its Commissioner of Finance until 1946.[12]

On 1 April 1946 the First Presidency announced the appointment of Oscar W. McConkie as president of the California Mission, succeeding Elijah Allen.[13] Oscar's mission proved to be a wonderful, productive, and spiritual time for him, during which he had many choice experiences that greatly blessed his life and the lives of others.

Oscar had learned that in order to serve the Lord the way he should, he would need the blessings of heaven. For example, when confronted with a particularly serious problem he said:

> In the California Mission...I prayed to God for strength, for wisdom, for understanding sufficient to enable me to accomplish my work, and I shall never forget how it was brought home to me that humility and righteousness are necessary in this work. As I arose from my knees, the voice of the Spirit spoke to my spirit, for I had asked God to give me faith like unto Enoch and Elijah, because I felt that I must have that kind of faith to accomplish the purpose I was required to seek to accomplish. And the voice of the Spirit said to me: "Enoch and Elijah obtained their faith through righteousness."[14]

It seems that Oscar was indeed blessed with faith similar to that possessed by these ancient prophets. His mission and life reveal a continuous series of miraculous, faith-promoting spiritual experiences as he labored in the service of the Lord.

Elder Harold B. Lee, while a member of the Twelve, toured Oscar's mission with him and made this comment about his companion: "President McConkie gave his usual forceful sermons in his strident, senatorial voice, but he displays a kindliness to the people and a marked deference to me that evidences a depth of humility."[15] Oscar and Elder Lee traveled quite a bit together while they toured the mission, and they had plenty of time to talk and exchange stories and spiritual experiences with each other. One story Oscar told involved "a dream in which he had gone to the home of Satan, and later told of an experience when Satan had appeared to him and his son James."[16]

Of this experience Bruce's son Joseph relates: "The Lord showed James' father a vision in which he saw Lucifer and saw James turn his back on him and continue playing the piano for the Lord's purposes."[17] After Elder Lee gave Oscar his opinion of what the dreams meant, he told an experience of his own. When a stake president, he had been summoned to the home of a member of his stake who was possessed of an evil spirit. The woman had spoken strangely to him, saying, "Great physician...head of the Church,...you are not going to send me from this world." Elder Lee had then cast out the evil spirit. At this point, Oscar offered Elder Lee his interpretation, as reported by Elder Lee, "that the evil spirit in the woman had spoken of not that which now was, but of that which Satan knew I was to become."[18] Years later, in 1972, Oscar's prediction was fulfilled when Harold B. Lee became the tenth President of the Church.

Elder Lee noticed a high degree of spirituality among the missionaries and investigators in Oscar's mission: "We had time to hear faith promoting experiences which included conversions of those who had been shown in dreams the coming of the elders and instant healings, etc."[19] Elder Lee also observed that "more great spiritual experiences were taking place there than anywhere else in the Church."[20]

Later, after Elder Lee's tour, Oscar learned that the President of the Church, George Albert Smith, was seriously ill. At the time he was convalescing in a private home the Church owned in California. Since Elder Lee was no longer present, Oscar was the nearest available Church leader to go to the prophet and give him a blessing. He picked up a young missionary as a companion and went to see President Smith. "In administering to President Smith, it was made known to President McConkie by the Spirit that the Prophet would be restored to health and so he promised him. It was further made known to him that the Lord wanted His Prophet to leave a last great testimony with the world before he passed away. President McConkie said he did not tell that to President Smith, because it was not his place to instruct the Prophet of God. President Smith regained his health, and in the next General Conference bore a powerful testimony to the world. He passed away a few weeks later."[21]

At another critical time, Oscar received a glimpse through the veil that helped him solve a difficult situation which had developed in his mission and that gave him insight into what takes place on the other side of the veil after the faithful depart this life:

A Cochapa Indian by the name of Mark Johnson Vest was baptized in President McConkie's mission, which at that time included parts of Arizona. Mark Vest was a giant of a man with a spirit to match. He stood six feet five inches tall and weighed over three hundred pounds. By birth he would have been the chief of his tribe had his people been following the traditions of their fathers. After he had been in the Church a short time he was called to be the branch president over a small Indian branch. Within six months he had increased the branch to seventy-five members. Brother Vest became ill and in the course of his illness lost over a hundred pounds. Both President McConkie and Elder Harold B. Lee administered to him but without lasting effect. Despite his illness, Mark Vest continued in his work with his people until his death a short time later.

When President McConkie received word that Mark had died he immediately boarded a train for Arizona to attend the funeral. All night long as he traveled, he prayed to know why the Lord had allowed this great missionary to be taken. As he prayed, a vision was opened to him of the spirit world. He saw Mark Johnson Vest standing in front of a large group of Lamanites, which he estimated to be twenty to thirty thousand. As he did so, one of the Indians in the middle of the group stood up and said; "Do not listen to this man! He is not a Lamanite. He is a Nephite!" President McConkie saw Mark Vest rise to the full stature of his height and say; "I am not a Nephite! I am a Lamanite, and when I died I was cremated according to the custom of my people." At this point the vision closed up.

Upon his arrival in Mesa, and as he drove to the chapel where the funeral was to be held, President McConkie was advised of a conflict between Mark Vest's tribe and the tribe from which his wife came. Mark's family wanted him buried in a cemetery while his wife's people wanted to cremate his body according to their traditions. The matter had become so heated that Mark's wife's tribe had threatened to dig up his body and take it if their demands were not met. When they arrived at the chapel President McConkie learned that he was to be the speaker. In his sermon, he was able to resolve the difficulty, explaining the importance of Mark complying even in death with the customs of those among whom he had now been called to labor.[22]

Oscar was famous for his method of delivery in giving his talks. One young man who often heard Oscar preach was future General Authority John K. Carmack. He reminisced about that delivery in these words:

If you've heard Bruce you've heard the father, only he spoke with more emotion, more like a Southern Baptist preacher. He'd get worked up and perspiration would fall off his face. He was an unusual person. He spoke from the heart, saying just what he believed. He couldn't find scriptures very easily, but he quoted them. He wasn't like Bruce, knowing chapter and verse on virtually everything, but he could quote them, and he knew them well. He'd read and studied them....

One of the things I remember about Oscar McConkie is the beautiful, delicate, loving way he treated his wife. She always came to conferences with a corsage he'd given her....She was as small as he was large. She was totally devoted to him and he was totally devoted to her. Sometimes he would get really worked up and then he'd stop and say in a voice much like Bruce's, "I've been a darn fool again, Mother." It was that kind of a tender rapport between them that I thought was so impressive.

Oscar would sometimes speak about his son Oscar Jr., who was serving a mission in New England. That's where he got the idea of putting his mission into the mode of going without purse or scrip. Oscar Jr. was doing that up in his mission, so Oscar Sr. had the California mission serve without purse or scrip. It was very hard because California was heavily Catholic in those days. It was hard on the missionaries but they had some great experiences.[23]

The sacrifices and hardships of going without purse or scrip (money) and thus relying on the Lord and the people to feed and house you are significant. It is a most difficult method of missionary work, and is a test that can make or break a missionary. However, since sacrifice brings forth the blessings of heaven, it is understandable that many of the missionaries under Oscar would have choice experiences.

While he was mission president, the number of members in the mission multiplied by two and a half times. There were more baptisms per missionary than there had ever been before.[24]

On his return from a highly successful four-and-a-half year mission, Oscar was invited by the Brethren to give his mission report in general conference. Much of the talk was filled with Oscar's expressions of gratitude to God for the many blessings he had received on his mission and during his life. He was grateful to God for the blessings of the gospel, and he expressed love for the Brethren who lead the Church under the Lord's direction. Throughout his address he bore a powerful testimony of the gospel:

> I am grateful to the Lord that he gave me a good parentage in this Church, that my father accepted the Gospel in this valley, that he remained here, that peace and righteousness settled down upon him and his wife, and that I was privileged to be born under the covenant in the Church of Christ.

I thank God for my testimony that he lives, and I am happy today as I stand before you that I have held myself in readiness all the days of my life to fulfill to my best ability whatever requirement has been made of me.

I have faith in this work. The energies of my life have been devoted unto it. There has never been anything that has been equal to it so far as I am concerned.

I have a testimony of this work. I love these Brethren who are called to preside. I sustain every one of them....

I have a testimony that Jesus Christ lives. I never expect to know that any better than I know it now. I have a testimony that Joseph Smith was and is a prophet of the mighty God. I know that God the Father and Jesus Christ, the Son, appeared unto him, and that heavenly messengers continued to visit him in the restoration of all of the keys and all of the powers and all of the authorities of the plan of salvation, and I know, and I reverence him with all my heart, that the present president of the Church is called of God as actually as was Joseph Smith, and that these men who are associated with him are called of God, even as the Prophets of old, and that the Lord speaks through them.

I know and have a testimony that the Book of Mormon is true, and that if you will read it and comprehend it, you will grow closer to the Lord than in the reading and comprehending of any other book, and I have a testimony that if I myself, have salvation, I will have to be faithful in obedience to the commandments of the Gospel, and I will have to endure unto the end.[25]

During his life, Oscar McConkie authored two books. The first, *A Dialogue at Golgotha*, published in 1945, is a scholarly discussion showing the oneness of the teachings of the ancient prophets and Jesus Christ. His second book, *The Holy Ghost*, was published in 1952. It examines the many purposes, functions, and powers of the Holy Ghost.[26] Both books sold well and were well written, full of sound doctrinal information.

In other Church service, Oscar served as bishop in Monticello, as a couselor in that stake's presidency, as a member of the Ensign Stake high council (after moving to Salt Lake City), and as a counselor in that stake presidency for five years.[27]

One characteristic for which Oscar was well known was his deep, powerful speaking voice that could be easily heard by even the most elderly. Some joked that you did not have to go to church to hear Oscar preach—you could hear him from your living room at home.

Oscar and Vivian had five sons and one daughter. Each of them followed the example of their parents by being married in the temple. Vivian served in the Relief Society for forty-six years, and was considered by her husband as his unquestionable superior. She served faithfully at his side in the many different capacities to which they were called.

Bruce Redd was their eldest child. Then came France Briton, named after two prominent countries involved in World War I. Brit later became a war hero, a lawyer, a stake patriarch, a counselor in two stake presidencies, a temple president and counselor, a mission president in Los Angeles, and a sealer in the temple.

James Wilson, the third son, was a musical genius, earning a master's degree in music at 18 years of age. He pursued a musical career as a concert pianist. He taught music at the University of Minnesota, but died of polio on August 21, 1953.

Their fourth son, Oscar Walter, played some football in college and served a mission. He became a gifted lawyer and served for many years as the Church's legal counsel.

The fifth son, William Robert, also became a lawyer, using his legal expertise in government work.

The sixth child was their first and only daughter, Margaret. She followed the example of her mother in Church service. She has traveled extensively and has been employed as a religion teacher at Brigham Young University.[28]

Oscar passed away 9 April 1966, after a long illness, at the age of 79. He left behind a great legacy for his family and others. The full extent of his example, service, and teachings cannot be measured in mortal terms. He was a spiritual giant with few peers.[29]

His wife, Vivian, lived for a much longer time. In 1984, the *Church News* ran a story about her grandchildren serving missions. It also mentioned that she performed four endowment sessions daily and three on Saturday. All this at the age of 94.[30] A year later, when her son Bruce passed away, she learned of it in the celestial room of the temple, as she performed the work she loved, serving those who could not do it for themselves. It is worthy of note that just three weeks (22 days) after her son's death, she passed away (11 May 1985), at the age of 95. She had been serving in the temple until just a week prior to her death. She lived a good and long life, served the Lord well, and raised a faithful family.

Oscar W. McConkie Sr.

As has been noted, Oscar W. McConkie was a man of great faith and spirituality. He saw visions, received revelations, healed the sick, heard the voice of the Lord, obtained and exercised great faith, had a profound testimony, and served the Lord diligently all his life in many important callings and leadership positions. Though he had the ability, the purity, the spirituality, and the faith to be numbered among them, he was never called to be a General Authority of the Church. To appreciate the greatness of the man, it should be observed that he lived as they live; he experienced the same kind of spiritual experiences they do; he enjoyed the same respect of the members of the Church they do, and received the same divine approbation they do. Perhaps Oscar has found himself with new and expanded stewardships in the next life, where the need for missionary work and preaching the gospel is so great and for which he was so gifted. His son Bruce declared: "My father has been transferred to another sphere of activity. He continues as a living, intelligent, sentient being, on the Lord's errand, working for God's kingdom and for the principles of righteousness."[31]

Notes

1. See Joseph Fielding McConkie, The Biography of Oscar W. McConkie, an unpublished graduate religion paper available in the LDS Church Historical Library, p. 2. Hereafter cited as Biography.

2. See S. Dilworth Young, "Elder Bruce R. McConkie of the Council of the Twelve," *Ensign*, Jan. 1973, p. 5. Hereafter cited as Young.

3. Biography, p. 3.

4. Mark L. McConkie, ed. *Doctrines of the Restoration* (Salt Lake City: Bookcraft, 1989), pp. 387-88. Hereafter cited as Mark McConkie, *Restoration*.

5. Oscar W. McConkie Jr., "Ye Are My Witnesses...That I Am God," Salt Lake Institute of Religion Devotional, 29 Oct. 1971, p. 6. Emphasis in original.

6. Biography, p. 4.

7. See Biography, p. 5.

8. Biography, p. 6.

9. See Biography, p. 7.

10. See Biography, p. 8; Young, p. 7.

11. Biography, p. 8.

12. See Biography, pp. 10-11.

13. See *Improvement Era*, May 1946, p. 303.

14. Oscar W. McConkie, Conference Report, Oct. 1952, pp. 56-57. Elder Neal A. Maxwell later referred to this experience in an address to the BYU student body: "The father of Elder Bruce R. McConkie, President Oscar W. McConkie, Sr., in a situation of stress years ago prayed for adequacy. He prayed that he would be able to carry out his heavy assignment and that he could be given the faith of Enoch. The answer to his prayer was Enoch's faith came through personal righteousness." ("Insights from My Life," BYU Devotional Address, *Devotional Speeches of the Year*, 1976 [Provo, Utah: Brigham Young University Press, 1976], p. 198. Hereafter cited as *Speeches*.)

15. L. Brent Goates, *Harold B. Lee: Prophet and Seer* (Salt Lake City: Bookcraft, 1985), p. 218. Hereafter cited as Goates.

16. Goates, p. 219.

17. Biography, p. 18. James was an excellent musician.

18. Goates, pp. 219-20.

19. Francis M. Gibbons, *Harold B. Lee: Man of Vision, Prophet of God* (Salt Lake City: Bookcraft, 1993), p. 269. Hereafter cited as Gibbons.

20. Biography, p. 11.

21. Biography, p. 14.

22. Robert L. Millet and Joseph Fielding McConkie, *The Life Beyond* (Salt Lake City: Bookcraft, 1986), pp. 55-56. Hereafter cited as *Beyond*.

23. Unpublished typescript of interview with Elder John K. Carmack, conducted by the author, 19 March 1997, p. 1. Hereafter cited as Carmack Interview.

24. See Conference Report, Oct. 1952, p. 56.

25. Conference Report, Oct. 1952, pp. 56-57.

26. See Biography, p. 15.

27. See *Improvement Era*, May 1946, p. 303.

28. See Biography, pp. 18-20.

29. See Biography, p. 20.

30. See *Church News*, 20 May 1984, p. 11.

31. Bruce R. McConkie, "Choose an Eternal Companion," BYU Devotional Address, 3 May 1966, pp. 5-6.

Chapter Two

Birth, Childhood, and First Mission

Bruce Redd McConkie was born 29 July 1915 in Ann Arbor, Michigan, where his father was studying law at the University of Michigan. His entry into this world was both difficult and miraculous. "My mother," said Bruce years later, "was on the operating table for a critical number of hours. By some happy coincidence, the best obstetrician in Ann Arbor just happened to be there and he worked for hours to save her life. They concluded that I was gone, that there was no use even bothering with me. I was a forceps delivery. I still have the scars on my temple. They just laid me aside. After some appreciable period someone just happened to think there might be some life in the baby."[1]

About a year after his son's birth, Oscar moved the family to Monticello, Utah, where he began practicing law. Here Bruce grew up on the family farm, doing the things that normal farm children do: chores, tending animals, milking cows, weeding the garden, and the like.[2]

The following description of Bruce's youth was included in an article decades later introducing him as a new General Authority: "As a young boy, Bruce exhibited those traits of character that a Latter-day Saint teacher would wish in a student. He was a thoughtful, obedient lad of a sober disposition, faithful and true, courteous in all his action, but ever ready to defend the truth. Even as a child, he possessed an unusual knowledge of the scriptures."[3] He gained that early knowledge from study: "At age 11, young Bruce would gather his brothers and sisters about him to read to them the Book of Mormon."[4]

In 1926, a year before Bruce became a deacon, the McConkie family moved from Monticello to Salt Lake City, where Oscar continued to serve as a judge. They kept their rural ties, however, as Bruce and his brothers returned to the farm every summer to work.[5]

Bruce's close friend Elder S. Dilworth Young shared his understanding of Bruce's early life in this way:

> During these growing years in Salt Lake City, he patronized heavily the public library and read avidly many books for boys. Among his favorites were the works of Ernest Thompson Seton, whose animal stories excited the imagination of that generation of boys. Breathing, talking and living the principles of the gospel made life in the McConkie home a constant joy. Meals were served family style. Father McConkie was an expert at making just the right conversation. Gospel subjects were the chief topic of discussion. The truth was carefully taught, repeated over and over in many ways, until real love of the doctrine came into their lives. Sundays were faithfully kept. At Sunday dinner each one told what he had learned at Sunday School, and the father added what he deemed necessary to illuminate the subjects discussed. The family car was put away for the day. All walked to and from the Sunday meetings. The neighborhood was healthy and the boys added to its vigor. They engaged in boyhood neighborhood activities.[6]

Joseph Fielding McConkie, Bruce's eldest living son, verified this practice of teaching in the home: "If you were to ask my dad where he learned the gospel he'd say, 'I learned it at the dinner table after Sunday School when my father would review with us what we'd been taught, and correct it.'"[7]

Teaching and learning the gospel at home was a way of life for Oscar and his children. He made sure that they knew gospel doctrine and loved it as he did. As time passed, father and sons continued to meet weekly to discuss the gospel. This practice ensured a family-centered pursuit of gospel truth.[8] Bruce explained:

> I had a very spiritual home life. My father had a practice in the family of talking about the gospel to the children, with the result that at the dinner table or Sunday dinner or in the evening or what have you, he somehow managed to get us involved in discussion and everlastingly he taught us the gospel. I would be surprised if there were anyone that I'd ever run across who spent as much time just deliberately discussing and thereby teaching gospel principles to his children as my father did. He was a great conversationalist and he just kept me everlastingly thinking and evaluating on principles of the gospel, and the environment had the effect of getting my mind centered in those channels and the result, obviously, is that when I talk I'm talking on a doctrinal subject.[9]

One early experience Bruce remembered well, and one which exemplified the spiritual sensitivities of his father, was an occasion of divine intervention:

> One of my earliest childhood recollections is of riding a horse through an apple orchard. The horse was tame and well broken, and I felt at home in the saddle. But one day something frightened my mount, and he bolted through the orchard. I was swept from the saddle by the overhanging limbs, and one leg slipped down through the stirrup. I desperately hung to an almost broken leather strap that a cowboy uses to tie a lariat to his saddle. Suddenly the horse stopped, and I became aware that someone was holding the bridle tightly and attempting to calm the quivering animal. Almost immediately I was snatched up into the arms of my father. My father had been sitting in the house reading the newspaper when the Spirit whispered to him: "Run out into the orchard." Without a moment's hesitation, not waiting to learn why or for what reason, my father ran. Finding himself in the orchard without knowing why he was there, he saw the galloping horse and thought, "I must stop this horse." He did so and found me. I was saved from death or serious accident because my father hearkened to the voice of the Spirit. If he had not responded instantly to the whisperings of the still small voice, my life might have ended then or had its course totally changed.[10]

When Bruce was twelve years old, he was ordained a deacon and his family moved back to Ann Arbor so Oscar could study law for another year. They then returned to Utah, where Oscar's work awaited him in Salt Lake City. During most of his time in Salt Lake, Bruce went to school and made friends, but "each summer they went [back] to Monticello, Utah, to be on the farm until school began in the fall. Bruce learned all of the farm skills: handling horses, milking cows, raking hay, and helping generally. He was truly raised on the farm."[11]

Bruce went to high school at the old LDS University where the Church Office Building now stands, graduating in 1931. Then he went on to the University of Utah, where he attended for three years. Between summers on the farm and his university studies, Bruce was finding himself increasingly out of the familiar family nest. Indeed, he carried a vivid memory of his father impressing strongly upon him how he should act when on his own, away from home:

> My father often said to his children on those occasions when one member of the family was to be separated from the others, "Remember who you are

and act accordingly." This meant to us that since we were members of a family in which the light of Christ was present; in which we were taught the truths of the gospel; in which the power of faith, the power of the priesthood, and the influence of the Holy Spirit were present—that when we were outside the family fold, we should continue to live in the way we had been taught; we should continue to walk in the light of gospel truths and principles.

My wife tells me that her father said exactly the same thing to the children in his family. As a matter of fact, I have heard her father say—and his name is Smith—that, "All people had the name of Smith in the beginning, and their names were changed when they committed sin." I am not exactly sure what that means with reference to her becoming a McConkie.[12]

Aside from the humor of the story, it indicates how Bruce was expected to behave when he left home. That time was at hand.

In late fall of 1934, having just turned 19, Bruce Redd McConkie was called to serve a mission to the Eastern States, entering the mission home in October. A close friend commented on his preparation: "He had read the Book of Mormon three times, had read the other standard works, and had had the long years of family discussions. He had patterned his life to the truth. He was ready when the call came."[13]

Soon after entering the mission home in Salt Lake City, he contracted hepatitis. Since the time for his farewell had already been set, the ward went ahead with it, and members of his family spoke, though he was unable to attend. Soon thereafter, just as it was time to leave for the mission field, he got well. He considered it a miraculous recovery.[14]

Upon arriving in the mission field, he participated in the dedication ceremonies for the monument atop the Hill Cumorah in upstate New York.[15] He then learned that the mission president was preparing the Hill Cumorah Pageant. Since he was involving all the missionaries and using them according to their abilities, Bruce was asked to participate. He later recalled his experience: "Here was somebody who played the trumpet and somebody who was Moroni and someone else did something else. Everybody acted according to their talents. Well, I was there two years that they did this, and I never even saw the pageant. I parked cars out in the field."[16]

In September 1935, Elder Joseph Fielding Smith visited Elder McConkie's mission. In Vermont they "paused to view the impressive granite monument that honors the Prophet" Joseph Smith's birthplace,

Farewell Testimonial

IN HONOR OF

ELDER BRUCE R. McCONKIE

Prior to His Departure for the
Eastern States Mission

TO BE GIVEN IN THE

Twentieth Ward Chapel

Corner 2nd Ave. & G St.

Sunday Evening, Oct. 14th, 1934

Program at 6:30   Voluntary Contributions

and then visited Fort Henry. That night, Elder Smith recorded in his diary that he "met Elder Bruce R. McConkie, a most excellent Elder." In all of Elder Smith's ministry, though he recorded on the pages of his diary many names of missionaries he met, he never spoke of another one so highly as being "a most excellent Elder."

Young Elder McConkie spent thirteen months of his two years in the area of Palmyra, New York and the Hill Cumorah.[17] It must have been thrilling for him to work and proselyte in the "backyard" of the Prophet Joseph Smith. His service as a missionary was the same area in which the Prophet began his own great ministry. Though nearly a hundred years had passed and many things had changed, it was still the same location where so many spiritual events in the history of the Church had taken place.

He was called by his mission president, Don B. Colton, to serve as president (now called zone leader) of the Seneca and Albany Districts.[18]

"He had all of the usual experiences a good missionary had in that mission. There were times when patience was the order of the day. There were times when vigor should be exercised. There were times of crisis. Elder McConkie was ready for each," said a good friend.[19] This missionary service would prove to be important preparation for his later experience as a General Authority. The growing and learning experience of mission life added mental and spiritual maturity to a young man of promise.

After a successful mission, Bruce returned home in October 1936 and finished the last year of his four year-degree, receiving his B.A. in the spring of 1937.

Notes

1. Dell Van Orden, "Elder Bruce R. McConkie: A Challenging Future," *Church News*, 21 Oct. 1972: p. 3. Hereafter cited as Van Orden.

2. See Young, pp. 7-8.

3. Marian C. Sharp, "Bruce Redd McConkie Sustained a Member of the First Council of the Seventy," *Relief Society Magazine,* vol. 33, no. 12 (Dec. 1946), p. 818.

4. *Improvement Era*, Nov. 1967, p. 57.

5. See *Church News,* 31 July 1965, p. 16.

6. Young, p. 8.

7. Sheri L. Dew, "Bruce R. McConkie: A Family Portrait," *This People,* Dec. 85/Jan. 86, p. 52. Hereafter cited as Dew.

8. See Young, p. 8.

9. Van Orden, p. 3.

10. Address given by Elder Boyd K. Packer at the funeral service of Elder Bruce R. McConkie, 23 April 1985. Cited in: Boyd K. Packer, *Let Not Your Heart Be Troubled,* (Salt Lake City: Bookcraft, 1991), pp. 260-61. Hereafter cited as Packer.

11. Young, p. 8.

12. Bruce R. McConkie, "Households of Faith," BYU Devotional Address, 1 Dec. 1970, p. 1.

13. Young, p. 9.

14. See Van Orden, p. 3.

15. See *Church News,* 31 July 1965, p. 16.

16. Van Orden, p. 3.

17. See Henry A. Smith, "Bruce R. McConkie: of the First Council of the Seventy," *Improvement Era,* Nov. 1946 (vol. 49), p. 692. Hereafter cited as Smith.

18. See *Church News,* 7 Oct. 1972, p. 3.

19. See Young, p. 9.

Chapter Three

Education, Marriage, Military, Employment

Bruce met Amelia Smith while he was a freshman at the University of Utah and she was a senior at East High School.[1] The two young people soon found themselves socializing with the same group of friends. One Saturday night, Bruce was at a party at the Smiths' home. When it got late, he told Amelia's mother that he needed to be home by midnight, since the next day was the Sabbath. Because of this incident, Bruce came to be regarded highly by Amelia's parents.[2]

"The first time I ever saw him," Amelia later recalled, "was at a party, and I thought, 'He sure is tall.' My first date with him was a dance [Amelia asked him], up at Memory Grove in Salt Lake City, and after the dance he took me out and got me a malt,"[3] which she accidentally spilled down the front of her formal.

They corresponded regularly during his mission to the Eastern States. He sometimes sent her copies of talks he'd given, which she showed her father, Elder Joseph Fielding Smith. He told her he thought they were very good. Amelia once went on a date with another suitor and got a lecture from her father. Elder Smith "was in Bruce's corner from the beginning." Besides Elder Smith noticing Bruce while he served his mission, he became well acquainted with him upon Bruce's return, for Bruce immediately resumed his courtship with Amelia.

Joseph Fielding Smith's diary records that he, "in the evening [of 7 February 1937] with Julina [another daughter], Amelia, and Bruce, attended the joint meeting of the Yale, Yalecrest and 33rd Wards in the Bonneville Stake conference."[4] Not long after this, Elder Smith "accompanied Amelia and Lewis [a son] through the temple when they obtained their endowments. Present also were Julina and Amelia's fiancee, Bruce R. McConkie."[5]

They attended the University of Utah together during their courtship; after Bruce walked her home in the evening, he would then walk the long distance to his own home.[6] These long walks were customary for Bruce to get anywhere, including attending to his university endeavors. He later recalled how he used this time:

> When I was going to the University, it took me about 45 minutes to walk there and 45 minutes to walk home. I began to think in outlines. I would arbitrarily choose some subject and imagine that I had been notified to give a talk on this subject.
>
> I would then say the first word on the subject and the last word, and then in the 40 minutes or whatever time I allotted myself, I would attempt to cover the subject in some intelligent way, just for the purpose of training myself to think in outlines. So, if somebody said faith, I'd immediately think, well, it's 1, 2, 3, and 1a, and 2b, and 3c.[7]

Later in life when he was asked if he still relied on that early system when called to speak, he said, "Oh, I don't pay any attention to it now except that it had the obvious effect of training me to think in a channel so that I'd keep intelligently on a subject. It set the pattern for the way that I always talk."[8]

Accustomed to hard work, Bruce delivered ice for the Hygeia Ice Company while attending the University of Utah law school.

Amelia and Bruce's courtship culminated on 13 October 1937, when they were sealed in marriage in the Salt Lake Temple by her father. At the time, Amelia was keeping house for her father and brothers, for when her mother passed away the duty had fallen to her. Upon marriage, the new couple moved into the basement apartment in the Smith home, where she continued this service until her father remarried.[9]

Years later Bruce made these interesting comments about his decision to marry Amelia:

> Maybe it will be a little shock to you, but never in my life did I ever ask the Lord whom I ought to marry. It never occurred to me to ask him. I went out and found the girl I wanted; she suited me; I evaluated and weighed the proposition, and it just seemed a hundred percent to me as though this ought to be. Now, if I'd done things perfectly, I'd have done some counseling with the Lord, which I didn't do; but all I did was pray to the Lord and ask for some guidance and direction in connection with the decision that I'd reached. A more perfect thing to have done would have been to counsel

with him relative to the decision and get a spiritual confirmation that the conclusion, which I by my agency and faculties had arrived at, was the right one.[10]

After Bruce and Amelia were married, they began the practice of reading the scriptures together before retiring each night. From this consistent habit, they were able to go through the standard works several times.[11] "I recall sitting on one side of the dining room table," said Amelia, "while he sat on the other and I read from the [King] James version of the Bible while he followed in the Joseph Smith Translation and made a note of every single solitary change that the prophet had made, and it taught me how to read [scripture more carefully]."[12]

"Well, we had fun," she continued. "Everything that he had to say to me wasn't prefaced by something from one of the standard works or anything like that. Some people seem to think that's what my life must have been, just a constant diet [of scripture]. He was perfectly normal. It was fun—there was never a dull moment really, because...this ready wit of his was always there."[13] "He was a real character with those he knew well. With others he was very proper."[14]

During the first two years of their marriage, Bruce continued his law studies. In 1939 he received a bachelor of laws degree. After graduation, he and three friends opened a law practice, and in September 1938 Amelia delivered Bruce Jr., their first child. "We were just married a year when that baby was born," said Amelia, "and he was with us just two months, and then he [Bruce Jr.] was called on a mission."[15]

Years later, while a General Authority, Bruce completed a Juris Doctorate degree at the University of Utah. This was quite an accomplishment considering the work load of a General Authority and the small amount of spare time he had. It is also an indication of his genius, for a law degree is not easily obtainable under the best of circumstances.

As mentioned, upon graduation in 1939, he and three friends opened a law practice. This venture was short-lived, and in 1940 he was named assistant Salt Lake City attorney and Salt Lake City prosecutor.[16]

Even at this point in life, Bruce had become a capable public speaker and found himself in demand to speak in sacrament meetings around the Wasatch Front for several years.[17] He also was "a member of Delta Phi, the missionary fraternity. He taught M-Men and Gleaner classes, genealogy and gospel doctrine classes; served as instructor of two quorums of seventies; in the Sunday School superintendency, the stake

M-Men presidency, and in various priesthood positions. He was a member of the 261st Quorum of Seventy and the senior president of the 340th quorum, both in Bonneville Stake."[18]

"World War II began at Pearl Harbor December 7, 1941. Believing in the inspired destiny of this country, Elder McConkie had joined the ROTC during his university days. He served in that organization for four years. Then when the war started he served four more years on active duty in the Ninth Service Command. He began his service as a first lieutenant and retired at the end of the period a lieutenant colonel. His work was in security and intelligence."[19] The Ninth Service Command was headquartered at Fort Douglas in Salt Lake City.[20]

Through his four years of intelligence work for the military he supported his growing family. But it was also during this time that he reconsidered the direction his life should take. As the time of his military service came to an end, he made a significant decision to leave his practice of law. Amelia observed that "he had to prosecute petty criminals" and that he had to deal with the prostitutes, and he didn't like it. "He much preferred to write, and so he got into the reporting and editorial writing business and worked at the *Deseret News*."[21]

This new occupation was one which suited him well, although it cannot be said that newspaper reporting totally excludes one from the bad elements of society. The difference was that Bruce did not have to deal personally with criminals. They were no longer his responsibility, except as he wrote about them. Furthermore, as Amelia stated, Bruce enjoyed writing a great deal and found it to be much more rewarding than getting petty criminals off the hook.

He reported many stories for the *Deseret News*, under the supervision of Elder Mark E. Peterson, who was simultaneously serving as Apostle and managing director of the newspaper. Bruce wrote a number of editorials which appeared on the front page of the *Church News* section. But even this new employment did not last long, for the Lord had a greater work for him to do.

Notes

1. See Young, p. 9.

2. Dew, pp. 51-52.

3. Unpublished typescript of video biography of Elder Bruce R. McConkie, produced by The Church of Jesus Christ of Latter-day Saints, 1987, p. 1; punctuation corrected for clarity. Hereafter cited as Video Biography.

4. Francis M. Gibbons, *Joseph Fielding Smith: Gospel Scholar, Prophet of God*, (Salt Lake City: Deseret Book, 1992) p. 271. Hereafter cited as Gibbons, *Smith*.

5. Gibbons, *Smith*, p. 273.

6. See Dew, p. 52.

7. Van Orden, p. 3. Elder S. Dilworth Young related the following about his understanding of his friend's mental exercises during this time: "It was during these long walks that Bruce trained and disciplined his mind. It was then that he learned to memorize outlines for talks, memorize scriptures, and put them together in a meaningful way. One associate relates that he would 'think of a subject in the gospel...and would then, in his mind, make up an outline for a sermon on the subject. He would from memory add the appropriate scripture and material supporting the outline. He had memorized a verse of scripture a day while in the mission field, and so he had a large amount to draw upon. Doing this daily as he walked gave him practice in analysis and logic on doctrinal subjects. He continued until this method of thinking has become second nature to him.'" (Young, p. 9.)

8. Van Orden, p. 3.

9. See Young, p. 9.

10. Bruce R. McConkie, "Agency or Inspiration—Which?" BYU Devotional Address, 27 Feb. 1973, p. 111.

11. See *Ensign,* Jan. 1973, p. 9.

12. Video Biography, p. 2.

13. Video Biography, p. 4.

14. Dew, p. 51.

15. Video Biography, pp. 1, 2.

16. See Bruce R. McConkie, "Knowest Thou the Condescension of God," *Speeches,* 1969, introductory material, pp. 1-2.

17. See Smith, p. 692. On one occasion, this author's grandfather was called into a bishopric on the same day he was to speak in a sacrament meeting. The stake

president "mentioned Bruce McConkie, son of his first counselor, who is an excellent speaker." Bruce's services as substitute were secured. (Dennis B. Horne, comp., *Proud That My Name Is Horne: A History of Walter and Marie Horne and Some of Their Ancestors* [privately published by the Horne family, 1992], p. 149.)

18. "Knowest Thou the Condescension of God," *Speeches*, 1969, p. 1; introductory material.

19. Young, p. 9.

20. It may be that it was during his four years of military service that he began work on *Mormon Doctrine*. (See Video Biography, p. 2.)

21. Video Biography, p. 2.

Education, Marriage, Military, Employment

Chapter Four

Call to the First Council of Seventy

Bruce had worked for the *Deseret News* for about a year[1] when his life was dramatically changed: he was called by the Lord to do something that he had been born to do—preach the gospel. His age and preparation at the time of his call were extraordinary. Though his talents and training enabled him to function well as an attorney, reporter, and author, his unique abilities truly blossomed and improved with his service as a leader and teacher among the Saints of Zion.

On 28 May 1946, Elder John H. Taylor, a member of the First Council of Seventy, passed away. With the resulting vacancy, the usual speculation began to circulate among the members of the Church. Who would be called? Who would fill the vacancy? When the October 1946 general conference convened, Bruce was at the *Deseret News* reporters' table covering the conference for the first time, taking notes on each speaker and address. Quietly, before the Sunday afternoon session began, he was called aside to speak with President David O. McKay, a Counselor in the First Presidency. President McKay then issued the call for him to be the new member of the First Council of the Seventy. "Still stunned from this shocking news, he returned to the press table and carried on his assignment." This could not have been easy. At the beginning of the afternoon session, the names of the Brethren were read for sustaining vote by President McKay: the First Presidency, the Twelve, and then the Seventy—Levi Edgar Young, Antoine R. Ivins, Oscar A. Kirkham, S. Dilworth Young, Milton R. Hunter, and then, thirty-one-year-old Bruce R. McConkie.[2]

The emotional shock that goes with such a call is well known to the Brethren as a shared experience. Along with the immediate stress of the moment, they experience a dramatic change in their lifestyle and in the public perception of the new General Authority.

Bruce was now in the public eye. His life's work became the Lord's work, and the constant demands were nearly overwhelming physically, emotionally, and spiritually.[3] This would be his calling and total commitment for the rest of his life.

Of course the call affected his wife as well. Amelia shared her experience, "I was home watching the children and heard [it] on the radio, and then immediately after conference was over, the first people that came to the house [were] my father and Aunt Jessie [President Smith's third wife]. And my father said, 'Just keep your feet on the ground.'"[4]

Bruce was set apart to the First Quorum of the Seventy on Thursday, October 10, 1946, by President George Albert Smith in the Salt Lake Temple.[5] On November 7, Elder McConkie was in President Smith's office receiving instructions about his new responsibilities. Interestingly, in referring to this visit in his journal, President Smith misspelled the new Seventy's name as "McKonkie," indicating that though Elder McConkie was an extended relative by marriage, he was not well known to President Smith.

This also seems to indicate something about the inspiration of the call itself, for President Smith had strong feelings about avoiding nepotism in the leading councils of the Church. Here is found supporting evidence of direct revelation from God to His prophet regarding this call.[6]

Elder Boyd K. Packer later added this insight: "I am sure there were snide remarks about nepotism, for he had married the daughter of Joseph Fielding Smith of the Council of the Twelve Apostles. People making such remarks did not know that the President of the Church had kept [Elder McConkie's] call from her father until it had to be announced."[7]

On 12 October, 1946, the *Church News* section of the *Deseret News* carried the following announcement:

Introducing the New General Authority
Seventy's Vacancy Is Filled

We introduce to the membership of the Church herewith the newest General Authority—Elder Bruce R. McConkie....Elder McConkie was sustained to this position at the closing session of the 117th Semi-Annual Conference.... His appointment brought a 31 year old youth into a position of great responsibility, the youngest to be named a member of the First Council of Seventy since 1888.

He is a tall good-looking young man, standing six-foot-four and weighing slightly over 200 pounds. He has a pleasant, almost bashful personality, and is friendly and courteous. Though he is unassuming, Bruce R.

McConkie is a capable, keen student of the Gospel, a dependable leader and, for his age, a most powerful speaker.

He has had a wide experience despite his years and is a four year veteran of World War II. He will carry a youthful viewpoint into the presiding councils of the Church, enhanced by his experiences and training as an attorney, ex-serviceman, and newspaperman.[8]

Accompanying this announcement was a large picture of Bruce, Amelia, and their family, consisting at this point of two sons, Joseph and Stanford, and two daughters, Vivian and Mary.

It is amusing yet revealing to catch the several references in this article to Elder McConkie's youth. His young age was not lost on the author of this news item, nor was his admiration.

At this point it might be interesting to try to gauge, to some extent, the level of Elder McConkie's gospel and spiritual knowledge at this time. After all, relatively few men are called to be General Authorities at or before age 31. Two intriguing stories convey insight into his remarkable early understanding of gospel principles.

As seen in chapter 1, Elder McConkie's father, Oscar, was a highly spiritual and doctrinally knowledgeable man. When he was serving as a mission president, one of his missionaries (who later became a prominent BYU religion professor and author) asked him a question and received a surprising answer:

> Oscar McConkie was a very capable man in his own right. One day we missionaries asked him a question: he thought a little while and said, "I don't know the answer, but I'd like to ask my son, Bruce." I asked him how old his son was: when he told me he was only thirty, I said, "How is it that you—being his father, a judge, a mission president—feel that you have to ask your son for the answer?" He replied, "You just don't know Bruce!"[9]

A Church magazine reported that prior to Bruce's call, he had

> undertaken a subject study of the standard works of the Church and has several loose-leaf books filled with an analytical study of the Book of Mormon and is now at work on the Doctrine and Covenants. He has searched the scriptures carefully and gleaned from them every bit of information available on a total of one hundred fifteen subjects. For example, under "Faith," he has, he thinks, every reference contained in the

> Book of Mormon on that subject, written fully enough so that he need not again refer to the original source. This scriptural study has taken years to do, but he has found it a most valuable training in preparation for preaching and teaching the gospel.[10]

This concentrated study became the basis for his book *Mormon Doctrine*, which would be published twelve years later.

Another source that revealed his unusual gospel understanding at this time is the content of his earliest general conference talks. These sermons show a solid foundation of knowledge without the compromise or rationalization that one might expect in someone so young and relatively inexperienced. For example, for his first sermon in conference, he first bore unequivocal testimony of Jesus Christ, the reality of the Restoration of the gospel, and the fact that the keys and authority of the priesthood reside with the prophets. Then he said, "It is all well and good to sing praises to the ancient prophets and build sepulchers to their names, but there is no salvation in that fact standing alone. If men in this world in our day want to go back to our Father's kingdom, it is incumbent upon them to come to the Living Oracle and have exercised in their behalf the authority of the priesthood. They must accept and live in harmony with the counsels of those men whom God has chosen today."

He concluded his talk with this instructive testimony:

> I do not know anything in this world that is greater than to have the constant companionship of the Holy Ghost...and I do not think there is anything greater in eternity than to have the companionship of those of the celestial world, to have exaltation and eternal lives....
>
>   Now there is nothing in this world that I would rather do than have the privilege of preaching the gospel and of devoting such time and abilities as the Lord may bless me with to the building up of his kingdom. I am grateful beyond any ability that I have to express for the privilege of being a member of the First Council of the Seventy and mingling with you Latter-day Saints and traveling in the stakes of Zion, and I pray that the Lord will bless me and will bless you and pour out his spirit upon the Saints.[11]

A year later he said, "I have read the Book of Mormon more times than I have fingers; I believe it, sincerely and wholeheartedly. I know that it is a true witness of Christ and an accurate revealer of the Doctrines of

Christ."[12] Such was the depth of knowledge and understanding of the gospel that Elder McConkie had acquired.

It was now time to embark on his ministry. Elder McConkie was a member of the First Council of the Seventy for 26 years. Here he developed the spiritual stature and skills that led him to be worthy and prepared for his future apostolic call. Also while a member of this quorum, he wrote several of his books and preached most of his sermons.

There is insufficient space in a work of this size to do more than review a few highlights of Elder McConkie's ministry as a member of the First Council of the Seventy. Over the years he served as serviceman's coordinator (for 15 years), was managing director of the full-time and stake missions, worked with the regional representatives, and was a mission president.[13] He spoke at general conference; toured missions; gave numerous talks, most without prepared notes; wrote articles for Church magazines; and traveled extensively. This, of course, includes the stake conference visits on most weekends throughout the year, and a constant flow of training meetings, writing lesson manuals, reviewing and approving the writings of others, correspondence, and so on.

With his background of military service he was well qualified to oversee the Church's program for the servicemen. Also, many of his early talks reflect the emphasis in his life on missionary work as it was applicable to military and to full-time mission experience. As a member of the First Quorum of the Seventy, a continuing responsibility was the many facets of missionary work.

One of Elder McConkie's early assignments was to accompany Elder Harold B. Lee, then of the Council of the Twelve, to California for the reorganization of the Gridley Stake. They interviewed the various brethren and installed the new stake president. They also dedicated a new chapel in Yuba City. Elder Lee reflected upon this trip: "I had a delightful visit with Bruce McConkie on the way home and found him entirely responsive to my suggestions relative to the work of the First Council of the Seventy and missionary work."[14] This trip was the second time the two had traveled together within a year. These visits, taken together with Elder Lee's recent tour of the California Mission with Oscar McConkie Sr., helped this Apostle become much better acquainted with the McConkie family, which proved fortuitous in future years.

Five years into his ministry (at the October 1951 general conference), Elder McConkie shared a special incident which indicates how the Lord was strengthening his testimony: "May I just tell you one experience that

I had? I have never told this to any person before, except my wife. Six months ago in the Solemn Assembly, when the First Presidency of the Church were sustained, as I sat down here behind one of these lower pulpits, the voice of the Lord came into my mind as certainly, I am sure, as the voice of the Lord came into the mind of Enos, and the very words were formed, and it said, 'These are they whom I have chosen as the First Presidency of my Church. Follow them.'"[15]

The most important duty that devolves upon a General Authority is serving as a witness of Jesus Christ—that he is the Son of God and that he was crucified for the sins of the world. This duty seems to be the one which Elder McConkie enjoyed the most and which he took most seriously. Just two years after his call he said, "As I understand it, our mission to the world in this day, is to testify of Jesus Christ. Our mission is to bear record that he is the Son of the Living God and that he was crucified for the sins of the world; that salvation was, and is, and is to come, in and through his atoning blood; that by virtue of his atonement all men will be raised in immortality, and those who believe and obey the gospel law both in immortality and unto eternal life."[16]

This is the testimony which Elder McConkie bore early in his ministry, and although his future testimonies were born with similar words, the spirit and power that accompanied them grew as he served.

In 1952 Elder McConkie toured the West Central States mission. His visit had a great impact, especially on one elder serving there, John K. Carmack, who would later become a General Authority. He remembered that Elder McConkie "gave approximately thirty talks all across the mission, no one of which was alike. In none of them did he use any notes; and all of which were at least an hour in duration. They were all on different doctrinal topics—every one of them. It was one of the most impressive performances of any I have witnessed, before or since. As he would start he would say, 'As the Spirit directs I would like to speak about (naming the topic)....' He would then speak for an hour on that topic."[17]

Elder McConkie himself commented on his method of speaking: "I don't use notes to speak of. It isn't once in a thousand times I ever have a note, and as I give talks week after week I approach the subject differently. For instance, last Sunday in Moab I talked about the family unit with a totally different approach than I'd ever talked about the family unit before."[18] "Sometimes he would quote a scripture," remembered Elder Carmack. "He would open the scriptures and he would be reviewing on the right-hand of the page while he was quoting the left-hand side. He would continue quoting the whole scripture, word perfectly. He would, perhaps, be reviewing just a little bit. He could do that."

Elder Carmack continued:

> He talked to all the missionaries in each district. In each, he would ask "Who is the scriptorian in this district." In the Butte District, Elder Jim Hill suggested he call on Elder Carmack. So Elder McConkie said, "Where is Elder Carmack? Please stand and give us a ten-minute talk on Acts 3:19-21." Then he would cross-examine us. He similarly called on Aldin Porter (who is now in the Seventy). We, along with other missionaries, became disciples of Elder McConkie. He changed the mission in that tour.
>
> He was there for about two weeks. He would start his talk to all the missionaries like this. "A missionary day starts at 6 o'clock. If you don't get up by training and habit and practice at 6 o'clock, get an alarm clock, and set it at 6 o'clock. When it goes off you get up. If you can't get up by that means, then you...put it across the room and get up and turn it off and stay up." Then he quoted D&C 112:5. He said this was a call to missionary work. "Morning after morning, afternoon after afternoon, evening after evening, constantly for two years." Then he opened it up for questions and had a testimony meeting.[19]

In June 1968 Elder McConkie was assigned as an assistant to Elder Ezra Taft Benson to supervise missionary work in the Orient. In late November he and Sister McConkie began a month-long trip with Elder and Sister Benson, visiting Japan, Okinawa, Taiwan, Korea, Hong Kong, Singapore, the Philippines, Vietnam, Thailand, and India, touring the missions and setting the Church in order. It was a grueling excursion, but they felt buoyed up by what they found. "There are no better missionaries anywhere," they said. "We expect to see a great harvest in the Orient and Asia in the days ahead. This spirit of optimism seems to be shared by all. The outlook is most encouraging." Elder McConkie spent time in Japan interviewing the missionaries and speaking at conferences in Tokyo and Sendal.[20] Speaking of the burden of constant travel associated with his calling, Elder McConkie observed:

> I've traveled so much that it's a way of life. It adds a great deal of variety to life. Obviously you get tired or you have long schedules or you fly all night or something, but that's life and everybody does that sort of thing.

Ei McCrackin and Ezra, Ted, and Elsa Rowan tour the Orient

It's an interesting experience to go over the nations of Asia or to travel throughout South America. Although in many respects, what you see is between the airport and the church; it isn't like being a tourist. But still, it's the people that count, and everywhere you go you find the best and finest people in the world—that is one of the beauties of this.

You're with the saints and with the portion of them that are faithful and trying to keep the commandments, so you have pleasant associations. And pretty soon you have friends and acquaintances and people that you esteem very highly all over the world.

People seem to think that it's an enjoyable thing when the brethren come traveling in their areas, but on the other hand, it's a source of great personal satisfaction to all of the brethren to get out and be with the Latter-day Saints.[21]

Thus began the ministry of Elder Bruce R. McConkie, General Authority.

Notes

1. The two sources used to approximate the time Bruce spent working for the *Deseret News* conflict. See the May, 1985 *Ensign,* "News of the Church" editorial, which gives the time as "less than a year," and the Video Biography, which gives it as "a year and a half."

2. *Church News,* Oct. 1971, p. 3; Smith, p. 692; Lawrence R. Flake, *Mighty Men of Zion* (Salt Lake City: Butler, 1974), p. 296.

3. The author has made a detailed study of the experiences related by many General Authorities concerning their calls. Without exception each of these Brethren experienced some degree of emotional or spiritual shock and feelings of inadequacy. Elder McConkie was no exception.

4. Video Biography, p. 3.

5. See Smith, p. 692.

6. Francis M. Gibbons, *George Albert Smith: Kind and Caring Christian, Prophet of God* (Salt Lake City: Deseret Book, 1990), pp. 42, 44, 85, 133, 320-21.

7. Packer, p. 263.

8. *Church News,* 12 Oct. 1946, p. 5.

9. *Ensign,* June 1985, p. 18. See also Dew, p. 52.

10. Smith, p. 692.

11. Conference Report, April 1947, pp. 38, 41.

12. Conference Report, April 1948, p. 91.

13. See "Advocate for Truth," *New Era,* June 1985, p. 9; see also Young, p. 10. Elder Young wrote, "He has written numerous articles and handbooks and read hundreds of manuscripts submitted for his appraisal. His sermons at conferences have been consistently doctrinal in nature, pointing out the basic gospel principles that lead to exaltation....His value in counsel has been wise, clear, and in harmony with the true principles of the gospel. His gift to write and speak concisely and with clarity amounts almost to genius, and he exercises these gifts willingly for the benefit of the work of the Lord whose name he reveres." (Young, p. 10.)

14. Gibbons, *Lee,* pp. 269-70.

15. Conference Report, Oct. 1951, p. 149.

16. Conference Report, Oct. 1948, p. 23.

17. Carmack interview, p. 2.

18. Van Orden, p. 3.

19. Carmack interview, pp. 2-3.

20. Sheri L. Dew, *Ezra Taft Benson: A Biography* (Salt Lake City: Deseret Book, 1987), pp. 401-2; *Church News,* 21 Dec. 1968, pp. 1, 12.

21. Quotations from interview by David Croft, *Church News,* 24 January 1976.

Various editions and bindings of *Mormon Doctrine*.

Chapter Five

Mormon Doctrine

In 1958 Elder McConkie published, through Bookcraft, a remarkable book entitled, *Mormon Doctrine: A Compendium of the Gospel.* More than anything else which he did, this book brought him notoriety, criticism, admiration, respect, and gratitude. It filled a need and established him as a competent doctrinal authority among the leaders of the Church. Forty years later, it is still one of the most used, studied, and quoted books in LDS literature[1]

It should be noted that not all of the story behind *Mormon Doctrine* is known, at least to this author. With the passing away of most of the principal participants and the unavailability of some primary sources, it is difficult to reconstruct the full picture. What is related here are those parts of the story that have become known to the author. There are undoubtedly facets that bear on the subject which are missing from this overview. This chapter should be viewed as only a portion of the full picture.

The *Mormon Doctrine* story began before Bruce was called as a General Authority. At age 19 he analyzed and cross-referenced every verse in the Book of Mormon, accumulating a stack of papers over a foot high. This gave him an extraordinary understanding of Book of Mormon doctrine at an early age. "But he threw them out," said his daughter Vivian. "The papers weren't important, he said. The understanding they had given him was."[2] Later, Bruce "undertook a subject study of the standard works of the Church," compiling several loose-leaf binders filled with information about gospel subjects, complete with exhaustive references.[3] This seems to have been the actual beginning of *Mormon Doctrine.* His exhausting study of the standard works was indeed a remarkable effort, undertaken in a day when all research was manual.[4]

The preface itself explains Elder McConkie's feelings about the effort: "This work is unique—the first book of its kind ever published. It is the first major attempt to digest, explain, and analyze all of the important doctrines of the kingdom. It is the first extensive compendium of the whole gospel—the first attempt to publish an encyclopedic commentary covering the whole field of revealed religion."[5] He also included a disclaimer, informing readers that he alone was responsible for the doctrinal and scriptural interpretations.

He pointed out that where needed he had relied on doctrinal explanations from certain past and present Church leaders whom he considered to be "recognized doctrinal authorities." These select men were Joseph Smith, Brigham Young, Orson Pratt, John Taylor, and Joseph Fielding Smith.[6]

Elder McConkie's disclaimer deserves close attention because it reveals the proper place of *Mormon Doctrine* and any book written by a General Authority or any Church member. As one member of the Quorum of the Twelve informed the author in 1990: "For a number of years it has been Church policy to include a disclaimer in works published by General Authorities which are not official declarations of the Church. This policy was adopted in order that those statements and declarations by the President of the Church or by the First Presidency which are official declarations might be separated from the many books and publications written by General Authorities. The publications, therefore, must speak for themselves, but are not to be accepted in the same category as if the President of the Church was making an official declaration."[7]

At the time Elder McConkie wrote *Mormon Doctrine*, such a disclaimer was not yet standard practice. Thus, books written by General Authorities were sometimes mistakenly looked upon as representing the official position of the Church.

Elder McConkie wrote with a naturally authoritative tone. Undoubtedly part of the reason for this was his extraordinary understanding of the doctrines of the Church. He was rarely misunderstood. Yet this very strength might cause some who read the book without noticing the disclaimer to place prophetic weight on the teachings within the book. For this reason (and others less significant) the First Presidency and Council of the Twelve Apostles decided to give the new book specific attention.

Before reviewing the deliberations of the Brethren about *Mormon Doctrine*, it would be helpful to review how these men handle disagreements among themselves. Each has a high regard for the other, whatever their differences. As Elder Dallin H. Oaks has expressed it: "During the twenty years I have been intimately acquainted with the leaders of The Church of Jesus Christ of Latter-day Saints, I have marveled at how effectively they live the commandment to avoid disputation and contention. They are not always in agreement, but they are always in harmony. They are not uniform in opinions, but they are united in effort. They are many, but they are one."[8] Some of the story behind *Mormon Doctrine* provides evidence of the practical application of this principle.

On 5 January 1959, President David O. McKay assigned Elder Marion G. Romney to read Elder McConkie's book and report what he learned. Elder Romney did so, and on 28 January he wrote President McKay a lengthy letter detailing his findings.[9] Most of Elder Romney's report dealt with Elder McConkie's usage of forceful, blunt language; some strongly worded statements about ambiguous doctrine and matters of opinion; and the overall authoritative tone throughout the book, though in general Elder Romney had a high regard for *Mormon Doctrine* and felt it filled an evident need remarkably well.

After Elder Romney submitted his report, a year passed in which we have no information on any actions or discussions taken by the Brethren, beyond the inference from Elder Romney's letter that a committee was at some point appointed to look further into the matter.

Then, on 7 January 1960, "The First Presidency met with Elders Mark E. Petersen and Marion G. Romney. They submitted their report upon their examination of the book *Mormon Doctrine* by Elder Bruce McConkie." The discussion centered on the concerns that *Mormon Doctrine* had not been reviewed by the Brethren before publication and that Joseph Fielding Smith, Elder McConkie's father-in-law and at that time President of the Council of the Twelve, "did not know anything about it until it was published."[10]

At this point, Elder Mark E. Petersen had studied his own copy of the book. He seems to have given it a very thorough and exacting examination, for he had marked a total of 1,067 "corrections," affecting "most of the 776 pages of the book."[11] As an astute, capable, student of the gospel with a wide range of writing experience, Elder Peterson would undoubtedly have had many insights and opinions of his own, not all in perfect accordance with Elder McConkie's.[12]

It has also been suggested, that because of the distrust of the RLDS publication of the Inspired Version of the Bible, prevalent in the LDS

Church during this time, Elder Petersen may have marked every reference to it as a concern.[13] This explanation may well account for some recommended changes, but certainly not all of them. Using a computer search, this author found only 170 references to the Inspired Version (Joseph Smith Translation).[14]

Each of these three men—Elders Romney, Petersen, and McConkie—was an extraordinary man. Each was, or became, an Apostle of the Lord Jesus Christ, a special witness of Him, and each paid a significant price for personal spirituality and gospel knowledge. The Church is much better off today because of the tremendous service rendered by each of these Brethren.

The First Presidency decided that because the corrections which seemed necessary were so numerous that a second edition should not be published. They worried that it might have the effect of discrediting, to some degree, the General Authority author. They even entertained the possibility of some form of mild public correction to inform Church members that the book was the sole responsibility of Elder McConkie, but abandoned this idea. President McKay then decided to inform the Twelve of their conclusions.

On 8 January, the First Presidency again considered the matter of *Mormon Doctrine*, confirming the decision that it should not be republished. They also mentioned that they had been told that Elder McConkie had "made corrections in his book" for another edition, but remained firm that it would still be best not to proceed.

On Wednesday, 27 January, at 3:00 P.M., President McKay called President Joseph Fielding Smith and told him that the First Presidency had disapproved Elder McConkie's book as an "authoritative exposition" of the gospel:

> [President McKay] then said: "Now, Brother Smith, he is a General Authority, and we do not want to give him a public rebuke that would be embarrassing to him and lessen his influence with the members of the Church, so we shall speak to the Twelve at our meeting in the temple tomorrow, and tell them that Brother McConkie's book is not approved as an authoritative book, and that it should not be republished, even if the errors...are corrected." Brother Smith agreed with this suggestion to report to the Twelve, and said, "That is the best thing to do."

President McKay also asked President Smith to caution Elder

McConkie in writing letters and speaking on some of the controversial subjects included in his book, and further told him of their decision that General Authorities not publish books until they had been approved.[15]

On 28 January, President McKay reported his conversation with President Smith to his Counselors. They spoke of "handling the matter to avoid undermining Brother McConkie's influence." They also decided to "inform Brother McConkie before he learns of our decision from some other source."

It is moving to observe the consideration the First Presidency had for the welfare and influence of their fellow servant. They did not wish to impair his ability to carry out his calling in any manner, despite their concerns with his book.

At this point, Elder McConkie was invited to meet with the First Presidency. He was informed "of the desire of the First Presidency with reference to his book not being republished, to which he agreed." He said, "I am amenable to whatever you Brethren want. I will do exactly what you want. I will be as discreet and as wise as I can."

The caliber of Elder McConkie's character is revealed in his humble response to his leaders. It was a test, and it showed the teachable, correctable spirit of Bruce McConkie. Some others have not and would not do so well in such a position. It must have been painful to him to receive such direction from his Brethren, but he rose admirably to the test.

Later that day, President McKay reported to the Twelve the decisions reached and actions taken. He noted that the book had "caused considerable comment throughout the Church" and reiterated their concerns: it had not been reviewed before publication by the Brethren, Elder McConkie must take full responsibility for it, no public statement of correction would be made, and it would not be republished.[16]

As previously mentioned, Elder McConkie had already made some changes, anticipating a new edition. But with the decision not to republish, he simply dropped the matter and went on with his important work in the ministry. Thus it stood for several years, until around 1965-66. At about this time, the First Presidency reconsidered the matter. They then assigned Elder Spencer W. Kimball to work with Elder McConkie in producing a revised edition of *Mormon Doctrine*. Elder Kimball, a senior member of the Quorum of the Twelve, approached Elder McConkie and informed him of the Brethren's new decision in connection with the project. He (Elder Kimball) would act as an advisor.

Elder McConkie with Sister and President David O. McKay and Oscar McConkie Sr.

Upon the strength of this counsel, Elder McConkie proceeded to work with his publisher to come out with a second edition.[17]

In 1966, the second edition with its approved revisions was published. A careful review of the changes suggests that the most obvious difference between the two editions is a more moderate tone.[18]

The most noted change was within the entry entitled, "Church of the Devil," which was altered from designating the Catholic church as the church of the devil to mean all churches that teach false doctrines and oppose the kingdom of God on earth.

A second and equally notable entry discussing blacks and the priesthood had been cited by some who attempted to expose doctrinal errors in Elder McConkie's writings. More information on this entry is found in chapter 11, "The 1978 Revelation on the Priesthood." The changes made in this entry were not included in the second edition until after President Kimball received the 1978 revelation announcing that all men could now receive the priesthood, regardless of race, based solely on worthiness. All printings after this time have a revised entry.

Beyond these two most notable revisions, many less significant changes were made. For example, entries on "Communism" and "Conceived in Sin" were enlarged and added, respectively. Significant amounts of text were added to "Forgiveness" and "Good Works." Other entries dealing with doctrines found in other churches were dropped or revised. In this context, the most common word changed was *apostate* which was either removed or softened to read "uninspired," "false," "sectarian," or "modern." In all, approximately 313 pages contained one or more changes.[19]

A few other doctrinally interesting examples include the following:

Firmament: "Such was rather the apostate view of the apostate church in the dark ages" was changed to, "Such was rather the false view of the church...."

Gazalem: "Presumptively these and other names used...have particular meanings; it well could be that they are names taken from the pure language of Adam" was changed to "...have particular meanings, which are not now known to us."

King of Kings: "...those who gain exaltation are ordained kings and queens, priests and priestesses, to rule and reign in the house of Israel forever" was changed to "...ordained kings and queens, priests and priestesses, in which positions they shall exercise power and authority in the Lord's eternal kingdoms forever."

Millennium: "The sealed part of the Book of Mormon, for one thing, probably will not come forth until the millennium" was changed to, "If the sealed part of the Book of Mormon has not already been revealed, it will come forth in that day."

By late 1966 Elder McConkie again felt free to quote from *Mormon Doctrine* in his sermons, though when he did he included the self-deprecating comment "[that his book was] reputed to have said more than it ought to have said on some subjects."[20]

The concerns of Elder McConkie's fellow Brethren seem to have been in large measure allayed, though some reservations may still have remained. In July 1968, some two years after the publication of the revised, second edition, Elder Harold B. Lee took occasion to clarify the position of the Brethren relative to books written by authors in nonofficial positions. He spoke to Church Educational System teachers, telling them: "There is a vast difference between a book coming from the President of the Church containing his writings which we label gospel doctrine and a book coming from a writer not in such an authoritative position who labels his book, 'gospel doctrine.'"[21] Although Elder Lee did not specifically name Elder McConkie's book, it is likely that he was referring to it and others like it in order to teach how these writings should be viewed.

In the process of time, Elder McConkie changed or modified his position on certain doctrines published in *Mormon Doctrine*. One of the most significant and interesting of these pertains to the identity of the "Spirit of the Lord" spoken of in 1 Nephi 11. In *Mormon Doctrine* he wrote: "When we read the account of the appearance of 'the Spirit of the Lord' to Nephi (1 Ne. 11), we are left to our own interpretive powers to determine whether the messenger is the Spirit Christ or the Holy Ghost. Presumptively it is the Spirit Christ ministering to Nephi much as he did to the Brother of Jared, for such is in keeping with the principles of Advocacy, intercession, and mediation."

Many years later, in May 1984, in a *New Era* article, he taught the following: "The heavens were opened and John saw the Holy Ghost descending in peace and serenity, like a dove, to be and abide with the Lamb of God forever. This is one of *possibly two occasions* in all history, of which we have record, in which the personage of the Holy Ghost was seen by mortal man" (see Matt. 3:11-17; emphasis added). Undoubtedly, the only other instance recorded in scripture that Elder McConkie could refer to is in 1 Nephi 11.[22]

Today, *Mormon Doctrine* seems to have increased in favor among members of the Church. Because of Elder McConkie's prominent role with the scriptures publications project for the new LDS editions of the scriptures, he had a direct and profound influence on such scripturally interpretive helps as chapter and section headings, footnotes, and the Bible Dictionary. This last item, which he contributed substantially to, is one of the most valuable informational aids available in the Church. A careful examination shows that the doctrine contained in it closely mirrors that found in many entries of *Mormon Doctrine*. In fact, one article in the Bible Dictionary, "Abraham, covenant of," is word for word exactly the same in all but one paragraph as found under "Abrahamic covenant" in *Mormon Doctrine*. Other Bible dictionary articles such as Fall of Adam, Adam, Eve, Flesh, Death, Only Begotten, and Replenish also teach identical concepts with closely paralleled wording.

Some of these subjects have not always been regarded by the Brethren as proper material to be published with the scriptures. At one time, the Brethren felt it would be inappropriate to officially state that there was no death before the Fall, or that there were no pre-Adamites.[23] Partially because of Elder McConkie's influence and insight, these doctrines have been clarified and published by the Church in the Bible Dictionary.

Considering the sheer size, number of pages, number of entries, and scope of *Mormon Doctrine*, Elder McConkie basically performed a literary miracle in writing it. He had no computer or word processor to help him. The doctrinal, historical, secular, geographical, scholarly, and scriptural content all came from his voracious mind and comprehensive research. Never before had any Church member put so much sound doctrinal material together so ably.

Mormon Doctrine continues to be one of the most popular, most quoted, and most studied books in LDS publishing. It has broadened the gospel scholarship and doctrinal understanding of many members of the Church. When a talk needs to be given, a sermon preached, a lesson prepared, a manual or study guide written, or a host of other needs, it is one of the most common and reliable resources used.

A valuable lesson was learned by Elder McConkie from his experience with writing *Mormon Doctrine*, a lesson that could be summed up by relating an experience from the life of Elder Marion G. Romney. Shortly after being called as one of the new Assistants to the Twelve, "Marion soon found that there was more diversity in the personal opinions held by the General Authorities than he had ever suspected. Each one was an individual with a strong personality, and no one seemed inclined to yield his opinion until after a thorough consideration of the facts and issues. Some, it seemed, were not inclined to yield at all, especially to the reasoning and suggestions of a relatively young Assistant to the Twelve. Marion took comfort, however, from the fact that the final position of the Brethren was well considered and very apt to be sound."[24] Such was also the spirit of Elder Bruce R. McConkie.

Notes

1. An advertisement for *Mormon Doctrine: A Compendium of the Gospel,* first appeared in the September 1958 *Instructor* magazine, with a short, poorly worded description of its contents. At that time its price was $5. In November 1966, when the *Church News* noted the publication of the "enlarged *Mormon Doctrine,*" second edition, it sold for $6.95. This notice carried a strong endorsement of the book, though it included mention of the disclaimer. In 1985, a *Church News* article stated that 376,000 copies had been printed since 1958. It has now been through at least 40 printings, including the paperback edition. It is interesting to note that at the time of this publication (2000), a first edition in excellent condition sells for around $150-$250. If it contains Elder McConkie's signature and has a dust jacket, it can sell for as much as $400. Most copies of the first edition have a green cloth cover; however, some copies are in existence that have a black cloth binding. These copies have the same cover design with the figure of the Prophet Joseph Smith in the lower right corner of the front.

2. Dew, p. 52.

3. Smith, p. 692. The Video Biography states that it was during Bruce's military service that he began the actual work on *Mormon Doctrine.*

4. See Dew, p. 53.

5. *Mormon Doctrine,* Preface, 1st. ed.

6. See *Mormon Doctrine,* Preface, 1st. ed.

7. Correspondence, Boyd K. Packer to Dennis B. Horne, 24 April 1990.

8. Dallin H. Oaks, *The Lord's Way* (Salt Lake City: Deseret Book, 1991), p. 150.

9. Correspondence from Elder Marion G. Romney to President David O. McKay, dated 28 Jan. 1959. Copy in author's possession.

10. The following information on deliberations of the First Presidency comes from an unpublished document entitled, "Items from David O. McKay's Office Journal Relating to the Publication of Bruce R. McConkie's '*Mormon Doctrine*.'" This consists of four journal entries dated January 7, 8, 27, and 28. Hereafter cited as McKay Journal.

11. McKay Journal.

12. Elder Mark E. Petersen's daughter and biographer, Peggy Petersen Barton, wrote, "If Mark was aware that any of the General Authorities...might be preaching doctrine not in harmony with Church teachings, he never hesitated to point out the error in their thinking" (Peggy Petersen Barton, *Mark E. Petersen: A Biography* (Deseret Book: Salt Lake City, 1985), p. 167). Hereafter cited as Barton.

Since Elder Petersen's own opinions disagreed with some of Elder McConkie's opinions expressed in *Mormon Doctrine*, this sentence helps us understand why he stepped forward with his concerns.

13. See Thomas E. Sherry, *Attitudes, Practices, and Positions toward Joseph Smith's Translation of the Bible: A Historical Analysis of Publications, 1849-1987,* unpublished thesis, LDS Church Historical Dept, pp. 6-8. See also, Mark E. Petersen, *As Translated Correctly* (Salt Lake City: Deseret Book, 1966), pp. 29-31. Elder Petersen's personal misgivings toward the Inspired Version are here enumerated.

14. This computer search was done on the second edition of *Mormon Doctrine*. The author is assuming that there is little variance in this number between the two editions.

15. President McKay himself answered letters of inquiry about *Mormon Doctrine* by saying that it was not an official publication of the Church and that its author alone was responsible for the views expressed in it. For example, in a reply to a letter from a professor, President McKay said, "Neither '*Man, His Origin and Destiny*' by Elder Joseph Fielding Smith, nor '*Mormon Doctrine*' by Elder Bruce R. McConkie, is an official publication of the Church." (Correspondence, President David O. McKay to Dr. A. Kent Christenson, dated 3 February 1959; copy of unpublished letter in author's possession.)

16. It is the opinion of this author that President McKay did not read *Mormon Doctrine* in detail. It seems more likely that he relied on the reports and recommendations of the appointed committee (Elders Romney and Petersen).

17. Author's notes from telephone interview with Joseph Fielding McConkie, son of Bruce R. McConkie, 11 January 1997, and 26 July 1997.

18. It should be noted here that Elder Romney's report and letter were apparently not used in making the changes. Many of the items which Elder Romney reported

on were left untouched or received only slight revision.

19. The question naturally arises as to whether the majority of the revisions changed doctrinal meaning, or really did harm the authoritative credibility of the author. Though this is something of a matter of semantics, the opinion of this author is no. Doctrinal concepts may be reworded without significant change. Persons with their own mature background in gospel understanding will still gather what Elder McConkie is teaching. The continued high creditability of *Mormon Doctrine* is seen by the frequent use the book has received by the Brethren themselves in quotations found in Church manuals and publications, conference talks, etc.

20. Bruce R. McConkie, "Are the General Authorities Human?" Salt Lake Institute of Religion, LDS Student Association Devotional, 28 Oct. 1966, p. 2.

21. Harold B. Lee, "Viewpoint of a Giant," Summer School Devotional Address, 18 July 1968. p. 7; available in LDS Church Historical Department.

22. Bruce R. McConkie, "A Man Called John," *New Era*, May 1984, p. 6. In changing his position, Elder McConkie harmonized with others of the Brethren who have given their opinion that the personage of the Holy Ghost is the identity of the "Spirit of the Lord," mentioned in 1 Nephi 11. These Brethren include Elder James E. Talmage, *Discourses on the Holy Ghost*, comp. N. B. Lundwall (Salt Lake City: Bookcraft, 1959), p. 13; *The Articles of Faith,* 42nd. ed. (Salt Lake City: LDS Church, 1982), p. 159; President Marion G. Romney, "The Holy Ghost," *Ensign*, May 1974, p. 90; President Joseph F. Smith and his son Elder Hyrum M. Smith (James R. Clark, comp. *Messages of the First Presidency,* vol. 4 [1901-1915] (Salt Lake City: Bookcraft, 1970), p. 32; and Elder LeGrand Richards, *A Marvelous Work and a Wonder* (Salt Lake City: Deseret Book, 1950), p. 119.

23. James B. Allen, "The Story of the Truth, the Way, the Life," *BYU Studies* (vol. 33, no. 4), pp. 704-41.

24. F. Burton Howard, *Marion G. Romney: His Life and Faith.* Salt Lake City: Bookcraft, 1988. p. 160.

Chapter Six

Mission President

During the week preceding 18 February 1961, life changed again for Elder McConkie when he was notified by the First Presidency of his appointment as president of the Southern Australian Mission. After fifteen years as a member of the First Council of the Seventy, actively involved with missionary work worldwide, Bruce was given a chance for some hands-on experience, leading and teaching the missionaries himself.

After learning of his new assignment, Elder McConkie took Amelia on a hike up Ensign Peak. Standing together at this historic site overlooking the Salt Lake Temple, he told her they had been called to leave their home for a season and travel to Australia to continue their service to the Lord.[1] They had about five months to prepare for the new calling. So it was that on 20 July 1961, they flew to San Francisco, where they took a boat bound for Australia. Nine days later Bruce celebrated his forty-sixth birthday aboard ship. They took six of their children with them. Joseph Fielding was on a mission in Scotland, and their eldest daughter, Vivian, who had married by this time, remained in Salt Lake City. The children going with them ranged from ages 4 to 17 and of course found this to be a major change in their young lives as well.

Mission headquarters was located in Toorak. Upon arriving in Australia, President McConkie had a picture taken with some incoming missionaries and the outgoing mission president. Then it was time to go to work.

Excellent information on President McConkie's service in Australia is found in two articles from the *Church News*. A news item from 6 October 1962, when President McConkie was visiting Salt Lake City for general conference after having been in Australia for over a year, states:

> From the "Land Down Under," President Bruce R. McConkie of the Southern Australian Mission, brought word of an all-time high mark in

mission converts and willingness of members to build new chapels. A total of 12 new chapels is on the building program. Three are under construction. One is due to start in three weeks and sites have been purchased for eight others scheduled to start within a year.

There has been no difficulty getting six building missionaries to work on each chapel under supervision of supervisors called from the states. Members readily contribute their share of building costs. "These new buildings aid greatly in missionary work, giving dignity and stature to the Church," said President McConkie.

Missionaries are finding success in public surveys made on the streets. People willingly respond to questions about their knowledge of the Mormon Church, some of its prominent men and athletes, and the Tabernacle Choir. They frequently invite the missionaries to visit them in their homes to hear more about the Church. There is freedom to worship in Australia as in the United States, although a quota of 300 missionaries from outside of Australia has been allotted the Church. In addition to the 150 missionaries in the Southern Australia Mission, there [are] 16 missionaries called from Australian states.

The mission, in area, is one of the largest missions in the Church with some members living 3,000 miles away from headquarters in Victoria. President McConkie does most of his traveling by plane. Missionaries have cars for transportation. Melbourne Stake in the Southern Australian Mission is one of three stakes now organized in all of Australia.

The second *Church News* article contains information obtained from President McConkie while in Salt Lake City during his third trip away from his mission (April 1964) while attending General Conference:

Copies of the Book of Mormon are being sold by missionaries in Australia at the rate of 75,000 a year. President Bruce R. McConkie of the First Council of the Seventy and president of the Southern Australian Mission, in Salt Lake City for General Conference, said this book of scripture is one of the main reasons conversions are soaring in "The Land Down Under."

In the past six years, conversions have increased from 228 in 1958 to 1,574 converts in 1963 in the Southern Australian Mission alone. There was an approximate total of 4,000 converts in all of Australia's stakes and missions, President McConkie said. "The number of conversions promises to be even larger in 1964. We had 204 join the Church in February, the mission's biggest month so far," he said. "We are happy to report that most of the converts are complete families containing mature people willing and capable of accepting responsibilities and provide good leadership. While Melbourne Stake is the only stake organized in our mission, the type of people being baptized will make it possible to organize at least three more stakes before long. In the city of Adelaide alone, we have five branches and a membership near the 2,000 mark," said President McConkie.

The Church has graduated from the "cult group" and is now recognized by the public as a sound and stable organization, especially since the erection of many fine chapels. Under direction of Church Building Supervisors and with the aid of Church builders, a total of 43 chapels have been completed and 13 more are under construction.

President McConkie said the Southern Australian Mission covers half a continent, including the states of Victoria, South Australia, Western Australia and the island state of Tasmania. There are members 4,500 miles from mission headquarters in Melbourne. He has piled up a total of 250,000 miles of air travel during the three years he has been president of the mission. There are 260 missionaries laboring in the Southern Australian Mission and 190 in the Australian Mission. These missionaries are assisting the local membership to assume leadership responsibilities so that the growing self-government of the missions, patterned after stake organizations can quickly assume stake responsibilities when the First Presidency so directs, President McConkie said.

Quarterly conference visitors to the Australian stakes also visit the mission branches, attending mission conferences in Perth, Adelaide, and Hobart in Tasmania. Members look forward to the visits of General Authorities and general board members from the various auxiliaries. Modern methods of missionary work including films, visual aids, flannel boards, use of the illustrated Mormon Story and sale of the Book of Mormon aid missionaries to deliver the Gospel message. "Our missionaries love Australia and the people. While they naturally are strong in their feelings toward the British Empire, they are appreciative of America in many fields of social and cultural activities. It is a wonderful country, cities and urban area modern in every way and plenty of wide open spaces for expansion," said President McConkie.[2]

President McConkie was able to visit Church headquarters in Salt Lake City three times as a mission president, speaking in general conference each time. In October 1962, he spoke about the divine mission and calling of the Prophet Joseph Smith, suggesting that the "greatest question in the spiritual realm today is this: Was Joseph Smith called of God?" He said that "you cannot argue with a testimony" of Joseph Smith and the book he translated or the gospel he restored.

In April 1964 he again focused on Joseph Smith as a prophet of God.

In his sermon he reviewed the main events of Church history during which Joseph Smith restored the gospel, with its keys and powers and revelations.

Finally, for the sermon of his third visit, he spoke of the crucial need for all men to come unto Christ, for that is where salvation is found. Apostles and prophets deliver His message and must be accepted, for without belief in them men cannot believe in Christ.

It is natural that Bruce would talk about these basic and important subjects in his addresses while a mission president, for it is in missionary work that the most basic, fundamental truths and doctrines of the gospel are taught. The Book of Mormon, the Prophet Joseph Smith, and the Restoration of the Church are the first things an investigator is taught and must pray about in order to get a testimony.

The missionaries quickly came to love their new mission president. His leadership style was one which fostered independence in the missionaries: "He led them, and they really just came to idolize him," remembered Amelia. "What he did was to make them learn to stand on their own feet. They would come and say, 'How do we do this? What should we do about that?' and he would say, 'What would you do? You go back and do what you think ought to be done.'"[3]

One native Australian missionary recalled his experience with mission president McConkie:

> I have to admit to a great deal of apprehension the day I climbed aboard the plane to answer the call....I will never forget the feeling of comfort I got when he met me at the airport and took me in his arms and then spent the weekend taking me everywhere he went, talking to me, teaching me, and getting me ready to serve.
>
> I remember one occasion when he invited his missionaries to a meeting at the top of a 4,000 foot mountain. The catch was that they had to walk. When they got to the top, worn, tired, and panting, they found Elder McConkie sitting fresh as a daisy, waiting for them.
>
> On another occasion, he called me out of the shower at 6 a.m. to ask me to gather all of the missionaries in the region for an all-day meeting. The most surprising thing about that invitation was that I was a very junior missionary and he was about 2,000 miles away at the time.
>
> I began to call the other missionaries to tell them about the meeting. Most thought it was an April Fool's joke, but eventually all of them, including the regional elders, assembled for the meeting.

The missionaries waited for over an hour for their mission president to arrive, many wondering if the young elder had understood the message accurately. Just as some were ready to call the meeting a hoax, President McConkie drove into the parking lot.

> That day we sat at his feet and were taught in vintage McConkie style, straight scripture—for seven hours.
>
> He started by saying he had asked us to meet to discuss one scripture. I remember to this day, more than two decades later, the exact verse because he elaborated on it, took it apart, examined every related reference and historical context for seven hours. When he had finished, we had spent the entire day on one verse. He stopped because it was obvious we couldn't take any more, not because he had no more to give. He was just getting started.[4]

President McConkie related another incident of enjoyment he had with his missionaries:

> One day in Hobart, Tasmania, I said to my missionaries, "We will hold our meeting on the top of Mount Wellington"—a tremendous mountain that overlooks the city and the bay. They did not realize I was serious at first, but after I told them that all great men, Moses, the brother of Jared, Nephi, and so on, climbed mountains, they consented. While it was scarce dawn we assembled at the foot of the mountain and spent a good many weary hours climbing to the top.
>
> On the top we found some television relay stations. Since we were there, we gained permission to be shown through. There was a very bright young man who, using language we did not understand, but speaking with a tone of authority, explained in detail the things that were involved in relaying television broadcasts. I was totally unable to comprehend or understand what was involved, but I knew that the thing did take place.

President McConkie held his meeting with the missionaries and then they climbed back down the mountain: "That night, down in the valley again—two of my young sons were with me—we stayed in a room where there was a television set. They tuned the wave band of that set to the broadcast that came from the top of the mountain." President McConkie went on to explain the connection between how television is broadcast and received, and how the visions and revelations of eternity are sent and received, and how if an elder put himself in tune with the Spirit, by conforming to spiritual law, he might receive these revelations.[5] Elder

McConkie used this example to teach this principle more than once throughout his life. He knew the importance of the Spirit of revelation and inspiration in missionary work. "When I was the President of the Southern Australian Mission," he later said, "we, meaning the missionaries and members, set out to find a slogan, some succinct thought that would crystalize in our minds the course that, in wisdom, we all wanted to pursue. We came up with the statement: 'Seek the Spirit.'"[6]

Along with imparting to the missionaries the benefits of scripture study and inspiration, Bruce had some fun with them as well. Since the McConkies had left a recently married and very pregnant daughter behind when they came to Australia, Amelia was anxious about her welfare.

> One morning a telegram arrived at the mission home in Melbourne, and a well-meaning missionary delivered it to President McConkie. Later, at lunch, the elder asked about the telegram from Salt Lake City. "What telegram?" Amelia immediately demanded. "You got a telegram from home?" Her husband looked up from the other end of the table and replied, stoicly, "I might have." "Did Vivian send the telegram?" "No." Pause. Amelia pursued. "Was it her husband, Carlos?" "It might have been." "Did she have her baby?" Amelia's voice was rising in pitch with each question. "Something like that." "Is she okay? Is it a boy or a girl?" The questions poured as Amelia tried to get something substantive out of her husband. "The missionaries were getting the biggest wallop out of him, that rascal. Finally he told me our daughter had had a baby boy."[7]

On 2 December 1963 President Joseph Fielding Smith and his third wife, Jessie, visited them in Australia for ten days. Besides catching up on family news, he dedicated the new mission home; visited with the missionaries, members, and investigators; and presided at the Melbourne Stake conference. It was a joy for them to see each other again.[8]

Because of the limited means which come from the fixed living allowance of the Brethren, Amelia had become efficient and sparing with spending money. Once in Australia, where they worked with a new monetary system and a mission budget, Amelia continued to solicit advice from Bruce about how much to spend and what to buy. Because her husband was so busy running the mission, these questions tended to annoy him. One day she found he had typed her a short note which read:

> Dear Amelia. If the question can be answered by "Yea," or "Nay," the answer is "Yea." If it is a matter of "Do" or "Don't," then "Do." If it is

a question of "Shall I" or "Shall I not," you "Shall." If it is one of "Buy" or "Not Buy," you "Buy." Anything you do, I approve. Your acts are my acts. Please use your own judgment. And do not trouble me anymore on these matters. Your loving husband, Bruce R. McConkie. P.S. It's only money, and we only live once.[9]

Amelia got a hearty laugh from that note, as she knew it was his way of telling her to do whatever she liked.

President McConkie was careful to listen to the advice of those around him who knew more about certain things other than missionary work but were still under his jurisdiction and affected the mission. Stanford, who served under his father as a missionary, recalled, "[Dad] had a 19 year old mission secretary who knew more about cars than he did, so when they bought cars for the mission he listened to that elder's advice."[10]

Bruce also had a practical joke streak in him, though it was reserved for close friends and family. He once enjoyed the following joke with his wife. Amelia tried often to get rid of Bruce's old ties that he kept wearing, "One morning he put one of them on, then asked innocently, 'Amelia, would you like me to throw out this tie?' She quickly grabbed it, said, 'Yes!' and threw it in the garbage. The next morning he again put on a tie, looked at his wife questioningly, and asked, 'Would you like me to throw out this tie?' Again, she grabbed the tie and tossed it in the trash. The scenario was repeated for four days. 'All of a sudden one morning I realized it was the same tie. [He] kept pulling it out of the trash. That was a typical Bruce McConkie stunt.'"[11]

President McConkie had an unusual experience at a district conference in Perth. Several people in attendance at the Sunday afternoon session were on the brink of baptism, but were hesitating. When informed of this, he decided to speak on the subject of baptism. He had been told that the baptismal font was full, but as yet there was no one to baptize in it. So he stood and preached a powerful sermon on the need for baptism. At the conclusion of his talk, he called upon all there who had not been baptized to come forward. Nine people came up and asked for the privilege of receiving the ordinance. He and his elders were happy to oblige.[12]

The life of a mission president is exceptionally busy and time consuming. Bruce spent most of his time in travel, meetings, teaching and preaching, deciding missionary transfers, and strengthening his missionaries. Of course, any mission president has problems with their missionaries on occasion, but he was overall pleased with the success of the work. In addition to the supervision of the mission, he was also in charge of the many branches and wards—and the one stake—throughout the vast mission territory. He had to call and release, set apart and ordain, train and instruct, and teach and testify among all these areas where members lived as well. As noted, chapel construction was a high priority for him, for progress in this area meant that the Church was becoming firmly established and was growing rapidly. Twenty years later it was a special source of joy and satisfaction for him to preside at the ground-breaking ceremony for the first Australian temple.

According to one mission history, President McConkie flew to Perth monthly, holding meetings with the missionaries, officiating at ground-breaking and dedication ceremonies for chapels, and touring with visiting General Authorities. On 21 November 1962, Elder Ezra Taft Benson accompanied him to the opening ceremony of the commonwealth games held in Perth. They sat in the VIP box with the prime minister and Prince Philip of Great Britain. Others of the Brethren who visited during President McConkie's tenure were Elders Howard W. Hunter and Gordon B. Hinckley. On one occasion when he had visitors from the Mutual Improvement Association general board, they went sightseeing, including watching kangaroos in the wild.

President McConkie spent great effort and time teaching and training the elders in their duty and strengthening their faith. The following are a few recorded gems of wisdom and inspiration he gave to his missionaries:

> We need youth converts by the thousands and the tens of thousands in the mission. The destiny of the mission and of the Church rests with the rising generation.

> We need young people who will get their feet on the ground, marry in the Church, raise families and lay the foundation for an Australian Zion that soon will surpass in glory and beauty anything we have ever supposed.

> Mental assent to the truth of our message is not sufficient. To be converted, and thus ready for baptism, people must be touched by the Spirit. They must achieve a witness from the Holy Ghost that the work is true.

> Every missionary begins with a clean slate. Look forward and not backward. We have no failures, no problems we can't solve, with the

Lord's help.

How can anything but success attend our labors, when the Lord, by his Spirit, is our companion.

Above all else in life we should and do desire the companionship of the Holy Ghost.

Please take special occasion to thank the Lord for his goodness to us, and give the honor and glory to him for all that has been and will be accomplished in our work here.

We are called to do everything in our power to bring souls to Christ. Ours is the greatest work in the world, the greatest commission ever given to mortal man. We are sent to prune the vineyard the last time, to prepare a people for the second coming of the Son of Man.[13]

After serving their three years in Australia, the McConkies returned home to Salt Lake City. Bruce resumed his full-time service as a General Authority in the First Council of Seventy, though now with more first-hand, practical knowledge of the needs of the missionary program that he supervised.

He made a great impact on the work of the Lord in Australia and came to love the people dearly, always retaining a soft spot in his heart for them. One elder who was called to serve in Australia shortly after the McConkies left commented on the feelings the people had for him: "I had the privilege of meeting with members of the Church who had come to know Brother McConkie personally, and I could not help being impressed as they related to me what a spiritual impact he had had in their lives and what a tremendous leader he really is."[14]

Notes

1. See Van Orden, p. 10.

2. *Church News,* April 4, 1964, p. 5.

3. Video Biography, pp. 3-4.

4. *Ensign,* June, 1985. See also *the Provo Daily Herald,* 21 Apr. 1985.

5. Bruce R. McConkie, "Seek the Spirit," *Instructor,* Jan. 1966, p. 22.

6. Bruce R. McConkie, "Lectures in Theology: Last Message Series," Salt Lake Institute of Religion Devotional Address, 22 Jan. 1971, p. 2.

7. Dew, p. 51.

8. Joseph Fielding Smith, Jr., and John J. Stewart, *Life of Joseph Fielding Smith* (Salt Lake City: Deseret Book, 1972), pp. 317-18. Hereafter cited as Smith and Stewart.

9. Dew, p. 51.

10. Dew, p. 58.

11. Dew, p. 51.

12. See *Church News,* 29 Aug, 1964, p. 5; *Church News,* 31 July, 1965, p. 16.

13. Unpublished manuscript titled, "Southern Australia Mission History, 1961-1964: They came, they saw, they conquered." 4 pages. No author given. Available in Archives Division, LDS Historical Department. Copy in possession of the author.

14. Bruce R. McConkie, "Lectures in Theology: Last Message Series," Salt Lake Institute of Religion Devotional Address, 22 Jan. 1971; see introduction by Bob Williams.

Mission President

Chapter Seven

Author

Because of Elder McConkie's legal training, newspaper reporting experience, and love for the scriptures, it would seem surprising if he had not become a student and subsequent author of gospel-centered writings. His nearly forty years of service as a General Authority was marked by a continuous flow of literary projects. He seemed to have an innate need to write about, compile, and teach the doctrine of the kingdom. He had his own peculiar style of writing, though it varied somewhat over the years. His early sermons and articles, written largely for Church publications, have a distinctive style, and as he grew in his service in the ministry his power and depth in doctrinal expression increased.

His first book, *Mormon Doctrine,* was encyclopedic in format and was written as concisely as Elder McConkie could. There was not a great deal of room to wax eloquent. Years later, when he wrote his books dealing with the life of Christ and the biblical prophets, he did not hold to such confinement. In both his speaking and writing, Elder McConkie emulated the spirit of the Old Testament. As close examination of his writings reveals, it was not unusual for him to restate, in similar language, the same doctrinal principle or concept multiple times. It was as though he naturally emulated the Hebrew style of repetition when praising the Lord and his doctrine.

Another McConkie trademark was his tendency to write with a rather formal, Jacobean English phraseology. He reverenced the formal biblical language and therefore adopted it in his writing style, especially when treating a subject he considered especially sacred or important. He even blended it into his prayerlike prose on occasion.

Though repetition can be unnecessarily redundant, in his case it was an effective teaching method; as was the case with many great teachers, Elder McConkie used repetition to embed a principle in the mind of a student. Furthermore, though the formal language of scripture may be cumbersome to the modern reader, it has its advantages. It challenges the mind and invites the reader to discover the beauty of scriptural language. Because of the prodigious amount of time he spent reading it, scriptural language became second nature to Elder McConkie. Indeed it was at times difficult to determine where the scripture quotation ended and his own language began, unless one were well acquainted with the scripture passage itself.

Over his lifetime, Elder McConkie wrote a great deal. In addition to the 11 major books he wrote, he authored many articles for Church magazines. He wrote lesson manuals for Church auxiliaries and he critiqued, edited, reviewed, and approved (or disapproved) others' writings for similar publications. He also wrote several pamphlets on basic doctrinal subjects (such as the Godhead), which were used as missionary tracts.

He became noted for his serious and direct writing style. One certainly understood his intent after reading his work. He often prefaced his writings with a notice that he had sought the Spirit of the Lord in preparation for the task and his only desire was to write what the Lord wanted him to write. In this, he succeeded admirably.

It is fair to say that by the end of his life, his final manuscripts reached a zenith. His last book, *A New Witness for the Articles of Faith,* is a masterwork. It is his magnum opus. He reaches a doctrinal level that few have equaled.

In the early fifties, Elder McConkie compiled selected "sermons, statements, correspondence," and other sources authored by his father-in-law, Joseph Fielding Smith. He did this by "working early and late (during what his wife, Amelia, half jokingly called 'her' time) and in intervals...when he could squeeze out a few minutes for the task from his duties as a General Authority."[1] These materials were eventually compiled by subject matter into three volumes entitled *Doctrines of Salvation.* Volume 1 came off the press in late 1954 and became an immediate success. Volumes 2 and 3 followed in 1955 and 1956, respectively. They were quick sellers and soon became standard references for the hungry student, attesting to their being a valuable contribution to the doctrinal literature of the church.[2]

Readers found that President Smith had spoken on numerous subjects for which there was little authoritative commentary available. His doctrinal analysis and reasoning was clear and unmistakable. Students of the gospel appreciated this clarity. He spoke simply, without flowery,

Elder McConkie presents volume one of *Doctrines of Salvation* to Joseph Fielding Smith, 13 November 1954.

verbose expression. Since their original release, these books have been among the most popular and influential LDS books ever published. They are especially significant for their unequivocal stand against false doctrine and the theories of men, which President Smith sought so diligently to eradicate. Untold thousands of Latter-day Saints have thus become the beneficiaries of Elder McConkie's time and effort.

In the December 1955 *Improvement Era,* an advertisement appeared promoting a book entitled *Sound Doctrine: The Journal of Discourses Series,* vol 1., edited by Bruce R. McConkie. The caption read, "At long last a great wealth of authoritative information comes to light from a series of books unknown and unavailable to this generation. This vital doctrinal source contains important sermons of the Presidency and the Council of the Twelve during the all important 40 year period in which most of the doctrines of the church were being revealed and recorded. These sermons, delivered by men who knew the Prophet Joseph and were taught by him in public and private, are published in full."

The book pictured in the advertisement was a bound volume of blank pages, with a dust jacket wrapped around it. *Sound Doctrine* was to be a ten-volume series, containing sermons selected from the *Journal of Discourses* and edited by Elder McConkie. The project never got off the ground and was discontinued. Later, Elder McConkie gave the contract for the series to his son Joseph, who assembled a single book called *Journal of Discourses Digest.* This was the only volume ever published. Marvin Wallin, the manager of Bookcraft, decided it would be more profitable to sell the actual 26-volume *Journal of Discourses* set than a 10-volume set of excerpts, thus halting the project permanently.[3]

During the same time that Elder McConkie was working on the *Doctrines of Salvation* he was also working on *Mormon Doctrine,* which was published in 1958 (See chapter 6, *"Mormon Doctrine"*).

In 1961, Elder McConkie wrote a comparatively short, 38-page treatise entitled *Cultism as Practiced by the so-called Church of the Firstborn of the Fullness of Times.* It was not publically published and today can only be found in archive repositories.[4] The document contains Elder McConkie's analysis and refutation of the claims of an apostate fundamentalist group whose members were excommunicated from the Church. It provides an excellent summary of the doctrines of the LDS Church concerning such subjects as conferral of priesthood authority, the law of common consent, revelation for the Church, witnesses, priesthood offices, the keys of the kingdom, authority of the Twelve Apostles, the office of Church Patriarch, the name of the true Church, plural marriage, "the one mighty and strong," the future destiny of the LDS Church, the history of the priesthood authority of Brigham Young and Benjamin F. Johnson, and other related matters which fall within the scope of various apostate groups claims. In this skillful treatise, Elder McConkie quoted extensively from the revelations, especially the Doctrine and Covenants.

In the years 1966, 1971, and 1973 respectively, Elder McConkie published three volumes of *Doctrinal New Testament Commentary* (referred to as *DNTC* in this chapter), which provide a detailed commentary of the teachings of the Lord Jesus Christ during his mortal ministry and of the successive prophets and apostles of the meridian day. These three volumes, totaling about 2,000 pages, remain the most complete and reliable examination and explanation of the New Testament text that exists. They make use of the best available secular scholarship while remaining anchored in the light of modern revelation. Elder McConkie made special use of the Inspired Version, or Joseph Smith Translation, of the Bible, commenting frequently on the added insight this revelation gives to biblical passages.

He understood that his New Testament commentary filled a need:

> Even in the true Church there are few sound scriptorians and theologians who have a comprehensive knowledge of revealed truth. So far this dispensation has not been noted for the diffusion of real gospel scholarship among the elders and saints generally. There are few modern experts on the gospel. Few have paid the price of intense study, of determined self-discipline, and of righteous living necessary to gain a broad knowledge of the truths of salvation. Nearly all members of the Church need to study the revealed word far more than they now do.[5]

This observation also points out the deficiencies that Elder McConkie perceived in the way Church members study the gospel. The basic problem was that not enough study was happening. His statement should serve as a catalyst for all who fall short of regular, meaningful effort. His interest in the subject made it easy for him to set an example: "One of the things that I enjoy doing more than anything else is just the simple matter of studying the doctrines of the gospel and organizing them by subject and solving and analyzing doctrinal problems. That, of course, is what I was doing when I wrote *Mormon Doctrine* and, in a very large degree, what I was doing on this New Testament commentary."[6]

Elder McConkie also desired to help the Saints avoid the doctrinal traps of the extant sources of Christian scholars:

> This [*DNTC*] is designed as a tool to aid the saints to gain a knowledge of the Lord's dealings with his people in the meridian of time. Needless to say, the many New Testament commentaries prepared by the scholars of the world are of slight value to the saints. Such books are all written without reference to the great flood of gospel truth now available through latter-day revelation; their authors speak from the perspective of an apostate Christendom, without having a comprehensive knowledge of the whole plan of salvation. In many instances their evident purposes are to minimize, question, or out-and-out deny the divinity of our Lord. In almost every instance they reach false doctrinal conclusions.[7]

This substantial doctrinal guide to the New Testament was sorely needed, yet some wondered about his direct manner. Once asked why he wrote so critically when conveying his opinion of non-LDS biblical commentaries, Elder McConkie said: "If I'm working on something like this *Doctrinal New Testament Commentary* obviously I read what the commentators of the world have said about these things, but I certainly don't read them to learn. I read them primarily because they make me angry at the modernistic and unstable views that are presented. In consequence of which, I write from our perspective with a good deal more vigor than I would have done if I hadn't seen the absurd, sectarian delusions that fill them."[8] Even today, Elder McConkie's commentaries are the most detailed and thorough in the Church. Other scholars and General Authorities have written fine works on New Testament subjects and history, but no one has yet approached the scope of *DNTC*.

The following are a few interesting and revealing "McConkie" observations from the pages of *DNTC*. They are statements selected to exemplify the flavor, boldness, and incisive insights of his writings on New Testament doctrines.

Volume 1

THE BIRTH OF JESUS

"Gabriel came to Mary before her conception, and to Joseph after it became apparent that his espoused wife was with child."

"Mary was a virgin...until after the birth of our Lord. Then, for the first time, she was known by Joseph, her husband; and other children, both sons and daughters, were then born to her....She conceived and brought forth her Firstborn Son while yet a virgin because the Father of that child was an immortal personage."

"Just as Jesus is literally the Son of Mary, so he is the personal and literal offspring of God the Eternal Father, who himself is an exalted personage having a tangible body of flesh and bones."

"Our Lord was destined to have all of the essential experiences of mortality, including conception and birth in the natural and literal sense." (*DNTC*, 1:82-83.)

THE TRANSFIGURATION

"Until men attain a higher status of spiritual understanding than they now enjoy, they can learn only in part what took place upon the Mount of Transfiguration. From the New Testament accounts and from the added light revealed through Joseph Smith it appears evident that...

"...John the Baptist, previously beheaded by Herod, apparently was also present. It may well be that other unnamed prophets, either coming as translated beings or as spirits from paradise, were also present."

"It appears that Peter, James, and John received their own endowments while on the mountain....It also appears that it was while on the mount that they received the more sure word of prophecy, it then being revealed to them that they were sealed up unto eternal life."

"Apparently God the Father, overshadowed and hidden by a cloud, was present on the mountain, although our Lord's three associates, as far as the record stipulates, heard only his voice and did not see his form."

"It is not to be understood that John the Baptist was the Elias who appeared with Moses to confer keys and authority upon those who then held the Melchizedek Priesthood....Rather, for some reason that remains unknown—because of the partial record of the proceedings—John played some other part in the glorious manifestations then vouchsafed to mortals."[9] (*DNTC*, 1:399-401, 404.)

MARRIAGES IN HEAVEN

"[Jesus] is not *denying* but *limiting* the prevailing concept that there will be marrying and giving in marriage in heaven....Because he does not choose to cast his pearls before swine, and because the point at issue is not *marriage* but *resurrection* anyway, Jesus does not here amplify his teaching to explain that there is marrying and giving of marriage in heaven only for those who live the fulness of gospel law—a requirement which excludes *worldly* people."

"And for that matter, there is no revelation, either ancient or modern, which says there is neither marrying nor giving in marriage in heaven itself for righteous people. All that the revelations set forth is that such is denied to the Sadducees and other worldly and ungodly people." (*DNTC,* 1:606-7.)

WASHING OF FEET

Washing of feet is a gospel ordinance; it is a holy and sacred rite, one performed by the saints in the seclusion of their temple sanctuaries. It is not done before the world or for worldly people." (*DNTC,* 1:708; see also pages 709-11.)

Volume 2

THE PROMISE OF THE FATHER

"This promise was twofold: 1. They would receive the gift of the Holy Ghost; and 2. They would receive a holy and sacred endowment, one reserved for the faithful, and of such a nature as to prepare them in all things to work out their salvation." (*DNTC,* 2:22.)

SPIRITUAL EXPERIENCE

"Paul and other pillars of spiritual strength have been caught up into heaven and have seen and heard marvelous things which cannot be revealed to the less spiritually talented and indeed can only be comprehended by those who do hear and see." (*DNTC*, 2:446; see also pages 445-47.)

Volume 3

CALLING AND ELECTION

"To have one's calling and election made sure is to be sealed up unto eternal life; it is to have the unconditional guarantee of exaltation in the highest heaven of the celestial world; it is to receive the assurance of godhood; it is, in effect, to have the day of judgment advanced, so that an inheritance of all the glory and honor of the Father's kingdom is assured prior to the day when the faithful actually enter into the divine presence to sit with Christ in his throne." (*DNTC*, 3:330; pages 323-55 constitute one of the most detailed explanations of the doctrine of one's calling and election being made sure that is available in LDS literature.)

THE TRANSLATION OF MOSES

"It appears, then, that Satan—ever anxious to thwart the purposes of God—'disputed about the body of Moses' meaning that he sought the mortal death of Israel's lawgiver so that he would not have a tangible body in which to come—along with Elijah, who also was taken up without tasting death—to confer the keys of the priesthood upon Peter, James, and John." (*DNTC*, 3:423.)

These brief examples are but a minuscule sample of the thousands of choice, insightful, and informative doctrinal explanations of Biblical passages that constitute the treasures found in this commentary for LDS Bible students.

Elder McConkie relied heavily upon his own previous writings in *Mormon Doctrine*, making limited use of certain sectarian commentaries where they were helpful for historical, geographical, and cultural purposes.[10] He also quoted from *Teachings of the Prophet Joseph Smith* extensively. And because of his heavy use of the Inspired Version of the

Bible (now known as the Joseph Smith Translation, or JST), it began to be more accepted as a resource for members of the Church.[11]

Elder McConkie was called as a member of the Council of the Twelve Apostles about the same time that his third volume of the *New Testament Commentary* was published. Within a few short years, he began a comprehensive work on the Messiah, a six-volume series that took a broader look at the Lord's eternal ministry. (See chapter 12 for further information.)

During the last years of his life Elder McConkie wrote his final book, *A New Witness for the Articles of Faith* (hereafter *A New Witness*), the manuscript for which was delivered to the publisher shortly after his passing. Because of the serious state of his struggle with cancer when he wrote *A New Witness*, Elder McConkie undoubtedly wrote it while experiencing severe pain. His last two years were anything but easy, yet he completed the manuscript enough for the publication process to begin.[12] It was the first draft, and he did not "have the opportunity to review the text in the several stages of the publication, as was his custom. With his other published works he had the opportunity to provide a detailed reference to every quotation, to read and polish, to reorganize and clarify up to the day that the finished work was 'locked up' and the press would roll."[13] These limitations are not immediately obvious, for the first draft (plus any editing performed by others) is consistently good.

As deep, profound, insightful, and astute as his other books were, *A New Witness* seems to sound even greater depths in the gospel's treasure house. Elder McConkie had come to the conclusion and climax of his apostolic ministry and had spent a lifetime studying the gospel, as recorded in the standard works and in the teachings of the Prophet Joseph Smith. This fact is manifest throughout the work. It is not perfect and does exhibit some of his propensity for repetition. It contains an abundance of his characteristic poetic and formal language, but toward the end becomes more concise and pointed.

The publishers of *A New Witness* included Elder McConkie's last general conference talk as the preface, noting that it was the concluding act of his ministry. (Further information on this remarkable sermon is found in chapter 14 of this book.)

This chapter could not be complete without a closer look at some of the doctrinal contributions found in *A New Witness*. The following examples are some the author felt important and highlight the feel and the doctrine of this excellent book.

TALENTS

"[Joseph Smith] was born with all of the scriptural talents and capacities he had acquired through long ages of obedience and progression among his fellow prophets. Men are not born equal in talents and capacities; mortality commences where preexistence ends, and the talents earned in the life that went before are available for use in this mortal life." (P. 4; see also pp. 33-34.)

BELIEVING BLOOD

"What then is believing blood? It is the blood that flows in the veins of those who are the literal seed of Abraham—not that the blood itself believes, but that those born in that lineage have both the right and the special spiritual capacity to recognize, receive, and believe the truth. The term is simply a beautiful, a poetic, and a symbolic way of referring to the seed of Abraham to whom the promises were made. It identifies those who developed in preexistence the talent to recognize the truth and to desire righteousness." (P. 38-39.)

"THE MENACE OF MORMONISM"

"We do not, of course, believe all that our enemies, for their purposes, ascribe to us. Those in the sects of the world whose delight it is to expose us, as they suppose, and to warn all mankind against the menace of Mormonism, do not know and do not want to know what we really believe. Their self-assigned mission is to say that we believe this or that absurdity and then to warn others against us and our supposed doctrines. So be it. All must choose for themselves what they will believe; and true beliefs save, while false beliefs damn." (P. 42.)

TERRESTRIAL BEINGS

"Those destined to inherit the terrestrial kingdom are: (1) those who died 'without law' those heathen and pagan people who do not hear the gospel in this life, and who would not accept it with all their hearts should they hear it; (2) those who hear and reject the gospel in this life and then accept it in the spirit world; (3) those 'honorable men of the earth, who are blinded by the craftiness of men'; and (4) those who are lukewarm members of the true church and who have testimonies, but who are not true and faithful in all things. (See D&C 76:71-80.)" (P. 146.)

BECOMING AS GOD

"If men become like [God], they ascend the throne of eternal power, are exalted to the highest state that exists in all the endless expanse of created things, and are themselves gods. Thus salvation is not only the greatest of all the gifts of God, it is also the chief and most glorious of all the fruits of faith." (P. 196.)

FAITH

"In the eternal sense, because faith is the power of God himself, it embraces within its fold a knowledge of all things. This measure of faith, the faith by which the worlds are and were created and which sustains and upholds all things, is found only among resurrected persons. It is the faith of saved beings. But mortals are in process, through faith, of gaining eternal salvation.

"The brother of Jared stands out as a good illustration of how the knowledge of God is gained by faith, and also of how that perfect knowledge, from a mortal perspective, replaces faith." (Pp. 209, 211.)

THE LIGHT OF CHRIST

"There is a spirit—the Spirit of the Lord, the Spirit of Christ, the light of truth, the light of Christ—that defies description and is beyond mortal comprehension. It is in us and in all things; it is around us and around all things; it fills the earth and the heavens and the universe. It is everywhere, in all immensity, without exception; it is an indwelling, immanent, ever present, never-absent spirit. It has neither shape nor form nor personality. It is not an entity nor a person nor a personage. It has no agency, does not act independently, and exists not to act but to be acted upon.

"It is the light of Christ; it is the life that is in all things; it is the law by which all things are governed; it is truth shining forth in darkness; it is the power of God who sitteth upon his throne. It may be that it is also priesthood and faith and omnipotence, for these too are the power of God." (P. 257.)

PRIESTHOOD AND FAITH

"Priesthood is the very power of God himself. In the broadest sense, priesthood and faith, the two wielded together as one, constitute the power by which the worlds were and are and everlastingly shall be made. Through the priesthood, the sidereal heavens were framed. By this power, worlds without number have been created, peopled, and redeemed." (P. 309.)

PRIESTHOOD IS ETERNAL

"There were priesthood holders in preexistence; there are many who have held and hold priestly powers in this probationary estate; and exalted beings will rule with this divine power to all eternity." (P. 310.)

THE CHURCH OF THE FIRSTBORN

"The Church of the Firstborn is the church among exalted beings in the highest heaven of the celestial world. It is the church among those for whom the family unit continues in eternity. In a sense it is the inner circle within the Lord's church on earth. It is composed of those who have entered into that patriarchal order which is called the new and everlasting covenant of marriage." (P. 337.)

THE CHURCH IN THE MILLENNIUM

"Our avowed belief in 'the same organization that existed in the

Primitive Church' means that we have the same keys, the same priesthood, and the same priesthood offices as were had in the meridian of time, though this has not always been the way the earthly kingdom has been organized. Paul promised that apostles, prophets, evangelists, pastors, and teachers would remain in the true church until that Millennial day when there was a 'unity of the faith.'" (P. 348.)

GIFTS OF THE SPIRIT

"Healing and being healed and raising the dead are only the beginning of miracles. Properly gifted persons control the elements, move mountains, turn rivers out of their course, walk on water, quench the violence of fire, are carried by the power of the Spirit from one congregation to another, are translated and taken up into heaven, or–and this above all–gain for themselves an eternal inheritance in the presence of Him who is Eternal. Miracles are now, have always been, and always will be part and portion of the true gospel of that God who is a God of miracles. They are the gifts of the Spirit." (P. 373.)

WE HAVE SEEN GOD

"In ages past we dwelt as spirits in the divine presence on some distant sphere; we saw God, heard his voice, and knew he was our Father; we then walked by sight." (P. 475.)

THE TALENT OF SPIRITUALITY

"The greatest and most important talent or capacity that any of the spirit children of the Father could gain is the talent of spirituality. Most of those who gained this talent were chosen, before they were born, to come to earth as members of the house of Israel.

"Though all mankind may be saved by obedience, some find it easier to believe and obey than others." (P. 512.)

LOCATION OF LOST TRIBES

"There is something mysterious and fascinating about believing the Ten Tribes are behind an iceberg somewhere in the land of the north, or that they are on some distant planet that will one day join itself with the earth....They are scattered in all the nations of the earth, primarily in the nations north of the lands of their first inheritance." (P. 520.)

THE ARTICLES OF FAITH

"It is the hope and prayer of this disciple that the doctrines announced and the truths taught in the Articles of Faith may live in the hearts of the Latter-day Saints and of all who will yet join with them in striving to gain that eternal life which is the greatest of all the gifts of God." (P. 702.)

As is apparent from the foregoing examples, Elder McConkie expressed himself plainly on doctrines that some may consider "mysteries." To him, they were not mysteries, for a thing is only a mystery to those who do not understand it. Once something is learned, it is no longer a mystery. For Elder McConkie, a multitude of issues that are mysteries to many in the Church, were not so to him.

The many cited examples in this chapter also serve to point out that Elder McConkie knew how to write—to clearly and correctly express his mind and knowledge. He used well the rules of grammar, punctuation, and spelling, and organized his material logically. When he turned in his final draft, he submitted a polished manuscript. Eleanor Knowles, an employee of Deseret Book who edited some of Elder McConkie's books, remembered that "his manuscripts were wonderful to work on. Elder Bruce R. McConkie was one of the finest writers in the Church. We [did] less editing on his work than on any other. He is very accurate and uses excellent grammar. His are the most carefully thought-out manuscripts I have ever seen."[14]

For Elder McConkie, the writing of thousands of pages of solid, insightful, doctrine had to be sandwiched into the arduous schedule which dominates the life of a General Authority. A reporter once asked him when he found the time and was told, "[I work] early in the morning and late at night. [I] open a book every chance [I] get, on an airplane or in an airport."[15] He also said, "I have research and writing projects that would never, ever get done if I didn't have Mondays and holidays."[16]   A colleague offered this observation, "Years of toil late into the night and in the early morning hours" is how he accomplished so much. "How did he ever find time to be a busy member of the Council of the Twelve and also write those six large volumes on the life and ministry of Christ? Undoubtedly, early morning and late night lamps burned brightly in his study. The Spirit rested upon him as he wrote and testified of Christ."[17]

This precious, sweet spirit which rested upon him as he studied and wrote distilled within him the knowledge and insight which pervades his books and articles. He once described this process to a group of Church leaders:

> I have spent many hours poring over and pondering the scriptures. In seeking to learn the doctrines of salvation, I have studied, weighed, and compared what the various prophets have said about the same subjects.
>
> Time and again, after much praying and pondering about a given point, new and added concepts have burst upon me showing deep and hidden truths that I had never before known.[18]

On another occasion he added:

> It would be a great surprise to most people, I think, to know that the very large percent of any study I do is on the scriptures themselves.
>
> I think that people who study the scriptures get a dimension to their life that nobody else gets, and that can't be gained in any way except by studying the scriptures.
>
> There's an increase in faith and a desire to do what's right and a feeling of inspiration and understanding that comes to people who study the gospel—meaning particularly the Standard Works—and who ponder the principles, that can't come in any other way.[19]

Students of gospel doctrine are greatly blessed by the inspiration found within the covers of the many books he has authored. His fellow Brethren have also recognized his abilities and genius, magnified by the inspiration of heaven and manifested in his written works. President Ezra Taft Benson was one who felt strongly about them: "I loved to read his scholarly writings. Thanks be to God that Elder McConkie's written words of testimony remain to continue to bless a world that needs them desperately."[20]

President Gordon B. Hinckley also spoke of the power found in Elder

McConkie's discourses, which apply to his books as well, when he said: "No one can discount the immensity of his understanding. No one can shrink the breadth of his knowledge. He had his own unique style. With measured words, firm and unequivocal and with order and logic, he wove the patterns of his discourses. His language was clear, its meaning unmistakable. There was a cadence to it. There was a peculiar strength and beauty in its pattern."[21]

Perhaps Elder Boyd K. Packer said it best when he stated, "Perhaps one day we will see how great a man has walked among us. He was not less than Elder Talmage or the others we revere from the past. His sermons and writing will live on. In these, he will live longer than any of us."[22]

In 1989, just four years after Elder McConkie's death, his son Mark L. McConkie arranged a compilation of his father's writings in a book entitled *Doctrines of the Restoration: Sermons and Writings of Bruce R. McConkie.* This excellent book contains some of the less-known sermons and articles of Elder McConkie's that are not always easily accessible. It is patterned after Elder McConkie's compilation of his father-in-law's books, *Doctrines of Salvation,* being divided into subject categories. Each category has an introduction written by Mark which contains excellent explanatory material. Also, there are a number of helpful notes which give added commentary on certain doctrinal and historical details mentioned in the book. These notes are improved by Mark's connection with the family and his personal knowledge of certain related circumstances.

Notes

1. Gibbons, *Smith,* pp. 390-91.

2. See Gibbons, *Smith,* p. 391. For further information, see the books themselves.

3. Telephone interview with Joseph Fielding McConkie, son of Bruce R. McConkie, 11 Jan. 1997.

4. This author has found it in both the LDS Historical Department, Salt Lake City, Utah; and the BYU Special Collections Department, Harold B. Lee Library, Brigham Young University, Provo, Utah.

5. *DNTC*, p. 59.

6. Quotation from interview by David Croft, *Church News,* 24 January 1976.

7. *DNTC*, p. 59.

8. Quotation from interview by David Croft, *Church News,* 24 January 1976. Joseph Fielding McConkie related the following story and commentary about his father, Elder McConkie:

"As he waited for his flight to be announced, my father buried himself in a book by a renowned New Testament scholar. He was delighted to discover material by a sectarian scholar that constituted a marvelous defense of Mormonism. As he boarded the flight he met Marion G. Romney, then a member of the First Presidency. He said, 'President Romney, I have got to read this to you. This is good.' And proceeded to share his newfound treasure. When he finished, President Romney said, 'Bruce, I have to tell you a story. A few years ago I found something that I thought was remarkable written by one of the world's great scholars. I read it to J. Reuben Clark, and he said, "Look, when you read things like that, and you find that the world doesn't agree with us, so what? And when you read something like that and you find they are right on the mark and they agree with us, so what?"' My father thought that a good lesson....

"My father read widely. He had a fine library of well-read books. He read the best of Latter-day Saint writers and the best of secular scholars. His standard of measure, however, was always the revealed gospel." (Joseph Fielding McConkie, *Here We Stand* [Salt Lake City: Deseret Book, 1995], pp. 113-14.

9. JST, Mark 9:1.

10. These were by J. R. Dummelow and Jamieson, Fausset, and Brown. See the Abbreviations page in any volume of *DNTC* for further information.

11. See chapter 13 for more information on Elder McConkie's use of the Joseph Smith Translation.

12. The "Publisher's Preface" to *A New Witness* states: "The first draft of the manuscript was delivered to the publisher [Deseret Book] shortly before he passed away."

13. *A New Witness*, Publisher's Preface.

14. *Church News,* 28 April 1985, p. 14.

15. *Church News,* 28 April 1985, p. 14.

16. Quotation from interview by David Croft, *Church News,* 24 January 1976.

17. John K. Carmack, "The Testament of Bruce R. McConkie," BYU Fireside Address, 5 May 1985, pp. 109, 111. Hereafter cited as Carmack, "Testament."

18. *Ensign*, Dec. 1985, p. 59.

19. Quotation from interview by David Croft, *Church News,* 24 January 1976.

20. Ezra Taft Benson, unpublished funeral remarks, typescript, p. 2. Copy in author's file.

21. Gordon B. Hinckley, unpublished funeral remarks, typescript, p. 14. Copy in author's file.

22. Packer, p. 263.

19 January 1976. Amelia talks about being a general authority's wife during interview.

Chapter Eight

Amelia and Family Life

Amelia Smith McConkie is the seventh child of Joseph Fielding Smith and his second wife, Ethel. She was named Amelia in honor of her grandmother Amelia Jane Reynolds, wife of George Reynolds, who was known throughout the Church because of his being the famous test case on the constitutionality of polygamous marriages before the Supreme Court. When he lost the case he became the first polygamous Mormon to spend time in the state penitentiary. George served much of his life as a secretary to several Presidents of the Church and was later called as a General Authority himself. He was also a prolific author and noted doctrinal authority, especially on the Book of Mormon.

Amelia Smith was born 21 June 1916 in Salt Lake City.[1] She was raised with a very large family as the daughter of a prominent General Authority and became accustomed to that kind of life. On 26 August 1937 her mother, Ethel, passed away. She had been ailing for several months and finally died of a cerebral hemorrhage.

A month and a half later, Amelia married Bruce. Over their years of marriage together, they had nine children: Bruce R. Jr. (who died as an infant), Vivian, Joseph Fielding, Stanford Smith, Mary Ethel, Mark Lewis, Rebecca, Stephen Lowell, and Sarah Jill.[2]

Elder S. Dilworth Young gave this synopsis of Amelia:

> And what about Amelia McConkie? She has stood by his side, a true helpmeet. In their young married life when money was scarce she enlarged it by her skill in handling a home, in cooking, sewing, and household work. With eight children to care for, she found time to be by his side on hikes, camps, socials, and in the physical labor of making a home. She is an expert seamstress and has for years made her own clothes as well as those of her girls.
>
> Sister McConkie has taught in Sunday School, Primary, and YWMIA. She was a stake Relief Society president before going to Australia and on

her return held the same post in a university student stake where she [was] revered by hundreds of young women. She [taught] Relief Society social relation lessons in her ward.

She has brought to the home culture and womanly refinement. The music of her piano has filled the house, and her landscapes hang with happy color on her walls. She is an excellent lapidarist and makes beautiful jewelry for her friends. She reminds one of Mary Fielding Smith in her courage and devotion and loyalty to principle. She is as strong in these virtues as was her great-grandmother.

She upholds her husband as head of the home and teaches her children that she and they are under his presidency. As one enters her home, one sees her in her true place, a devoted mother who is indeed the queen of the household. She is a noble example of Latter-day Saint womanhood and a worthy helpmeet to her husband. Out of the mouth of her youngest daughter comes the whole sum of the home she and Elder McConkie have created. Sara said that when she gets married she hopes she can have as much fun as Daddy and Mother have had. And one is sure of the love and security of this home when one calls on the phone and asks if President McConkie is at home and is told that, yes, he is home and is teaching and explaining the Book of Mormon to Sara. These are the simple things, the homey things, the Spirit overruling all.[3]

Bruce and Amelia were a celestial couple. They lived as an example to all Latter-day Saint families. Though Bruce would have liked to have been home more, still they were able to raise their children up righteously and teach them correctly.

His children had a precise understanding of how he felt about their mother. Bruce told them their mother was perfect. Then, when President David O. McKay interviewed him, he asked, "How is your wife?" Bruce answered, "She's practically perfect." President McKay then replied, "She is perfect, my boy." His children teased him about hedging on his answer to the prophet. But they knew where Amelia stood with their father. Their son Mark remembered that:

My father and mother were a perfect team. I remember being in a sleeping bag with the family up the canyon and having mother tell us pioneer stories and dad tell us Book of Mormon stories. She is a perfect complement to dad. They were demonstrably affectionate. There was no embarrassment about holding hands or kissing. Frankly, there were times when dad would leave in the morning and by the way he kissed mother you'd think he was off to Japan for three weeks. When they were in the same room dad wanted mother sitting next to him. Obviously that physical closeness symbolized the emotional, spiritual and intellectual closeness they shared.[4]

"For me, life married to a General Authority was perfectly normal," said Amelia. "I know that's not the case for other women who are plunged into it suddenly. But I wasn't. I did, though, in large part have to raise the children alone. When he was home Bruce would chide me for jumping out of the car without waiting for him to open the door, and things like that. But I told him, 'You're away most of the time, and I do these things for myself. So don't get upset because I do what I have to do when you're not here.'"[5]

Bruce had a humorous story he made up about choosing his wife. His daughter Vivian remembers that he said, "his appreciation for mom began in premortal life when a large group of women had gathered around him, clamoring to choose him for their husband. He said, 'I'll handle this,' looked over the group, saw mother and said,. 'I'll take that one.'"[6] Bruce knew that he could not obtain exaltation without her, but he wouldn't have wanted it without her either:

> My wife and I were having a serious discussion recently, in which we were counting our many blessings, We named a host of things that have come to us, because of the Church, because of our family, because of the glorious restoration of eternal truth that has taken place in this day; and then she [concluded] the discussion by asking this question: "What's the greatest blessing that has ever come into your life?" Without a moment's hesitation I said, "The greatest blessing that has ever come to me was on the thirteenth day of October in 1937, at 11:20 a.m., when I was privileged to kneel in the Salt Lake Temple at the Lord's altar and receive you as an eternal companion." She said, "Well, you passed that test."[7]

But sometimes Bruce's methods of rearing the children conflicted with Amelia's. It may be that since he was gone so much, he didn't understand the daily labor of taking care of a large family as well as she did. One biographer said, "Bruce wasn't...stern with his children. Once in a while he'd offer a, 'Now look here, Junior,' or something equivalent, but a strict disciplinarian he was not. As the eldest son Joseph got older he loved sports and became annoyingly consistent at getting home late for dinner. Finally one day when Joseph came home late yet again, an exasperated Amelia demanded, 'Bruce, you say something to this boy!' Bruce looked at his son and replied, 'Well, hello Joseph.'" With these mild discipline practices, combined with the steady influence of the gospel in the home, each of his children turned out right, each one stayed faithful to the Church, and each went on to make important contributions to the kingdom. "Frankly, we're a peculiar family," said Joseph. "When we had a family reunion we didn't spend the time boating or in some other form of recreation. What we did was talk the gospel, into the late hours of the night. We'd sit by the hour and pump dad for all he was worth, to the point that our wives would say, 'Now, settle down. You McConkies think you're the only people in the Church who understand anything.'"[8]

Yet Bruce did not force feed the gospel to his children. "Never in our lives were we told that [we must learn the gospel]," said Joseph. "We never got up and read scriptures as a family. This was before the present emphasis on family home evening, and we didn't have many. But we caught something, we sensed something. We inherited by exposure. There was never any pretense. There was never any attempt to squeeze religion into us. But dad lived the gospel, he breathed it, he loved it. And he taught us more than answers. He taught us how to get answers. We don't have to stop learning because he is gone. McConkies are supposed to know something. But that's not because dad sat us down and taught us. It's because we loved our father and grew to love what he loved, which was the gospel."[9]

Bruce and Amelia enjoyed the adventure of their lives together. She told of one humorous incident which occurred when she accompanied her husband on a stake conference assignment to Santiago, Chile:

> During the afternoon session the congregation rose to sing a hymn. As Amelia glanced down at the hymnbook, the "page began to dance around." She took several deep breaths but still felt dizzy. The song ended, and before she could sit down her husband put his hand on her back, pushed her towards the pulpit, and said, "it's your turn to speak." I began, "My dear brothers and sisters," and then looked to see if the interpreter was with me. Amelia says, "That's the last thing I remember until I came to, stretched out on the floor behind the pulpit." When she fainted, the only time in her life, members of the congregation started popping up, straining for a glimpse of what had happened. Elder Robert E. Wells, who was present, looked questioningly at Elder McConkie, who said, "She'll be all right," stepped over her, and began to preach his sermon.

"This is no ordinary guy," Joseph commented, as he laughed. "His wife passes out, he takes his place at the pulpit and not a syllable is lost.

But to him, the kingdom rolls on. His wife just fell out of the wagon, but the caravan rolls on."[10]

Elder McConkie did not mind telling a good story on himself either:

> When we [the family] were celebrating Washington's birthday, I was down at my mother's sawing a log in the backyard. She came out to give me some direction and see how I was doing it, and she wasn't very pleased. She thought I ought to do it differently. She went back into the house and in a few minutes my younger brother arrived. She [had] said to him, "I think you'd better go out in the backyard and give Bruce some help and see that he does this thing right." And then she said to him, "Bruce isn't very bright."[11]

Besides his writing, Bruce took up two main hobbies, both of which were outgrowths of a family member's encouragement or needs. His hobbies became very important to him. When he had spare time, he devoted it to them. It was a way of keeping his mind and body busy, expending the nervous energy which he had such an abundance of.

Most his life Bruce was an avid walker, taking long walks through the city and in the foothills behind their home. He could walk long distances with his great strides, for occasionally excessive periods of time, which sometimes worried his wife. Amelia said the reason he walked was so he could clarify "things in his mind." Then she coaxed him into watching a television show on fitness, which started his next obsession: jogging. "He bought books about jogging and read them all," she said. "He got the kind of clothes and shoes he needed. And he set goals, which troubled me, because he'd have rather died than not complete the number of miles he'd committed to run. Sometimes he was so worn out by the time he got through that he was no good the rest of the day. But he got his miles in." One jogging shirt he wore had "Lengthening My Stride," printed across the front, a reference to President Kimball's slogan for the Church. This hobby became a substantial source of fitness and good health for Bruce, but Amelia thought he did it too much. "I told him that if he dared say another word about jogging I'd clobber him. I came third—right behind the Church and jogging."[12]

These times out walking or jogging alone had some needed side benefits which helped Bruce mentally and spiritually: "He'd leave home and go somewhere and then call me," remembers Amelia, "from wherever he might be, and the distance he had covered [was] twelve miles or so,

12 January 1980. Elder McConkie jogs to maintain physical fitness. *Lengthening My Stride* shirt is a gift from a son.

and all this time he was pondering and thinking about things and doing whatever he felt he needed to do to get the answers to things he wanted to know."[13]

Since jogging is a physical sport, it had its share of risk. For example, a stake president who was visiting Church headquarters stopped in to visit with Elder McConkie in his office, only to find his foot in a cast propped up on his desk. When he asked Elder McConkie how it had happened, he was told that Bruce "was jogging and didn't see the new wire fence around the neighbor's yard which he normally cut through."[14]

Even near the end of his life, after he had been diagnosed with cancer, Bruce continued jogging as much as he could. He felt strongly about the health benefits and conditioning it provided him.

The other hobby Bruce took up was rock hunting, or lapidary work. When his daughter Sara came home from school with a geology assignment and asked him for help, his interest was sparked:

> I go on the theory that someone who is working with his mind all the time needs to do something with his hands. I've taken up rock hounding, which means that my wife and I go out in desert and mountainous areas looking for gemstones, agates, jasper, petrified wood and the like. And then I cut these things with a diamond saw into shapes and slabs.
>
> The great problem is that, at least ever since I've been in the Twelve, I've had very little time to do it. Rock hunting itself is a summer activity here in Utah, because of the weather, but the polishing and preparing of items of jewelry could be a year-round thing, depending on the time.
>
> I've said jocularly that I have an ambition to cut a petrified log, and find, in the inside, a replica of the Salt Lake Temple with the Angel Moroni, and then see it published on the cover of the Lapidary Journal.
>
> I get a real genuine satisfaction; it's a creative thing. There's a sense of accomplishment and there's a sense of expectancy and wonder at what you're going to get when you cut something.[15]

Over the years he put together quite a large collection. His rock hunting didn't always make for peaceful walks in the hills though. He told how it once brought him into danger:

> We [Elder McConkie and a friend] were up Salina Canyon on a ledge along the side of the mountain, digging into a vein. We were digging in the pocket which was about a yard deep under an overhanging cliff. We'd been doing this for about five hours, lying on our sides with a sledge hammer and a

chisel and with a crowbar, wrenching out rocks. We started at opposite ends and we worked toward each other. We'd come to the point where we were right together and we were so close that I could no longer use my crowbar, so I was going to move back and start over again. I stood up to move back and start over again, and as I laid down again, the whole cliff caved in and a couple of tons of rock came tumbling down.

One rock about 18 inches or two feet in diameter came down where my head and shoulders had just been five seconds before. It came so close to my head that I felt it go through the top of my hair. At that same instant, Finn Paulsen, still lying on his side where he'd been, without knowing why, just started to roll. The cliff came so close to him that it caught his trousers where his legs were but he got out from under it. Neither one of us had a scratch on us. All we lost was his chisel which was under two tons of rock.[16]

Elder McConkie's reaction to the narrow escape is revealing of his personality: "We just got up and picked up our rocks and put them in a sack and we climbed down the mountain to the car without any nervousness or being upset or perturbed, either one of us."[17]

Elder McConkie filled his home with rocks. He even made things from them: book ends, paper weights, and jewelry. He gave some special polished rocks to Elder James E. Faust and his wife, and many others. His double garage in the basement was converted into a rock shop, where he installed saws, grinders, buffers, polishers, and other equipment necessary to turn ordinary chunks of rock into magnificent pieces of beauty. "Before I knew it," said Amelia, "I was trotting all over with him looking for rocks. He went overboard with it. We had a yard full of rocks we'd found and when he polished them he'd rub his hands against those abrasive wheels until his fingers bled, but he'd just keep at it. A little pain didn't stop him. He'd say the blood of Israel was in those stones."[18] He considered it a "family type hobby." Amelia ended up with a rock egg collection which includes egg-shaped rocks from many parts of the world, including marble from Athens, jasper from Hong Kong, rose quartz from Brazil, and bloodstone from Hong Kong.[19]

Even if he went overboard with his hobbies, he still had his priorities straight. His two greatest loves were (1) his wife and family and (2) the gospel. He wrote a poem that put these loves in perspective for him and which gives insight into the eternal view which Bruce had for his family:

I stood before God's mighty throne;
The time had come to leave my home;
My pilgrimage before me lay;
This was the long-expected day.

For ages past I'd walked by sight;
Now faith must be my guiding light;
To find the Truth, the Light, the Way,
I must be housed in mortal clay.

Before I left, my Father spoke;
"Go now, my son, bear well thy yoke;
I send thee forth to keep my law,
To worship me with reverent awe.

"Thy first concern in that new sphere;
Find her whom though hast chosen here;
These children I shall send to thee;
Choice shall thy chosen family be."

And so I came as Adam's son,
To seek all that may be won,
By those who love and serve their God,
And bow beneath his gospel rod.

To me has come that law divine,
By which I may my name enshrine,
In realms of light and life and love,
In those eternal courts above.

And God be praised, she here is found
Who in celestial garments gowned,
By me shall stand as ages roll,
To comfort, guide, and cheer my soul.

To us have come those spirits dear,
Whom we must lead and guide and rear,
And teach to love and serve the Lord,
And sing as one each gospel chord.

Our home is one where joy abounds,
Where God is served and praise resounds;
Where gospel light in splendor shines,
And each of us its truth enshrines.[20]

Bruce and Amelia, 21 October 1972.

Notes

1. Further information on Amelia Smith McConkie may be found in the various biographies written about her father, Joseph Fielding Smith.

2. Smith and Stewart, p. 350.

3. Young, p. 11.

4. Dew, p. 62.

5. Dew, p. 61.

6. Dew, p. 62.

7. Bruce R. McConkie, "Agency or Inspiration—Which?" BYU Devotional Address, 27 Feb. 1973, p. 108.

8. Dew, p. 53.

9. Dew, p. 54.

10. Dew, p. 61.

11. Bruce R. McConkie, "Agency or Inspiration—Which?" BYU Devotional Address, 27 Feb. 1973, p. 116.

12. Dew, p. 60.

13. Video Biography, p. 4.

14. Incident taken from unpublished notes made by Lloyd J. Cope, former president of Paradise Stake, California.

15. Quotation from interview by David Croft, *Church News,* 24 January 1976.

16. Van Orden, p. 3.

17. Quotation from interview by David Croft, *Church News,* 24 January 1976.

18. Dew, p. 54.

19. Van Orden, p. 3.

20. Poem in the prefatory pages of Joseph Fielding McConkie, *Sons and Daughters of God* (Salt Lake City: Bookcraft, 1994).

Chapter Nine

Call to the Twelve

In his last general conference talk as a member of the First Council of Seventy, Elder McConkie bore testimony of the Savior:

> I asked the Lord what he would have me say on this occasion and received the distinct and affirmative impression that I should bear testimony that Jesus Christ is the Son of the living God and that he was crucified for the sins of the world.
>
> I have what is known as "the testimony of Jesus," which means that I know by personal revelation from the Holy Spirit to my soul that Jesus is the Lord; that he brought life and immortality to light through the gospel; and that he has restored in this day the fulness of his everlasting truth, so that we with the ancients can become inheritors of his presence in eternity.[1]

After twenty-six years as a member of this Council, another change came into Elder McConkie's life. From the perspective of hindsight, it is apparent that the Lord set His hand to weave together several events which proved of great consequence to the Church and to Elder McConkie. The major players in these events were Elder McConkie himself; his father-in-law, President Joseph Fielding Smith; and President Harold B. Lee. The passing away of a President of the Church, the transfer of the prophetic mantle to new shoulders, and the calling of another to fill the resultant vacancy in the Quorum of the Twelve are highly spiritual, deeply significant occasions during which the veil typically becomes thin and the Lord grants an increased measure of inspiration to his servants.

At the time of his passing, President Joseph Fielding Smith was living with Elder McConkie's family. The days leading up to his death were active, productive, and scarcely indicative of what was about to happen. At 9:25 P.M. on 2 July 1972, as he sat in his favorite chair, while Elder McConkie held his hand, the prophet's pulse stopped and he passed to the other side. Bruce and Amelia gave him oxygen in an effort to revive him but found that his spirit had indeed departed. With President Smith's passing, the mantle of the prophet fell upon President Harold B. Lee, now the senior Apostle on earth. He and the other Brethren were quickly notified of their file leader's passing.

President Smith's funeral services were held on 6 July with Elder McConkie contributing as both family member and General Authority speaker. His sermon was deeply spiritual, reviewing President Smith's life of faith and service, speaking of his glorious reward earned by remaining true and faithful. He quoted Elder Ezra Taft Benson saying, "The saving of the souls of men is the greatest work that is going on in the whole universe. It is going on on both sides of the veil, and I sometimes think it doesn't matter which side of the veil we are working on." Elder McConkie reviewed a portion of President Smith's patriarchal blessing and the fulfillment of those promises. He would one day, "sit in counsel with [the] brethren and preside among the people," the blessing read. Bruce also spoke of how President Smith's mother, Julina, "went before the Lord and...'vowed a vow.' Her promise: that if the Lord would give her a son, 'she would do all in her power to help him be a credit to the Lord and to his father.' The Lord hearkened to her prayers, and she kept her promise to him; and he also manifest to her, before the birth of the child, that her son would be called to serve in the Council of the Twelve."

Included within information Elder McConkie later published with his funeral remarks, he said: "[President Smith] is now in the midst of a joyous reunion with his family and friends in the paradise of God. In that spirit sphere he continues to labor as he did so long and valiantly during a faith-filled sojourn among mortal men."[2]

Later, in remarks to a gathering at a Joseph F. Smith family reunion, Elder McConkie referred to this funeral service and stated that, "Joseph F. Smith had attended the funeral of his son, doing so to manifest his interest in the family."[3]

The following day, Harold B. Lee was set apart by the Twelve to be the next President of the Church, and he chose Marion G. Romney to be his Second Counselor. This choice created a vacancy in the Quorum of the Twelve. The responsibility then devolved upon President Lee to fill the vacancy, with the inspiration of the Lord and the approval of his fellow Apostles. At this point he decided to defer calling a new Apostle until the next general conference.

In August the new First Presidency invited Elder McConkie to accompany them to the Mexico area conference held in Mexico City. This event proved to be another significant occasion for him. He spoke on the latter-day gathering and restoration of scattered Israel. In this sermon he taught that "the place of gathering for the Mexican Saints is in Mexico; the place of gathering for the Guatemalan Saints is in Guatemala; the place of gathering for the Brazilian Saints is in Brazil; and so it goes throughout the length and breadth of the whole earth."[4] Elder McConkie was here expounding a major doctrinal concept that those who are taught the gospel, are baptized, and come into the Church should no longer seek to join with the Saints in Utah; rather, they should consider their own country their place of gathering.

In the earliest days of the restored Church, Church leaders encouraged converts to gather physically to Church headquarters in order to strengthen Zion. Though converts were now no longer instructed to move to Utah, Zion was still considered to be in and around Church headquarters. Elder McConkie did not denounce the notion and practice of a geographical gathering, he simply taught that the time spoken of by the prophets in the scriptures had come, the time of the gathering of Israel into "the folds of the Lord, of Israel being gathered to the lands of their inheritance, of Israel being established in all their lands of promise, and of their being congregations of the covenant people of the Lord in every nation."[5] This seems to be a unique instance in which a member of the First Council of the Seventy publicly reinterpreted a gospel principle and its attendant policies and immediately thereafter received the total support of the President of the Church.

At the next general conference of the Church, "President Lee noted that in the early days of the Church the Lord had appointed specific gathering places, but now, in concurrence with the teachings of Elder Bruce R. McConkie at the Mexico City area conference, President Lee instructed that, with the Church membership distributed over the earth in seventy-eight countries and the gospel being taught in seventeen different languages, the gathering place for the saints was in their own native countries. Rather than move to a 'Utah Zion,' they must make their homes and local stakes the places of refuge and strength by keeping the commandments of God. The Church would reach out to stakes throughout the world."[6] In his sermon President Lee quoted extensively from Elder McConkie's remarks at the Mexico conference, using the scriptures and arguments Elder McConkie had used to make his point.[7]

But the most dramatic event which took place at this area conference in Mexico City for Elder McConkie was not his announcement of new policy, but rather a deeply personal, private experience. It happened in connection with the presenting of the names of the Apostles for the members' sustaining vote. After the reading of the eleventh and final name—Marvin J. Ashton—Bruce then heard his own name spoken, although it had not been read.[8]

President Lee reported in his journal, "When I talked with Brother McConkie he related an experience he had at the recent Mexico City area conference. When the General Authorities were sustained, following the reading of Elder Marvin J. Ashton's name (the eleventh Apostle in seniority), he heard his own name spoken. Since that time he had wrestled with this forewarning in the temple for a long time, and seemed to feel, as President Grant had expressed himself when he was called, that he 'seemed to see' a council of the Brethren on the other side, where they were advocating his name."[9]

Elder McConkie's reference to the call of President Heber J. Grant to the Twelve is highly instructive and adds considerable insight to Elder McConkie's call. President Grant had been bothered by doubts as to the divine origin of his call to the apostleship. To help him overcome these doubts, the Lord gave him the following spiritual experience:

> I seemed to see, and I seemed to hear, what to me is one of the most real things in all my life. I seemed to hear the words that were spoken. I listened to the discussion with a great deal of interest....In this council the Savior was present, my father was there, and the Prophet Joseph Smith was there,...and they discussed as to whom they wanted to occupy those positions [vacancies in the Quorum of the Twelve], and decided that the way...was to send a revelation. It was given to me that the Prophet Joseph Smith and my father mentioned me and requested that I be called to that position....It was given to me that because of my father's having practically sacrificed his life,...having been practically a martyr, that the prophet Joseph and my father desired me to have that position, and it was because of their faithful labors that I was called.[10]

With this information relative to President Grant's call, and Elder McConkie's statement to President Lee that he had had a similar experience, it is possible to draw some inferences concerning Elder McConkie's call; namely, while struggling in prayer in the temple: (1) Elder McConkie seemed to see and hear a council in the spirit world at which his father, Oscar Sr., and others were present; (2) the revelation was reaffirmed to him that he had indeed been called to the apostleship; (3) Bruce's father advocated his son's name to fill the vacancy in the Quorum of the Twelve Apostles; (4) the calling was made, at least partially, in honor of Oscar McConkie's valiant service in the Church; (5) Elder McConkie was foreordained to the apostleship, as are all men who are called to such positions in the kingdom of God.[11]

Though Elder McConkie now knew these things, the call had yet to be extended by the prophet. Of that decision President Lee wrote: "Today while fasting, I went to the most sacred room in the temple.[12] There for an hour I prayerfully considered the appointment of a new apostle. All seemed clear that Bruce R. McConkie should be the man. When I told my counselors they both said that from the first they seemed to know also it was to be Elder McConkie."[13] When President Lee extended the call, Elder McConkie told him of his experience in the temple which paralleled President Grant's so closely.

After the call had been officially extended to him by the prophet, Elder McConkie desired to share it with Amelia. Together they drove up to the mouth of Emigration Canyon to the This Is the Place monument. Upon their arrival, they walked to the base of the monument, because Elder McConkie said he "wanted to be among friends." Then he disclosed his new calling to Amelia.

When he later spoke to President Marion G. Romney (the newly appointed Counselor in the First Presidency) about the call, President Romney said, "I think Granddad Redd [Lemuel Hardison Redd] will be glad to receive us." Elder McConkie said, "I am going to live so I will be worthy to go where he is." President Romney responded, "So am I."[14]

Elder McConkie took the opportunity in the next conference to bear his testimony and speak of his tender feelings:

> I am grateful beyond any measure of expression, beyond any utterance in my power, for the blessings the Lord has so abundantly showered upon me, [and] upon my family.
>
> As members of the church and kingdom of God on earth, we enjoy the gifts of the Spirit—those wonders and glories and miracles that a gracious and benevolent God always has bestowed upon his faithful saints. The first of these gifts listed...is the gift of testimony....This gift is elsewhere described as the testimony of Jesus, which is the spirit of prophecy. This is my gift. I know this work is true.
>
> I have a perfect knowledge that Jesus Christ is the Son of the living God

and that he was crucified for the sins of the world.

I know there is revelation in the Church because I have received revelation. I know God speaks in this day because he has spoken to me.

Elder McConkie also repeated what the Spirit had literally spoken to him twenty years before: "With reference to these brethren who hold the keys of the kingdom of God at this hour, the voice of the Lord to his people is: 'These are they whom I have chosen as the First Presidency of my Church. Follow them.'"[15]

Thus Elder McConkie's apostolic ministry began on a note of testimony, and he did not depart from it. He rejoiced in bearing his testimony and witness of the Savior, which testimony was powerful. As an Apostle of the Lord, his chief duty and obligation was to testify of Jesus Christ and Him crucified. He relished this duty, and had many opportunities to do so throughout his ministry.

It seems that often his most spiritual times were when he stood before the Saints of God to proclaim his errand. Elder Russell M. Nelson remembered one instance in which he witnessed the Spirit inspiring Elder McConkie. Elders Nelson and McConkie were part of a group which had accompanied President Kimball to Tahiti. When the governor of the country had met them, he expressed concern and doubt as to the propriety of their visit. President Kimball "won him over in a very short time and invited the governor to come to the area conference, which he did. Elder Bruce R. McConkie gave a talk at that meeting which visibly moved the governor. Elder McConkie was inspired to set aside the text that had been prepared for the translators and gave instead an extemporaneous address on the Church, its divine origin, the apostasy, and the restoration. It was one of the best talks I've ever heard."[16]

On another occasion Elder McConkie attended a stake conference and "stood to give a prepared talk, and no sooner had he begun to preach, than he found himself teaching doctrines that he did not know, about how the gospel is taught in the spirit world. He learned that it is taught by a family, to their own family, that we teach the gospel to our own progenitors."[17]

These two accounts illustrate Elder McConkie's ability to rely on the Spirit and teach what the Lord directed him to teach. One of the most significant times this happened to him was at the April 1981 general conference. A purported historical document called "the Joseph Smith III blessing" had caused considerable stir both in and out of the Church. A

Elder Russell M. Nelson shakes hands with Elder McConkie as Elder L. Tom Perry looks on.

few members had seen in the document reason to doubt the historical authenticity of the pattern of priesthood leadership succession in the Church. Elder McConkie was uncomfortable with the document and its implications, in part because it failed to mention priesthood keys. At the conclusion of his prepared remarks for the conference, he said:

> And may I add, speaking as an Apostle of the Lord, Jesus Christ, that mingled and intertwined with the testimony which we bear and which was borne by the ancients—and I speak for myself and for my Brethren of the Twelve—that we know that God has in these last days restored again the fulness of his everlasting gospel for the salvation of all men on earth who will believe and obey; and that he has called Joseph Smith, Jr., to be his latter-day prophet, to be the first and chief Apostle in the dispensation of the fulness of times, and has given him every key and priesthood and power that Peter and the Apostles and the ancient prophets held in the days of their ministry; and that these keys and this holy apostleship have descended in this manner: Joseph Smith, Brigham Young, John Taylor, Wilford Woodruff, Lorenzo Snow, Joseph F. Smith, Heber J. Grant, George Albert Smith, David O. McKay, Joseph Fielding Smith, Harold B. Lee, and Spencer W. Kimball; and that this holy apostleship and these keys will continue to descend from one apostle to another until the Lord Jesus Christ comes in the clouds of heaven to reign personally upon the earth. And this I say not of myself, but in the name of the Lord, standing as his representative and saying what he would say if he personally were here.[18]

After concluding this inspired testimony, Elder McConkie sat down. Later, in a speech to Church Educational System teachers, he explained in greater detail what had happened when he gave that sermon:

> I was doing what we are pretty much required to do now. I was reading the expressions I was making. And then at the end I said a few sentences extemporaneously. As I said then,...I felt impressed...to bear witness of what was involved in succession in the presidency. And I named all of the Presidents from Joseph Smith to Spencer W. Kimball and said that down that line the power and authority and keys of the kingdom had come. Then I said something that highly offended all the intellectuals. I said, "What I am saying is what the Lord would say if he were here." Now, the only way you can say a thing like that is to be guided and prompted by the power of the Holy Spirit.[19]

Those who listened to Elder McConkie bear this testimony were then placed in a position of either accepting or rejecting it. The Spirit had borne record, and receptive hearts had understood. Those who chose not to believe were later embarrassed and ashamed when the supposed "discoverer" of this document was convicted of forgery and murder and was sentenced to life in prison. Time had vindicated the prophets. The spontaneous inspiration the Lord had given his Apostle, safely guided and strengthened faithful Saints. And thus it was, and ever will be the pattern of the Spirit: Elder McConkie taught what the Lord wanted taught, for he was directed by inspiration.

In March 1977, Elder McConkie spoke by the spirit of prophecy. The occasion was an area conference in Santiago, Chile. As he opened his remarks, he said:

> I shall tell you the vision that I have for the people of Chile. I foresee the day when the seven stakes here will be seven times seventy. I foresee the day when the two hundred and fifty native Chilean missionaries will be numbered in the thousands. I foresee the day when the thirty thousand members of the Church in this great nation will become the two thousands of Ephraim and the thousands of Manasseh of whom the scriptures speak. I foresee the day when The Church of Jesus Christ of Latter-day Saints will be the most powerful influencing leaven in this whole nation.
>
> Stakes of Zion will multiply in Chile. This is a blessed land. This is a place where the Lord wants his kingdom to grow. This is a place where it will grow. You have tasted in small measure an outpouring of the Spirit of the Lord. This is just a sample of what is to be. I said publicly in Santiago, in April of 1976, that the day would come when there would be a temple in Santiago. I repeat that; you can write it in your journals; it will come to pass. I do not say when, but surely it will be.[20]

While some of this prophecy is still in the process of being fulfilled, one part was fulfilled on 2 April 1980 when President Kimball announced that the Church would build a temple in Santiago. It was dedicated in September 1983 by President Gordon B. Hinckley.

In 1982, Elder McConkie received an assignment that was a special privilege for him personally. He was sent to Sydney, Australia, the country in which he had served as mission president, to break ground for the first temple in Australia. He said it was "the most memorable day in the history of this great nation." Later that evening he spoke to 1,500 Australian Saints in the Sydney Hebersham Stake center. "We have done something that will do more for the salvation and exaltation of this great land than practically any other single thing we could have done," he said. He referred to Isaiah's prophecy of "the mountain of the Lord's house," saying that it was "figurative language for places where temples will be built." Furthermore: "This temple is a fulfillment, as far as Australia is concerned, of that prophecy of Isaiah. I cannot use language that is too emphatic. There is no way to over emphasize what we are presenting—the fact that a house of the Lord is about to rise in Australia will be the crowning event for the Church here at this time, when the blessings and ordinances of the gospel are made available. We want temples in great numbers, and we shall have them just as soon as the numbers of members warrant their construction."[21] This was a personally precious time for Elder McConkie, as he was able to watch the Church grow rapidly in a country where he himself had labored to bring souls to Christ. This temple was dedicated in September 1984, just seven months before Elder McConkie passed away.

In December 1983, Elder McConkie was in Idaho Falls, Idaho, reorganizing a stake. With him was mission president John K. Carmack (later of the Seventy), who remembers that the incoming and outgoing stake presidencies both spoke as quickly as possible so that they might get to listen to Elder McConkie preach. "He stood and said that the Spirit had directed him to speak on the doctrine of Christmas. He led out with Isaiah 53 where Isaiah says, 'Who shall declare his generation,' referring to Christ, and he said, 'I boldly declare his generation.' Then he spoke on what the whole doctrine of Christmas meant. It was approximately an hour. It was a great sermon on Christmas, as good as I've ever heard. It was totally extemporaneous. He used no notes, he just used his scriptures."[22]

An interesting responsibility that Elder McConkie was given as an Apostle was the task of assigning new missionaries to their fields of labor.[23] One colleague remembered how Elder McConkie went about this duty: "I was with him a number of times when he would assign missionaries. He was so sure-footed on that. He wouldn't miss a step. He would just take the list and he would assign them, 'This one should go here, this one should go there,' and it was just like a cadence."[24]

Beyond such special assignments, Elder McConkie's life consisted of touring missions, attending stake conferences for the purposes of reorganization, meetings with the Council of the Twelve and the First Presidency (every Thursday), lengthy travel, and anything else he could fit into his schedule that needed to be done. This last category included participating as a member of the Scriptures Publications Committee.[25] It also included the sobering task of speaking at funerals, where he did his best to speak words of solace and comfort. Once in a while he would find himself speaking at the funeral of someone he knew well or had worked with (sometimes a fellow General Authority). One such occasion was the funeral of Elder S. Dilworth Young, with whom Elder McConkie had served for many years in the First Council of Seventy. In this particular sermon, he chose to speak of the reward that awaits those who live the kind of life Elder Young lived. He said:

> If we die in the faith, that is the same thing as saying that our calling and election has been made sure and that we will go on to eternal reward hereafter. As far as faithful members of the Church are concerned, they have charted a course leading to eternal life. This life is the time that is appointed as a probationary estate for men to prepare to meet God, and as far as faithful people are concerned, if they are in the line of their duty, if they are doing what they ought to do, although they may not have been perfect in this sphere, their probation is ended. Now there will be some probation for some other people hereafter. But for the faithful saints of God, now is the time and the day, and their probation is ended with their death, and they will not thereafter depart from the path.[26]

After teaching this interesting and comforting doctrine, Elder McConkie then shared a personal spiritual experience he had when blessing Elder Young shortly before his death:

> When I placed my hands upon his head, it was as though I [was] in a dark room. There was no light at all. The room was dark and I was against a black wall. There was no promise and no assurance and no hope of recovery or improvement or betterment. Simply a prayer to the Lord that he might have rest of body and be free from unnecessary pain. And that night he had a measurably good night, I am told.
>
>   Now, a few minutes after that, I did a similar thing to Dilworth's beloved [wife]. I gave her a blessing to comfort her in the ordeal she was then undergoing. And when I did it, it was as though the light had turned on in the room. And I could be fluent and expressive and manifest to her what the Spirit prompted. Because her destiny of the moment was different than the destiny of the moment of her husband.[27]

It was rare for Elder McConkie to speak so intimately about a spiritual impression received during a blessing such as this. But it does teach the principle that all things must be done as the Lord wills, which is not always as we want, even when we love the suffering individual as much as Bruce did his friend "Dil."

Elder McConkie once shared his feelings about his fellow servants in the ministry: "I don't think anybody would have any feeling except one of gratification and appreciation to associate with the brethren. They're congenial and most of them have a very rich sense of humor. They enjoy the work they're doing, as normally they should. The brethren, all of them, are very human, very personable, very gifted and talented in various ways. It's an inestimable privilege for all of us to sit, as it were, at the feet of [the First Presidency]."[28]

But along with the solemn and sorrowful occasions, there were some humorous times as well. Elder L. Tom Perry told of an incident when Elder McConkie was running down the stairs in the Church Administration Building. Part of the way down he decided to ride the banister and slide down. He landed right in the middle of President Harold B. Lee and Elder Marion G. Romney. President Lee looked up and said, "Oh, Bruce, it's you. I thought it was a messenger from heaven."[29]

Another time, Elder McConkie was on assignment with Elder Spencer W. Kimball in Mexico City. While relaxing on a chapel lawn, they removed their suit coats because of the heat. When the time came to begin their meeting inside, they purposely picked up and put on each other's coats. "Elder Kimball's coat reached just halfway down [Elder McConkie's] forearm. Elder McConkie's swallowed the shorter man's hands. All the missionaries around raced for their cameras. Later at Oaxaca the two authorities were shown a round column. There was a legend that if a man reached his arms around the column, the number of finger widths still left between his hands was the number of years he had left to live. Elder Kimball discovered he had sixteen left. But Elder McConkie, with his huge arm-span, encircled the column and overlapped a little. Elder Kimball told him that meant he was already dead and didn't know it."[30] These light-hearted incidents reveal the mirthful personality of Bruce McConkie, unknown to those who only saw him when he spoke.

His speaking style was virtually always commanding and direct. Sometimes in smaller settings he was less formal. He preached doctrine from the scriptures and the writings of the Prophet Joseph Smith, and little else. He told few stories, but when he did, they were short, to the point, and unembellished. When he spoke, his audience often sub-

consciously divided themselves into two groups: (1) those who were spiritually prepared and mature enough to drink deeply from the living waters he imparted, and (2) those who lacked spiritual and doctrinal understanding of what he taught and consequently often found themselves fighting sleep. Elder McConkie did have a solemn and somewhat monotone delivery, and he purposely avoided some of the more entertaining approaches and techniques used by some speakers. With that said, it is also true that his sermons were always instructive and rewarding for the seeker. On one occasion he taught:

> We should seek to get in tune with the Holy Spirit and to gain a witness, not simply of the truth and divinity of the work in which we are engaged but also of the doctrines that are taught by those who preach to us. We come into these congregations, and sometimes a speaker brings a jug of living water that has in it many gallons. And when he pours it out on the congregation, all the members have brought is a single cup and so that's all they take away. Or maybe they have their hands over the cups, and they don't get any to speak of.
>
> On other occasions we have meetings where the speaker comes and all he brings is a little cup of eternal truth, and the members of the congregation come with a large jug, and all they get in their jugs is the little dribble that comes from a man who should have known better and who should have prepared himself and talked from the revelations and spoken by the power of the Holy Spirit.[31]

Elder McConkie understood that both the speaker and the hearer had responsibility for a successful edifying and faith-promoting experience to take place. As to what to do when asked to speak on a different subject than the one the Lord would have them speak on, Elder McConkie counseled his sons that "when they are called on to speak and the person extending the invitation does not ask them to talk on what they ought to, they should have the sense to do it anyway."[32]

There were times (albeit few) when he injected some humor into his talks. On one such occasion he said, "I told Brother _____ before the meeting that the thing I was going to talk about was that three things are essential to salvation: Baptism, celestial marriage, and short hair. And I suggested further that in his case I thought he had it made."[33] The man was mostly bald.

Another time when Elder McConkie was mistakenly introduced as "Elder Smith," he said, "I've been many places with my wife when, as we

Elder McConkie visits with Freda Joan Lee and Camilla Eyring Kimball (wives of Presidents Lee and Kimball) at conference.

have met members of the Church, stake presidencies, high councils, and the like, they've said to me: 'We're surely glad to meet you, Brother McConkie, and we're most pleased to have Sister Smith with us.' I've assured her that that was all right with me, as long as they didn't call me Brother Smith. And now that's happened." Then after talking a few minutes he changed the subject and told another story: "I hold here a little piece of amorphous quartz that's clear as transparent glass. I picked this up in a wilderness area outside of a little community called Crystalina, in...Brazil, in South America. The Brethren thought I was off touring missions, but actually I was doing a little rock hunting."[34]

One of the most memorable quips made by Elder McConkie was at the beginning of a talk he gave at a Brigham Young University devotional. He said: "When the announcement was made that I was a graduate of the University of Utah, a voice in the background spoke up, 'That's a forgivable sin.' I'm pleased to certify that I have repented."

On a similar par with that occasion was a time when, speaking about those people who believe the theory that God is eternally progressing in knowledge, he joked, "I have been sorely tempted to say at this point that any who so suppose have the intellect of an ant and the understanding of a clod of miry clay in a primordial swamp—but of course I would never say a thing like that."[35] Because of his concern that this joke did not go over well in print, he edited it from the published version, but it is still classic McConkie humor. He realized that people rarely glimpsed the humor within his personality, observing—

> I have a keen sense of humor, actually, but it doesn't project over the pulpit and it's not generally known. For instance, one of the brethren who came in the Twelve said, "The greatest shock of my life was to find out what Bruce McConkie is really like."
>
> Life surely isn't eternally a long-faced thing. I get a great deal of enjoyment out of life and associating with people.
>
> There have been a good many instances where some elaborate and extensive practical jokes have been pulled on me by Dilworth Young or someone else, that add a savor and an interest to what's going on.[36]

Though Elder McConkie was virtually tone deaf and often lip-synced when hymns were sung, he did write the lyrics to the hymn, "I Believe in Christ."[37] In writing the words to this song, he bore powerful testimony of Jesus Christ and his atoning sacrifice. He later read some of the lyrics to an accompaniment by the Tabernacle Choir, which was recorded and issued on compact disc. Though he could not always sing in tune, in this manner he could still worship through music. He wanted to take advantage of every possible way to reverence and worship the Lord whom he served.

Notes

1. *Ensign,* July 1972, p. 109.

2. *Ensign,* Aug. 1972, pp. 24, 27-30; see also, Heidi S. Swinton, *In the Company of Prophets* [Personal Experiences of D. Arthur Haycock with Heber J. Grant, George Albert Smith, David O. McKay, Joseph Fielding Smith, Harold B. Lee, Spencer W. Kimball, and Ezra Taft Benson](Salt Lake City: Deseret Book, 1993), pp. 67-68, and Smith and Stewart, pp. 376-82.

3. *Beyond,* p. 81.

4. Bruce R. McConkie, "Report of Mexico City Area Conference," p. 4.

5. Bruce R. McConkie, "Report of Mexico City Area Conference," p. 4.

6. Goates, p. 516.

7. *Ensign,* July 1973, pp. 4-5.

8. Goates, pp. 494-95. As President Lee afterwards related to a visitor, "As the General Authorities were being sustained in the conference, only eleven names of Apostles were read, inasmuch as Elder Romney had been elevated. Elder McConkie at that moment heard his name read as the twelfth apostle, even though it hadn't actually been read. He tried to put such thoughts out of his mind, but the Holy Spirit told him again that he would be called to fill the vacancy in the Quorum of the Twelve. Elder McConkie also heard this same message from the Spirit after returning to his home." (Related by President Harold B. Lee to Gerald B. Quinn, a former mission president. Cited in L. Brent Goates, *He Changed My Life,* p. 156.)

9. Goates, pp. 494-95.

10. Francis M. Gibbons, *Heber J. Grant: Man of Steel, Prophet of God* (Salt Lake City: Deseret Book, 1979), pp. 54-55. The author has slightly edited the original narrative for clarity and context.

11. For further information see Goates, pp. 494-96.

12. The "most sacred room in the temple" usually means the Holy of Holies, access to which is controlled by the President of the Church (see Daniel H. Ludlow, ed., *The Encyclopedia of Mormonism* [New York: MacMillan, 1992], p. 651). Hereafter cited as *Mormonism.*

13. Goates, p. 494.

14. *Ensign,* Jan. 1973, p. 36.

15. *Ensign,* Jan. 1973, pp. 36-7.

16. Russell M. Nelson, *From Heart to Heart* (privately published by Russell M. Nelson, 1979), p. 183.

17. Account from author's notes of remarks by Joseph Fielding McConkie at a Doctrine and Covenants Symposium held at the Ogden, Utah, LDS Institute, 23 Jan. 1993.

18. *Ensign,* May 1981, p. 77.

19. Mark McConkie, *Restoration,* p. 322.

20. Bruce R. McConkie, "Remarks Given at Area Conference," March 1977, Santiago, Chile, p. 2. Available in LDS Church Historical Dept.

21. *Church News,* 21 Aug. 1982.

22. Carmack Interview, p. 2.

23. This assignment should not be confused with *calling* new missionaries, a duty which devolves on the President of the Church after a bishop has made the recommendation. The signature on the official call is that of the President of the Church.

24. Carmack Interview, p. 3.

25. For further details on Elder McConkie's work with this committee, see chapter 13.

26. Remarks of Elder Bruce R. McConkie at the funeral of Elder S. Dilworth Young, as cited in *Beyond,* p. 141.

27. Quotation taken from typescript of unpublished remarks of Elder Bruce R. McConkie at the funeral of Elder S. Dilworth Young, in possession of the author.

28. Quotation from interview by David Croft, *Church News,* 24 January 1976.

29. Incident taken from unpublished notes made by Lloyd J. Cope of talk given by Elder L. Tom Perry at Chico, California, stake conference, 11 August 1974.

30. Edward L. Kimball and Andrew E. Kimball, *Spencer W. Kimball* (Salt Lake City: Bookcraft, 1977), pp. 281-82.

31. Bruce R. McConkie, "The Seven Deadly Heresies," BYU Fireside Address, 1 June 1980, p. 80.

32. Joseph Fielding McConkie and Robert L. Millet, *Sustaining and Defending the Faith* (Salt Lake City: Deseret Book, 1985), p.115.

33. Bruce R. McConkie, "Making Our Calling and Election Sure," BYU Fireside Address, 25 March 1969, p. 1.

34. Bruce R. McConkie, "Agency or Inspiration—Which?" BYU Fireside Address, 27 Feb. 1973, pp. 112-13.

35. Bruce R. McConkie, typescript of sound recording, BYU Fireside Address, "The Seven Deadly Heresies," 1 June 1980.

36. Quotation from interview by David Croft, *Church News,* 24 January 1976.

37. *Hymns,* no. 134.

Chapter Ten

True Doctrine

Perhaps Elder Bruce R. McConkie's greatest contribution to the Church and the world was his doctrinal teachings. Because of him, many doctrines, principles, and truths are now better understood and less obscured by the theories of men. It is a sure foundation upon which the student builds who studies the writings and sermons of Elder Bruce R. McConkie.[1]

"Truth—pure, diamond truth—truth unmixed with error, truth and truth alone can lead a soul to salvation."[2] So taught Elder McConkie to those with ears to hear, eyes to see, and hearts to understand. To teach true doctrine and only true doctrine was his greatest desire. Paralleling that was another great desire: he wanted others to teach and believe true doctrine also. Anything else was, to one degree or another, heresy. This did not always mean that if a belief disagreed with his own it was wrong; he just wanted to ensure that people didn't hang their testimonies on the hook of the philosophies of men.

One biographer said: "To Bruce McConkie, there was no democracy where truth was concerned. The scriptures were everything. Others' interpretations of scripture didn't interest him."[3] Elder McConkie's son Stanford offered this insight: "He felt that when he was called to teach and preach and exhort, he'd ought to teach and preach and exhort. It was not his duty to tell jokes and stories."[4] Another son, Joseph, expanded on this attitude: "My father preached and lived a practical religion, but you miss the point if you don't know that he knew he was an apostle. You knew where he stood. There was absolutely nothing phony about him. He refused to assume any authority, any knowledge that wasn't his. But on the other hand, in the area of his competency he refused to be falsely modest. He knew what he knew, and he knew what he didn't."[5] The same biographer also said, "Because he wrote doctrine, Bruce McConkie attracted critics—lots of them, in and out of the Church."[6]

Special insight into the struggles faced by this teacher of true doctrine comes from one who could empathize with him—Elder Boyd K. Packer:

It was not granted to Brother McConkie to judge beforehand how his discourses would be received and then to alter them accordingly. He could not measure what ought to be said and how it ought to be said by, "What will people think?" Would his sermons leave any uncomfortable? Would his bold declarations irritate some in the Church? Would they inspire the critics to rush to their anvils and hammer out more "fiery darts," as the scriptures call them?

Would his manner of delivery offend? Would his forthright declarations, in content or in manner of presentation, drive some learned investigators away? Would he be described as insensitive or overbearing? Would his warnings and condemnations of evil undo the careful work of others whose main intent was to have the world "think well of the Church?" Perhaps it was given to other men to measure their words in that way, but it was not given to him.

He and I have talked of this. And when he was tempted to change, the Spirit would withdraw a distance and there would come that deep loneliness known only to those who have enjoyed close association with the Spirit, only to find on occasion that it moves away. He could stand what the critics might say and what enemies might do, but he could not stand that. He would be driven to his knees to beg forgiveness and plead for the renewal of that companionship with the Spirit which the scriptures promise can be constant. Then he would learn once again that what was true of Holy men of God who spoke in ancient times applied to him as well. He was to speak as he was moved upon by the Holy Spirit. What matter if it sounded like Bruce R. McConkie, so long as the Lord approved! I knew him well enough to know all of that.[7]

Elder McConkie never hesitated to say or write what he thought and felt when motivated by the Spirit. If it offended some, he lived with the consequences, however painful. His concern was declaring truth, exposing heresy, or giving erring individuals needed correction. Sometimes this direct approach to his duty as a "watchman on the tower" opened him to personal attacks from those who were upset by both the correction and his various methods of dispensing it. At other times erring parties humbled themselves sufficiently to receive the correction as it was intended and subsequently repented.

One example of Elder McConkie's commitment to true doctrine is found in his willingness to expose false doctrine for what it was no matter where he found it. He seemed more concerned with the false doctrine being taught than diplomacy in refuting it. Thus he was understandably bold, direct, and uncompromising in his denunciation of views which deviated from the scriptural truths he taught and loved.

Perhaps the most blunt warning Elder McConkie ever gave was issued in the form of a letter written to an erring university professor. The letter gave strong counsel on following the *living* prophet and avoiding improper intellectualism. Unfortunately, a copy of the private letter found its way into the possession of unscrupulous individuals who un- successfully tried to use it to compromise the integrity of the teachings of Church leaders.

Another occasion when Elder McConkie conveyed needed correction occurred in March 1982. Some difficulties arose at Brigham Young University when some misguided students became caught up in a spiritually dangerous fad of trying to gain an extreme, special, personal relationship with Jesus Christ, leading them into improper prayer patterns and practices.[8]

Elder McConkie saw a need to check this before it grew to more excessive proportions. He focused on the doctrinal problem, logically and prayerfully evaluated the proper refutation, and then gave it in a straightforward, frank manner, without regard for how critics would receive what he said. The truth was declared, the testimony borne, the duty of the special witness accomplished. Then it was up to the individuals involved to repent.

He spoke on the subject in question at a BYU devotional, thus reaching as many students and faculty as possible, getting to the root of the problem quickly. To open his address he stated:

> I shall speak of our relationship with the Lord and of the true fellowship all Saints should have with the Father. I shall set forth what we must believe relative to the Father and the Son in order to gain eternal life. I shall expound the doctrine of the Church relative to what our relationship should be to all members of the Godhead and do so in plainness and simplicity so that none need misunderstand or be led astray by other voices.
>
> I shall express the view of the Brethren, of the prophets and apostles of old, and of all those who understand the scriptures and are in tune with the holy Spirit. These matters lie at the very foundation of revealed religion. In presenting them I am on my own ground and am at home with my subject. I shall not stoop to petty wrangling about semantics but shall stay with matters of substance. I shall simply go back to basics and set forth

fundamental doctrines of the kingdom, knowing that everyone who is sound spiritually and who has the guidance of the Holy Spirit will believe my words and follow my counsel.

Please do not put too much stock in some of the current views and vagaries that are afloat, but rather, turn to the revealed word, get a sound understanding of the doctrines, and keep yourselves in the mainstream of the Church. Now, it is no secret that many false and vain and foolish things are being taught in the sectarian world and even among us about our need to gain a special relationship with the Lord Jesus. I shall summarize the true doctrine in this field and invite erring teachers and beguiled students to repent and believe the accepted gospel verities as I shall set them forth.

After teaching the true doctrine involved, he then said:

As far as I know there is not a man on earth who thinks more highly of Him [Jesus] than I do. It just may be that I have preached more sermons, taught more doctrine, and written more words about the Lord Jesus Christ than any other man now living. I have ten large volumes in print, seven of which deal almost entirely with Christ, and the other three with him and his doctrines. I do not suppose that what I have here said will be an end to controversy or to the spread of false views and doctrines. The devil is not dead, and he delights in controversy. But you have been warned, and you have heard the true doctrine taught.[9]

When occasion required correction, he gave it. Then, after it was given, he felt he had done his duty to the best of his ability and was personally absolved of future consequences. The sin would no longer be required at his hands for not doing his duty. One far and future day, he might be summoned to stand as a witness against one who did not heed the warning, painful though that might be. (See D&C 75:21-22).

So Elder McConkie focused on teaching only true doctrine. The real challenge was often learning which true doctrine a particular audience was most in need of. He explained: "There are times when I struggle and strive to get a message over and just do not seem to myself to be getting in tune with the Spirit. The fact is, it is a lot harder for me to choose what ought to be said, what subject ought to be considered, than it is for me to get up and preach it. I am always struggling and trying to get the inspiration to know what ought to be said at general conference, or in a stake conference, or whatever."[10] On occasion Elder McConkie shared

with his audience the struggle he had been through in choosing his subject, as in the following two examples:

To the BYU student body: "I have prayed and pondered earnestly to learn what the Lord wants me to say on this occasion. In the early hours of the morning, as I tossed and turned in bed and kept my wife awake, I concluded upon a subject."[11]

To a BYU fireside gathering: "When I consulted with Brother ____, he told me that it would be most appropriate if I spoke on a Thanksgiving Theme, since it would fit in well with the music. I decided to do that, and prepared my mind and an outline, and gathered some quotations, but since arriving here tonight I have had nothing but a stupor of thought, nothing but uncertainty in my mind as to that subject. Rather, I think, if I may be guided by the power of the Spirit and say what will please the Lord, I shall talk to you [about eternal marriage]."[12]

Once he had decided upon a subject, he then, with reliance upon the Spirit, taught what he considered to be the truth. As he himself said, "It is my pattern and custom simply to teach and testify. I do not debate and I do not argue. If someone wants to contend to the contrary, he is just as welcome as the day is long to do so. But let us understand this. When we deal with God and his laws, when we get in the realm of spiritual things, we are dealing with the things that save souls, and at our peril we are obligated to find the truth."[13] On another occasion, to reinforce and emphasize his single-minded purpose of teaching truth in the face of controversy, he opened his sermon with an important clarification:

I shall depart from my normal and usual pattern and read portions of my presentation because I want to state temperately and accurately the doctrinal principles involved and to say them in a way that will not leave room for doubt or question. I shall speak on some matters that some may consider to be controversial, though they ought not to be. They are things on which we ought to be united, and to the extent we are all guided and enlightened from on high we will be.[14]

In many of his sermons, Elder McConkie went to great lengths to talk about the need for the members of the Church to learn to discern or distinguish between true and false doctrine. Since personal salvation hung in the balance, it was very important to him to fulfil his calling as an

Apostle, in exposing heresy and false doctrine. Though this made him unpopular with certain liberal and extremist elements within and without the Church, nevertheless he did not falter in his duty. Each false theory in its turn, as espoused by various dissident groups, received Elder McConkie's attention, including fundamentalists (polygamists), feminists, evolutionists, intellectual dissidents, and cultists.

"We are saved or damned by what we believe," he said. "Nearly the whole educational world goes blithely along, espousing the false theories of organic evolution, which rule out the fall of man and the atonement of Christ. Men worship at the shrine of intellectuality without ever realizing that religion is a thing of the Spirit and that 'the things of God knoweth no man, but the Spirit of God.' Our schools teach some principles of socialism, of communism, of so-called women's liberation, of curtailing population growth and the like—much of which runs counter to revealed gospel truths."[15] Truly, Elder McConkie was not one that could be misunderstood.

Because of his reputation as a gospel scholar and authority, coupled with his position as a member of the Quorum of the Twelve Apostles, he often found himself buried under a pile of endless correspondence—letters asking myriad gospel questions. In a letter to an acquaintance he once expressed his procedure for handling questions: "Ordinarily I probably would not do more than make some passing comment or expression in reply to a letter of the sort you wrote me..."[16]

When the flood of mail had simply become too burdensome, Elder McConkie needed to find a way to manage the situation more efficiently. Then he hit upon a solution. On 1 July 1980, he wrote an "open" letter directed to "Honest Truth Seekers," which he often sent as a reply to incoming correspondence. In it he explained his dilemma and justified his solution:

> I receive a flood of letters asking questions about the doctrines, practices, and history of the Church. Several thousand questions are presented to me each year. Recently I received a single letter containing 210 major questions plus numerous lesser ones. To answer the questions in this one letter alone would have taken several hundred pages. Frequently I have a stack of unanswered letters which is six or eight inches high. There are times when weeks go by without an opportunity even to read the letters let alone attempt to answer them.
>
> Thoughtful persons will realize that if I devoted all my waking hours to the research and work involved in answering the questions which come to

me, I still would not be able to answer all of them. But—and this is far more important—if I were able to perform this service it still would not be the right thing to do nor be in the best interests of those who present their problems to me.[17]

The letter then gives counsel on how an individual can find their own answers to gospel questions. Elder McConkie felt strongly that this is how it should be done; the inquirer should spend the time and effort to search out their own answers. Personally he felt that when someone asked him a question, they were abrogating the responsibility to find their own answers. "People eternally ask me questions," he once said, that "they ought to figure...out [for] themselves. I mean, I don't have any more obligation than they do to know what the answers to these things are and they have the same sources to look to that I do."[18] Further, "The answers to nearly all important doctrinal questions are found in the Standard Works or in the sermons and writings of the Prophet Joseph Smith. If they are not found in these sources, they probably are not essential to salvation and may well be beyond our present spiritual capacity to understand."

> The way to achieve a high state of gospel scholarship is first to study and ponder and pray about the Book of Mormon and then to follow the same course with reference to the other scriptures. The Book of Mormon contains that portion of the Lord's word which he has given to the world to prepare the way for an understanding of the Bible and other revelations now had among us. We have been commanded to search the scriptures, all of them; to treasure up the Lord's word, lest we be deceived; to drink deeply from the fountain of holy writ, that our thirst for knowledge may be quenched. It is far better for us to gain our answers from the scriptures than from something someone else says about them. It is true that we often-times need an inspired interpreter to help us understand what apostles and prophets have written for us in the Standard Works. But it is also true that many explanations given by many people as to the meaning of scriptural passages are somewhat less than true and edifying.
>
> We are in a far better position if we are able to drink directly from the scriptural fountain without having the water muddied by others whose insights are not as great as were those of the prophetic writers who first penned the passages found in the accepted canon of holy writ. I am not rejecting proper scriptural commentaries; I know and appreciate their value and have written volumes of them myself; I am simply saying that people with the ability to do it would be far better off to create their own

commentaries. There is something sacred and solemn and saving about studying the scriptures themselves. We should train ourselves in this direction.

After offering this advice, Elder McConkie spoke of the need to make sure the doctrine we believe is in harmony with the scriptures: "The Standard Works are scripture. They are binding upon us. They are the mind and will and voice of the Lord. He never has, he does not now, and he never will reveal anything which is contrary to what is in them. No person, speaking by the spirit of inspiration, will ever teach doctrine that is out of harmony with the truths God has already revealed."

Next he emphasized the importance of harmonizing the scriptures with the statements of the prophets:

> Truth is always in harmony with itself. The word of the Lord is truth, and no scripture ever contradicts another, nor is any inspired statement of any person out of harmony with any inspired statement of any other person. Paul and James did not have differing views on faith and works, and everything that Alma said about the resurrection accords with Section 76 in the Doctrine and Covenants. When we find seeming conflicts, it means we have not as yet caught the full vision of whatever points are involved.
>
> The Lord expects us to seek for harmony and agreement in the scriptures and among the Brethren rather than for seeming divergences of views. Those who have faith and understanding always seek to harmonize into one perfect whole all the statements of the scriptures and all pronouncements of the Brethren. The unfortunate complex in some quarters to pounce upon this bit of information or that and conclude that it is at variance with what someone else has said is not of God.
>
> My experience is that in most instances—nay, in almost all instances—the seeming divergencies can be harmonized, and when they cannot be it is of no moment anyway. The Spirit of the devil champions division and debate and contention and disunity.
>
> Are all prophetic utterances true? Of course they are! This is what the Lord's system of teaching is all about. Anything which his servants say when moved upon by the Holy Ghost is scripture....
>
> But every word that a man who is a prophet speaks is not a prophetic utterance. Joseph Smith taught that a prophet is not always a prophet, only when he is acting as such. Men who wear the prophetic mantle are still men; they have their own views; and their understanding of gospel truths is dependent upon the study and inspiration that is theirs.

Elder McConkie then dispensed some practical counsel: "Leave the mysteries alone and avoid gospel hobbies." He explained:

> We do not and...cannot comprehend all things. It is unwise to swim too far in water over our heads. My experience is that people who get themselves ensnared in fruitless contention over the meanings of deep and hidden passages of scripture are usually those who do not have a sound and basic understanding of the simple and basic truths of salvation.
>
> People who ride gospel hobbies, who try to qualify themselves as experts in some specialized field, who try to make the whole plan of salvation revolve around some field of particular interest to them—it is my experience that such persons are usually spiritually immature and spiritually unstable. This includes those who devote themselves—as though by divine appointment—to setting forth the signs of the times; or, to expounding about the Second Coming; or, to a faddist interpretation of the Word of Wisdom; or, to a twisted emphasis on temple work or any other doctrine or practice. We would do well to have a sane, rounded, and balanced approach to the whole gospel and all of its doctrines.

Other concerns which Elder McConkie addressed were: "Be not overly concerned about unimportant matters. ('I know it is not essential to my salvation, but I would really like to know how many angels can dance on the head of a pin...');" and "Withhold judgment, if need be, on hard questions. (If you cannot believe all of the doctrines of the gospel, withhold judgement in the areas in question. Do not commit yourself to a position which is contrary to that espoused by the prophets and apostles who preside over the kingdom. Study, pray, work in the Church and await further light and knowledge.)"

Elder McConkie commented on anti-Mormon literature, and the imperative need to leave the cults alone:

> There are of course, answers to all of the false claims of those who array themselves against us—I do not believe the devil has had a new idea for a hundred years—but conversion is not found in the dens of debate. Most members of the Church would be better off if they simply ignored the specious claims of the professional anti-Mormons.
>
> If the false claims about salvation by grace alone, or whatever the anti-Mormon literature is proclaiming, if these claims trouble you, search out the answers. They are in the scriptures. Anyone who cannot learn from the Bible that salvation does not come by simply confessing the Lord with one's lips, without reference to all the other terms and conditions of the true plan

of salvation, does not deserve to be saved.

And as to the cults—they are the gate to hell. Members of the Church who espouse the cultist practice of plural marriage, for instance, are adulterers, and adulterers are damned. The common approach of those who propagandize for this practice is to pit the sayings of the dead prophets against those of the living prophets. Anyone who follows a dead prophet rather than a living prophet will follow him to death rather than life.

Then Elder McConkie quickly reviewed the fact that "there are no private doctrines"; that we need to "maintain an open mind (our espousal and defense of a false doctrine will not make it true)"; and that "the responsibility to study is a personal one." Amplifying this last point, he said, "Now let us come to the conclusion of this whole matter;...each person must learn the doctrines of the gospel for himself. No one else can do it for him. Each person stands alone where gospel scholarship is concerned."

He concluded his letter with a summary of how a person learns the gospel in the Church (namely, through personal study, teaching others, and learning from Church auxiliaries and organizations such as the CES program) and then stated: "The foregoing expressions are made in an attempt to be helpful; to encourage gospel scholarship; and to guide truth seekers in a wise and proper course."[19]

It is possible that thousands of people have received this letter. As previously noted, it was one of many determined efforts Elder McConkie made to cultivate and ensure the learning and teaching of true doctrine.

Perhaps the most widely known effort he made for this purpose was a BYU fireside talk entitled "The Seven Deadly Heresies." This sermon singled out seven false doctrines (heresies) that he perceived as growing problems in the Church. Further exploration of those subjects is found in the teachings section of this book.

Probably the greatest acknowledgment of Elder McConkie's doctrinal and scriptural acumen came from his fellow Brethren in the Twelve and the First Presidency. "Often when a doctrinal question came before the First Presidency and the Twelve," said President Ezra Taft Benson, "Elder McConkie was asked to quote the scripture, or to comment on the matter."[20]

President Gordon B. Hinckley said, "He had his own unique style. With measured words, firm and unequivocal and with order and logic, he wove the patterns of his discourses. His language was clear, its meaning

Gordon B. Hinckley, Marvin J. Ashton, Bruce R. McConkie, and L. Tom Perry visit briefly after general conference.

unmistakable. There was a cadence to it. There was a peculiar strength
and beauty in its pattern. He spoke from a cultivated mind, but also from
a sincere heart."[21]

Notes

1. Since this book is about the life and teachings of Elder McConkie, it
purposefully points out his particular strengths and gifts. However, this author
appreciates the fact that a balanced overall view of Church doctrine comes from the
study of the scriptures, the inspiration of the Lord, and the study of the teachings of
all the prophets and apostles. No one should study or subscribe *exclusively* to the
teachings of just one man, however astute. Elder McConkie was among the elite of
the doctrinal authorities of this dispensation, but this does not excuse us from
studying the words of the other prophets and apostles. Proper perspective is
essential to sound gospel study.

Having said this, let no one shrink from a deep and exhaustive study of Elder
McConkie's teachings, for they are of inestimable worth, and the student who does
so will be richly rewarded.

2. *Ensign,* Nov. 1984, p. 83.

3. Dew, p. 53.

4. Dew, p. 50.

5. Dew, p. 58.

6. Dew, p. 53.

7. Packer, pp. 263-64.

8. Author's interview with Joseph Fielding McConkie, summer 1988. These
improper prayer practices included praying to Jesus instead of God the Father,
climbing mountains to pray, day-long prayers, and excessive length of fasting.

9. Bruce R. McConkie, "Our Relationship with the Lord," BYU Devotional
Address, 2 March 1982, pp. 97, 103.

10. Bruce R. McConkie, "The Foolishness of Teaching," Address to Seminary and
Institute Personnel, 1981. Published by The Church of Jesus Christ of Latter-day
Saints. Cited in Mark L. McConkie, *Restoration,* p. 336.

11. Bruce R. McConkie, "Who Shall Declare His Generation," BYU Devotional
Address, 2 Dec. 1975, p. 1.

12. Bruce R. McConkie, "Celestial Marriage," BYU Fireside Address, 6 Nov.
1977, p. 169.

13. Bruce R. McConkie, "The Lord God of Joseph Smith," BYU Devotional Address, 4 Jan. 1972, p. 7.

14. Bruce R. McConkie, "The Seven Deadly Heresies," BYU Fireside Address, 1 June 1980, p. 74.

15. Bruce R. McConkie, "The Ten Commandments of a Peculiar People," BYU Devotional Address, 28 Jan. 1975, p. 37.

16. Correspondence, Bruce R. McConkie to Walter M. Horne, 2 Oct, 1974, p. 2; original letter in author's file. In this particular case, Elder McConkie answered the question in some detail (see chapter on preexistence).

17. Correspondence, Bruce R. McConkie to Honest Truth Seekers, open letter dated 1 July 1980, copy in author's file. The following quotations are from this letter.

18. Quotation from interview by David Croft, *Church News,* 24 January 1976.

19. The preceding quotations are all taken from the specified letter to truth seekers. This author has chosen only highlights to use as quotations. The letter was seven single-spaced typed pages long. An excellent source of the full text of the letter is found in Mark McConkie, *Restoration,* pp. 228-35.

20. Unpublished typescript of remarks of Ezra Taft Benson at funeral services of Bruce R. McConkie, p. 3.

21. Unpublished typescript of remarks of Gordon B. Hinckley at funeral of Bruce R. McConkie, p. 14.

Chapter Eleven

The 1978 Revelation on the Priesthood

As with most other General Authorities, Elder McConkie occasionally found himself dealing with the issue of blacks being denied the privilege of bearing the priesthood. Though the restriction dated from the time of Adam and was upheld from the days of the Prophet Joseph Smith, the Lord had revealed no doctrinal explanation behind the restriction, and it fell to each individual to evaluate the issue and receive the Church's position as a matter of faith. Because the restriction was of divine origin, any changes to this policy must necessarily come from Him who is the Head of the Church through revelation to His prophet.

In 1958, with the publication of the first edition of *Mormon Doctrine*, Elder McConkie offered the Church his understanding relative to the subject. As to why the priesthood was withheld from those born through the lineage of Cain, he wrote:

> In the pre-existent eternity various degrees of valiance and devotion to the truth were exhibited by different groups of our Father's spirit offspring. One-third of the spirit hosts of heaven came out in open rebellion and were cast out without bodies, becoming the devil and his angels. The other two-thirds stood affirmatively for Christ: there were no neutrals. To stand neutral in the midst of war is a philosophical impossibility.
>
> Of the two-thirds who followed Christ, however, some were more valiant than others. Those who were less valiant in pre-existence and who thereby had certain spiritual restrictions imposed upon them during mortality are known to us as the negroes.
>
> Negroes in this life are denied the priesthood; under no circumstances can they hold this delegation of authority from the Almighty.
>
> The present status of the negro rests purely and simply on the foundation of pre-existence. Along with all races and peoples he is receiving here what

he merits as a result of the long pre-mortal probation in the presence of the Lord. The principle is the same as will apply when all men are judged according to their mortal works and are awarded varying statuses in the life hereafter.

In making these statements, Elder McConkie was but echoing similar sentiments to the opinions of various other Brethren.[1] It had been common for enemies of the Church, not understanding the pre-existence nor believing this doctrine, to use statements such as this one as an excuse to label the Church and its leaders as racist. To those who properly understood the doctrine this was ridiculous. It was not men who imposed these restrictions, but God. One sign of the true Church is that it does not blow about with every wind of doctrine or attempt to always be politically correct. Some members, judging the Church's doctrines by their own worldly measurement, could not stand this refiner's fire and apostatized. They often did this in the name of racial equity or some other high sounding ideal. Some have tried to use Elder McConkie's statement as a means to weaken the veracity of his other teachings. They say something like, "Bruce McConkie said that the blacks would never receive the priesthood." This simply is not true. What he said was: "President Brigham Young and others have taught that in the future eternity worthy and qualified negroes will receive the priesthood and every gospel blessing available to any man."

Also, at the *time* he said that "Negroes in this life are denied the priesthood; under no circumstances can they hold this delegation of authority from the Almighty," it was true that they could not. These statements have been twisted and misinterpreted by certain people for their own purposes.

Concluding his article, Elder McConkie said: "Certainly the negroes as children of God are entitled to equality before the law and to be treated with all the dignity and respect of any member of the human race. Many of them certainly live according to higher standards of decency and right in this life than do some of their brothers of other races."[2]

Over the years (especially in the 60s and 70s), the Church had come under intense pressure from various organizations to change its position. Groups with private political agendas saw it as an opportunity to attract media attention and draw public sympathy to their cause. Ironically, such groups did not even believe the Church's claim to the priesthood. Some groups held rallies and demonstrations, and others boycotted BYU athletic events. Though religious practices are independent from civil rights, antagonists still carried the banner of civil rights to help stir up uninformed outcries and sometimes hysterical emotions. Because unscrupulous people are not shackled by fairness and truth, the Church became a "victim of the times."

Occasionally, the Brethren found it necessary to clarify the position of the Church relative to the restriction of the priesthood from black members. The following is such an example:

> In view of confusion that has arisen, it was decided at a meeting of the First Presidency and the Quorum of the Twelve to restate the position of the Church with regard to the Negro both in society and in the Church.
>
> First may we say that we know something of the sufferings of those who are discriminated against in a denial of their civil rights and Constitutional privileges....We as a people have experienced the bitter fruits of civil discrimination and mob violence.
>
> It follows therefore, that we believe the Negro as well as those of other races, should have his full Constitutional privileges as a member of society, and we hope that members of the Church everywhere will do their part as citizens to see that these rights are held inviolate. Each citizen must have equal opportunities and protection under the law with reference to civil rights.
>
> However, matters of faith, conscience, and theology are not within the purview of the civil law. The first amendment to the Constitution specifically provides that "Congress shall make no law respecting an establishment of religion, or prohibiting the free exercise thereof."
>
> The position of The Church of Jesus Christ of Latter-day Saints affecting those of the Negro race who choose to join the Church falls wholly within the category of religion. It has no bearing upon matters of civil rights. In no case or degree does it deny to the Negro his full privileges as a citizen of the nation.
>
> This position has no relevancy whatever to those who do not wish to join the Church. Those individuals, we suppose, do not believe in the divine origin and nature of the Church, nor that we have the priesthood of God. Therefore, if they feel we have no priesthood, they should have no concern with any aspect of our theology on priesthood so long as that theology does not deny any man his Constitutional privileges.
>
> From the beginning of this dispensation, Joseph Smith and all succeeding presidents of the Church have taught that Negroes, while spirit children of a common Father, and the progeny of our earthly parents Adam and Eve, were not yet to receive the priesthood, for reasons which we believe are

known to God, but which He has not made fully known to man.

Our living Prophet, President David O. McKay, has said, "The seeming discrimination by the Church toward the Negro is not something which originated with man; but goes back into the beginning with God."

Until God reveals His will in this matter, to him whom we sustain as a prophet, we are bound by that same will. Priesthood, when it is conferred on any man, comes as a blessing from God, not of men.

Were we the leaders of an enterprise created by ourselves and operated only according to our own earthly wisdom, it would be a simple thing to act according to popular will. But we believe that this work is directed by God and that the conferring of the Priesthood must await the revelation. To do otherwise would be to deny the very premise on which the Church is established.

We recognize that those who do not accept the principle of modern revelation may oppose our point of view. We repeat that such would not wish for membership in the Church, and therefore the question of priesthood should hold no interest for them. Without prejudice they should grant us the privilege afforded under the Constitution to exercise our chosen form of religion just as we must grant all others a similar privilege. They must recognize that the question of bestowing or withholding priesthood in the Church is a matter of religion and not a matter of Constitutional right.

We join with those throughout the world who pray that all of the blessings of the Gospel of Jesus Christ may in the due time of the Lord become available to men of faith everywhere. Until that time comes we must trust in God, in His wisdom and in His tender mercy.[3]

This statement from the Brethren served to help sincerely interested people understand the position of the Church regarding the priesthood restrictions. Others who still needed publicity for their own causes continued to harass the Church and its leaders.

In early May 1978, barely a month before the revelation was given, Elder LeGrand Richards, one of the senior members of the Council of the Twelve, was given a spiritual experience which was later seen as something of a prelude and premonition to the revelation on the priesthood. At the conclusion of a Thursday testimony meeting held by the Twelve in an upper room of the Salt Lake Temple, Elder Richards asked for the opportunity to speak. He said he had seen, "a man seated above the organ there and he looked just like [President Wilford Woodruff]":

I saw him just as clearly as I see any of you Brethren. He was dressed in a white suit and was seated in an armchair. I thought at the time that the reason I was privileged to see him was probably that I was the only one there who had ever seen President Woodruff while he was upon the earth. I had heard him dedicate the Salt Lake Temple and I had heard him give his last sermon in the Salt Lake Tabernacle before he died.[4]

The timing of this experience is surely not coincidental. One author has offered this explanation: "The significance...of this appearance [is] apparent. Here, appearing through the veil in the upper room of the temple, was the prophet who, almost a hundred years before, had wrestled with a critical problem, plural marriage, which was resolved by revelation, the same way the problem President Kimball faced would be resolved."[5]

With this experience, the veil between the world of spirits and the world of mortality seemed to become thin and even part as the time for change drew nearer.

The following statements are taken from the accounts of those who were either closely involved or were actual participants in and witnesses to the momentous events surrounding the revelation. They are given here as sequentially as possible; taken together they unfold a sacred, precious story:

Bruce R. McConkie:

Obviously, the Brethren have had a great anxiety and concern about this problem for a long period of time, and President Spencer W. Kimball has been exercised and has sought the Lord in faith. When we seek the Lord on a matter, with sufficient faith and devotion, he gives us an answer....One underlying reason for what happened to us is that the Brethren asked in faith; they petitioned and desired and wanted an answer—President Kimball in particular. And the other underlying principle is that in the eternal providences of the Lord, the time had come for extending the gospel to a race and a culture to whom it had previously been denied, at least as far as all of its blessings are concerned. So it was a matter of faith and righteousness and seeking on the one hand, and it was a matter of the divine timetable on the other hand. The time had arrived when the gospel, with all its blessings and obligations, would go to the Negro.[6]

Francis M. Gibbons[7]:

On March 23, 1978, President Kimball advised his counselors that he had had a wakeful night struggling with the question of priesthood restrictions and felt they should be lifted. No action was taken at the time. On April 20, 1978, the prophet advised the Twelve of his prayerful efforts to receive divine guidance on the issue and asked them to join him and his counselors in their prayers to that end. There followed personal interviews between President Kimball and members of the Twelve to discuss the matter.[8]

Boyd K. Packer:

President Kimball spoke in public of his gratitude to Elder McConkie for some special support he received in the days leading up to the revelation on the priesthood.[9]

Boyd K. Packer:

He [President Kimball] handed me his scriptures and said he'd like me to read to him from the revelations. So we started with the one from Doctrine and Covenants 124:49 that I had read in the temple. For a couple of hours we just moved back and forth through the Doctrine and Covenants, the Book of Mormon, and the Pearl of Great Price, and then talked about what we read. The spirit of revelation seemed to be brooding upon the prophet that day.[10]

Spencer W. Kimball:

We met with the Council of the Twelve Apostles, time after time, in the holy room where there is a picture of the Savior in many different moods and also pictures of all the Presidents of the Church.[11]

Gordon B. Hinckley:

The question of extending the blessings of the priesthood to blacks had been on the minds of many of the Brethren over a period of years. It had repeatedly been brought up by Presidents of the Church. It had become a matter of particular concern to President Spencer W. Kimball.[12]

Spencer W. Kimball:

I remember very vividly that day after day I walked to the temple and ascended to the fourth floor where we have our solemn assemblies and where we have our meetings of the Twelve and the First Presidency. After everybody had gone out of the temple, I knelt and prayed. I prayed with much fervency. I knew that something was before us that was extremely important to many of the children of God. I knew that we could receive the revelations of the Lord only by being worthy and ready for them and ready to accept them and put them into place. Day after day I went alone and with great solemnity and seriousness in the upper rooms of the temple, and there I offered my soul and offered my efforts to go forward with the program. I wanted to do what he wanted. I talked about it to him and said, "Lord, I want only what is right. We are not making any plans to be spectacularly moving. We want only the thing that thou dost want, and we want it when you want it and not until."[13]

Gordon B. Hinckley:

President Kimball was bold in petitioning the Lord for this revelation. He wrestled over it. He worked at it. He went to the Lord again and again. And when the revelation came, there was among the Twelve a tremendous feeling of gratitude for this unspeakable blessing.[14]

Spencer W. Kimball:

I want you to know, as a special witness of the Savior, how close I have felt to him and to our Heavenly Father as I have made numerous visits to the upper rooms in the temple, going on some days several times by myself. The Lord made it very clear to me what was to be done.

Finally, we had the feeling and the impression from the Lord, who made it very clear to us, that this was the thing to do to make the gospel universal to all worldly people.

We had the glorious experience of having the Lord indicate clearly that the time had come when all worthy men and women every where can be fellow heirs and partakers of the full blessings of the gospel.[15]

Gordon B. Hinckley:

I was present and was a participant and a witness to what occurred on Thursday, June 1, 1978. My memory is clear concerning the events of that day.

We heard testimonies from some of the brethren, and we partook of the sacrament of the Lord's Supper. It was a wonderfully spiritual meeting, as are all such meetings in these holy precincts and under these circumstances. Then the members of the First Quorum of the Seventy and the Presiding Bishopric were excused, while there remained the President of the Church, his two Counselors, and ten members of the Council of the Twelve—two being absent, one in South America and the other in the hospital.[16]

Bruce R. McConkie:

I was present when the Lord revealed to President Spencer W. Kimball that the time had come, in His eternal providences, to offer the fulness of the gospel and the blessings of the holy priesthood to all men. I was present, with my brethren of the Twelve and the counselors in the First Presidency, when all of us heard the same voice[17] and received the same message from on high. All of us were together in an upper room in the Salt Lake Temple. We were engaged in fervent prayer, pleading with the Lord to manifest his mind and will concerning those who are entitled to receive his holy priesthood. President Kimball himself was mouth, offering the desires of his heart and of our hearts to that God whose servants we are.

In his prayer President Kimball asked that all of us might be cleansed and made free from sin so that we might receive the Lord's word. He counseled freely and fully with the Lord, was given utterance by the power of the Spirit, and what he said was inspired from on high. It was one of those rare and seldom-experienced times when the disciples of the Lord are perfectly united, when every heart beats as one, and when the same spirit burns in every bosom.

We...had come together in the spirit of true worship and with unity of desire. We were all fasting and had just concluded a meeting of some three hours' duration that was attended by nearly all of the General Authorities. That meeting was also held in the room of the First Presidency and the Twelve in the holy temple. In it we had been counseled by the First Presidency, had heard the messages and testimonies of about fifteen of the Brethren, had renewed our covenants, in the ordinance of sacrament, to serve God and keep his commandments that we might always have his Spirit to be with us, and, surrounding the holy altar, had offered up the desire of our hearts to the Lord. After this meeting, which was one of great spiritual uplift and enlightenment, all of the Brethren except those of the Presidency and the Twelve were excused.

When we were alone by ourselves in the sacred place where we meet weekly to wait upon the Lord, to seek guidance from his Spirit, and to transact the affairs of his earthly kingdom, President Kimball brought up the matter of the possible conferral of the priesthood upon those of all races. This was a subject that the group of us had discussed at length on numerous occasions in the preceeding weeks and months. The President restated the problem involved, reminded us of our prior discussions, and said he had spent many days alone in this upper room pleading with the Lord for an answer to our prayers. He said that if the answer was to continue our present course of denying the priesthood to the seed of Cain, as the Lord had theretofore directed, he was prepared to defend that decision to the death. But, he said, if the long sought day had come in which the curse of the past was to be removed, he thought we might prevail upon the Lord so to indicate. He expressed the hope that we might receive a clear answer one way or the other so the matter might be laid to rest.

At this point President Kimball asked the Brethren if any of them desired to express their feelings and views as to the matter in hand. We all did so, freely and fluently and at considerable length, each person stating his views and manifesting the feelings of his heart. There was a marvelous outpouring of unity, oneness, and agreement in council. This session continued for somewhat more than two hours. Then President Kimball suggested that we unite in formal prayer and said, modestly, that if it was agreeable with the rest of us he would act as voice.

It was during that prayer that the revelation came. The Spirit of the Lord rested mightily upon us all; we felt something akin to what happened on the day of Pentecost and at the dedication of the Kirtland Temple. From the midst of eternity, the voice of God, conveyed by the power of the Spirit, spoke to his prophet. The message was that the time had now come to offer the fulness of the everlasting gospel, including celestial marriage, and the priesthood, and the blessings of the temple, to all men, without reference to race or color, solely on the basis of personal worthiness. And we all heard the same voice, received the same message, and became personal witnesses that the word received was the mind and will and voice of the Lord.

President Kimball's prayer was answered and our prayers were answered. He heard the voice and we heard the same voice. All doubt and uncertainty fled. He knew the answer and we knew the answer. And we are all living witnesses of the truthfulness of the word so graciously sent from heaven.[18]

Bruce R. McConkie:

Thus...on the first day of June 1978, the First Presidency and the Twelve, after full discussion of the proposition and all the premises and principles that were involved, importuned the Lord for a revelation. President Kimball was mouth, and he prayed with great faith and great fervor; this was one of those occasions when an inspired prayer was offered....It was given President Kimball what he should ask (D&C 50:30). He prayed by the power of the Spirit, and there was perfect unity, total and complete harmony, between the Presidency and the Twelve on the issue involved.

And when President Kimball finished his prayer, the Lord gave a revelation by the power of the Holy Ghost....

On this occasion, because of the importuning and the faith, and because the hour and the time had arrived, the Lord in his providences poured out the Holy Ghost upon the First Presidency and the Twelve in a miraculous and marvelous manner, beyond anything that any then present had ever experienced. The revelation came to the President of the Church; it also came to each individual present. There were ten members of the Council of the Twelve and three of the First Presidency there assembled. The result was that President Kimball knew, and each one of us knew, independent of any other person, by direct and personal revelation to us, that the time had now come to extend the gospel and all its blessings and all its obligations, including the priesthood and the blessings of the house of the Lord, to those of every nation, culture and race, including the black race. There was no question whatsoever as to what happened or as to the word and message that came.[19]

Bruce R. McConkie:

There is no way to describe in language what is involved. This cannot be done. I cannot describe in words what happened; I can only say that it happened and that it can be known and understood only by the feeling that can come into the heart of man.[20]

Gordon B. Hinckley:

On this occasion he raised the question before his Brethren—his Counselors and the Apostles. Following this discussion we joined in prayer in the most sacred of circumstances. President Kimball himself was voice in that prayer. I do not recall the exact words that he spoke. But I do recall my own feelings and the nature of the expressions of my Brethren. There was a hallowed and sanctified atmosphere in the room. For me, it felt as if a conduit opened between the heavenly throne and the kneeling, pleading prophet of God who was joined by his Brethren. The Spirit of God was there. And by the power of the Holy Ghost there came to that prophet an assurance that the thing for which he prayed was right, that the time had come, and that now the wondrous blessings of the priesthood should be extended to worthy men everywhere regardless of lineage.

Every man in that circle, by the power of the Holy Ghost, knew the same thing. It was a quiet and sublime occasion. There was not the sound "as of a rushing mighty wind," there were not "cloven tongues like as of fire" as there had been on the Day of Pentecost. But there was a Pentecostal spirit, for the Holy Ghost was there.

No voice audible to our physical ears was heard. But the voice of the Spirit whispered with certainty into our minds and our very souls. It was for us, at least for me personally, as I imagine it was with Enos, who said concerning his remarkable experience, "And while I was thus struggling in the spirit, behold, the voice of the Lord came into my mind."[21]

David B. Haight:

I was in the temple when President Spencer W. Kimball received the revelation regarding the priesthood. I was the junior member of the Quorum of the Twelve. I was there. I was there with the outpouring of the Spirit in that room so strong that none of us could speak afterwards. We just left quietly to go back to the office. No one could say anything because of the powerful outpouring of the heavenly spiritual experience....I was a witness to this revelation. I was there. I witnessed it. I felt that heavenly influence. I was part of it....it was truly a revelation from God....I was a witness to it.[22]

Bruce R. McConkie:

On this occasion, because of the importuning and the faith, and because the hour and the time had arrived, the Lord in his providences poured out the Holy Ghost upon the First Presidency and the Twelve in a miraculous and marvelous manner, beyond anything that any then present had ever experienced.[23]

Bruce R. McConkie:

In the days that followed the receipt of the new revelation, President Kimball and President Ezra Taft Benson—the senior and most spiritually experienced ones among us—both said, expressing the feelings of us all, that neither of them had ever experienced anything of such spiritual magnitude and power as was poured out upon the Presidency and the Twelve that day in the upper room in the house of the Lord. And of it I say; I was there; I heard the voice; and the Lord be praised that it has come to pass in our day.

President Kimball is a man of almost infinite spiritual capacity—a tremendous spiritual giant. The Lord has magnified him beyond any understanding or expression and has given him His mind and will on a great number of vital matters that have altered the course of the past.[24]

Gordon B. Hinckley:

We left that meeting subdued and reverent and joyful. Not one of us who was present on that occasion was ever quite the same after that....All of us knew that the time had come for a change and that the decision had come from the heavens. The answer was clear. There was perfect unity among us in our experience and in our understanding.[25]

Boyd K. Packer:

[President Kimball had] asked me, assuming that the revelation was to come, how it might best be announced to the Church, and asked that I put something in writing. This I did and handed it to him a day or two later. He had asked one or two of the others to do the same.[26]

Francis M. Gibbons:

On Wednesday, June 7, 1978,...letters were read from three members of the Twelve, which President Kimball had requested, containing suggested wording for the public announcement of the decision. Using these three letters as a base, a fourth statement was prepared and then reviewed, edited, and approved by the First Presidency. This document was taken to the council meeting with the Twelve on Thursday, June 8...The document was read and, with minor editorial changes, was approved.[27]

Bruce R. McConkie:

This revelation that came on the first day of June 1978 was reaffirmed by the spirit of inspiration one week later on June 8, when the Brethren approved the document that was to be announced to the world. And then it was reaffirmed the next day, on Friday, June 9, with all of the General Authorities present in the temple....All received the assurance and witness and confirmation by the power of the Spirit that what had occurred was the mind, the will, the intent, and the purpose of the Lord. This is a wondrous thing; the veil is thin. The Lord is not far distant from his church.[28]

Mark E. Petersen (then in South America on assignment):

I was delighted to know that a new revelation had come from the Lord. I felt the fact of the revelation's coming was more striking than the decision itself. On the telephone I told President Kimball that I fully sustained both the revelation and him one hundred percent.[29]

Bruce R. McConkie:

The revelation came to every member of the body that I have named. They all knew it in the temple.

In my judgment this was done by the Lord in this way because it was a revelation of such tremendous significance and import; one that would [change] the whole direction of the Church, procedurally and administratively; one that would affect the living and the dead; one that would affect the total relationship that we have with the world; one, I say, of such significance that the Lord wanted witnesses who could bear record that the thing had happened.

Now, if President Kimball had received the revelation and had asked for a sustaining vote, obviously he would have received it and the revelation would have been announced. But the Lord chose this other course, in my judgment, because of the tremendous import and the eternal significance of what was being revealed.

This affects what is going on in the spirit world, because the gospel is preached in the spirit world preparatory to men's receiving the vicarious ordinances that make them heirs to salvation and exaltation. This is a revelation of tremendous significance.

This means that the same revelation had to be given to the Brethren in the Church in the spirit world, so that they can conform their preaching of the gospel to our new system on earth. This revelation is something in the same category as the revelation which caused Wilford Woodruff to issue the Manifesto.[30]

Bruce R. McConkie:

Once again a revelation was given that affects this sphere of activity and the sphere that is to come. And so it has tremendous significance; the eternal import was such that it came in the way it did. The Lord could have sent messengers from the other side to deliver it, but he did not. He gave the revelation by the power of the Holy Ghost. Latter-day Saints have a complex; many of them desire to magnify and build upon what has occurred, and they delight to think of miraculous things. And maybe some of them would like to believe that the Lord himself was there, or that the Prophet Joseph Smith came to deliver the revelation, which was one of the possibilities. Well, these things did not happen. The stories that go around to the contrary are not factual or realistic or true....This thing came by the power of the Holy Ghost, and...all the Brethren involved, the thirteen who were present, are independent personal witnesses of the truth and divinity of what occurred.

I think I can add that it is one of the signs of the times. It is something that had to occur before the Second Coming. It was something that was mandatory and imperative in order to enable us to fulfil all of the revelations that are involved.[31]

Once the revelation was announced to the world, the reaction was predictable. For unbelievers, the response might have been encapsulated in the word "claimed."[32] Intellectual dissidents presumed to take credit for pressuring the Church into announcing a "policy" change.[33] As for faithful members of the Church, it was greeted with joy and thanksgiving. "There has been a tremendous feeling of gratitude and thanksgiving in the hearts of members of the Church everywhere," said Elder McConkie. "For all general purposes there has been universal acceptance; and everyone who has been in tune with the Spirit has known that the Lord spoke, and that his mind and his purposes are being manifest in the course the Church is pursuing."[34]

What about the entry in the first edition of *Mormon Doctrine* quoted at the beginning of this chapter? What about the statements Elder McConkie quoted from the other early Brethren given before 1978? To those who still wondered and puzzled and researched the question he said:

There have been these problems, and the Lord has permitted them to arise. There is not any question about that. We do not envision the whole reason and purpose behind all of this; we can only suppose and reason that it is on the basis of preexistence and of our premortal devotion and faith.

There are statements in our literature by the early Brethren that we have interpreted to mean that the Negroes would not receive the priesthood in mortality. I have said the same things, and people write me letters and say, "You said such and such, and how is it now that we do such and such?" All I can say is that it is time disbelieving people repented and got in line and believed in a living, modern prophet. Forget everything that I have said, or what President Brigham Young or President George Q. Cannon or whoever has said in days past that is contrary to the present revelation. We spoke with a limited understanding and without the light and knowledge that now has come into the world.

It doesn't make a particle of difference what anybody ever said about the Negro matter before the first day of June 1978. It is a new day and a new arrangement, and the Lord has now given the revelation that sheds light out into the world on this subject. As to any slivers of light or any particles of darkness of the past, we forget about them. We now do what meridian Israel did when the Lord said the gospel should go to the Gentiles. We forget all the statements that limited the gospel to the house of Israel, and we start going to the Gentiles.[35]

Although we may wonder, analyze, and debate the reason for things that have not been revealed, God is in His heaven and knows all things and reveals light and knowledge sufficient for the day. In the meantime, faith leads us on with safety and success until we are prepared for greater responsibility, opportunity and revelation.

In all printings of *Mormon Doctrine* after 1978, Elder McConkie removed his old entry on the subject and instead included an announcement of the joyous revelation, some attendant commentary, and the wording of the official declaration as it now appears in the Doctrine and Covenants. Changes were also made in all other entries which dealt with the priesthood restriction issue.

Notes

1. The following are samples of statements of opinion given by a few prominent Church leaders, which, though unofficial, constituted the prevailing personal beliefs shared by the Brethren in general:

a) President David O. McKay taught, "I believe...that the real reason [for the restriction] dates back to our pre-existent life." (Unpublished letter to a BYU Student, 3 Nov. 1947; copy in author's file.)

b) Elder Melvin J. Ballard taught, "Why is it in this Church we do not grant the priesthood to the negroes? It is alleged that the Prophet Joseph said—and I have no reason to dispute it—that it is because of some act committed by them before they came into this life. It is alleged that they were neutral, standing neither for Christ nor the devil. But, I am convinced it is because of some things they did before they came into this life that they have been denied the privilege. The races of today are very largely reaping the consequences of a previous life." (Melvin J. Ballard, "The Three Degrees of Glory," *Melvin J. Ballard: Crusader for Righteousness*, Salt Lake City: Bookcraft, 1966, p. 218.)

c) Elders Mark E. Petersen and Joseph Fielding Smith both taught similar doctrines. (See Mark E. Petersen, unpublished talk given at Paris, France, at a missionary meeting, 24 Jan. 1963, LDS Church Historical Dept., and Joseph Fielding Smith, "Status of the Negro," unpublished talk given 11 Oct. 1958, LDS Church Historical Dept., and *The Progress of Man,* Salt Lake City: Genealogical Society of Utah, p. 32.)

2. *Mormon Doctrine,* 1st ed., pp. 476-77. This entry is the same for the second edition also, with the change not being incorporated until printings after 1978.

3. *Church News* "Policy Statement of Presidency," 10 Jan. 1970, p. 12 (signed by Presidents Hugh B. Brown, and N. Eldon Tanner of the First Presidency; President McKay was very ill at the time and died shortly thereafter.)

4. Lucile C. Tate, *LeGrand Richards: Beloved Apostle* (Salt Lake City: Bookcraft, 1982), pp. 291-92.

5. Francis M. Gibbons, *Spencer W. Kimball: Resolute Disciple, Prophet of God* (Salt Lake City: Deseret Book, 1995), p. 294. Hereafter cited as Gibbons, *Kimball.*

6. Mark McConkie, *Restoration,* pp. 165-66.

7. Francis M. Gibbons was secretary to the First Presidency at the time the revelation was given.

8. Gibbons, *Kimball,* pp. 293-94.

9. Packer, p. 264.

10. Lucille C. Tate, *Boyd K. Packer: A Watchman on the Tower* (Salt Lake City: Bookcraft, 1995), p. 226. Hereafter cited as Tate, *Packer.*

11. Edward L. Kimball, ed., *The Teachings of Spencer W. Kimball* (Salt Lake City: Bookcraft, 1982), p. 451. Hereafter cited as Kimball.

12. *Ensign,* Oct. 1988, pp. 69-70.

13. Kimball, pp. 450-51.

14. Sheri L. Dew, *Go Forward with Faith: The Biography of Gordon B. Hinckley* (Salt Lake City: Deseret Book, 1996), p. 362.

15. Kimball, pp. 451-52.

16. *Ensign,* Oct. 1988, p. 70.

17. Elder McConkie did not here mean to imply he heard a physically audible speaking voice. See Gordon B. Hinckley's statements quoted in this chapter.

18. Mark McConkie, *Restoration,* pp. 159-61.

19. Mark McConkie, *Restoration,* pp. 166-67.

20. Mark McConkie, *Restoration,* p. 169.

21. *Ensign,* Oct. 1988, p. 70.

22. *Ensign,* May 1996, p. 23.

23. Mark McConkie, *Restoration,* pp. 166-67.

24. Mark McConkie, *Restoration,* pp. 161-62, 169-170.

25. *Ensign,* Oct. 1988, p. 70.

26. Tate, *Packer,* p. 226.

27. Gibbons, *Kimball,* p. 295.

28. Mark McConkie, *Restoration,* p. 169.

29. Barton, p. 176.

30. Mark McConkie, *Restoration,* pp. 167, 170-71.

31. Mark McConkie, *Restoration,* pp. 168-69.

32. *Ensign,* May 1996, p. 23.

33. Gibbons, *Kimball,* pp. 296-97.

34. Mark McConkie, *Restoration,* p. 170.

35. Mark McConkie, *Restoration,* pp. 163-65.

Chapter Twelve

The Messiah Series

In the mid-1970s, not long after the completion of *Doctrinal New Testament Commentary,* Elder McConkie began another major project, which grew to a six-volume series on the ministry of the Messiah, the Lord Jesus Christ. He explained:

> My original intent, as this opus and its companion volumes took form in my mind, was to write two volumes, one dealing with the Messianic prophecies and the First Coming of the Messiah; the other with the prophetic utterances and revealed realities relative to his Second Coming. I had not dared even to think of assuming the prerogative of writing an account of the life [of Jesus Christ]. After all, I reasoned, I already had in print a nearly nine-hundred-page doctrinal commentary on the four Gospels, which in the very nature of things dealt primarily with the doings and sayings [of Jesus].[1]
>
> In addition...I have a deep and profound respect for *Jesus the Christ,* the scholarly work of Elder James E. Talmage, one of my most prominent predecessors. Why, I thought, should I step into the most difficult of all fields of gospel writing—that of composing something akin to a "Life of Christ"? But as I pondered and prayed and put into words, in the first volume of this series, the true meaning of the many Messianic messages,... and as I envisioned more fully the faithless and uninspired nature of almost everything that worldly men have recorded about the marvelous works and message [of the Lord], there came into my heart an overpowering desire to put into words, as best I might, for all to read, what we believe and know about the greatest life ever lived.
>
> [Elder James E. Talmage's] work is profound and sound and should be studied by every member of the true Church. But I think I hear his voice, vocal and penetrating above those of all others qualified to speak in the specialized field here involved, saying, "Now is the time to build on the foundations I laid some seventy years ago, using the added knowledge that has since come by research and revelation, and to pen a companion volume to the one I was privileged to write."[2]

Elder McConkie's reference to Elder James E. Talmage and the spiritual impression about him is especially enlightening. Elder Boyd K. Packer, speaking at the funeral of his close friend Bruce R. McConkie, said these words: "Perhaps one day we will see how great a man has walked among us. He was not less than Elder Talmage or the others we revere from the past. His sermons and writings will live on. In these, he will live longer than any of us."[3] This authoritative pronouncement by Elder Packer regarding Elder McConkie's stature and greatness is most meaningful. In 1962, Elder Marion G. Romney wrote an article in which he described the qualifications of Elder Talmage to write *Jesus the Christ.* This description applies equally well to Elder McConkie and his Messiah series. Because of Elder Packer's statement, might it not be respectful to Elder McConkie to substitute his name for that of Elder Talmage, in the following quotation from Elder Romney?

[Elder Bruce R. McConkie] was peculiarly qualified to write a treatise on the life of Jesus. His attainments testify to this. He was a scholar of... [high] repute. He was an accomplished writer, already acknowledged as an authority in [his] field.

Among the religious books he had written were [*Mormon Doctrine* and three volumes of *Doctrinal New Testament Commentary*], which [have] few if any peers in [their] field. He was a mature and righteous man; he revered Jesus as the literal son of God, the Redeemer of mankind and of the world. This reverence he had demonstrated by obedience to all his commandments. He had entered, through the initiatory principles and ordinances of the gospel, The Church of Jesus Christ of Latter-day Saints.

He had received the priesthood of God and all its saving ordinances. So complete was his dedication that the Lord had called him to be an apostle—a special witness of Jesus Christ in all the world.

All these circumstances combined to give him the most important qualification he possessed—namely, the companionship and guidance of the Holy Spirit. No one had a clearer conception than did he of man's inability, without the guidance of that Spirit, to portray correctly the life and mission of the world's Redeemer. He knew and followed the Lord's admonition, "Remember that that which cometh from above is sacred, and must be spoken with care, and by constraint of the Spirit..." (D&C 63:64), and "...if ye receive not the Spirit ye shall not teach." (D&C 42:14.)

Anyone who reads [the Messiah series] under the influence of the Spirit will be convinced that the author was inspired in his understanding of the sacred records concerning the life and mission of Jesus, and that he wrote his treatise by the same inspiration.[4]

Their similarity in knowledge, ability, and spiritual insight is remarkable and profound. They each knew of whom they wrote. The qualifications of the one were as those of the other. Their works stand together in teaching and testifying to the world of the divinity of the Lord Jesus Christ.

Elder McConkie would call his six volumes a "near-biography," considering it impossible for a mere mortal to write a true, complete, and comprehensive biography of the Savior.[5]

Elder McConkie's first book in the set, *The Promised Messiah*, came off the press in 1978. It was closely followed by book 1 of *The Mortal Messiah* in 1979. Books 2 and 3 were printed in 1980, closely followed by book 4 in 1981. Then *The Millennial Messiah* was published in 1982. In approximately seven years, Elder McConkie wrote around 3,200 pages of commentary, analysis, and doctrine centering on the Son of God. It was a monumental task, as he described to religious educators at BYU:

> I read the standard works from cover to cover, as though I'd never read them before, and elicited from them everything that had anything to do with the promise of a messiah. Then I organized and wrote *The Promised Messiah*. Now I'll tell you how I wrote *The Millennial Messiah*. I read the standard works from cover to cover, as though I'd never read them before, and elicited from them everything that had anything to do with the Millennial Messiah and the return of Christ. Then I organized and wrote the book.[6]

Toward the end of this labor, Elder McConkie wrote, "[I] have written this work—in agony and in ecstasy; in sweat and in tears; in depression and in elation; through seasons of sorrow and in times of unbounded joy—all to the end that men might believe and know that God's Almighty Son ministered as a Man among men, and that believing, perchance, they might be faithful and gain eternal life."[7]

Nor did Elder McConkie lose his humility in the course of the work, even though he wrote so powerfully and poignantly. "Throughout this whole work, with inept and faltering fingers," said he, "[I] have sought to weave, page by page, those threads which belong in the Lord's eternal tapestry, and chapter by chapter have attempted to describe the scenes the Lord has envisioned from the beginning."[8]

Elder McConkie once gave an inspired address entitled "The Bible: A Sealed Book," in which he spoke of two symbolic seals which kept people from reading and understanding the marvelous truths within its covers. He named them ignorance and intellectuality.[9] His point was that because of illiteracy, religious dictatorship, and carelessness, accompanied by uninspired reason and intellect, the Bible has gone undiscovered and unused by countless people. He then offered several keys of varying worth, which he declared would help to remove these unwanted seals.

The Messiah series seems to have some minor seals of its own, though different in nature from the Bible. This chapter will attempt to provide keys for removing these seals, thus providing a brief glimpse into a treasury of gospel truth, preciously deep and sacred.

One seal is that the six rather lengthy volumes of this comprehensive work could seem somewhat intimidating. Once opened and perused, a second seal is encountered. As mentioned in an earlier chapter, the language style that Elder McConkie used is often rather formal, wordy, and poetic. At times he sounds a bit like the prophet Isaiah; for example: "Hear, O ye heavens, and give ear, O earth; let mortal men and angelic ministrants join hands; let all who belong to the family of the Father, whether on earth or in heaven, rejoice in the great atonement."[10] Another time, for a chapter title he used the biblical sounding "Messiah Bringeth the Resurrection."[11] Both these descriptions are quite true and important, but they can be difficult for the inexperienced to read.

After the reader has digested a fair number of pages, another seal may become apparent—repetition. If the direction of his writing took him across ground he had already traveled, he often covered it once more, using very similar phraseology to express the same doctrinal concepts once again. Dealing with this sometimes ponderous repetition is part of the reality of working through this sizeable set, which unfortunately has encouraged some to use the series as a reference tool only. Such repetition is intended to offer a certain doctrinal familiarity to the student, delightfully exposing him to scriptural terms and phrases, and should not be a deterrent in discovering the Savior through this magnificent doctrinal treasury.

In the preface to the *Promised Messiah,* Elder McConkie wrote, "And so...having no private views to expound, no personal doctrines to set forth, no ideas that originate with me alone—I desire to present those things which will cause men of good will everywhere to believe [in Christ]." There is absolutely no doubt that his purpose was to write things that would cause men and women to believe in Christ. Some have doubted whether he presented personal views, and ideas that might not be familiar to most readers. It should be perfectly clear that Elder McConkie had a profound and deep knowledge of gospel truths. He understood the scriptures, and the Spirit of the Lord had enlightened his mind and taught him. As he said: "What a spirit of exhilaration and peace comes into the heart of a gospel student each time a new truth is manifest to him! Each time his views expand to catch the full vision of some prophetic passage! Each time his soul both learns and feels the import of what the revelations say about some great principle!"[12] It is clear that this was a familiar process for Elder McConkie. It does not mean that he knew things no one else knew, but it does suggest he knew things few others knew. He had earned his knowledge by obeying the laws upon which such divine truths are predicated, and he shared some of these truths with those willing to search them out from the pages of his books.

In order to understand and appreciate the precious gospel food found in this voluminous series, short excerpts from each volume are hereafter provided to help remove some of the seals for the student. It should be remembered that they are out of context. Therefore they should be read in the full text of the *Messiah Series* for better understanding.

The Promised Messiah

THE SECOND COMING

And he [Jesus] shall come again—perhaps while some of us on earth yet live as mortals—first, to dwell and reign on earth a thousand years, and then, after a short season, to transform this earth into his own celestial home. (P. 2.)

BASIC GOSPEL KNOWLEDGE

It is helpful—indeed, almost imperative—that those of us who seek to know the deep and hidden things about Christ and his coming first gain an overall knowledge of the plan of salvation. (P. 42.)

UNDERSTANDING SCRIPTURE

But in the final analysis, there is no way—absolutely none (and this cannot be stated too strongly!)—to understand any Messianic prophecy, or any other scripture, except to have the same spirit of prophecy that rested upon the one who uttered the truth in its original form. Scripture comes from God by the power of the Holy Ghost. It does not originate with man. It means only what the Holy Ghost thinks it means. To interpret it, we must be enlightened by the power of the Holy Spirit. (P. 44.)

WORLDS WITHOUT NUMBER

Where Christ himself was concerned, this small planet was but one speck of dust in a storm swirling over the Sahara. There is not one earth, but many; not one planet inhabited by our father's children, but an infinite number.

Worlds without number! Innumerable unto man! There is not a finite way to envision the extent of the worlds created by Christ at the behest of his Father. Count the grains of sand on all the seashores and Saharas of the world, add the stars in the firmament for good measure, multiply the total by like sums from other worlds, and what do we have? Scarcely a dot in the broad expanse of an infinite universe—all created by Christ. (P. 55.)

THE FATHER CREATED MAN

However, from other sacred sources we know that Jehovah-Christ, assisted by "many of the noble and great ones" of whom Michael is but the illustration, did in fact create the earth and all forms of plant and animal life on the face thereof. But when it came to placing man on earth, there was a change in Creators. That is, the Father himself became personally involved. All things were created by the son, using the power delegated by the Father, except man. In the spirit and again in the flesh, man was created by the Father. There was no delegation of authority where the crowning creature of creation was concerned. (P. 62.)

PRE-ADAMITES

Implicit in the doctrine of the fall and the consequent atonement is the bitter reality—if such it must be to those whose spiritual understanding has not yet been opened to the full truth—that there were no pre-Adamites, for mortality, death, and procreation began with Adam. And there is no salvation provided for any except Adam's seed, for it is they for whom Christ died. (P. 226.)

GOSPEL ON OTHER WORLDS

Further, the gospel is in operation in all the worlds created by the Father and the Son. Their work and their glory, in all the infinite creation that their hands have made, is to bring to pass immortality and eternal life for the children of the Father. Through the atonement of Christ, the inhabitants of all these worlds have power to become his sons and his daughters. (P. 286.)

SANCTIFICATION, A PROCESS

Sometimes men are born again miraculously and suddenly, as was Alma. They become alive to the things of the Spirit and completely reverse the whole course of their life almost in an instant. But for most members of the Church the spiritual rebirth is a process that goes on gradually. The faithful are sanctified degree by degree as they add to their faith and good works. (P. 351.)

LIKENESS OF CHRIST AND MOSES

Moses was in the similitude of Christ, and Christ was like unto Moses. Of all the hosts of our Father's children, these two are singled out as being like each other.

...All men are endowed with the characteristics and attributes which, in their eternal fulness, dwell in Deity. But it appears there is a special image, a special similitude, a special likeness where the man Moses and the man Jesus are concerned. It is reasonable to suppose that this similarity, this resemblance, is both physical and spiritual; it is a likeness where both qualities and appearance are concerned. (P. 442.)

MANNER OF CHRIST'S BIRTH

Some words scarcely need definition. They are on every tongue and are spoken by every voice. The very existence of intelligent beings presupposes and requires their constant use. Two such words are father and son. Their meaning is known to all, and to define them is but to repeat them. Thus: a son is a son is a son, and a father is a father is a father. I am the son of my father and the father of my sons. They are my sons because they were begotten by me, were conceived by their mother, and come forth from her womb....

And so it is with the Eternal Father and the mortal birth of the Eternal

Son....The one begat the other. Mary provided the womb from which the Spirit Jehovah came forth, tabernacled in clay,...There is nothing figurative or hidden or beyond comprehension in our Lord's coming into mortality. He is the Son of God in the same sense and way that we are the sons of mortal fathers. It is just that simple. (P. 468.)

KNOWLEDGE OF THE FATHER

Matthew, Mark, Luke, and John, the four New Testament Gospels, contain more revealed truth about the nature and kind of being that God is than all the rest of the scriptures combined, simply because they reveal the personality, powers, and perfections of the Son of God, which is in the express image and likeness of the Father. (P. 475.)

WHOM WE PRAY TO

Proper prayers are not addressed to the Blessed Virgin, although we may suppose she was the greatest mortal of her sex. They are not addressed to Eve, the mother of all living, nor to Sarah, who with Abraham has entered into her exaltation and sits at her husband's side on the throne of eternal power. Proper prayers are offered to the Father, and to him only, but they are always offered in the name of his Only Begotten Son. (P. 558.)

THE PURPOSE OF THE ENDOWMENT

To those of understanding we say: The purpose of the endowment in the house of the Lord is to prepare and sanctify his saints so they will be able to see his face, here and now, as well as to bear the glory of his presence in the eternal worlds. (P. 583.)

THE FATHER SPEAKS WITH ENOCH

The Father dealt directly with Adam before the fall, and he apparently (as we shall note shortly) dealt directly with Enoch after that prophet was translated. Otherwise, all the dealings of Deity with men on earth have been through the Son.

Then Enoch "was high and lifted up, even in the bosom of the Father, and of the Son of Man," which is to say that he saw both the Father and the Son and conversed with them. There are then recorded some three and a half pages of these conversations, some statements being made by the Father, others by the Son. (Moses 7.) (Pp. 597, 599.)

The Mortal Messiah, Book 1

MARY'S AGE

And so we find Mary, about fifteen years of age and inexperienced in meeting the trials of life, under contract to marry one she loved, but with child by the power of the Holy Ghost. (P. 322.)

JESUS' YOUTH

It seems perfectly clear that our Lord grew mentally and spiritually on the same basis that he developed physically. In each case he obeyed the laws of experience and of learning and the rewards flowed to him. The real issue of concern is not that he grew and developed and matured—all in harmony with the established order of things, as is the case with all men—but that he was so highly endowed with talents and abilities, so spiritually sensitive, so in tune with the Infinite, that his learning and wisdom soon excelled that of all his fellows. His knowledge came to him quickly and easily, because he was building—as is the case with all men—upon the foundations laid in preexistence. He brought with him from that eternal world the talents and capacities, the inclinations to conform and obey, and the ability to recognize truth that he had there acquired.

Of the Lord Jesus the scripture says: "God giveth not the Spirit by measure unto him" (John 3:34), which is to say that he enjoyed, at all times, the fulness of that light and guidance and power which comes by the power of the Holy Ghost to the faithful." (Pp. 369-70.)

GOSPEL OF JOHN THE BAPTIST

John the Baptist also is destined to write of the gospel of that Lord whose witness he is, but his account, perhaps because it contains truths and concepts that the saints and the world are not yet prepared to receive, has so far not been given to men. On May 6, 1833, however, the Lord did reveal to Joseph Smith eleven verses of the Baptist's writings. (D&C 93:6-18.) (P. 426.)

The Mortal Messiah, Book 2

FAITH IN FAMILIES

In the first Twelve called in this dispensation, Parley P. and Orson Pratt were brothers, as were Luke S. and Lyman E. Johnson. Joseph Smith, the Prophet, and Hyrum Smith, the Patriarch, were brothers; their brother William served in the Twelve, and their father, Joseph Smith Sr., was the first Patriarch to the Church. Brigham Young Jr., a son of President Brigham Young, was one of the Twelve. George A. Smith, John Henry Smith, and George Albert Smith constitute three generations of apostles, as do Franklin D. Richards, George F. Richards, and LeGrand Richards, and Amasa, Francis M. and Richard R. Lyman. President Joseph F. Smith, and two of his sons, Hyrum Mack and Joseph Fielding, served in the Twelve. Lorenzo and Erastus Snow were related. John Taylor and his son John W., Wilford Woodruff and his son Abraham O., Mathias F. Cowley and his son Matthew, and George Q. Cannon and his son Sylvester were all apostles. Joseph F. Merril was a son of Marriner W. Merril, Ezra Taft Benson a great-grandson of the original Ezra T. Benson, and Stephen L. Richards a grandson of Willard Richards. President Spencer W. Kimball is a grandson of Heber C. Kimball, and Gordon B. Hinckley a nephew of Alonzo A. Hinckley—plus the fact that there are many instances of cousins and more distantly related family members, all called to positions of apostolic power. Truly, faith runs in families, in all dispensations. (Pp. 113-14.)

WALKING ON WATER

[As the disciples' ship foundered in the storm, Jesus] came to them "walking on the sea": his weight was borne by the foaming liquid beneath his feet; it was as though the watery waves were a stone-set street. The storm-tossed Sea of Galilee was as a dusty Galilean lane because Jesus willed it. He walked on the water—literally, actually, and in reality....

And come Peter did. He too walked on the water. Jesus and Peter were both supported by the liquid highway beneath them. (Pp. 359-60.)

The Mortal Messiah, Book 3

GOSPEL POWERS ON BOTH SIDES OF VEIL

Now on the Mount of Transfiguration, a heavenly voice—that of the Almighty Father who is visiting his Son on planet earth—bears holy witness of the same divine Sonship. And now Jesus and angelic visitants, who do his bidding, join in conferring upon Peter, James, and John the promised keys of the kingdom with their sealing powers. And these angelic ministrants...also speak with Jesus of his coming death and resurrection. The bearing of testimony, the use of the keys of the kingdom, the reality of the atonement—all these are operative on both sides of the veil. Both men on earth and the angels of God in heaven are saved and blessed by the same eternal laws. (Pp. 54-55.)

MOUNT OF TRANSFIGURATION

Elohim was there in the cloud. That he was seen by the Son we cannot doubt. Whether our Lord's three companions saw within the veil we do not say. We do know that even now those who have been sealed up unto eternal life, whose calling and election has been made sure, have the privilege of receiving the Second Comforter; and that this Comforter "is no more nor less than the Lord Jesus Christ Himself," who then appears to them "from time to time,"; and that "He will manifest the Father," and "they will take up their abode" with him, and the visions of heaven will be opened unto them. (*Teachings,* pp. 150-51.) Let each man determine for himself what happened there on the slopes of Mount Hermon in the summer or autumn of A.D. 29. (Pp. 61.)

CHILDREN OF THE DEVIL

And further, just as surely as the obedient receive the adoption of sons, becoming children of God, so the disobedient are adopted into the Church or kingdom of the devil, thus becoming children of the devil. (P. 164.)

REVELATION ON THE PRIESTHOOD

A new and grander vision of those called into the Master's service at the eleventh hour is seen in the revelation, received June 8, 1978, offering the full blessings of the gospel, including the priesthood and the blessings of the temple, to those of every race and color. All such, called at the eleventh hour, have the same obligation of priesthood service that the divine Householder has given to any of his servants, and they shall be rewarded on an equal basis. (P. 309.)

FATE OF WICKED JEWS

Jesus sends apostles and prophets among the Jews of his day....Even he himself ministers among them, testifying with words such as no other man ever spake....All this they reject, and they are damned; no man can reject the light of heaven and be saved—of course they are damned....They shall die in their sins. Thus saith Jesus.

But this is not all. They [the scribes and pharisees] are accountable for the sins of their fathers who through ignorance rejected the message of salvation. Such is the worst of woes, the crowning curse—to be accountable, not alone for their own sins, but for the sins of those who might have been saved had these spiritual leaders done their duty. (Pp.404-5.)

The Mortal Messiah, Book 4

WASHING OF FEET

The full significance of this [John 13:1-17] is not apparent to the casual reader, nor should it be, for the washing of feet is a sacred ordinance reserved to be done in holy places for those who make themselves worthy. [Jesus] had re-instituted one of the holy ordinances of the everlasting gospel. Those who have been washed in the waters of baptism, who have been freed from sin and evil through the waters of regeneration, who have come forth thereby in a newness of life, and who then press forward with a steadfastness in Christ, keeping the commandments and walking in paths of truth and righteousness, qualify to have an eternal seal placed on their godly conduct. They are thus ready to be endowed with power from on high. Then, in holy places, they cleanse their hands and their feet, as the scripture saith, and become "clean from the blood of this wicked generation...."

It should be clear to all, however, that just as the act of immersion in water only hints at the true significance and power of baptism, so the act of the washing of feet is far more than the cleansing and refreshing of dusty and tired pedal extremities. It is an eternal ordinance, with eternal import, understood only by enlightened saints....

And in conclusion, well might we ask: If true disciples are to wash each other's feet, where among the sects of Christendom is this done? And how could it be done except by revelation? Who would know all that is involved unless God revealed it? Is not this holy ordinance one of the many signs of the true Church? (Pp. 38-41.)

The ordinance of the washing of feet was a manifestation of Jesus' eternal love for his own, a love that impelled the Loving One to do all in his power to seal his friends up unto eternal life in his fathers kingdom." (P. 48.)

THE FAITHFUL RECEIVE GREATER TESTS

Every man's tests...are those which are suited to him and him alone. But we do know that in principle the higher one of the Lord's servants stands in the hierarchy of righteousness, the more severe are the tests to which his faith will be subjected. (P. 120.)

QUOTING FARRAR

No man of whom I know has written so consistently and so well...about... the life of our Lord as has Conan Farrar, whose words I have freely quoted from time to time in this work. It is my observation that when either I, or Elder Talmage, or Edersheim, or other authors—and all of us have done it—when any of us put the thoughts of Farrar in our own words, however excellent our expression may be, it loses much of the incisive and pungent appeal found in the language of our British friend from the Church of England. With this realization in mind...I shall feel free in this and the remaining chapters of this work to draw more heavily than otherwise upon the genius of Farrar....

May I express the hope—nay, offer the prayer—that both Farrar and Edersheim, and others who had faith and believed in the Messiah, according to the best light and knowledge they had, now that they are in the world of spirits where Elder Talmage continues his apostolic ministry, may have received added light and knowledge and will have pursued that strait and narrow course that will make them inheritors of the fulness of our Father's kingdom. (See Notes, pp. 180-81.)

THE SPIRITUALITY OF WOMEN

We know that women in general are more spiritual than men, and certainly their instincts and desires to render compassionate service exceed those of their male counterparts. (P. 265.)

JESUS' RESURRECTION AND BURIAL CLOTHING

To his account Mark adds that the women...[became] eye witnesses that His [Jesus'] body was gone and that the burial clothes were left in such a way as to show that his resurrected body had passed through their folds and strands without the need of unwinding the strips or untying the napkin. (P.268; see also pp. 262, 266, and 280.)

SECTARIAN BIBLICAL COMMENTARIES

At this point a word about almost all sectarian commentaries and biographies about Christ might not be amiss. It is my judgment that most of the modern publications are far from faith promoting. In most cases it is necessary to go back a hundred years or so to find authors who believed in the divine Sonship with sufficient fervor to accept the New Testament passages as meaning what they say. (P. 425.)

The Millennial Messiah

TIME OF SECOND COMING ALREADY FIXED

The time for the Second Coming of Christ is as fixed and certain as was the hour of his birth. It will not vary as much as a single second from the divine decree. He will come at the appointed time. The Millennium will not be ushered in prematurely because men turn to righteousness, nor will it be delayed because iniquity abounds.

So shall it be with his return in glory. He knows the set time and so does his Father. Perhaps a latter-day prophet will hear the Divine Voice on the day the veil parts and the heavens roll together as a scroll. But there is this difference between his two comings: The fixed and known time of his triumphal return has not been and will not be revealed until the set hour and the fixed time and the very day arrives. (Pp. 26-27.)

WATCH AND BE READY

Hence, the day when he shall return always has been and always will be a matter of uncertainty. Thus, no matter when they live, all his saints are placed in a position of anxious expectation. All are to await his return as though it were destined for their day. Written in words of fire, they have ever before them the command: Watch and be ready. (P. 33.)

DEFINITION OF FALSE CHRISTS

True, there may be those deranged persons who suppose they are God, or Christ, or the Holy Ghost, or almost anything. None but the lunatic fringe among men, however, will give them a second serious thought. The promise of false Christs who will deceive, if it were possible, even the very elect, who will lead astray those who have made eternal covenant with the Lord, is a far more subtle and insidious evil.

A false Christ is not a person. It is a false system of worship, a false church, a false cult that says: "Lo, here is salvation, here is the doctrine of Christ. Come and believe thus and so, and ye shall be saved." It is any concept or philosophy that says that redemption, salvation, sanctification, justification, and all of the promised rewards can be gained in any way except that set forth by the apostles and prophets. (P. 48.)

DANGERS IN THE WORK OF THE LORD

What is not as well understood among us as it should be is that the harvest is to go forward under increasingly difficult circumstances. It could not be otherwise in a world that is ripening in iniquity. War and pestilence and desolation shall cover the earth before the Lord comes, and the preaching of his holy word must and shall go forward in the midst of these. (P. 137.)

THE MARK ON LAMANITES

Lehi's seed divided into two nations—the Nephites, who maintained their membership in the true Church and who worshipped the true God, and the Lamanites, who forsook the faith, rejected the gospel, and turned to the worship of false gods. These latter were cursed by the Lord for their rebellion, and he placed a mark upon them—a dark skin—lest the Nephites should intermarry with them and sink into their loathsome and degraded state.

For a thousand years these Lehite peoples alternately flourished and prospered on the one hand, or dwindled in darkness and struggled without civilization and decency on the other. In the main the Nephites were righteous and the Lamanites were wicked, though on occasion this was reversed. Ordinarily when Nephites apostatized and joined the Lamanites, they became Lamanites, but there was one glorious period when the Lamanites were converted, wherein they joined with and became Nephites, and when they received back skins that were white. (P. 207.)

BUILDING THE TEMPLE IN JERUSALEM

The temple in Jerusalem will not be built by Jews who have assembled there for political purposes as at present. It will not be built by a people who know nothing whatever about the sealing ordinances and their application to the living and the dead. But it will be built by Jews who have come unto Christ, who once again are in the true fold of their ancient Shepherd, and who have learned anew about temples because they know that Elijah did come...to the Kirtland Temple on April 3, 1836 to Joseph Smith and Oliver Cowdery. The temple in Jerusalem will be built by The Church of Jesus Christ of Latter-day Saints.

...This city, a city that shall be built before the Second Coming,...is this city, the New Jerusalem in Jackson County, that the house of the Lord unto which all nations shall come in the last days shall be built....

When the appointed time comes, the Lord will reveal it to his servants who preside over his kingdom from Salt Lake City, and then the great work will go forward. They will direct the work; they hold the keys of temple building; the temple will be built by gathered Israel and particularly by Ephraim, for it is unto Ephraim that the other tribes shall come to receive their temple blessings in due course. Some Lamanites may assist and some Gentiles may bring their wealth to adorn the buildings, but the keys are with Ephraim. (Pp. 279-81.)

TIME AND EXTENT OF GEOLOGIC CHANGES IN EARTH

In the days of Noah came the flood, a universal flood, a flood that immersed the earth and destroyed men and beasts. We suppose that at this time the continents and islands were divided, with the division becoming complete in the days of Peleg.

...At the time of the crucifixion there was a great earthquake. In the Americas this was of such immeasurable proportions that the whole surface of the continents was changed. Mountain ranges arose, valleys disappeared, cities sank into the sea, and almost a whole civilization was destroyed. (P. 356.)

NO SEASONS BEFORE FLOOD

Seed time and harvest, in the sense of one season following another, exist because the axis of the earth is tilted twenty-three and a half degrees from the upright. This is the reason we have summer and winter, spring and fall. The first reference in the scriptures to seasons as we know them is in connection with the flood of Noah. There is a presumption that prior to the flood there were no seasons because the axis of the earth was upright, and a similar presumption that when the Millennium comes and the earth returns to its original paradisiacal state, once again the seasons as we know them will cease and that seed time and harvest will go on concurrently at all times. The whole earth at all times will be a garden as it was in the days of Eden. (P. 413.)

A VIEW OF THE SECOND COMING

We have woven the doctrine of the Second Coming, including much of the prophetic word relative to that glorious day of promise, into one great tapestry that is as broad as eternity and as beautiful as any of the paintings that hang in celestial galleries. Or, rather, we have pierced the veil as best we could, to let those who seek the face of the Lord gain glimpses of what the Master Weaver has himself woven on the tapestries of eternity. (P. 562.)

A VIEW OF THE SECOND COMING FOR THE FAITHFUL

And in the center of all things standeth Christ. Lo, he comes, as it is written of him. Angelic hosts attend; tens of thousands of his saints make up his train; the holy apostles and the prophets of all ages are on his right hand and on his left, having crowns of gold upon their heads. And the tapestry stretches on into eternity. No man can view it all, and we marvel at what we have seen and prepare ourselves to see more. We know that what we have seen is hidden from the world; the view is reserved for those whose spiritual eyes are open. (P. 564.)

PROPHETIC ACCOUNTS OF THE MILLENNIUM

Using the best language at their command, our inspired forerunners have recorded some of the visions vouchsafed to them relative to the new heaven and the new earth, and they have written down some of the revelations they received about the wonders of the Millennium. In their accounts we read of mountains becoming plains, of valleys ceasing to be, and of the very landmasses of the earth uniting into one grand continent. We read of deserts becoming gardens and of the whole earth yielding her fruit as in Eden of old. (P. 619.)

PEOPLE DURING THE MILLENNIUM CHANGED

Those who abide the day of the Lord's coming will be changed so as to stand the fire and the glory of that dread time; they will be changed when they are caught up to meet the Lord in the air, and they will be changed again when they attain their prescribed age and gain their immortal glory. (Pp. 629-30.)

DIFFERENT STATES OF THE EARTH

This earth was created first spiritually. It was a spirit earth. Nothing then lived on its face, nor was it designed that anything should. Then came the physical creation, the paradisiacal creation, the creation of the earth in the Edenic day and before the fall of man. After the fall, the earth became telestial in nature; it fell from the terrestrial to the telestial state; it became a fit abode for mortal life. Such is the state in which it now is. When the millennial day dawns, the earth will be renewed and receive its paradisiacal glory; it will return to its Edenic state; it will be (as contrasted with its present state) a new heaven and a new earth. In the process of change the earth will be burned; it will dissolve; the elements will melt with fervent heat, and all things will become new. There will also be a short postmillennial period of which we know very little, and finally the earth will become a celestial sphere and will shine like the sun in the firmament. (pp.642-43.)

TWO KINDS OF PEOPLE DURING THE MILLENNIUM

During the Millennium there will, of course, be two kinds of people on earth. There will be those who are mortal, and those who are immortal. There will be those who have been changed or quickened or transfigured or translated (words fail us to describe their state), and those who have gone through a second change, in the twinkling of an eye, so as to become eternal in nature. There will be those who are on probation, for whom earth life is a probationary estate, and who are thus working out their own salvation, and those who have already overcome the world and have entered into a fulness of eternal joy. There will be those who will yet die in the sense of being changed from their quickened state to a state of immortality, and those who, having previously died, are then living in a resurrected state. There will be those who are subject to the kings and priests who rule forever in the house of Israel, and those who, as kings and priests, exercise power and dominion in the everlasting kingdom of Him whose we are. (Pp.644-45.)

After reading the foregoing excerpts, which are only a minuscule selection from among many, one begins to acquire an appreciation both for the work Elder McConkie did and for what he knew. Without question, anyone who studies these books will vastly increase their knowledge of God, His Son, and their great eternal plan for us.

One of the amazing things about the Messiah series is that most of it is original with Elder McConkie.[13] It is written from his knowledge and on his authority. It is not a compilation of what others said or wrote. If he quoted someone else, it was usually the Prophet Joseph Smith. Elder McConkie trusted firmly in his own inspiration and insight. His son Stanford commented on a criticism which the Messiah series received in some circles after it was published: "There were complaints that in the entire work dad had quoted only seven sources other than the scriptures. What those individuals didn't realize is that that was how it should have been done."[14]

A humorous yet insightful example of this penchant of Elder McConkie's to stand on his own authority comes from a story related by Elder John K. Carmack of the Seventy:

During a meeting of...priesthood leaders, which [Elder McConkie] held as part of [a] mission tour, he opened the meeting for questions. Young Russel Taylor [a now-deceased General Authority] asked Elder McConkie how Joseph [Smith] and Oliver [Cowdery] could be elders in the Church since they were ordained by Peter, James, and John before the Church was organized in 1829, the Church not being organized until April 6, 1830. Elder McConkie answered, "Well, they presented them to the Saints after the Church was organized and ordained them again as elders in the Church. Next question?"

Elder Taylor persisted, "That sounds logical, Elder McConkie, but what is your authority?" [Elder McConkie answered:] "Well, you can quote me. Next question?" He spoke as one having authority.[15]

Readers of this series quickly discern where they stand. And they know where Elder McConkie's stated conclusions and doctrines originate: the scriptures, the Prophet Joseph Smith, some excerpts from a few sectarian authors which were considered solid and sound, and Elder McConkie.[16]

Notes

1. *The Promised Messiah*, preface, p. xv.

2. *The Promised Messiah*, preface, pp. xvii-xviii.

3. Packer, p. 263.

4. *Improvement Era*, Nov. 1962, p. 805.

5. *The Promised Messiah*, preface, p. xvii.

6. Dew, p. 53.

7. *The Mortal Messiah*, 4:412.

8. *The Millennial Messiah*, p. 563.

9. Bruce R. McConkie, "The Bible: A Sealed Book," delivered at a Church Educational System Symposium held at BYU, 17 Aug. 1984. Cited in Mark McConkie, *Restoration*, pp. 276-96.

10. *The Mortal Messiah*, 3:57.

11. *The Promised Messiah*, chapter 16.

12. Mark McConkie,. *Restoration*, p. 235.

13. We are not inferring that others have not said similar things or written similar doctrine or even that this is new doctrine. We are saying that Elder McConkie seldom quoted other authors. He did his own thinking, interpreting, and evaluating.

14. Dew, p. 53.

15. Carmack,. *Testament*, p. 111.

16. Elder McConkie wrote, "Manifestly the portions [of non-LDS authors' writings] quoted in this work are deemed to be sound and proper" (*The Mortal Messiah*, 4:425). One study of the actual amount of quotations Elder McConkie used, concluded that for book 4, he had quoted these non-LDS authors significantly on 124 pages, or 28.3% of the book. (A copy of this study is in the author's file.)

Chapter Thirteen

The Scriptures Publications Committee and the Joseph Smith Translation

The Scriptures Publications Committee

The publication of the new editions of the LDS standard works is one of the great miracles of our time. Although many people contributed to this landmark work, probably the greatest contribution came from Elder McConkie. As Elder Boyd K. Packer stated, "It could not have been done without Elder Bruce R. McConkie."[1] As a life-long student of the word of God, he had uniquely prepared himself for this work. Elder Packer witnessed:

> If ever there was a man who was raised up unto a very purpose, if ever a man was prepared against a certain need, it was Bruce R. McConkie. All members of the First Presidency and the Quorum of the Twelve had important work to do in the publication of the new editions of the scriptures....Brother Monson and I served for years with Brother McConkie on the Scriptures Publication Committee. I know full well that the work could have been accomplished without me. I venture to suggest, as well, that Brother Monson was not crucial to that work. But it could not have been done without Elder Bruce R. McConkie. Few will ever know the extent of the service he rendered. Few can appraise the lifetime of preparation for this quiet, crowning contribution to the on-rolling of the restored gospel in the dispensation of the fullness of times.[2]

Anyone glancing over the new edition of LDS scripture will immediately recognize what a vast amount of work went into their preparation. But throughout such a mammoth undertaking was a need for accuracy. All who study them must be able to rely upon them. The helps needed to be historically, geographically, and most importantly, doctrinally correct. This is one reason that Elder McConkie was placed on the committee and given so much responsibility. He had the qualifications, he had the knowledge, and he had the ability. His contribution was singular and crucial. "Few will ever know the extent of the service he rendered," stated Elder Packer.[3]

The story behind the preparation of the new editions of LDS scripture is fascinating.[4] In the early 1970s, the Church decided it would be advantageous to publish an edition of the King James Version of the Bible for the Church itself. For many years the Church had been using at least three different editions of the Bible for various purposes. The Brethren and others came to view this as somewhat counterproductive. Thus, the First Presidency appointed a "Bible Aids" advisory committee composed of Elder Thomas S. Monson (as chairman), Elder Boyd K. Packer, and Elder Marvin J. Ashton. These Brethren would oversee the work of carefully chosen specialists, each assigned to work on a different aspect of the improvements. Soon after, on 21 September 1973, Elder McConkie was appointed to the committee, replacing Elder Ashton. Elder McConkie was asked to "oversee the project and to be the contact man with the General Authorities concerning any problems that might arise."[5]

The work was slow, tedious, and time consuming. Footnotes, indexes, a topical guide, chapter headings, introductory material, language translations, a dictionary—all had to be written and prepared. The Brethren had previously gone to BYU and the Church Educational System to locate men who had the requisite scriptural scholarship. Ellis Rasmussen, Robert Patch, Edward J. Brandt, Robert J. Matthews, and William James Mortimer (of the Church's printing services) were officially commissioned by letter to participate (27 Oct. 1972).[6] Their charge from Spencer W. Kimball was to "assist in improving doctrinal scholarship throughout the Church." Over the next nine years, intense labor, long hours, and less sleep became the order of the day for these and other men and women who worked on the project. Though the Bible was published in 1979, the triple combination was not printed until 1981. Overseeing their work were the General Authority members of the committee. There were laborious editing and revision needs to satisfy in the process, with important decisions being made regularly.

The project became significantly more time consuming than was originally considered. President Kimball had asked the committee to accomplish the work in a year and a half. It took about that much time just to get started.[7]

As part of the project, the Brethren studied the original printer's manuscript of the Book of Mormon, as well as early editions that had been edited by the Prophet Joseph Smith. This close attention to detail helped them find typographical and other errors that had crept into later printings, thus enabling a more accurate and faithful text. Elder McConkie explained: "There are...numerous important textual changes in the Book of Mormon and the Pearl of Great Price. All of these hark back to the original manuscripts or to corrections made by the Prophet."[8]

The Brethren carefully examined the revelations in the Doctrine and Covenants for printing errors and mistakes, including details as small as the placement of a comma. For example, during the committee's work on the Doctrine and Covenants, the subject of the comma in section 89, verse 13, came up for discussion. The presence, or lack thereof, of the comma between the words "used" and "only" can drastically change the meaning of the verse. Earlier publications of the Church which contained this verse were ambiguous, as some included the comma and others did not. Elder McConkie said that the subject had been discussed by the First Presidency and the Twelve a year or two earlier. At that time they asked Elder McConkie to research the subject, which he did. His findings were then approved, and it was decided that the comma as it now stands was in the proper place and should not be removed. Therefore, the Scriptures Publications Committee did not take any further action. Elders Monson and Packer, both of whom were at this meeting, concurred with the decision to leave it as is.[9]

The text of the King James Bible was retained as the official Bible of the LDS Church. Not one word was altered; however, appropriate explanatory language notes were added, giving the meaning of archaic words, non-English words, and words whose meaning had changed over time. One important addition to the footnotes were excerpts from the Inspired Version of the Bible, which the committee called the Joseph Smith Translation, or JST. These inspired additions, which were included in both footnotes and in a special 17-page section at the back of the book, are of tremendously important significance. Further examination of their importance follows later in this chapter.

The committee also added a high quality Bible dictionary to the study aids. The Church received permission from the Cambridge University Bible publishers, who were typesetting and proofreading the new LDS edition, to use as a foundation the Bible dictionary they published. Though an excellent dictionary, it was prepared by protestant scholars and needed a great deal of revision. Elder McConkie was one of several who worked on these alterations. In fact, most of the entry on the Covenant of Abraham was taken word for word from *Mormon Doctrine*.[10]

Of the many changes, deletions, and additions to this Cambridge Bible dictionary, the most significant resource for instruction and clarification was modern revelation. Many entries, most dealing with doctrinal subjects, include such phrases as "From modern revelation we learn that..." Thus we have a powerful evidence that latter-day prophets and revelation are of critical value in coming to a correct understanding of the doctrine of the Lord.

As it now stands, the Bible dictionary is a truly precious possession of the Church. It would be wise to remember, however, that it is not purported to be perfect, for we are at the mercy of limited Biblical scholarship. Consequently, such things as increased understanding of Bible history, new archeological discoveries, or new revelation could improve it. As one major contributor stated, "The new Bible dictionary is not intended as a revealed treatment or official version of doctrinal, historical, cultural, chronological, and other matters found in the Bible."[11] Nonetheless, having understood that it is not to be viewed with the same respect as the scriptures, it would be folly for any student of the gospel to ignore this precious aid to Biblical study. For all students who are seriously interested in gaining a sound, practical, and thorough knowledge of the Bible, especially from an LDS perspective, it is of priceless worth.

Readers can be assured that at least as far as doctrinal content is concerned, the information contained in the Bible dictionary is on solid ground. It was reviewed and approved by the Brethren, as were all the study aids that were included in the new edition. Elder McConkie taught, "Without question our latter-day scriptures are in a more nearly perfect form now than they have ever been since the beginning."[12]

Elder McConkie's most visible and weighty contribution to the project was the writing of the chapter and section headings. He wrote the chapter headings for every chapter in the entire standard works, including the heading for every section in the Doctrine and Covenants. Obviously, this labor required him to re-read, in close detail, all the standard works again in order to briefly summarize the doctrinal and historical content of each chapter. Modern students of the scriptures who may not understand difficult passages would be well advised to turn to the beginning of each chapter and review the summary heading. Following this procedure will result in an increased personal understanding of each of the standard works.

Edward Brandt shared his understanding of the task:

> Elder McConkie had the responsibility to...[write] the initial draft of the summaries of all of the chapters of all four of the standard works. It wasn't that he just handed it in and everyone assumed that it would be correct. He had to stand the evaluation, suggestions, and cross-examination, as it were, of all who worked on the project, particularly his own brethren.[13]

Robert J. Matthews, former dean of BYU Religious Education and also a co-worker, added this insight:

> One of Elder McConkie's major accomplishments on that committee was the individual chapter headings and section summaries. Although I read those headings before publication, I still frequently marvel and am re-impressed with the clarity and insight wherein few words say so much.
> Sometimes those of us who worked with the Committee discussed the headings with him before publication. He was always open and non-defensive, and never did I see him use the weight of his office to decide a point. He would often say in a friendly way, "If you fellows want to change the wording you may do so." We rarely did, and then only with his concurrence.[14]

An example of one chapter in the Book of Mormon where Elder McConkie's heading clarifies the meaning of some verses is found in 3 Nephi 28. Verses 12-13 relate that Jesus, "touched every one of them with his finger save it were the three who were to tarry, and then he departed. And behold, the heavens were opened, and they were caught up into heaven, and saw and heard unspeakable things." The text does not seem to make clear whether the three who were to remain as translated beings were translated at that very time or much later when their mortal lives would have come to an end. After all, the account says that Jesus touched the other nine, but not the three. The chapter heading states: "The Three Nephites desire and are given power over death so as to remain on the earth until Jesus comes again—They are translated and see things not lawful to utter...." This heading clearly indicates that the three were translated at that time.

Around December 1977 the Bible Aids Committee was renamed the Scriptures Publications Committee. Soon thereafter, they made a major decision to combine the planned concordance and index into a topical guide for the Bible. This saved valuable space, time, and expense, and still accomplished the objective. The Spirit of inspiration frequently influenced the progress and direction the Brethren took relative to the new editions.

On 4 March 1977 those laboring under the direction of the General Authority committee were brought together. Elder McConkie met with this group of men who had been working on the project and said, "Yes, the committee will be dissolved, all except for four members of the original committee. You and you are assigned to prepare the new combined concordance/topical guide."[15]

When the final format for the footnoting system was being considered, Brother Mortimer took some proofs to Elder McConkie's home to get tentative approval. Carefully he looked them over. "After what seemed to me an eternity of silence, he looked up, smiled, and said simply, 'why not?'"[16] Elder McConkie then got the approval of the rest of the committee and the Brethren.

On 28 February 1975, Elder McConkie made a recommendation to the First Presidency that the revelations now known as sections 137 and 138 of the Doctrine and Covenants be added to the canon of the scriptures. His reasoning for this recommendation was that they would need to be cross-referenced into the topical guide of the new LDS edition of the Bible *at that time* if they were going to be included.[17] The Brethren discussed the matter on several occasions. Elder McConkie divided the proposed sections into verses, and upon President Kimball's proposal, they were approved by the First Presidency and the Council of the Twelve in April 1976. They were initially included in the Pearl of Great Price, and then were later shifted, by administrative decision, to the Doctrine and Covenants in June 1979. In the case of D&C 138, the vision of the redemption of the dead, "President Kimball and all the Brethren," wrote Elder McConkie, "thought it should be formally and officially recognized as scripture so that it would be quoted, used, and relied upon more than the case would have been if it had simply been published as heretofore in various books. By putting it in the Standard Works formally, it gets cross-referenced and is used to better advantage by the saints."[18]

With the addition of these revelations and the inclusion of Official Declaration–2 (the revelation on the priesthood), the work of proofreading and typesetting began.

The Inclusion of the Joseph Smith Translation

As mentioned in an earlier chapter, for much of the Church's history (especially in the late 19th century and the early 20th century), there were some disagreeable feelings between leaders of the LDS and RLDS churches. One area in which this feeling manifested itself was the distrust which LDS leaders felt toward the RLDS publication of the Inspired Version of the Bible. Joseph Smith, by revelation, had dictated many corrections to his scribes, and these were written on manuscript sheets of paper. The manuscripts containing these restorations and corrections (later incorporated into the RLDS Bible publication entitled Holy Scriptures) was not made available to the LDS Church to examine in order to determine accuracy and reliability of printed texts. Therefore, many LDS Church leaders discouraged its use to varying extents.[19] However, as evidenced by his early and persistent use of the Inspired Version in his writings and references, Elder McConkie placed great confidence in these published corrections. But since he was an exception, and most of the other Brethren felt uncertain about the reliability of the RLDS publication, its use continued to be discouraged.

Robert J. Matthews, then a BYU religion professor, was given access by the RLDS Church to the Joseph Smith revision materials and manuscripts.[20] After his comprehensive examination and publication of the results, negative feelings began to dissipate. References to the JST cropped up in Church study guides and manuals, and sometimes the Brethren used it in their preaching. As Elder Dallin H. Oaks has expressed the feeling of the Brethren, "Now that the integrity of the Joseph Smith Translation has been established, we have no reason to refrain from using this valuable resource in our teaching and scholarship."[21]

As the committee's work of footnoting began, the suggestion was made that it would be beneficial to include excerpts from the Joseph Smith Translation in the new edition. This idea was presented to President Harold B. Lee. The Reorganized Church of Jesus Christ of Latter-day Saints owned the copyright for the Inspired Version of the Bible. President Lee said, "We will not offend them. We will ask for permission." Soon, a satisfactory agreement granting permission was made between the publishing houses of the two churches.

When BYU contracted with MacMillan Publishing in the early 1990s to publish the *Encyclopedia of Mormonism*, the chief editor, Daniel H. Ludlow, wrote Elder Neal A. Maxwell (an advisor to the project), requesting information about the Church's position regarding the JST at that time, and how it could be used with the encyclopedia.[22] In his response, Elder Maxwell said, "The Brethren 'crossed the bridge' concerning the use of the Joseph Smith Translation when they approved (and strongly endorsed) the use of excerpts from the Joseph Smith Translation in the footnotes of the LDS publication of the Bible in 1979, and even provided a special section for more lengthy excerpts."[23]

There is no question that Elder McConkie's positive use and support of the JST had a profound if not crucial impact on its gradual acceptance. He, along with others in the Church, originally did not have access to the JST historical materials in order to check for accuracy, but he did have sufficient spiritual insight to feel that its use was helpful and was doctrinally sound. In fact, Elder McConkie felt so strongly about the inclusion of JST material in the new edition that when space became an issue, he said, "If we lack room, let's have a little more JST and a little less dictionary."[24]

The following are some examples of Elder McConkie's strong emphasis on this precious source of revelation:

> In some minds there seems to be a nagging uncertainty about the so-called Inspired Version. After all, some say, the Prophet did not finish his work, and how can we be sure what he did finish is correct?
>
> May I be pardoned if I say that negative attitudes and feelings about the Joseph Smith Translation are simply part of the devil's program to keep the word of truth from the children of men.
>
> Of course the revealed changes made by Joseph Smith are true—as much so as anything in the Book of Mormon or the Doctrine and Covenants. Of course we have adequate and authentic original sources showing the changes....
>
> Of course we should use the Joseph Smith Translation in our study and teaching. Since when do any of us have the right to place bounds on the Almighty and say we will believe these revelations but not those?
>
> I think much of the prejudice of the past was based on a lack of understanding and has faded away since we have published our new Church edition of the King James Version with its repeated references to the Joseph

Smith Translation.

True, the Joseph Smith Translation, though completed to the point that the early Brethren were going to publish it at one time, has not been completed in the full and true sense. But for that matter neither has the Book of Mormon.

I am pleased to say...that this inspired work by the great Prophet of the Restoration is one of the great evidences of his divine calling. One of the reasons we know he was the mighty Prophet of the Restoration is the inspired translation and revision of the Holy Bible."[25]

Other Inspired Version changes are found in the footnotes of our new edition of the Bible. Those too lengthy for inclusion in the footnotes are published in a seventeen page section at the back of this Bible edition. All of these changes and additions are scripture and have the same truth and validity as if they were in the Pearl of Great Price itself. It is important that this is clearly understood.[26]

That there are other revelations which might appropriately be given this additional dignity and formal stamp of approval is obvious. All of the changes made by Joseph Smith in the King James Version of the Bible, for instance, are the voice of truth and revelation to the Latter-day Saints and carry the same verity as any of his revelations or inspired narrations.[27]

As every student knows, these inspired changes made by the Prophet throw a marvelous flood of light on a host of doctrines and are one of the great evidences of his divine calling.[28]

From these excerpts of Elder McConkie's remarks relative to the JST, it becomes clear how important it is and how highly he valued this work. He seemed frustrated over the lingering reluctance of some to fully embrace the JST.

The scholarly and editorial work on the new edition neared completion in early 1978, and the typesetting and binding phase of the project commenced.[29] By August 1979, just in time for seminary and institute classes to begin, the first Bibles rolled off the press.

Elder McConkie had great respect and admiration for both the final product and the men he worked with:

I feel very strongly, and have rejoiced individually, in the...spirit, the wonder and the glory that has attended this near-ten-year project that involves all of the standard works of the Church. I have no language which indicates how strongly I feel or how much I am assured that the work that has been done will benefit the members of the Church and the hosts of people who yet will hear the message of the Restoration. These brethren [with whom he worked] have just literally been raised up by the Lord at this time and season to do the particular, difficult, and technical work that has been required. The Lord's hand has been in it.

And there is no question that major decisions were made by the spirit of inspiration, and that the conclusions reached accord with the mind and will of the Lord. I have been close enough to the work to be aware of the inspiration that has attended it, and I want you to hear me bear my testimony to that effect.[30]

This admiration and praise for recognized talent and ability was reciprocated by those who worked with him. One committee member, Ellis Rasmussen, voicing the feelings of them all, said this of him: "I can't sing that man's praises enough—so perceptive, so appreciative, so quick to grasp a point, so knowledgeable and—something you might not know if you're only aquainted with him from behind the pulpit—such a delightful sense of humor."[31]

Elder McConkie also desired to convert the whole church to using the new LDS editions of the scriptures and was concerned when the members acceptance seemed slow. To dramatize the seriousness of his position, he stated:

I own an 1879 edition of the Doctrine and Covenants. It is the copy of Julina Lambson Smith, who is my wife's grandmother; she was the wife of President Joseph F. Smith himself. From a standpoint of sentiment and of feeling, I could make a good case in my mind for using these books, because of the heritage, as it were, that they have. But the revelations in these editions do not have one single footnote; there is not a single cross-reference. There are no teaching aids. There are some brief, single sentences at the head of the sections....I also have the copy my wife gave me when I went on my mission; it has been rebound and recovered three times. It has been in every state of the union, and in many of the nations of the earth. I could make a good case for using that book—but again, the improvement in the teaching aids that are part of the new LDS editions of the scriptures are so great that by using them I can increase the rate with which I learn about the gospel. We have in these new editions the best teaching aids that have ever been devised to include in any set of scriptures.[32]

Elder Packer was in an excellent position to watch Elder McConkie's labors over the years and appreciated the tremendous work which he had done: "During the long scripture-publication process, the anchor to the spiritual significance of it all was Bruce McConkie. We know from the revelations and from reading Church history that...some men are raised up unto a specific purpose, and Bruce McConkie in this great scriptural project was obviously one of them."[33]

Elder McConkie also recognized the deep significance of the work: "I am very grateful to have been a part of the work that has made these standard works available. I...don't think there will be anything in my ministry among men that I will do that will have a more far-reaching effect than what is involved in preparing and disseminating these new LDS editions of the standard works."[34]

Elder McConkie considered the project with its attendant benefits to be one of "the three things that have happened in our lifetime which will do more for the spread of the gospel, for the perfecting of the Saints, and for the salvation of men" than anything else.[35]

It is instructive to consider that Elder McConkie served on the Scriptures Publications Committee for nearly his entire length of service as an Apostle: from 1973, not long after the project began, until 1985 (the year he passed away) and four years after its completion, when the First Presidency broadcast a fireside, in which he took part, specifically to promote use of the new LDS editions of the scriptures.

Notes

1. Packer, p. 262.

2. Packer, pp. 61-62.

3. Packer, p. 262.

4. The historical information on the work of the Scriptures Publications Committee, if not documented with its own reference, comes from the following: *Ensign,* "Church Publishes First LDS Edition of the Bible," Oct. 1979, pp. 8-18; *Ensign,* "The Coming Forth of the LDS Editions of Scripture," Aug. 1983, pp. 35-41; *Ensign,* "The Church Publishes a New Triple Combination," Oct. 1981, pp. 8-19; *Ensign,* "Using the New Bible Dictionary in the LDS Edition," June 1982, pp. 47-50; *Ensign,* "I Have a Question," July 1985, pp. 17-19; *Ensign,* "Discovering the LDS Editions of Scripture," Oct. 1983, pp. 55-58.

5. Edward J. Brandt, "The Development of the New LDS Bible," Salt Lake Institute of Religion Devotional Address, 19 Oct. 1979, p. 2. Hereafter cited as Brandt, *Development.*

6. *Ensign,* Oct. 1979, p. 12.

7. See Brandt, *Development,* p. 3.

8. Mark McConkie, *Restoration,* pp. 240, 251.

9. This incident was told to the author by a prominent member of the committee who asked to remain anonymous since he was not the official spokesman.

10. See "Abrahamic Covenant," *Mormon Doctrine.* 2nd ed.

11. Robert J. Matthews, "Using the Bible Dictionary in the New LDS Edition," *Ensign,* June 1982, p. 48.

12. Mark McConkie, *Restoration,* p. 240.

13. Edward J. Brandt, "The New Editions of the Scriptures and a New Generation of Scripture Literacy," Salt Lake Institute of Religion Devotional Address, 20 Feb. 1983, p. 4. Hereafter cited as Brandt, Literacy.

14. *Ensign,* June 1985, p. 19. *See also* Video Biography, p. 5.

15. Brandt, *Development,* p. 4.

16. William James Mortimer, "The Coming Forth of the LDS Editions of Scripture," *Ensign,* 1983, p. 41. Another account of this conversation related this comment from Elder McConkie upon being shown the new footnote system: "Why hasn't anyone thought of this before?" (Lavina Fielding Anderson, "Church Publishes First LDS Edition of the Bible," *Ensign,* Oct. 1979, p. 16.)

17. Unpublished memo, Bruce R. McConkie to Ezra Taft Benson, 28 Feb. 1975. Copy in author's file.

18. Letter, Bruce R. McConkie to Robert L. Millet. Cited in *Hearken: O Ye People, Discourses on the Doctrine and Covenants* [Sperry Symposium, 1984] (Sandy, Utah: Randall Book Co., 1984), pp. 264, 266.

19. Dallin H. Oaks, "Scripture Reading, Revelation, and Joseph Smith's Translation of the Bible," cited in Robert L. Millet and Robert J. Matthews, eds., *Plain and Precious Truths Restored: The Doctrinal and Historical Significance of the Joseph Smith Translation* (Salt Lake City: Bookcraft, 1995), pp. 8-9. Hereafter cited as Millet/Matthews. For more detailed information on the Inspired Version of the Bible, see Robert J. Matthews, *Joseph Smith's Translation of the Bible: A History and Commentary* (Provo, Utah: Brigham Young University Press, 1985).

20. Millet/Matthews, p. 10.

21. Millet/Matthews, p. 10.

22. Notes from author's telephone interview with Robert J. Matthews, 17 Feb. 1997.

23. Millet/Matthews, p. 177.

24. Millet/Matthews, p. 174.

25. Bruce R. McConkie, "The Doctrinal Restoration," cited in Monte S. Nyman and Robert L. Millet, eds., *The Joseph Smith Translation: The Restoration of Plain and Precious Things* (Provo, Utah: BYU Religious Studies Center, 1985), pp. 14, 22.

26. Bruce R. McConkie, "Come, Hear the Voice of the Lord," *Ensign,* Dec. 1985, p. 58.

27. Bruce R. McConkie, "A New Commandment: Save Thyself and Thy Kindred," *Ensign,* Aug. 1976, pp. 7-8.

28. Mark McConkie, *Restoration,* pp. 239-40.

29. *Encyclopedia of Mormonism,* vol. 1, pp. 110-11.

30. Mark McConkie, *Restoration,* pp. 241, 244.

31. *Ensign,* Oct. 1979, p.18.

32. Mark McConkie, *Restoration,* p. 245.

33. Tate, *Packer,* p. 221.

34. Mark McConkie, *Restoration,* p. 246.

35. Mark McConkie, *Restoration,* p. 236. The other two were the organization of the Seventy into their proper quorums and the 1978 revelation on the priesthood.

Chapter Fourteen

Illness, Testimony, and Death

In August 1983, Elder McConkie received a thorough routine physical examination and was told he was fine. But two months later Amelia noticed a change in his appetite and a general feeling of tiredness. "He'd tell me all he needed was simple food." She said, "If I'd feed him bread, milk, some cheese and a little fruit every meal, he'd [be] happy. I got so frustrated trying to prepare things for him that I really got after him, and he finally admitted he didn't feel good. I tried like the dickens to get him to the doctor, but he insisted he didn't need a doctor, just simple food." Then in early January 1984, Amelia made him go to the doctor. He received many tests, which indicated that he had developed cancer and needed major surgery.[1] He went through that ordeal on January 20. Upon conclusion of the operation, the doctors told his family that he had but weeks to live. After recuperating sufficiently, he began taking chemotherapy treatments.

A month after the surgery, Elder McConkie was back in his office. He resumed stake conference and speaking assignments, although his schedule was altered to eliminate the burden of international travel. His condition improved steadily, and he started jogging again.[2] But it was not a lengthy reprieve. He confided to his close friend Elder Packer that things looked bleak. "One day, he talked to me," remembered Elder Packer. "He had received from his doctor the result of a recent test. There was a malignancy. It was estimated that he had about two months to live. I said, 'You can't do that to me,' and I forbade him to die. We were both chuckling but both of us were very serious over such a matter."[3] This incident serves to give insight into Elder McConkie's method of dealing with these physically and emotionally trying circumstances—serious, yet still not losing his sense of humor. When he visited the doctor's office for his treatment each week, he would face it with courage and pluck. Evidently this bemused his physician. Amelia told one acquaintance "that his doctor, who was not a member of the Church, did not quite know how to take Bruce. She said he would walk in on Friday for his shot, roll up his sleeve, and say, 'Seven more days of life, Doc!'"[4]

The truth is that Elder McConkie believed in his heart that this was simply a trial for him to undergo and he would eventually be healed. According to Amelia:

> He never thought he wasn't going to get better. He told me time and time again that this was the Lord's test for him, and that he had enough faith in and of himself to be healed. Bruce was so confident he'd be healed that when he was home I'd feel optimistic. But when he was away, it was easy to get very discouraged. All the uncertainty was so hard to deal with, though I believed as he did.[5]
>
> He had absolute faith that the Lord would heal him, that this was just a test that the Lord was putting him through for some reason and that he was going to triumph, and he would quote to me, and say, "The Lord chasteneth him whom he loveth and scourgeth every son whom he receiveth." And he said "When this is over I will pick up my cross and go on."[6]

In his April 1984 general conference address, Elder McConkie shared tender feelings relative to his recent trials: "I am quite overwhelmed by deep feelings of thanksgiving and rejoicing for the goodness of the Lord to me. He has permitted me to suffer pain, feel anxiety, and taste his healing power. I am profoundly grateful for the faith and prayers of many people, for heartfelt petitions that have ascended to the throne of grace on my behalf."[7] Then in late 1984, he started to weaken again. By early 1985, he began to fail rapidly.[8]

The last major assignment Elder McConkie received was to go to the BYU Motion Picture Studio to tape the Churchwide fireside for the scriptures publication project. This was a tremendously difficult experience for him. "They had him standing up, the lights were hot, and I could tell he wasn't feeling well because every time they stopped taping he'd hang on to the pulpit," said Amelia. "I asked them to get him a chair, which they did, but I got more nervous as the day went on." After finishing a six-hour taping session, Amelia drove him home: "Bruce didn't say a word to me, [he] just got in the passenger's side, fell instantly asleep, and I drove home. He'd have never made it alone. He was sick."[9] Difficult as this day had been, it was one on which Elder McConkie was needed, since he had been such a moving force with the scripture project.

As Elder Packer stated: "I should not have felt right about participation in the recent satellite broadcast on the scriptures had Bruce been unable to participate. Only Amelia knows the pain he endured during the many hours it took to record that program."[10]

As hard as he tried to conceal it, the cancer was eating him up inside, draining his strength and weakening his body. Only family and close associates knew the truth of what was going on—the pain he was suffering and the toll the disease was exacting of him. Yet he had already outlived the doctor's time estimate. One son gave this summary: "The doctors gave him a couple of months, and he lived fourteen. He had a few more things to do, and when they were done, he was finished."[11]

As the time for general conference neared, Elder McConkie, sick as he was, penned the most powerful, eloquent, and inspired sermon he had ever written. It was the climactic moment of his life that he was preparing for, and he wrote his remarks by the spirit of inspiration. This would be his last talk, and he knew it. He was prompted to bear his testimony of the Savior's infinite and eternal Atonement and to declare the truth and reality of its power, efficacy, and virtue. These truths flowed from his heart as he wrote, and modern spiritual history was in the making. When he had completed his preparations, he sought out his beloved Amelia to share with her his finest work:

> And then this one Saturday sometime before conference (this was in March), he came into me [in the kitchen], and he said, "Would you like to hear what I have prepared for general conference?" I was making him a pie, because his appetite had begun to go down hill, and I thought, "Maybe he'd like an apple pie." I had the apples all ready to go in, and I was rolling up the dough, the oven was on, everything was ready. And he came in and sat down and started to read me his talk and the tears streamed down his face, and he didn't get more than a couple of sentences out and I thought to myself, "You don't make apple pies when somebody is saying these things to you." So I sat down, dropped everything, and listened to him. But I said, "How are you ever going to be able to get up and read this?" Because there he was, having a hard time saying what he was saying because he was so touched. And he said, "I don't know, but I'm going to do it."[12]

His ability to stand the strain of speaking on international television at general conference was not a concern shared by these two alone. His doctor also had some nervousness. On the Tuesday before conference, he called Amelia and said, "You've got a dying man on your hands. He's living on stored energy. You must not let him speak at conference. If he tries, he will collapse on...television. Keep him home, and make him comfortable. That's all you can do for him." The doctor told her he didn't know why Bruce hadn't lapsed into a coma already. This great burden was placed squarely upon Amelia: "The doctor wouldn't tell all this to Bruce. It was hard on me because I believed in Bruce and I had to do what he wanted. The doctor was so worried when he heard Bruce was going to speak, but I couldn't try to stop him."

"That Tuesday evening Mother called me," said Joseph. "She wished me happy birthday and then told me the doctor had said Dad was going to die. It crushed her. Up until that time we all still thought he was going to get better."

The day came: 6 April, 1985. Weak as he was, he took his place on the stand, and when his turn came, he stood at the pulpit and began to speak of the "purifying power of Gethsemane."[13]

Since this was no ordinary message, and since it falls under the definition of scripture, having been spoken by the power of the Holy Ghost, it deserves special consideration.[14]

No one could have written these things so perfectly if they did not have a comprehensive understanding of the final days of Christ's mortal ministry. This was Elder McConkie's gift. His narration of these events was flawless, dramatic, and moving. It seemed as though he had been taught these transcendent events in a special, spiritual manner, similar to that which Elder David B. Haight described in a like talk given four years later.[15] Detailed mental images of the traumatic injuries which Christ suffered at the hands of his persecutors were related with unerring accuracy. Other events were enumerated with special insight and reverence. Truly, Elder McConkie knew of him whom he testified.

He began:

> I feel, and the Spirit seems to accord, that the most important doctrine I can declare, and the most powerful testimony I can bear, is of the atoning sacrifice of the Lord Jesus Christ.
>
> His atonement is the most transcendent event that ever has or ever will occur from creation's dawn through all the ages of a never-ending eternity.
>
> It is the supreme act of goodness and grace that only a god could perform. Through it, all of the terms and conditions of the Father's eternal plan of salvation became operative.

With these opening lines, Elder McConkie captured the congregation's attention. A feeling that something special was taking place was spontaneously sensed by all.

> Through it are brought to pass the immortality and eternal life of man. Through it, all men are saved from death, hell, the devil, and endless torment.
>
> And through it, all who believe and obey the glorious gospel of God, all who are true and faithful and overcome the world, all who suffer for Christ and his word, all who are chastened and scourged in the cause of him whose we are—all shall become as their maker and sit with him on his throne and reign with him forever in everlasting glory.

Herein is detailed the infinite power and purpose of the atoning sacrifice of Jesus Christ. This meaningful doctrine is the most precious reality at the heart of the gospel, and Elder McConkie had an unshakably firm testimony of it.

> In speaking of these wondrous things I shall use my own words, though you may think they are the words of scripture, words spoken by other apostles and prophets.
>
> True it is they were first proclaimed by others, but they are now mine, for the Holy Spirit of God has borne witness to me that they are true, and it is now as though the Lord had revealed them to me in the first instance. I have thereby heard his voice and know his word.

The doctrine here expounded may be puzzling to some. On another occasion, Elder McConkie himself explained what he meant:

> His voice comes to us in many ways. He may speak audibly to attuned ears. His voice may come by the power of the Spirit. It may also be given by the mouths of his servants as they recite the words revealed to them. All of the Saints are entitled to hear his voice in each of these ways. But there is another way to hear the voice of the Lord, and, almost universally, it should be our first approach in seeking revelation. It is available to us all, but sadly is overlooked or ignored by many of us.
>
> If the Spirit bears record to us of the truth of the scriptures, then we are receiving the doctrines in them as though they had come to us directly. Thus, we can testify that we have heard his voice and know his words.[16]

Elder McConkie had received revelation by the power of the Holy

Ghost, giving him a perfect assurance of the truth of the scriptures; therefore, he proceeded to narrate the events of the Atonement.

This holy ground [Gethsemane] is where the sinless Son of the Everlasting Father took upon himself the sins of all men on condition of repentance.

We do not know, we cannot tell, no mortal mind can conceive, the full import of what Christ did in Gethsemane.

We know that he sweat great gouts of blood from every pore as he drained the dregs of that bitter cup his Father had given him.

We know that he suffered, both body and spirit, more than it is possible for man to suffer, except it be unto death.

We know that in some way, incomprehensible to us, his suffering satisfied the demands of justice, ransomed penitent souls from the pains and penalties of sin, and made mercy available to those who believe in his holy name.

We know that he lay prostrate upon the ground as the pains and agonies of an infinite burden caused him to tremble, and would that he might not drink the bitter cup.

We know that an angel came from the courts of glory to strengthen him in his ordeal, and we suppose it was mighty Michael who foremost fell that mortal man might be.

As near as we can judge, these infinite agonies—this suffering beyond compare—continued for some three or four hours.

After this—his body then wrenched and drained of strength—he confronted Judas and the other incarnate devils, some from the very Sanhedrin itself; and he was led away with a rope around his neck, as a common criminal, to be judged by the arch-criminals, who as Jews sat in Aaron's seat and who as Romans wielded Caesar's power.

Elder McConkie described the process and gave reality to the events associated with the Atonement of Jesus Christ, set forth in the most profound of terms. Then he made a transition from the exquisite sufferings in Gethsemane to the pernicious persecutions and abuses meted out by wicked Jews: the mock trial and undeserved punishments, the tortures inflicted upon him, and the devilish designs imposed by those who thirsted for his death.

They took him to Annas, to Caiaphas, to Pilate, to Herod, and back to Pilate. He was accused, cursed, and smitten. Their foul saliva ran down his face as vicious blows further weakened his pain-engulfed body.

With reeds of wrath they rained blows upon his back. Blood ran down his face as a crown of thorns pierced his trembling brow.

But above it all he was scourged with forty stripes save one, scourged with a multi-thonged whip into whose leather strands sharp bones and cutting metals were woven.

Many died from scourging alone, but he rose from the sufferings of the scourge that he might die an ignominious death upon the cruel cross of Calvary.

Then he carried his own cross until he collapsed from the weight and pain and mounting agony of it all.

These vivid, heartbreaking descriptions of the Lord's sufferings at the hand of his persecutors convey the intense drama as the scene unfolded. Elder McConkie then spoke of His crucifixion and death upon the cross.

Finally, on a hill called Calvary—again, it was outside Jerusalem's walls—while helpless disciples looked on and felt the agonies of near death in their own bodies, the Roman soldiers laid him upon the cross.

With great mallets they drove spikes of iron through this feet and hands and wrists. Truly he was wounded for our transgressions and bruised for our iniquities.

It is instructive that Elder McConkie knew that Jesus' disciples "felt the agonies of near death in their own bodies," as they witnesses the crucifixion of their Lord. This revelatory detail is not found in the scriptural accounts.

Then the cross was raised that all might see and gape and curse and deride. This they did, with evil venom, for three hours from 9 A.M. to noon.

Then the heavens grew black. Darkness covered the land for the space of three hours, as it did among the Nephites. There was a mighty storm, as though the very God of Nature was in agony.

And truly he was, for while he was hanging on the cross for another three hours, from noon to 3 P.M., all the infinite agonies and merciless pains of Gethsemane recurred. And finally, when the atoning agonies had taken their toll—when the victory had been won, when the Son of God had fulfilled the will of his Father in all things—then he said, "It is finished" (John 19:30), and he voluntarily gave up the ghost."

When the atoning sacrifice was completed, Jesus departed to join the faithful who were gathered in the spirit world in preparation for his coming.

As the peace and comfort of a merciful death freed him from the pains and sorrows of mortality; he entered the paradise of God.

When he had made his soul an offering for sin, he was prepared to see his seed, according to the messianic word.

These, consisting of all the holy prophets and faithful Saints from ages past; these, comprising all who had taken upon them his name, and who, being spiritually begotten by him, had become his sons and his daughters, even as it is with us; all these were assembled in the spirit world, there to see his face and hear his voice.

Elder McConkie recited one of the greatest and most important Messianic prophecies, foretelling the Lord's advent to spirit paradise. This visit is detailed in Doctrine and Covenants section 138, which Elder McConkie had himself divided into verses, which explains that he did not go personally into the spirit prison, but that he organized the righteous and opened the door for them to preach to the spirits in "prison."

After some thirty-eight or forty hours—three days as the Jews measured time—our blessed Lord came to the Arimathaean's tomb, where his partially embalmed body had been placed by Nicodemus and Joseph of Arimathaea.

Then, in a way incomprehensible to us, he took up that body which had not yet seen corruption and arose in that glorious immortality which made him like his resurrected Father.

He then received all power in heaven and on earth, obtained eternal exaltation, appeared unto Mary Magdalene and many others, and ascended into heaven, there to sit down on the right hand of God the Father Almighty and to reign forever in eternal glory.

His rising from death on the third day crowned the atonement. Again, in some way incomprehensible to us, the effects of his resurrection pass upon all men so that all shall rise from the grave.

As Adam brought death, so Christ brought life; as Adam is the father of mortality, so Christ is the father of immortality.

And without both, mortality and immortality, man cannot work out his salvation and ascend to those heights beyond the skies where gods and angels dwell forever in eternal glory.

The wonder and truth of the Resurrection and Ascension of Christ is here recounted in plain yet eloquent terms. Special care is taken to point out those parts of this transcendent event which are beyond our limited mortal understanding, but are nonetheless true.

> Now, the atonement of Christ is the most basic and fundamental doctrine
> of the gospel, and it is the least understood of all our revealed truths.
> Many of us have a superficial knowledge and rely upon the Lord and his
> goodness to see us through the trials and perils of life.
> But if we are to have faith like that of Enoch and Elijah, we must believe
> what they believed, know what they knew, and live as they lived.
> May I invite you to join with me in gaining a sound and sure knowledge
> of the atonement.
> We must cast aside the philosophies of men and the wisdom of the wise
> and hearken to that Spirit which is given to us to guide us into all truth.
> We must search the scriptures, accepting them as the mind and will and
> voice of the Lord and the very power of God unto salvation.

The Atonement is here singled out and set apart as the most basic and
important doctrine within the gospel plan. Yet we are also gently
reminded that as fundamental as it is, "it is the least understood of all our
revealed truths." Our collective understanding of the true depth and
breadth of the Atonement is superficial, yet when we are stretched to our
innate limits by the trials of life, we then humble ourselves individually
before God and find his waiting grace.

This kind of faith was exemplified in the life of Oscar McConkie Sr.,
who was told by the voice of the Spirit that Enoch and Elijah gained their
faith through righteousness. That sweet experience beautifully
demonstrates this true principle—that faith comes from knowledge and
righteousness. The way to gain this level of faith is to humble ourselves
before the Lord, strip ourselves of worldly wisdom, and learn his will by
feasting upon the holy scriptures.

Elder McConkie then reviewed three great spiritual realities in the
history of planet earth—the creation of the earth and life in an Edenic
paradise, the price of Gethsemane wherein the Lord began his atoning
sacrifice, and the garden of the empty tomb where Jesus broke the bands
of death before appearing to Mary Magdalene.

Elder McConkie's promise is that the perceptions in our minds will
change through a prayerful search of the scriptures. This promise he
spoke of in a rhetorical "we will see" sense, which may cause us to
wonder and marvel at what Elder McConkie had seen and heard and
knew for himself.

> Thus, creation is father to the Fall, and by the Fall came mortality and
> death; and by Christ came immortality and eternal life.

If there had been no fall of Adam, by which cometh death, there could have been no atonement of Christ, by which cometh life.

These facts are recited in beauty and simplicity. One event complemented and prepared the way for the next, with each providing the next step forward in fulfilling the Father's plan for his children.

And now, as pertaining to this perfect atonement, wrought by the shedding of the blood of God, I testify that it took place in Gethsemane and at Golgotha; and as pertaining to Jesus Christ, I testify that he is the son of the Living God and was crucified for the sins of the world. He is our Lord, our God, and our King. This I know of myself, independent of any other person.

I am one of his witnesses, and in a coming day I shall feel the nail marks in his hands and in his feet and shall wet his feet with my tears.

But I shall not know any better then than I know now that he is God's Almighty Son, that he is our Savior and Redeemer, and that salvation comes in and through his atoning blood and in no other way.

God grant that all of us may walk in the light as God our Father is in the light so that, according to the promises, the blood of Jesus Christ his Son will cleanse us from all sin.

In the name of the Lord Jesus Christ. Amen.

Here is set forth one of the most poignant, inspired, and powerful testimonies uttered in this dispensation. His voice cracked with emotion, moving an audience of Saints who had come to know this man as one who was usually so stoic at the pulpit. His sure witness, borne by the power of the Holy Ghost, was carried into the hearts of his hearers—and those who heard, knew he knew. Such witnesses are held in sacred trust, protected from the world. However, through this rather private disclosure, Elder McConkie opened a personal door just enough to assure all that he knew perfectly of the witness he bore.

With his final testimony, he washed his garments free from the blood of this generation in preparation of whatever the days ahead would bring. In so doing he also cast a bright ray of hope before the Saints, for all who will, may follow this same course.

Of this last testimony, and last official act in his ministry, his son Stanford said, "I don't think there's anything Dad wanted to do more than preach that last sermon at conference."[17] Echoing this thought, his son Joseph said, "It meant so much to him to bear his testimony of Christ that last time that he could not read his remarks without weeping.[18]

After expending his last reservoirs of energy in preaching this final sermon, he was too weak and sick to attend the rest of conference and instead stayed home in bed.

One of the Brethren who witnessed his final talk from close range said, "You saw and heard him at general conference. You saw a man as close to having one foot on the earth and another in paradise as you are likely to see. Once more he raised his voice to proclaim his testimony of and allegiance to Jesus the Christ. Soon he would join his Savior, but he must endure to the end. This he did with courage and power beyond anything I have witnessed. He never returned to his ministry after that talk."[19]

The next Sunday, his close friend and associate Elder Boyd K. Packer went to visit him at his home:

> We had talked...of his coming graduation from mortality. On those occasions, despite his great regret at leaving his family and his brethren, he spoke in terms of anticipation. He was absolutely devoid of any fear.
>
> As we said our good-byes I inquired whether I could do anything else for him. He asked for a blessing.
>
> In it I quoted from verses in section 138 of the Doctrine and Covenants. "I beheld that the faithful elders of this dispensation when they depart from mortal life, continue their labors in the preaching of the gospel of repentance and redemption, through the sacrifice of the Only Begotten Son of God, among those who are in darkness and under the bondage of sin in the great world of the spirits of the dead" (v. 57.). Following the blessing, Brother McConkie wept and said, "It is now all in the hands of the Lord." He affirmed his willingness to do as the Lord should wish.[20]

At the conclusion of this blessing, with tears in his eyes, Elder McConkie looked at his beloved Amelia and said, "Do you know what he just did? He sealed me [up] unto death." "As I showed Elder Packer out," said Amelia, "Bruce got up, changed his clothes and got under the covers. Always before he'd insisted that I make the bed and he'd lay on top of it, fully dressed. But this was his way of saying he was submitting. He later told me he didn't want anyone fasting or praying for him, that it was all up to the Lord. He desperately didn't want to die. He had been so sure he would live. For him, it was the ultimate test of obedience."[21]

Each Thursday the First Presidency and the Council of the Twelve meet together in the Salt Lake Temple to transact the business of the Church and to pray together in the unity of love and faith possible only in

that sacred edifice. When the next time for this meeting arrived, "the Brethren met in the temple, [and] the message came from him and from his Amelia that he was ready now to go. Would we ask the Lord?...That was done. The following day at Amelia's invitation his family knelt around the bed for a final family prayer. His son Joseph was voice. At last they were willing to let him go, and at the very moment they asked the Lord, his passing came."[22]

Of this passing, Elder Carmack said, "I believe with all my heart that Elder McConkie stepped from his own bed at home with his family, who at his request on his deathbed prayed for his release the very moment he passed to the other world, into the mansion of Jesus Christ in a glory and peace which passeth all understanding."[23]

Thus, Elder Bruce Redd McConkie passed away on Friday, 19 April 1985, and went into the paradise of God, there to continue his ministry by preaching the gospel to the departed spirits. His funeral services were held on 22 April in the Salt Lake Tabernacle. The proceedings were carried by television and radio to a large, somber audience. The meeting was conducted by President Gordon B. Hinckley, Second Counselor to President Spencer W. Kimball, who was in attendance and presided over the services but did not speak because of physical limitations. The speakers were President Ezra Taft Benson, Elder James E. Faust, Elder Boyd K. Packer, and President Gordon B. Hinckley. Each expressed great praise and tender feelings for their departed fellow laborer. Since portions of their collective comments are spread throughout this book, only the two following excerpts will be mentioned.

President Gordon B. Hinckley said: "Can any of us doubt that he has now reported to the Lord whom he loved? That he has felt of the nail marks in His hands and in His feet? And wet His feet with his own tears? I can well imagine that he has repeated the words that were spoken by Thomas of old, 'My Lord and my God' (John 20:28). I believe that he has received in response, 'Well done, thou good and faithful servant,... enter into the joy of thy Lord' (D&C 25:21)."[24]

And speaking of Elder McConkie's yet future state, Elder Packer, whom Elder McConkie's death "had affected...more deeply than any other," said, "Where is Bruce McConkie now? He is with his Lord. When the refining process is complete, I know something of how he will appear. He will be glorious! What will he do? Whatever the Lord wills him to do. I believe he shall be, as the revelation describes them, 'a chosen messenger, clothed with power and authority to go forth and carry

Bruce K. McConkie
April Conf - 1984

the light of the gospel to them that were in darkness'" (D&C 138:30-31).[25]

At the following general conference, when Elder M. Russell Ballard was called to fill Elder McConkie's place in the Council of the Twelve, Elder Packer said, "I'm sure Brother Bruce R. McConkie, with whom Brother Ballard worked on a daily basis in missionary work, is rejoicing this day in what has transpired."[26]

Even with the death of so mighty a man, the work of the Lord goes on. Others are called to fill the positions of those whom the Lord Himself has released from mortal care and sickness and has sent on ahead. And so a great light has been extinguished on earth, only to burn the brighter in the next sphere of action.[27]

Notes

1. Dew, p. 63.

2. Dew, p. 63.

3. Tate, *Packer,* pp. 221-22.

4. Carmack, *Testament,* p. 110.

5. Dew, p. 63.

6. Video Biography, p. 5.

7. *Ensign,* May 1984, p. 32.

8. Dew, p. 63.

9. Dew, p. 63.

10. Packer, p. 262.

11. Dew, p. 63.

12. Video Biography, p. 6.

13. The following quotations from Elder McConkie's talk are taken from the *Ensign,* May 1985, pp. 9-11. See also the preface to *A New Witness for the Articles of Faith,* by Bruce R. McConkie.

14. This author does not presume to have an adequate grasp of this masterpiece. The best that I or anyone else can do is to try to be in tune with the same Spirit Elder McConkie had when he wrote it, in order to make some humble observations concerning its precious content.

15. David B. Haight, "The Sacrament—And the Sacrifice," *Ensign,* Nov. 1989, pp. 59-60.

Bruce R. McConkie: Highlights From His Life & Teachings

16. *Ensign,* Dec. 1985, pp. 54-59. Cited in Mark McConkie, *Restoration,* p. 256.

17. Dew, p. 63.

18. Dew, p. 63.

19. Carmack, *Testament,* p. 110.

20. Packer, pp. 265-66.

21. Dew, p. 63.

22. Packer, p. 267.

23. Carmack, *Testament,* p. 109.

24. Unpublished typescript of remarks by Gordon B. Hinckley at funeral of Elder Bruce R. McConkie, p. 15.

25. Packer, p. 266.

26. *Ensign,* Nov. 1985, p. 80.

27. Elder Carmack gave his opinion of how Elder Bruce R. McConkie might speak of his own death: "It makes not a particle of difference whether I preach the gospel here or in the world to come. I will preach the gospel." (Carmack, *Testament,* p. 110.)

216

Section Two

Bruce R. McConkie

Highlights From His Teachings

Preface to Section Two

This section is made up of subject selections from Elder McConkie's sermons, articles, and correspondence that I felt to be especially doctrinally insightful *but are not available in other McConkie books and compilations.* I have searched through older sources as well as some unpublished materials to find these wonderful pearls of great price. Hence its greatest worth, for he said some remarkable things in talks and letters found in no other place. Consequently these teachings help inspire a greater appreciation for—and understanding of—this powerful doctrinal teacher and chosen servant of God.

Elder McConkie did not typically mince words when he taught. He was direct and to the point. It was not in his nature to be offensive but rather to give clear correction or explanation, and sometimes warning or rebuke. As an Apostle of the Lord Jesus Christ, he clearly felt this duty rested upon him.

There is a measure of unavoidable overlap between some of the following chapters. For example, the chapters on judgment and valiance also touch briefly on subject matter found in other chapters.

Since Elder McConkie often began sentences with a "Now," or "Well," I often removed them to improve readability. This occurred most often when the source material used was an unedited typescript of a talk that he had delivered without a prepared text.

He also consistently used a collective "men" or "man" when referring to people in general. In most instances, this meant both male and female. One exception was when he spoke of priesthood and keys. Though in today's politically correct climate this may be considered insensitive by some, it is obvious that Elder McConkie did not view his usage as such; rather he referred to all mankind as is the pattern in the scriptures.

It may seem to the reader that the flow of subject content jumps on occasion as they read. This occurs because portions of text not related to the subject were removed. To obtain appropriate context, the reader should refer to the original source.

I have added short comments at the beginning of a few selected chapters where introductory explanation seemed helpful. These are designated by use of brackets and are intended to shed historical or contextual light upon what follows. There are also a few footnotes containing details which should prove helpful to the reader.

The teachings in each chapter are assembled in chronological order, with complete documentation at the end of each quotation.

There were times when Elder McConkie broke into prayer at the conclusion of his sermons. I have not included these prayers, but the following is an example: "Oh, God our Father, wilt thou look upon thy children everywhere in love and mercy, grant them repentance, and lead them in thy holy way so they may gain peace in this life and eternal life in the world to come." (*Ensign*, Nov. 1980, p. 52.)

It is my own prayer that this small collection of doctrinal gems from this spiritual giant may deepen the understanding of those who study them and enhance their love and appreciation of this unique and dedicated Apostle, Bruce R. McConkie.

Chapter Fifteen

The Atonement of Jesus Christ

As I ANALYZE and view the matter, it seems to me that the greatest miracle that ever occurred was the miracle of creation: the fact that God, our Heavenly Father, brought us into being; the fact that we exist; that we were born as his spirit children; and that now we are privileged to abide in mortal tabernacles and partake of a probationary experience.

It seems to me that the second greatest miracle that has ever occurred, in this or any of God's creations, is the atoning sacrifice of his Son; the fact that he came into the world to ransom men from the temporal and spiritual death brought into this existence by the fall of Adam; the fact that he is reconciling us again to God and making immortality and eternal life available to us. This atoning sacrifice of Christ is the greatest thing that has ever happened since the creation....

The very heart and core and center of revealed religion is the atoning sacrifice of Christ. All things rest upon it, all things are operative because of it, and without it...the purposes of creation would be void, they would vanish away, there would be neither immortality nor eternal life, and the ultimate destiny of all men would be to become as Lucifer and his followers are. ("Who Shall Declare His Generation?" in *Speeches of the Year, 1975* [1976], p. 306.)

WE SPEAK NOW of the Christ who came into the world to die, to die upon the cross for the sins of men. And we speak also of the Christ who came to rise again from the dead, of the Christ who, in glorious immortality, invites us to follow him in life and in death and in life again.

In Gethsemane he bowed beneath a load none other could bear. There he sweat great gouts of blood from every pore as he bore the sins of us all on conditions of repentance....

Again, on Calvary, during the last three hours of his mortal passion, the sufferings of Gethsemane returned, and he drank to the full the cup which his Heavenly Father had given him.

In the garden and on the cross he paid the ransom and finished his atoning work. Early on the morning of the third day he burst the bands of death and came forth from the tomb to inherit all power on earth and in heaven.

There is no language to extol the wonders of his works and all that he has done for us. As our Advocate and Intercessor he now dwells eternally in the heavens....

And now in words of soberness we announce that the Lord Jesus, the Everlasting Christ, the Savior who was and is and is to be, shall soon come again.

Just as surely as the son of Mary came to dwell among his fellowmen, so shall the Son of God come, in all the glory of his Father's kingdom, to rule among the sons of men.

In that dread day the world that now is shall end; wickedness will cease; every corruptible thing will be consumed. And the glory of the Lord will shine daily upon all men from the rising of the sun until it sinks in the western sky.

Those among us who abide the day of his coming shall find joy and peace everlasting. The faithful Saints shall live and reign with him on earth for a thousand years and shall then go on to their celestial rest.

The second coming of the Son of Man will be a day of vengeance and burning and sorrow for the wicked and ungodly.

For those who love the Lord and live his law it will be a day of peace and triumph and glory and honor—the day when the Lord comes to make up his jewels. ("The Seven Christs," *Ensign*, Nov. 1982, pp. 33-34.)

THE ATONEMENT OF the Lord Jesus—it began in Gethsemane; in large measure in Gethsemane it was accomplished. The time was the Thursday night of what the scriptures call the Week of His Passion. He and the disciples, the Twelve, had spent the afternoon and evening in an upper room in a house in Jerusalem where they partook of the Feast of the Passover according to the tradition and custom that then prevailed. On that occasion, Jesus had washed the feet of the Twelve and then Judas had left and after that He had introduced the ordinance of the Sacrament, and preached some glorious doctrines and delivered the great Intercessory Prayer; and then He had taken the Eleven with Him out to this place on the Mount of Olives that is called Gethsemane.

The Garden of Gethsemane means the Garden of the Oil Press. It's very obvious that it was a site owned by a disciple and a friend. The scriptures say it was a place "they were wont to go." They'd been there before. When they got to this Garden, Jesus left eight of the Twelve at the gate and He took three of them with Him into the Garden and then told them to stay at a certain place. It says He went on about a "stone's cast distance" and fell on His face and began to pray to the Father. Now, Peter, James, and John were the three in the Garden. The account says that they went to sleep. We can piece it together, with reasonable certainty, and discover that they awoke on occasions and that about three separate things occurred: Jesus, by Himself, praying to the Father—one account says that He used this language: "Father, if it be possible, let this cup pass from me; nevertheless, not my will but thine be done."

On another occasion Peter, James, and John saw that an angel came down and strengthened Him for the great ordeal that He was then undergoing. On another occasion when they were awake, they saw what appeared to them to be great drops of blood falling to the ground. Now we know that, in literal fact, that's what took place from what I read in section 19—that He sweat great drops of blood from every pore.

We can make quite an accurate, shall we say guess, maybe it's a little more than that, as to the time that was involved. We can be certain from all the events that are recited that it was not less than 1 hour. It could have been easily as much as 3 hours that He was in the Garden. Now this is the time when, primarily, He took upon Himself the sins of the world on conditions of repentance. And as I have read, all men must suffer for their own sins unless they repent. And if they repent, meaning if they believe in Christ and join the Church and get the companionship of the Holy Spirit and keep the commandments; if they pursue that course then the Lord Jesus bore their sins in Gethsemane.

Now I say that's incomprehensible. We don't know how it operates, but suffice it to say that it does, and if we do not repent in the sense in which I have said—which means membership in The Church of Jesus Christ of Latter-day Saints, and it means keeping the commandments of God—if we don't repent and obey in that sense, we have to suffer for our own sins. He bore our sins on conditions of repentance and in *no* other sense.

He suffered there in body and in spirit more than it is possible for man to suffer—the angel told King Benjamin—except it be unto death. The Lord Jesus, in large measure, worked out the atoning sacrifice there in the Garden of Gethsemane. Somewhere around or after midnight, probably a bit after midnight, the arresting party came. The arresting party was led by Judas. He'd gone out from the upper room to connive with the members of the Sanhedrin. He had known about the Garden of Gethsemane and apparently speculated or concluded that's where they'd be; and he led the party. We know who were in the party. We know that the temple guards, and the members of the Sanhedrin were there representing the ecclesiastical power of the day. We know there were 600 Roman soldiers because it says they were commanded by a Tribune and that's the number he commands. It's obvious that they came from the Fortress of Antonia which was near the temple. When they came to arrest Jesus they were totally overawed by His presence and fell to the ground. He invited them to stand. Peter impetuously drew his sword and cut off the ear of a man named Malchus who was the servant of the high priest, which has to mean that he was the servant of Caiaphus. Jesus told Peter to put up his sword and He reached out His arm and He touched the ear and healed the servant, and this appears to be the last miracle of that sort ever performed. The miracle of the Atonement is the greatest of all miracles, but for healing miracles that was the last and obviously it would stand as an added witness against the High Priest.

Jesus asked them to let the Apostles go and the group of them did flee into the night. And then it says they led Him away. This is after the traitor's kiss. Incidentally, the traitor's kiss was not a kiss on the cheek. The word that's involved in the original language is different than the word kiss to us. It connotes a very effusive outpouring of affection. It was common to kiss each other in that day, men included; but on this occasion Judas was effusively and elaborately showering Jesus with kisses—according to the language in the original text. In any event they led Him away, and that's the New Testament language; their tradition and custom was to arrest someone and put a rope around their neck, and so that language means that that's what they did in Jesus' case. They took Him to Ananias for a very astute political reason but no legal reason. Ananias was a former high priest; but Ananias was the most influential, single man in all Jerusalem or in all the Holy Land among the Jews. He was extremely wealthy. His son-in-law, in fact, was the high priest. He had four sons who served as high priests, and one grandson. He commonly connived with the Roman authority. The reason for taking Him to Ananias was to get Ananias to condemn Him. And it was perfectly obvious that if Ananias took this stand because of his political influence no one else would rise against that judgment....

Ananias condemned Him and then they took Him to Caiaphas who was the legal High Priest. He illegally held the office...because he had been appointed by Rome instead of being the natural blood descendant of Aaron. But, in any event, he was exercising legal authority. He had two trials before Caiaphas; an initial trial and then along toward morning a second trial. He was condemned at both of them—the second one was to allow the Sanhedrin to assemble so that they could make the condemnation, which they did, and what they found Him guilty of was blasphemy and, according to their law, He should die.

He was taken from Caiaphas to Pilate and they wanted Pilate to "rubber-stamp" their decree that He was worthy of death, so they told him, "He is worthy of death." And Pilate said, "What has he done?" And they said it was a violation of their law, and he said, "Well, take ye him and judge him according to your law then." And they knew it was not propitious for them to issue a death sentence; legally they couldn't, although in practice they were doing it. So they immediately changed the charge of blasphemy and made it one of sedition and of treason, and the sedition consisted of preaching the gospel and stirring the people up against the established order, and the treason was that He made Himself a king and was, therefore, in opposition to Tiberius, the Roman emperor.

Pilate felt obligated to hear the charges of sedition and of treason, though he was attempting, realistically, to free Him. The reason Pilate didn't free Him is because his own hands were covered with blood and he didn't have the moral courage to go forward. In the course of the trial before Pilate, this first one, he heard it mentioned that Jesus was a Galilean, and so being an astute politician, he decided to send Jesus to Herod who ruled over the other area, Galilee. He was considered, or bore, informally, the title of King although, in fact, he wasn't a king. They took Him to Herod. This Herod is the son of the one who slaughtered the children in Bethlehem. This Herod is the one who had John the Baptist beheaded and he was a very lecherous and evil and corrupt man, and he had wanted to see Jesus to see if some miracle could be wrought. When Jesus got before Herod He remained mute, He didn't say a thing. This is the one occasion we know of in His whole ministry where He absolutely refused to speak to a human being. They put a white robe on Him, they mocked Him, they scorned Him, and finally Herod sent Him back to Pilate.

Pilate tried to free Him. Pilate asked whether they wanted Barabbas or Jesus released to them according to the tradition of releasing a prisoner at the Passover time. The crowd cried out that they wanted Jesus released, and immediately the chief priests and Sanhedrin went through the crowd and stirred them up and changed their minds and got them chanting that they wanted Barabbas and that they wanted Jesus crucified. And they kept saying, "Crucify him, Crucify him." And Pilate said, "What wrong hath he done?" And they said, "He's made himself a king." Pilate queried Him about that and they gave that horrendous cry, "His blood be upon us and upon our children." Finally the decree was issued to crucify Him.

Pilate let his soldiers take Him away and take off the white robe that He had on, and put on a scarlet one, and mocked Him, putting a crown of thorns on His head, and scourged Him—the most vicious form of torment that there is, that a man can withstand and live. It was not uncommon, as a matter of fact, for people to die in the scourging process....

[Pilate] was forced by his own sins to issue the decree, "Take ye him and crucify him." Which they then did, the Roman soldiers performing the crucifixion. We know what the tradition and custom and mode of crucifixion was in that day. It wasn't what you see in movies about Christ or what artists have painted. Artists take license and paint an elaborate cross and they paint Him as carrying some tremendous big cross. We don't know what He carried but we know what everybody did in that day, and it's unbelievable that things were different with Him. The way you carried a cross was to carry the cross bar on which your arms would be; and that consisted of two pieces of wood or a tree, and they tied them together at the ends and put your neck in between them so your arms were outstanding. And while you carried that, someone else took the pole—now it's conceivable that He carried the pole but if He did, out of the thousands of people who were crucified, He was the only one who did that. We don't know the details. But as He carried this cross and, in all probability, only the bar, it was beyond His physical capacity. He'd been up all night. He'd been tried and smitten and scourged. Above all, He'd suffered in Gethsemane for from one to three hours and He was weak and couldn't carry the burden. And they impressed someone else into the service to carry His cross. They took Him to this place that's called Calvary, in the Greek, and Golgotha, in the Hebrew. It apparently was outside the wall of Old Jerusalem. Some of you have been to Jerusalem, I suppose. Both President Kimball and President Lee have given it as their opinion that that site of the open tomb and adjacent to it the hill known as Calvary, a small hill, is the one place in Jerusalem where we can believe with some certainty, at least, that an actual event took place. Most of the recitations as to what happened there and so on are just speculation.

Interestingly enough, this is called "The Place of the Skull," and there's a big limestone cliff there with caves in it, and the caves are so situated that they give the impression that the whole hillside is the human skull. It could be that that's what's meant by "The Place of a Skull."

In any event, they took the Lord to the place where He was to be crucified. And the normal way to crucify a person was to tie him to the cross but in Jesus' case they drove nails into His hands and His feet. Occasionally, on other people, they did that. What they would do would be to lay him down on the ground and drive the nails into his hands, and then attach this crossbar and drive a nail through each foot alone or both feet together into the pole, and then lift it up and put it in a hole that's dug for the purpose. That was the normal way to handle a crucifixion. In order to sustain the weight of the body they put a little peg in the pole between the legs on which some of the weight rested. The great probability is that that's what they did with Him. And the likelihood is that He had some clothing on. The Romans crucified people naked, but in the case of Jews when they crucified them they humored the Jews because of their sense of modesty by letting them wear some clothing. At least we like to believe that in the case of Jesus He had that clothing.

Their practice was to take a person who was crucified and let him drink an opiate. They offered this to Jesus and He declined. Presumptively the two thieves accepted. Their practice also was to take a club and hit the individual over the chest in order to dull his sensitivities so that he could stand the crucifying act and his life would continue on and he'd suffer in a prolonged way. It's quite obvious that they did not do that to Jesus, at least there is no intimation in the text that they did, and we suppose that Jesus was declining all help that would have stopped the suffering.

Crucifixion, itself, is a very horrible death. Sometimes people were on the cross for days or even weeks until they died. We know exactly what time He was placed on the cross. It was 9 A.M. on Friday—that's specifically set forth. We know some conversations that He had that took place between 9 and 12 and we know what time He was taken off the cross, which was 3 P.M. We know that from noon to 3 P.M. there was darkness, the New Testament says, over all the earth. Now, that fits in marvelously well to the 3 hours of darkness that the Book of Mormon talks about when the rocks were rent and the great upheavals occurred in the Americas.

There isn't one syllable or indication in the New Testament of what took place during the three hours from noon to 3 P.M. But I've told you what took place in the Garden of Gethsemane and indicated to you that that's the occasion when Jesus took upon himself, in large measure, the sins of the world. The very interesting thing is that the Book of Mormon makes a very express point of saying that the atoning sacrifice took place upon the cross. Now that has the atoning sacrifice both in the Garden and upon the cross. And what Brother Talmage says in his book *Jesus the Christ*—and there can't be the slightest question about this—is that from noon until 3 P.M. as He hung on the cross there recurred all of the agonies and sufferings that took place in the Garden.

That means that either four hours as a minimum or six hours, which is more likely, was the time involved in working out the atoning sacrifice. Three hours on the cross and from one to three hours in the Garden. We can't comprehend this. We don't know what's involved. We don't understand the agonies. We can't comprehend creation. We can't comprehend redemption. We know we have been created. We know there has been a redemption. And this redemption brought immortality on one hand and eternal life on the other.

After He had been on the cross for the six hours, it was nearing the time of the Sabbath. The Sabbath started at sundown on Friday night. The Jews would have been offended to have someone hanging on the cross on the Sabbath day. It would have violated their Sabbath and they importuned Pilate that his soldiers might break the legs of the three people. They weren't breaking the legs to kill them as I, at least, always supposed until I knew better. They were breaking the legs to increase the suffering of the individual to compensate for the short time on the cross because they then killed the person either with a sword or a spear.

They did break the legs of the two thieves and then, obviously, they killed them and we would suppose with a spear because when they came to Jesus they didn't break His legs but found Him dead already; the roman soldier thrust the spear into Him. Leading us to suppose that that's the way they killed the two thieves.

This, to a degree, concluded the atoning sacrifice although there was something yet ahead—the hour of glory and triumph. Then they wanted to take the body off the cross. It was the practice to take someone who was crucified down and just put the body in a cart and take it out to a valley called the Valley of Hinnom or Gehenna, outside of Jerusalem where they burned their garbage. Presumptively that's what they did with the two thieves, but Jesus' friends wanted to do otherwise with Him. And there was one of them who was a member of the Sanhedrin who was very rich and very influential who importuned Pilate that he might have the body; and this was Joseph of Arimathaea. And Pilate was surprised that Jesus was dead and he inquired of the Centurion who had conducted the crucifixion to be sure that He was dead. And when he got the response that He was, he gave the body into the custody of Joseph of Arimathaea.

There was another member of the Sanhedrin, who was Nicodemus—this is the one who came to Jesus by night on the occasion of the first Passover and had the conversation about being born again. Nicodemus came to join Joseph of Arimathaea, either at the site of crucifixion or at the site of burial, we cannot tell. But Nicodemus brought some ointments that were costly and some linen cloth that was torn into strips.

The way they would take a person off the cross is to take the cross down and pull out the nails from the hands and the feet and, in preparation for burial, they would wash the body which they undoubtedly did with Jesus, and then they would annoint the body with things that had an embalming effect. They were working quite hastily and it could only be a partial embalmment because of the time and they wrapped the linen strips around His body and they took it and put it in Joseph's tomb. The account says a tomb in which never man had lain and as they did this there was a group of women standing off at a modest distance watching what was involved; Mary Magdalene and others.

They got Him in the tomb before the sun went down. Now the next thing that we become aware of is that He rose from the dead and He rose very early Sunday. We can make quite a good judgment, between 38 and 40 hours He lay in the tomb. This 38 or 40 hours was part of the three days, and the Jews had a system of counting days where they counted the beginning and the ending day, so to them that meant three days. I have no explanation for the nights involved. There's some defect in our accounts where they are concerned surely. But in any event, He was placed in the tomb and then the record says that while it was yet dark on Sunday morning, Mary Magdalene came, the angels were there, and so on. Mary saw Him in the Garden. She thought He was the gardener.

She said, "Sir, if thou hast taken him, show me where." She wanted to continue the embalming process of His body. He said to her, "Mary." And she then looked up and recognized Him and said, "Rabboni," which is "My Lord, my Master." And in an effusive outburst was going to throw her arms around Him and He stopped her from doing that. She did not, at least at that time, touch Him.

Then the record says when it began to be light the other women came. So shortly after this the other women came—a group of them. It says that they were permitted to throw their arms around His feet and hold Him. That's two appearances after the resurrection.

Some time that day—we don't know when—He appeared to Peter, which is a third appearance. We know that the afternoon of that Sunday He walked for two or three hours on the road from Jerusalem to Emmaus with two disciples. We know that one of them was Cleophas and we assume that the other one was Luke. This is the account where they said their hearts burned within them as He talked. When they got to Emmaus He was known to them in the breaking of bread and vanished out of their sight. And they went immediately back to Jerusalem and went to an upper room. This could well have been the same upper room in which the Feast of the Passover was held by them; it probably was.

In any event, in this room they were holding a little testimony meeting as they ate. A congregation of Saints in which, without question, women were present. They were bearing testimony of what had happened that day and they had barred the room because they were afraid of the Jews and so Jesus, then, stood in the midst of that room suddenly. And the account says they were terrified and afrighted and supposed that they had seen a spirit....And He said to them, "Handle me and see. He said, "A spirit hath not flesh and bones as ye see me have." They handled Him, they felt the nail marks in His hands and in His feet. Without question, although it doesn't say it, they thrust their hands in the spear wound.

We know that when He appeared to the Nephites they thrust their hands into the spear wound. He said to them, on that occasion, "Have ye here any meat?" Meaning food or a rhetorical question because they were there eating. The account says they brought Him a piece of a broiled fish and of a honeycomb and He took it and did eat before them. What He was doing was proving to them that He was not a spirit, that He was a resurrected being, that He had a tangible body of flesh and bones. Ten of the Twelve were there. Thomas was absent. There was a similar appearance a week later, it says eight days, because of this system of counting both days at the ends, a week later He appeared and Thomas was present and had a similar experience.

It went on like that. He appeared in due course—first He appeared on the Sea of Galilee to about 6 of them, then He appeared on the mountain in Galilee and He appeared on the Mount of Olives when He ascended. He was appearing over and over again to let them know and become witnesses that He'd been resurrected.

The Atonement really started Thursday night in the Garden and the suffering there was intense beyond belief....The Atonement continued on the cross without any question for the last three hours. But the climax of the Atonement, the glorious, wondrous thing was the bursting of the bands of death and His coming forth from the grave which He did on Sunday morning. Now, we don't comprehend this. He was the first fruits of them that slept. We know that in some way, beyond our understanding, the effects of the Resurrection of Christ passes upon all men. As in Adam all die, even so in Christ shall all be made alive, is what Paul says....

If there had been no atoning sacrifice there would be no eternal life. There'd be no continuation of the family unit. There'd be no blessings, and honor and dignity of any sort. There'd be no salvation. Everything that there is centers in the Atonement. The creation started the system rolling. The creation put the Father's plan into operation. The Atonement gives efficacy and virtue and power and force to the Father's plan.' That's why the gospel of God which is the Father's plan is called the Gospel of Jesus Christ. It's so named to center our attention in Christ and let us know that all blessings and all rewards and all good things come because of the Atonement....

What I've been saying here, really, is information that's pretty much available to all the world. It's not peculiar, secret knowledge that Latter-day Saints have....The reason we're able to put these things into position and into perspective is because of the latter-day revelation that we have received. We have a host of revelations about the atoning sacrifice. There are some glorious things in the third chapter of Mosiah; that's a sermon that was preached by an angel about the Atonement....

I guess as far as personal application is concerned, the most important thing for us to know is what was in that original passage and Section 19, that if we repent and believe and obey and live the law, then the suffering of Christ pays the penalty for our sins and that if we don't we have to pay the penalty for our own sins.

If He took upon Himself our sins on conditions of repentance, we become inheritors of the celestial world; but if we have to pay the penalty for our own sins, having paid it, we'll go to lesser kingdoms that are prepared, a telestial kingdom or, possibly, a terrestrial kingdom. ("The Atonement," [unpublished talk given at the Chico California Stake conference, 15 March 1981], pp. 3-10.)

DO I BELIEVE in the atonement of the Lord Jesus Christ?

As to this question, I give my own personal answer. It is:

I know that my Redeemer lives; with Job I testify. What though the ravages of disease destroy my body; what though I am slain by the sword of death—yet I know that he who bought me with his blood shall soon reign on earth and that "in my flesh shall I see God." (Job 19:26; see also v. 25.)

I am a witness that he was lifted up upon the cross of Calvary; that he was crucified, died, and rose again the third day; that he ascended into heaven, where, sitting on the right hand of God, the Father Almighty, he now reigns in everlasting glory; and that he will soon come again among the sons of men.

I know that he is the one Mediator between God and man, that he brings to pass the immortality and eternal life of man; that his is the ministry of reconciliation whereby fallen man can be reconciled with his Maker.

I know that salvation is in Christ and that only by faith in his name can we hope for the riches of eternity.

He is my Brother and Friend, but he is more. He is my Lord, my God, and my King, whom I worship in the full majesty of his Godhead and who will continue to be my Savior, my Redeemer, and my God through all the eternities that lie ahead. ("The Caravan Moves On," *Ensign*, Nov. 1984, pp. 82-83.)

THE TEACHER WHO uses the illustration of the nails in the board and concludes by saying, "The holes are always there" is mistaken. If a person has truly repented, the hole ceases to exist—the person is washed clean and pure. (Excerpt from unpublished talk given at the [Salt Lake

City] Emigration Stake conference, 31 August 1958.)[1]

---

1. In a letter to the author's grandfather, Walter M. Horne, Elder McConkie's father-in-law, Joseph Fielding Smith, said, "This idea, which has so often been taught, that the holes remain after the nails are withdrawn is a false doctrine when applied to the atonement for the truly repentant sinner."

Chapter Sixteen

The Creation and the Fall

THE THREE PILLARS of eternity, the three events, preeminent and transcendent above all others, are the creation, the fall, and the atonement. These three are the foundations upon which all things rest. Without any one of them all things would lose their purpose and meaning, and the plans and designs of Deity would come to naught.

If there had been no creation, we would not be, neither the earth, nor any form of life upon its face. All things, all the primal elements, would be without form and void. God would have no spirit children; there would be no mortal probation; and none of us would be on the way to immortality and eternal life.

If there had been no fall of man, there would not be a mortal probation. Mortal man would not be, nor would there be animals or fowls or fishes or life of any sort upon the earth. And, we repeat, none of us would be on the way to immortality and eternal life.

If there had been no atonement of Christ, all things would...vanish away. Lucifer would triumph over men and become the captain of their souls. And, we say it again, none of us would be on the way to immortality and eternal life....

We are speaking of the three pillars of heaven, of the three greatest events ever to occur in all eternity, of the three doctrines that are woven inseparably together to form the plan of salvation. We are speaking of the creation, the fall, and the atonement. And these things are one. And, be it noted, all things were created; all things fell; and all things are subject to the redeeming power of the Son of God....

Many among us have no difficulty envisioning that the atonement is infinite and eternal and applies to all forms of life. They know that the revelations say in so many words that all forms of life both lived as spirit entities and will be resurrected—animals, fowls, fishes—all things are eternal in nature.

But some among us have not yet had it dawn upon them that all things fell and became mortal so they could be resurrected. ("The Three Pillars of Eternity," in *Brigham Young University 1981 Fireside and Devotional Speeches* [1981], pp. 27, 31.)

THERE IS NO revealed recitation specifying that each of the "six days" involved in the Creation was of the same duration. Our three accounts of the Creation are the Mosaic, the Abrahamic, and the one presented in the temples. Each of these stems back to the Prophet Joseph Smith. The Mosaic and Abrahamic accounts place the creative events on the same successive days. The temple account, for reasons that are apparent to those familiar with its teachings, has a different division of events. It seems clear that the "six days" are one continuing period and that there is no one place where the dividing lines between the successive events must of necessity be placed.

The Mosaic and the temple accounts set forth the temporal or physical creation, the actual organization of element or matter into tangible form. They are not accounts of the spirit creation. Abraham gives a blueprint as it were of the Creation. He tells the plans of the holy beings who wrought the creative work. After reciting the events of the "six days" he says: "And thus were their decisions at the time that they counseled among themselves to form the heavens and the earth." (Abr. 5:3.)

Then he says they performed as they had planned, which means we can, by merely changing the verb tenses and without doing violence to the sense and meaning, also consider the Abrahamic account as one of the actual creation. ("Christ and the Creation," *Ensign*, June 1982, p. 11.)

THE PHYSICAL BODY of Adam is made from the dust of this earth, the very earth to which the Gods came down to form him. His "spirit" enters his body, as Abraham expresses it. (See Abr. 5:7.) Man becomes a living, immortal soul, body and spirit are joined together. He has been created "spiritually," as all things were because there is as yet no mortality. Then comes the Fall; Adam falls; mortality and procreation and death commence. Fallen man is mortal; he has mortal flesh; he is "the first flesh upon the earth." And the effects of his fall pass upon all created things. They fall in that they too become mortal. Death enters the world; mortality reigns; procreation commences; and the Lord's great and eternal purposes roll onward. ("Christ and the Creation," *Ensign*, June 1982, p. 14.)

Chapter Seventeen

Symbolism in the Garden of Eden

[This chapter contains quotations from several sources and relates Elder McConkie's symbolic or figurative interpretations of scriptural passages involving the "tree of life," the "tree of knowledge of good and evil," the "forbidden fruit," and other identifying phrases, each of which is found in the scriptural accounts of the events which took place in the Garden of Eden. Included in the footnotes is further information on these interesting and unique interpretations.]

AS TO THE FALL, the scriptures set forth that there were in the Garden of Eden two trees. One was the tree of life, which figuratively refers to eternal life; the other was the tree of knowledge of good and evil, which figuratively refers to how and why and in what manner mortality and all that appertains to it came into being.... (Moses 3:16-17.)[2]

Eve partook without full understanding; Adam partook knowing that unless he did so, he and Eve could not have children and fulfill the commandment they had received to multiply and replenish the earth. After they had thus complied with whatever the law was that brought mortality into being, the Lord said to Eve: "I will greatly multiply thy

---

2. Robert L. Millet: "We cannot always tell which items are literal and which are figurative. That is, we do not always know when the scriptures are giving us symbolic imagery or when they provide a record of literal events. We know, for example, that there was an Adam and an Eve, that there was a Garden of Eden, and that the Fall was an actual historical event. But what of the 'rib story?' Was Eve really created from Adam's rib, or is the scripture pointing to a greater doctrinal reality? *And what of the trees in the garden and the fruit? Elder McConkie has written:* [Here follows the text just quoted from NWAF.]" (*The Power of the Word*, Deseret Book: Salt Lake City. 1994, p. 66. Emphasis mine.)

sorrow and thy conception. In sorrow thou shalt bring forth children, and thy desire shall be to thy husband, and he shall rule over thee." To Adam the decree came: "Cursed shall be the ground for thy sake; in sorrow shalt thou eat of it all the days of thy life. Thorns also, and thistles shall it bring forth to thee." Thus the paradisiacal earth was cursed; thus it fell; and thus it became as it now is. (*A New Witness for the Articles of Faith,* 1985, p. 86.)

[MOSES 3:21-25] SAYS, speaking figuratively, that Eve was formed from Adam's rib....

As to the Fall itself we are told that the Lord planted "the tree of knowledge of good and evil" in the midst of the garden. (Moses 3:9.) To Adam and Eve the command came: "Of every tree of the garden thou mayest freely eat, But of the tree of knowledge of good and evil, thou shalt not eat of it, nevertheless, thou mayest choose for thyself, for it is given unto thee; but, remember that I forbid it, for in the day thou eatest thereof thou shalt surely die." (Moses 3:16-17.) Again the account is speaking figuratively. What is meant by partaking of the fruit of the tree of knowledge of good and evil is that our first parents complied with whatever laws were involved so that their bodies would change from their state of paradisiacal immortality to a state of natural mortality.[3]

Moses 4 gives the actual account of the Fall. Adam and Eve partake of the forbidden fruit and the earth is cursed and begins to bring forth thorns and thistles; that is, the earth falls to its present natural state. ("Christ and the Creation," *Ensign,* June 1982, p. 15; see also *Doctrines of the Restoration,* 1998, p. 189.)

[ADAM AND EVE] WERE...told that of every tree in the Garden of Eden they might eat excepting only the tree of the knowledge of good and evil.

For disobedience to this command death (*or in other words mortality*) was to enter the world. (Moses 3:17.) In order to have children it was

---

3. Mark L. McConkie, son of Elder McConkie: "Elder McConkie adds a number of insights which have escaped our general notice:...that the whole earth was Eden, and that Adam and Eve lived in a garden located 'Eastward in Eden' (Gen. 2:8); that the expression, 'the tree of knowledge of good and evil' is figurative (and he points out its meaning)." (*Doctrines of the Restoration,* Introduction to Part III, 1998, p. 175.)

necessary that they become mortal; and so in accordance with the divine plan they partook of the *forbidden fruit*, death and mortality entered the world, and the bodies of our first parents were so changed as to permit them to have offspring and thus fulfil the purposes of the Lord in the creation of the earth....

What the real meaning is of the expression forbidden fruit has not been revealed, and it is profitless to speculate. It is sufficient for us to know that Adam and Eve broke the law which would have permitted them to continue as immortal beings, or in other words they complied with the law which enables them to become mortal beings, and this course of conduct is termed eating the forbidden fruit.[4]

One thing we do know definitely: The forbidden fruit was not sex sin. (*Mormon Doctrine*, 2nd ed., pp. 289-290.)

FOR THOSE WHOSE limited spiritual understanding precludes a recitation of all the facts, the revealed account, in figurative language, speaks of Eve being created from Adam's rib. (Moses 3:21-25.) A more express scripture, however, speaks of "Adam, who was the son of God, with whom God, himself, conversed." (Moses 6:22.) In a formal doctrinal pronouncement, the First Presidency of the Church (Joseph F. Smith, John R. Winder, and Anthon H. Lund) said that "all who have inhabited the earth since Adam have taken bodies and become souls in like manner," and that the first of our race began life as the human germ or embryo that becomes a man. (See *Improvement Era*, November 1909,

---

4. Joseph Fielding McConkie, son of Elder McConkie: "What of the trees of Eden? Was there actually a tree whose fruit would make one wise, and another whose fruit would assure everlasting life?...

"If we were to reason that it was the fruit itself that brought about this change in the bodies of Adam and Eve, we would then have to suppose that our first parents fed some of the fruit to all the other living things upon the whole earth....Every plant and animal, including all sea life and the fowls of the air, would have been required to eat some of this fruit (and must also have been precluded from partaking of it either by design or accident before this point of time)....

"If...we assume the partaking of the fruit to have been a figurative representation of what actually brought about the transformation of the earth from a paradisiacal to a natural or mortal sphere, then it might follow that the speaking serpent would also have been figurative." ("The Mystery of Eden," in *The Man Adam* [Bookcraft: Salt Lake City, 1990], pp. 28-29.)

p. 80.)

Christ is universally attested in the scriptures to be the Only Begotten. At this point, as we consider the "creation" of Adam, and lest there be any misunderstanding, we must remember that Adam was created in immortality, but that Christ came to earth as a mortal; thus our Lord is the Only Begotten in the flesh, meaning into this mortal sphere of existence. Adam came to earth to dwell in immortality until the fall changed his status to that of mortality. Those who have ears to hear will understand these things.

God, meaning the Father, created Adam and Eve in his own image; male and female created he them. (Moses 2:27.) The woman was given to the man in eternal marriage, for there was no death. They were commanded not to partake of the tree of the knowledge of good and evil. But "when the woman saw that the tree was good for food, and that it become pleasant to the eyes, and a tree to be desired to make her wise," as the figurative language has it, "she took of the fruit thereof, and did eat, and also gave unto her husband with her, and he did eat. And the eyes of them both were opened." (Moses 4: 12-13.)

The name of Adam and Eve as a united partnership is Adam. They, the two of them together, are named Adam. This is more than the man Adam as a son of God or the woman Eve as a daughter of the some Holy Being. Adam and Eve taken together are named Adam, and the fall of Adam is the fall of them both, for they are one. ("Eve and the Fall," *Woman* [Deseret Book: Salt Lake City, 1979], pp. 60-64.)

Chapter Eighteen

The Godhead

THERE IS NO SALVATION in believing any false doctrine, particularly a false or unwise view about the Godhead or any of its members. Eternal life is reserved for those who know God and the One whom he sent to work out the infinite and eternal atonement.

True and saving worship is found only among those who know the truth about God and the Godhead and who understand the true relationship men should have with each member of that Eternal Presidency.

It follows that the devil would rather spread false doctrine about God and the Godhead, and induce false feelings with reference to any one of them, than almost any other thing he could do. The creeds of Christendom illustrate perfectly what Lucifer wants so-called Christian people to believe about Deity in order to be damned.

These creeds codify what Jeremiah calls the lies about God (see Jer. 16:19; 23:14-32). They say he is unknown, uncreated, and incomprehensible. The say he is a spirit, without body, parts, or passions. They say he is everywhere and nowhere in particular present, that he fills the immensity of space and yet dwells in the hearts of men, and that he is an immaterial, incorporeal nothingness. They say he is one-god-in-three, and three-gods-in-one who neither hears, nor sees, nor speaks. Some even say he is dead, which he might as well be if their descriptions identify his being.

These concepts summarize the chief and greatest heresy of Christendom. Truly the most grievous and evil heresy ever imposed on an erring and wayward Christianity is their creedal concept about God and the Godhead! But none of this troubles us very much. God has revealed himself to us in this day even as he did to the prophets of old.

We know thereby that he is a personal Being in whose image man was made. We know that he has a body of flesh and bones as tangible as man's, that he is a resurrected, glorified, and perfected Being; and that he lives in the family unit. We know that we are his spirit children; that he endowed us with the divine gift of agency; and that he ordained the laws whereby we might advance and progress and become like him.

We know that God is the only supreme and independent Being in whom all fullness and perfection dwell and that he is omnipotent, omniscient, and, by the power of his Spirit, omnipresent....

What is and should be our relationship to the members of the Godhead?

First, be it remembered that most scriptures that speak of God or of the Lord do not even bother to distinguish the Father from the Son, simply because it doesn't make any difference which God is involved. They are one. The words or deeds of either of them would be the words and deeds of the other in the same circumstance.

Further, if a revelation comes from, or by the power of the Holy Ghost, ordinarily the words will be those of the Son, though what the Son says will be what the Father would say, and the words may thus be considered as the Father's. Thus any feelings of love, praise, awe, or worship that may fill our hearts when we receive the divine words will be the same no matter who is thought or known to be the author of them.

And yet we do have a proper relationship to each member of the Godhead, in part at least because there are separate and severable functions which each performs, and also because of what they as one Godhead have done for us.

Our relationship with the Father is supreme, paramount, and preeminent over all others. He is the God we worship. It is his gospel that saves and exalts. He ordained and established the plan of salvation. He is the one who was once as we are now. The life he lives is eternal life, and if we are to gain this greatest of all the gifts of God, it will be because we become like him.

Our relationship with the Father is one of parent and child. He is the one who gave us our agency. It was his plan that provided for a fall and an atonement. And it is to him that we must be reconciled if we are to gain salvation. He is the one to whom we have direct access by prayer, and if there were some need—which there is not!—to single out one member of the Godhead for a special relationship, the Father, not the Son, would be the one to choose.

Our relationship with the Son is one of brother or sister in the premortal life and one of being led to the Father by him while in this mortal sphere. He is the Lord Jehovah who championed our cause before the foundations of the earth were laid. He is the God of Israel, the promised Messiah, and the Redeemer of the world.

By faith we are adopted into his family and become his children. We take upon ourselves his name, keep his commandments, and rejoice in the cleansing power of his blood. Salvation comes by him. From Creation's dawn, as long as eternity endures, there neither has been nor will be another act of such transcendent power and import as his atoning sacrifice.

We do not have a fraction of the power we need to properly praise his holy name and ascribe unto him the honor and power and might and glory and dominion that is his. He is our Lord, our God, and our King.

Our relationship with the Holy Spirit is quite another thing. This Holy Personage is a Revelator and a Sanctifier. He bears record of the Father and the Son. He dispenses spiritual gifts to the faithful. Those of us who have received the gift of the Holy Ghost have the right to his constant companionship.

And again, if it were proper—and I repeat, it is not!—to single out one member of the Godhead for some special attention, we might well conclude that member should be the Holy Ghost. We might well adopt as a slogan: Seek the Spirit. The reason of course is that the sanctifying power of the Spirit would assure us of reconciliation with the Father. And any person who enjoys the constant companionship of the Holy Spirit will be in complete harmony with the divine will in all things.

In spite of all these truths, which ought to be obvious to every spiritually enlightened person, heresies rear their ugly heads among us from time to time....

There are [those] who have an excessive zeal which causes them to go beyond the mark. Their desire for excellence is inordinate. In an effort to be truer than true they devote themselves to gaining a special, personal relationship with Christ that is both improper and perilous.

I say perilous because this course, particularly in the lives of some who are spiritually immature, is a gospel hobby which creates an unwholesome holier-than-thou attitude. In other instances it leads to despondency because the seeker after perfection knows he is not living the way he supposes he should.

Another peril is that those so involved often begin to pray directly to Christ because of some special friendship they feel has been developed....

Our prayers are addressed to the Father, and to him only. They do not go through Christ, or the Blessed Virgin, or St. Genevieve or along the beads of a rosary. We are entitled to "come boldly unto the throne of grace, that we may obtain mercy, and find grace to help in time of need" (Hebrews 4:16).

And I rather suppose that he who sitteth upon the throne will choose his own ways to answer his children, and that they are numerous. Perfect prayer is addressed to the Father, in the name of the Son; it is uttered by the power of the Holy Ghost; and it is answered in whatever way seems proper by him whose ear is attuned to the needs of his children.

Now I know that some may be offended at the counsel that they should not strive for a special and personal relationship with Christ. It will seem to them as though I am speaking out against mother love, or Americanism, or the little red schoolhouse. But I am not. There is a fine line here over which true worshipers will not step.

It is true that there may, with propriety, be a special relationship with a wife, with children, with friends, with teachers, with the beasts of the field and the fowls of the sky and the lilies of the valley. But the very moment anyone singles out one member of the Godhead as the almost sole recipient of his devotion, to the exclusion of the others, that is the moment when spiritual instability begins to replace sense and reason.

The proper course for all of us is to stay in the mainstream of the Church. This is the Lord's church, and it is led by the spirit of inspiration, and the practice of the Church constitutes the interpretation of the scripture. ("Our Relationship with the Lord," BYU Devotional Address, 2 March 1982, pp. 97-103.)

Chapter Nineteen

The Adam-God Theory

[The supposed Adam-God theory states that Adam is our father in heaven, that he created the spirit and body of Jesus Christ as well as the spirits of all mankind. It also states that he is the god whom we worship. The theory originates with certain perceptions of a few statements made by some of the early Brethren, most notably Brigham Young.[5] The theory has been officially denounced as being totally false by the First Presidency.[6] Though the theory itself has been rejected and repudiated, no *official* explanation of it has been given by the Brethren. Various

---

5. The following quotation from Brigham Young is given to illustrate these early teachings. It is followed by another contradicting quotation from him:

"He is Michael, the Archangel, the Ancient of Days! about whom holy men have written and spoken—He is our Father and our God, and the only God with whom we have to do." (*Journal of Discourses* 1:50.)

On another occasion he said, "I want to tell you,...that you are well acquainted with God the heavenly Father, or the great Eloheim. You are all well acquainted with Him, for there is not a soul of you but what has lived in His house and dwelt with Him year after year;...

"There is not a person here today but what is a son or a daughter of that Being. In the spirit world [preexistence] their spirits were first begotten and brought forth, and they lived there with their parents for ages before they came here." (*Journal of Discourses* 4:216.)

6. "We warn you against the dissemination of doctrines which are not according to the scriptures and which are alleged to have been taught by some of the General Authorities of past generations. Such, for instance, is the Adam-God theory. We denounce that theory and hope that everyone will be cautioned against this and other kinds of false doctrine." (President Spencer W. Kimball, in Conference Report, Oct. 1976, p. 115.)

LDS authors, including some General Authorities, have offered their observations concerning this theory.[7] This chapter includes excerpts of addresses and other statements made by Elder McConkie wherein he comments on the Adam-God theory.]

INTERESTINGLY PRESIDENT BRIGHAM YOUNG has said some...things [about Adam being God] which are in contradiction to other quotations from him. (Correspondence from Elder Bruce R. McConkie to Walter M. Horne, 13 September 1972.)

THERE ARE THOSE who believe or say they believe that Adam is our father and our god, that he is the father of our spirits and our bodies, and that he is the one we worship.

The devil keeps this heresy alive as a means of obtaining converts to cultism. It is contrary to the whole plan of salvation set forth in the scriptures, and anyone who has read the Book of Moses, and anyone who has received the temple endowment, has no excuse whatever for being led astray by it. Those who are so ensnared reject the living prophet and close their ears to the apostles of their day. "We will follow those who went before," they say. And having so determined, they soon are ready to enter polygamous relationships that destroy their souls.

We worship the Father, in the name of the Son, by the power of the Holy Ghost; and Adam is their foremost servant, by whom the peopling of our planet was commenced. ("The Seven Deadly Heresies," in *1980 Devotional Speeches of the Year* [1981], 1 June 1980, p. 78.)

EVERY WORD THAT a man who is a prophet speaks is not a prophetic utterance. Joseph Smith taught that a prophet is not always a prophet, only when he is acting as such. Men who wear the prophetic mantle are still men; they have their own views; and their understanding of gospel

---

7. For further information on the Adam-God theory, see Bruce R. McConkie, *Mormon Doctrine,* p. 18; Joseph Fielding Smith, *Doctrines of Salvation,* vol 1., pp. 96-106; Van Hale, "What About the Adam-God Theory," Mormon Miscellaneous response series, pamphlet; Rodney Turner, "The Position of Adam in Latter-day Saint Scripture and Theology," unpublished master's thesis, BYU, Provo, Utah, 1953.

truths is dependent upon the study and inspiration that is theirs.

Some prophets—I say it respectfully—know more and have greater inspiration than others. Thus, if Brigham Young, who was one of the greatest of the prophets, said something about Adam which is out of harmony with what is in the Book of Moses and in Section 78, it is the scripture that prevails. This is one of the reasons we call our scriptures the *Standard Works*. They are the standards of judgment and the measuring rod against which all doctrines and views are weighed, and it does not make one particle of difference whose views are involved. The scriptures always take precedence. (Open letter from Bruce R. McConkie to "All Truth Seekers," 1 July 1980, pp. 3-4.)

IT IS ALL THE RAGE in this modern world to worship false gods of every sort and kind....There are those who worship cows and crocodiles, and others who acclaim Adam or Allah or Buddha as their supreme being....

Neither Adam, nor Allah, nor Buddha, nor any person real or imaginary will ever bring salvation to fallen man. ("The Lord God of the Restoration," *Ensign*, Oct. 1980, pp. 51-52,)

I CAN'T THINK of a better illustration of [false doctrine] than this Adam-God philosophy that goes around. People say they believe that Adam is God, that we worship him, and that he is the father of our spirits as well as the father of our bodies. They want to believe that, and the reason is that they can quote somebody of the past who seems to have said it and somebody of the present who denies it's true. Then, they can say, "Well, Spencer Kimball says this and somebody of the past said something else, and I'll choose to believe what somebody in the past said," and that enables them then to say that somebody of the past believed in plural marriage and Spencer Kimball doesn't. ("The Probationary Test of Mortality," Salt Lake Institute of Religion Devotional, 10 January 1982, p. 11.)

THERE ARE THOSE deluded cultists, and others who, unless they repent, are on the road to becoming cultists, who choose to believe we should worship Adam. They have found or should find their way out of the Church. ("Our Relationship with the Lord," BYU Devotional Address, 2 March 1982, p. 102.)

Chapter Twenty

Eternal Progression

[During his ministry, Elder McConkie often encountered members of the Church who had an incorrect understanding of the doctrine of eternal progression. Some of these false ideas originated with opinions expressed by some of the early Church leaders who felt more at liberty to offer such opinions publicly than is true of today's Church authorities.[8] For example, some individuals began to believe and teach that God is still learning new truths and is progressing in knowledge and intelligence and will continue to do so eternally. Because of his concern that this false theory might become widely accepted within the Church, Elder McConkie spoke with strength and vigor against those erroneous views.]

I WOULD LIKE to teach and testify that there is a God in heaven who is everlasting and eternal; who is infinite in all his powers and attributes; who has all wisdom, all knowledge, all might, all power, and all dominion....

Let us get a concept instilled in our minds that God is omnipotent; that he is above all things; that the very universe itself is his creation and is subject to him; that he upholds, preserves, and governs it....

Where every attribute and every characteristic is concerned, the Lord is perfect and in him is embodied the totality of whatever is involved.

---

8. For a brief review of some statements made by some of the early leaders, see *Journal of Discourses* 1:349; 6:120; 19:326; 29:65. The position of the Church could be summed up by D&C 38:1-2, which says, "Thus saith the Lord your God,...the same which knoweth all things, for all things are present before mine eyes." For further scriptural references on this subject, see 2 Nephi 9:20; Alma 26:35; D&C 88:41.

Can anyone suppose that God does not have all charity, that he falls short in integrity or honesty, or that there is any truth that he does not know?...

God is almighty;...there is no power he does not possess, no wisdom that does not reside in him, no infinite expanse of space or duration of time where his influence and power are not felt. There is nothing that the Lord God takes into his heart to do that he cannot do. He has attained to a state of glory and perfection where he is from everlasting to everlasting. To be from everlasting to everlasting the same unchangeable, unvarying being means, in effect, that he is from one preexistence to the next. He is from one eternity to the next—the same in knowledge, in power, in might, and in dominion....

I am bold to testify that these doctrines are true; that God is all that the revelations say that he is; that there is no power, no might, no omnipotence, that excels him. (*The Lord God of Joseph Smith*, Brigham Young University Speeches of the Year [4 Jan.1972], pp. 2, 4, 7.)

THERE IS A STATEMENT in our literature that says that the Prophet and his associates learned, by translating the papyrus received from the catacombs of Egypt, that life had been going on in this system for 2,555,000,000 years. It seems reasonable to me that a god who has been creating, expanding, governing, and regulating worlds for a period that is so infinite that you and I have no way of comprehending its duration has attained a state where he knows all things and nothing is withheld. (*The Lord God of Joseph Smith*, Brigham Young University Speeches of the Year [4 Jan. 1972, p. 7.)

AS I UNDERSTAND IT, God is progressing in that his dominions and kingdoms become more extensive and complex, but is not progressing in charity, love, truth, and the other attributes of godliness, all of which he possesses in their eternal fulness. This is what I understand the scriptures to teach and it is certainly what the Prophet Joseph Smith taught in most emphatic, unequivocal language as recorded in the Lectures on Faith. About a year ago I spoke on this subject in the devotional at the BYU quoting extensively from the Prophet. My talk is published by the BYU under the title, "The Lord God of Joseph Smith." Interestingly President Brigham Young has said some similar things which are in contradiction to other quotations from him. I have never researched the various matters my friend...quotes, and do not know whether they are taken out of context or not....

I have heard President Joseph Fielding Smith say many times that all men are accountable for what they teach and that all teachings must be measured against the revealed statements in the Standard Works. I personally think there is no question about the doctrine involved and that in due course all the faithful brethren, whether in this life or in the spirit world, will have a perfect understanding and be united wholly and totally where the concepts are concerned. (Correspondence from Bruce R. McConkie to Walter M. Horne, 13 September 1972. Original letter in possession of the author.)

IN OUR FINITE CIRCUMSTANCES we have no ability or power to comprehend the might and omnipotence of the Father. We can look at the stars in the heavens, we can view the Milky Way, we can see all the worlds and orbs that have been created in their spheres, we can examine all the life on this planet with which we are familiar, and by doing this we can begin to get a concept of the glorious, infinite, unlimited intelligence by which all these things are—and all these things taken together and more dramatize the fulness of the glory of the Father. ("Celestial Marriage," in *1977 Devotional Speeches of the Year* [1978], p. 170.)

THERE ARE THOSE who say that God is progressing in knowledge and is learning new truths.

This is false—utterly, totally, and completely. There is not one sliver of truth in it. It grows out of a wholly twisted and incorrect view of the King Follett Sermon and of what is meant by eternal progression.

God progresses in the sense that his kingdoms increase and his dominions multiply—not in the sense that he learns new truths and discovers new laws. God is not a student. He is not a laboratory technician. He is not postulating new theories on the basis of past experiences. He has indeed graduated to that state of exaltation that consists of knowing all things and having all power.

The life that God lives is named *eternal life*. His name, one of them, is "Eternal," using that word as a noun and not as an adjective, and he uses that name to identify the type of life that he lives. God's life is eternal life, and eternal life is God's life. They are one and the same. Eternal life is the reward we shall obtain if we believe and obey and walk uprightly before him. And eternal life consists of two things. It consists of life in the family unit, and, also, of inheriting, receiving, and possessing the fulness of the glory of the Father. Anyone who has each of these things is an inheritor and possessor of the greatest of all gifts of God, which is eternal life.

Eternal progression consists of living the kind of life God lives and of increasing in kingdoms and dominions everlastingly. Why anyone should suppose that an infinite and eternal being who has presided in our universe for almost 2,555,000,000 years, who made the sidereal heavens, whose creations are more numerous than the particles of the earth, and who is aware of the fall of every sparrow—why anyone would suppose that such a being has more to learn and new truths to discover in the laboratories of eternity is totally beyond my comprehension.

Will he one day learn something that will destroy the plan of salvation and turn man and the universe into an uncreated nothingness? Will he discover a better plan of salvation than the one he has already given to men in worlds without number?

The saving truth, as revealed to and taught, formally and officially, by the Prophet Joseph Smith in the Lectures on Faith is that God is omnipotent, omniscient, and omnipresent. He knows all things, he has all power, and he is everywhere present by the power of his Spirit. And unless we know and believe this doctrine we cannot gain faith unto life and salvation.

Joseph Smith also taught in the Lectures on Faith "that three things are necessary in order that any rational and intelligent being may exercise faith in God unto life and salvation." These he named as—

1. The idea that he actually exists;
2. A *correct* idea of his character, perfections, and attributes; and
3. An actual knowledge that the course of life which he is pursuing is according to the divine will.

The attributes of God are given as knowledge, faith or power, justice, judgement, mercy, and truth. The perfections of God are named as "the perfections which belong to all of the attributes of his nature," which is to say that God possesses and has all knowledge, all faith or power, all justice, all judgment, all mercy, and all truth. He is indeed the very embodiment and personification and source of all these attributes. Does anyone suppose that God can be more honest than he already is? Neither need any suppose there are truths he does not know or knowledge he does not possess.

Thus Joseph Smith taught, and these are his words:

"Without the knowledge of all things, God would not be able to save any portion of his creatures; for it is by reason of the knowledge which he has of all things, from the beginning to the end, that enables him to give that understanding to his creatures by which they are made partakers of eternal life; and if it were not for the idea existing in the minds of men that God had all knowledge it would be impossible for them to exercise faith in him." (*Mormon Doctrine*, p. 264.) If God is just dabbling with a few truths he has already chanced to learn or experimenting with a few facts he has already discovered, we have no idea as to the real end and purpose of creation. ("The Seven Deadly Heresies," in *1980 Devotional Speeches of the Year* [1981], pp 75-76.)

AND THERE ARE even those who champion the almost unbelievable theory that God is an eternal student enrolled in the University of the Universe, where he is busily engaged in learning new truths and amassing new and strange knowledge that he never knew before.

How belittling it is—it borders on blasphemy—to demean the Lord God Omnipotent by saying...he is ever learning but never able to come to a knowledge of all truth (see 2 Tim. 3:7)....

He is omnipotent, omniscient, and omnipresent. He has all power, knows all things, and, by the power of his Spirit, is in and through all things....

And certainly a student god, with finite powers, who is just experimenting in the eternal laboratories, is not a being in whom I, at least, would feel inclined to repose an infinite trust....

Turn ye to the Lord our God. Repent of all your sins. Forsake false doctrines; flee from false gods; seek the truth.

Do not be deceived by the doctrines of men or of devils. Cleave unto the truth and be believing as was the case with those of old for whom the heavens were rent and who made their callings and election sure in the days of their mortal probation. ("The Lord God of the Restoration," *Ensign*, Nov. 1980, pp. 50-52.)

WHO IS ELOHIM? He is God the Eternal Father. He is a glorified and exalted personage. He has a body of flesh and bones as tangible as man's. In the language of Adam, Man of Holiness is his name. He is omnipotent, omniscient, and omnipresent. He knows all things and has all power—not simply as pertaining to us or in some prescribed sphere or realm—but in the absolute, eternal, and unlimited sense. In the ultimate sense, he is the Creator. And anything you may have heard to the contrary, whether in the creeds of Christendom or the mouthings of intellectuals who, in their own eyes, know more than the Lord, is false. ("The Three Pillars of Eternity," in *Brigham Young University 1981 Fireside and Devotional Speeches* [1981], pp. 31-32.)

SOMEBODY CAN TEACH that God is progressing in knowledge. And if he begins to believe it, and emphasizes it unduly, and it becomes a ruling thing in his life, then, as the *Lectures on Faith* say, it is not possible for him to have faith unto life and salvation. He is required to believe, in the Prophet's language, that God is omnipotent, omniscient, and omnipresent, that he has all power and he knows all things. ("The Foolishness of Teaching," address to seminary and institute personnel [The Church of Jesus Christ of Latter-day Saints, 1981], p. 12.)

THERE ARE OTHERS—in the main they are intellectuals without strong testimonies—who postulate that God does not know all things but is progressing in truth and knowledge and will do so everlastingly. These, unless they repent, will live and die weak in the faith and will fall short of inheriting what might have been theirs in eternity. ("Our Relationship with the Lord," p. 102.)

LET THERE BE no mistake about this. God has all power; he is the Almighty. He knows all things, and there is nothing in all eternity, in universe upon universe, that he does not know. Joseph Smith so taught, and all our scriptures, ancient and modern, bear a concordant testimony. He is not a student god, and he is not progressing in knowledge or learning new truths. If he knows how to create and govern worlds without number, and all that on them is, what is there left for him to learn? Also, he is omnipresent, meaning that by the power of his spirit he is in all things, and through all things, and round about all things. ("The Mystery of Godliness," in *Brigham Young University 1984-85 Devotional and Fireside Speeches* [1985], p. 52.)

Chapter Twenty-One

Intellectualism

WE HAVE NO INTEREST in teaching by the wisdom or learning or according to the precepts of men. We want to teach the gospel the way the Lord would have us teach it, and to do it under the power and influence of the Holy Ghost. If we will do that, we will teach sound doctrine. It will be the truth. It will build faith and increase righteousness in the hearts of men, and they will be led along that path which leads to the celestial world.

But if we teach without the Spirit of the Lord, if we are not guided by the Holy Ghost, we will be teaching at our peril. It is a serious thing to teach false doctrine, to teach that which is not true, to teach that which does not build faith in the hearts of men. ("The Message of the Restoration," *Improvement Era*, Nov. 1949, p. 727.)

THE ISSUE IS NOT what men purport to believe; it is whether, having believed the truth, they also get the power of God into their lives. Salvation does not come by reading about religion, by learning that holy men in former days had spiritual experiences. It is not found through research in musty archives; it does not spring forth as the result of intellectual dialogues about religious matters. Salvation is born of obedience to the laws and ordinances of the gospel; salvation comes to those who obey the statutes and judgements of that God who created it and ordained the laws whereby it might be gained. ("Our Gospel Came Not Unto You in Word Only...," *Improvement Era*, Dec. 1968, p. 103.)

TRUE RELIGION DEALS with spiritual things. We do not come to a knowledge of God and his laws through intellectuality, or by research, or by reason. I have an average mind—one that is neither better nor worse than the general run of mankind. In the realm of intellectual attainment I have a doctor's degree, and I hope my sons after me will reach a similar goal. In their sphere, education and intellectuality are devoutly to be desired.

But when contrasted with spiritual endowments, they are of but slight and passing worth. From an eternal perspective what each of us needs is a Ph.D. in faith and righteousness. The things that will profit us everlastingly are not the power to reason, but the ability to receive revelation; not the truths learned by study, but the knowledge gained by faith; not what we know about the things of the world, but our knowledge of God and his laws....

I know people who can talk endlessly about religion but who have never had a religious experience. I know people who have written books about religion but who have about as much spirituality as a cedar post. Their interest in gospel doctrine is to defend their own speculative views rather than to find out what the Lord thinks about whatever is involved. Their conversations and their writings are in the realm of reason and the intellect; the Spirit of God has not touched their souls; they have not been born again and become new creatures of the Holy Ghost; they have not received revelation. ("The Lord's People Receive Revelation," *Ensign*, June 1971, pp. 77-78.)

I DESIRE...TO COUNSEL the Latter-day Saints to take an affirmative, wholesome attitude toward world and national conditions; to turn their backs on everything that is evil and destructive; to look for that which is good and edifying in all things; to praise the Lord for his goodness and grace in giving us the glories and wonders of his everlasting gospel.

In view of all that prevails in the world, it might be easy to center our attention on negative or evil things, or to dissipate our energies on causes and enterprises of doubtful worth and questionable productivity.

I am fully aware of the divine decree to be actively engaged in a good cause; of the fact that every true principle which works for the freedom and blessing of mankind has the Lord's approval; of the need to sustain and support those who espouse proper causes and advocate true principles—all of which things we also should do in the best and most beneficial way we can. The issue, I think, is not *what* we should do but *how* we should do it; and I maintain that the most beneficial and productive thing which Latter-day Saints can do to strengthen every good and proper cause is to live and teach the principles of the everlasting gospel.

There may be those who have special gifts and needs to serve in other fields, but as far as I am concerned, with the knowledge and testimony that I have, there is nothing I can do for the time and season of this mortal probation that is more important than to use all my strength, energy and ability in spreading and perfecting the cause of truth and righteousness, both in the Church and among our Father's other children. ("Think on These Things," *Ensign*, Jan. 1974, pp. 47-48.)

WE ARE SAVED or damned by what we believe. If we believe in the Lord Jesus Christ and the saving truths of his everlasting gospel, we have a hope of eternal life. If our beliefs embrace the philosophies of men and the vagaries of the world, they may lead to destruction. Nearly the whole educational world goes blithely along, espousing the false theories of organic evolution, which rule out the fall of man and the atonement of Christ. Men worship at the shrine of intellectuality without ever realizing that religion is a thing of the Spirit....Our schools teach some principles of socialism, of communism, of so-called women's liberation, of curtailing population growth and the like—much of which runs counter to revealed gospel truths. ("The Ten Commandments of a Peculiar People," in *Speeches of the Year 1975* [1976], p. 37).

WE ARE CALLED Mormons. Many people look upon us as a singular sect as they cry: "Delusion, false prophets, polygamy," as once was so common; or "Racists, anti-women, patriarchal dictators," as some now say; or "Worshipers of Adam and deniers of Christ and his grace," as others falsely acclaim; or whatever sophistry of the moment will sow the seeds of prejudice among those who otherwise might learn who we are and what we believe.

Oftentimes it seems to us that these cries from shallow minds and these self-serving statements of those who resent our rapid growth and increasing influence in the world and these voices whose social and political views we do not espouse are but another evidence of the truth and divinity of the work itself. The devil is not dead, and as his voice was once raised in cries of "Crucify him, crucify him," so it now shrieks in shrilling hysteria against Christ's people in this day.

We feel it is not too much to ask, in this age of enlightenment and open dialogue, to let us be the ones who tell who we are, what we believe, and why our cause is going forward in such a marvelous way....

Among us, women and the family unit are held in higher esteem than anywhere else on earth. Our mothers and wives and daughters receive greater honors, perform more responsible labors, and develop their native talents to a greater degree than do any of the women of the world.

Indeed the whole aim and purpose of the gospel is to enable men and women—united as one in the Lord—to create for themselves eternal family units in eternity. Celestial marriage prepares us for the greatest joy and happiness known to mortals and for eternal life in the realms ahead.

May we say, as many have done before, that what men call Mormonism is the very system of laws and truths which will make of earth a heaven and of man a god. ("The Mystery of Mormonism,"*Ensign,* Nov. 1979, pp. 53, 55.)

I THINK THAT the great majority of the members of the Church believe and understand true doctrines and seek to apply true principles in their lives. Unfortunately, there are a few people who agitate and stir these matters up, who have some personal ax to grind, and who desire to spread philosophies of their own, philosophies that, as near as the judges in Israel can discern, are not in harmony with the mind and will and purpose of the Lord. ("The Seven Deadly Heresies," in *1980 Devotional Speeches of the Year* [1981], p. 80.)

PRESIDENT BRIGHAM YOUNG—of blessed memory who now reigns in heavenly courts—devised this rallying cry: "The Kingdom of God or nothing." It was echoed by his associates and might well be revived among us.

A wise cleric of a former day leaves us this counsel: "If you have not chosen the kingdom of God first, it will in the end make no difference what you have chosen instead."

The kingdom of God on earth is The Church of Jesus Christ of Latter-day Saints, which prepares men for an inheritance in the kingdom of God in heaven, which is the celestial kingdom.

When we put first in our lives the things of God's kingdom, we are speaking of the earthly kingdom which prepares us for the heavenly kingdom.

With us, in this life and in the life to come, it is and should be the kingdom of God or nothing.

The kingdom of God, both in time and in eternity, is governed by the spirit of inspiration. It always sends forth the mind and will of the Lord, whether by his own voice or by the voice of his servants it is the same. (See D&C 1:38.)

On every issue it behooves us to determine what the Lord would have us do and what counsel he has given through the appointed officers of his kingdom on earth.

No true Latter-day Saint will ever take a stand that is in opposition to what the Lord has revealed to those who direct the affairs of his earthly kingdom.

No Latter-day Saint who is true and faithful in all things will ever pursue a course, or espouse a cause, or publish an article or book that weakens or destroys faith.

There is, in fact, no such thing as neutrality where the gospel is concerned....

If we do not sustain and uphold and support the kingdom of God in all things, we are thereby aiding a cause other than the Lord's. ("The Caravan Moves On," *Ensign*, Nov. 1984, pp. 84-85.)

Chapter Twenty-Two

Evolution

THERE ARE THOSE who believe that the theory of organic evolution runs counter to the plain and explicit principles set forth in the holy scriptures as these have been interpreted and taught by Joseph Smith and his associates. There are others who think that evolution is the system used by the Lord to form plant and animal life and to place man on earth.

May I say that all truth is in agreement, that true religion and true science bear the same witness, and that in the true and full sense, true science is part of true religion. But may I also raise some questions of a serious nature. Is there any way to harmonize the false religions of the Dark Ages with the truths of science as they have now been discovered? Is there any way to harmonize the revealed religion that has come to us with the theoretical postulates of Darwinism and the diverse speculations descending therefrom?

Should we accept the famous document of the First Presidency issued in the days of President Joseph F. Smith and entitled "The Origin of Man" as meaning exactly what it says? Is it the doctrine of the gospel that Adam stood next to Christ in power and might and intelligence before the foundations of the world were laid; that Adam was placed on this earth as an immortal being; that there was no death in the world for him or for any form of life until after the Fall; that the fall of Adam brought temporal and spiritual death into the world; that this temporal death passed upon all forms of life, upon man and animal and fish and fowl and plant life; that Christ came to ransom man and all forms of life from the effects of the temporal death brought into the world through the Fall, and in the case of man from a spiritual death also; and that this ransom includes a resurrection for man and for all forms of life? Can you harmonize these things with the evolutionary postulate that death has always existed and that the various forms of life have evolved from preceding forms over astronomically long periods of time?...

I believe that the atonement of Christ is the great and eternal foundation upon which revealed religion rests. I believe that no man can be saved unless he believes that our Lord's atoning sacrifice brings immortality to all and eternal life to those who believe and obey, and no man can believe in the atonement unless he accepts both the divine Sonship of Christ and the fall of Adam.

My reasoning causes me to conclude that if death has always prevailed in the world, then there was no fall of Adam that brought death to all forms of life; that if Adam did not fall, there is no need for an atonement; that if there was no atonement, there is no salvation, no resurrection, and no eternal life; and that if there was no atonement, there is nothing in all of the glorious promises that the Lord has given us. I believe that the Fall affects man, all forms of life, and the earth itself, and that the atonement affects man, all forms of life, and the earth itself. ("The Seven Deadly Heresies," in *1980 Devotional Speeches of the Year* [1981], pp. 76-77.)

HERE ARE SOME DOCTRINES that weaken faith and may damn. It depends on how inured a person gets to them, and how much emphasis he puts on them, and how much the doctrine begins to govern the affairs of his life. Evolution is one of them. Somebody can get so wrapped up in so-called organic evolution that he ends up not believing in the atoning sacrifice of the Lord Jesus. Such a course leads to damnation. ("The Foolishness of Teaching," [address to seminary and institute personnel, published by The Church of Jesus Christ of Latter-day Saints, 1981], p. 12.)

AS THE INTERPOLATIVE exposition in the divine word explains, "I, the Lord God, planted a garden eastward in Eden, and there I put the man whom I had formed." (Moses 3:8.) Adam, our father, dwelt in the Garden of Eden. He was the *first man of all men* in the day of his creation, and he became the *first flesh of all flesh* through the Fall. Because of the Fall "all things" changed from their spiritual state to a natural state. And thus we read: "And out of the ground made I, the Lord God, to grow every tree, *naturally*, that is pleasant to the sight of man; and man could behold it. And it became also a living soul. For it was *spiritual* in the day that I created it." (Moses 3:9; italics added.)

There is no evolving from one species to another in any of this. The account is speaking of "every tree" and of "all things." Considering them as one collective unit, the account continues: "It remaineth in the sphere in which I, God, created it, yea, even all things which I prepared for the use of man; and man saw that it was good for food." (Moses 3:9.)...

These revealed verities about the creation of all things run counter to many of the speculations and theoretical postulates of the world. They are, however, what the inspired word sets forth, and we are duty bound to accept them. ("Christ and the Creation," *Ensign*, June 1982, p. 15.)

Chapter Twenty-Three

Gospel Scholarship, Teaching, and the Mysteries

I THINK WE HAVE the obligation, the great underlying responsibility, to learn the doctrines of the Church so that we will be able to serve in the kingdom, so that we will be able to carry the message of salvation to our Father's other children, and so that we will be able to live in such a manner as to have peace and joy ourselves, and gain this hope of glorious exaltation and eternal life. ("On Reading the Standard Works," *Improvement Era*, Dec. 1959, p. 935.)

THERE ISN'T ANYONE, I think, who more fervently and devotedly and sincerely believes that Latter-day Saints should be gospel scholars than I do. I think we ought to search the scriptures and learn the truths of salvation and be qualified from an intellectual standpoint and a reasoning standpoint to give a reason for the hope that is within us. I think we ought to know and understand the doctrines of salvation, insofar as is possible for mortal men in our circumstances to know them. (*Ye Are My Witnesses*, Brigham Young University Speeches of the Year, 14 Mar. 1967, p. 4.)

I KNOW THAT we talk about such a supposedly simple thing as faith, and we think, well, it is the *first* principle of the gospel, it is the foundation—why do we spend our time on that? Why don't we get off on some of the mysteries of the kingdom?

There will be time enough to get off on the mysteries of the kingdom. There will be time enough to know the deep and the hidden and the hard things of the laws pertaining to salvation when we have really laid a foundation of faith. As a matter of fact, the deep and the hidden and the hard things, and the things that some of us would like to seek, can only come to us after we have acquired this foundation of faith.

You cannot teach calculus to somebody until he first has all of the basic courses in arithmetic and algebra and geometry and so on. He has to have a foundation on which to build. We are in effect newborn babes in Christ. We have to grow up. We are working with milk now. The time will come when we have been fed enough of the bread of life and the spiritual things that we can eat and digest the meat of the gospel. But it will come to us through the process of enlarging and increasing our faith; and until we have done that, we are well off to center the faculties and capacities and abilities that we have in some of these things that we ordinarily have thought were basic and fundamental and something not as interesting perhaps as the mysterious and the hidden things. (*Lord, Increase our Faith,* Brigham Young University Speeches of the Year, 31 Oct. 1967, p. 10.)

IT JUST MAY be that my salvation (and yours also!) does in fact depend upon our ability to understand the writings of Isaiah as fully and truly as Nephi understood them. ("Ten Keys to Understanding Isaiah," *Ensign*, Oct. 1973, p. 78.)

WE HAVE IN THE CHURCH an untapped, almost unknown, treasury of inspiring and faith-promoting stories. They are the best of their kind and there are thousands of them.

One reason they are the best and most inspiring faith-promoting stories is because they were selected and edited by the Lord himself. They are the ones he had his prophets choose and place in the holy scriptures so that we would have samples before us of how to act and what to do in all the circumstances that confront us in life.

They are stories of real people who faced real problems and who solved them in a way that was pleasing to the Lord. They have been preserved for us so that we will know how to act and what to do in all the affairs of our daily lives....

There is, of course, nothing wrong with telling a modern faith-promoting story, one that has happened in our dispensation, one that occurred in the lives of living people whom we know, whose voice we can hear, and whose spirit we can feel. Indeed, this should be encouraged to the full. We should make every effort to show that the same things are happening in the lives of the Saints today as transpired among the faithful of old. Unless our religion is a living thing that changes the lives of people in whose nostrils the breath of life is now inhaled, it has no saving power....

Perhaps the perfect pattern in presenting faith-promoting stories is to teach what is found in the scriptures and then to put a seal of living reality upon it by telling a similar and equivalent thing that has happened in our dispensation and to our people and—most ideally—to us as individuals. ("The How and Why of Faith-promoting Stories," *New Era*, July 1978, pp. 4-5.)

REAL, TRUE, GENUINE, Spirit-born worship, in a sacrament meeting for instance, comes when a speaker speaks by the power of the Holy Ghost, and when a congregation hears by the power of the Holy Ghost. So the speaker gives the word of the Lord, and the congregation receives the word of the Lord. Now that is not the norm, I think, in our sacrament meetings. At least it does not happen anywhere nearly as often as it ought to happen. What happens is this: the congregation comes together in fasting and prayer, pondering the things of the Spirit, desiring to be fed. They bring a gallon jug. The speaker comes in his worldly wisdom and he brings a little pint bottle and he pours his pint bottle out and it rattles around in the gallon jug. Or else, as sometimes happens, the preacher gets his errand from the Lord and gets in tune with the Spirit and comes with a gallon jug to deliver a message, and there is not anybody in the congregation that brought anything bigger than a cup. And he pours out the gallon of eternal truth and people get just a little sample, enough to quench a moment's eternal thirst, instead of getting the real message that is involved. It takes teacher and student, it takes preacher and congregation, both of them uniting in faith to have a proper preaching or teaching situation. ("The Foolishness of Teaching," [address to seminary and institute personnel, published by The Church of Jesus Christ of Latter-day Saints, 1981], p. 9.)

LET ME SAY just a word about false doctrine. We are supposed to teach. Pitfalls we are supposed to avoid are the teaching of false doctrine; teaching ethics in preference to doctrine, compromising our doctrines with the philosophies of the world; entertaining rather than teaching, and using games and gimmicks rather than sound doctrine, coddling students, as President Clark expressed it. ("The Foolishness of Teaching," [address to seminary and institute personnel, published by The Church of Jesus Christ of Latter-day Saints, 1981], p. 11.)

THERE IS KNOWLEDGE and there are spiritual experiences to be gained from reading, pondering, and praying about the scriptures which can be gained in no other way. No matter how devoted and active members of the Church are in administrative matters, they will never gain the great blessings which come from scriptural study unless they pay the price of that study and thus make the written word a part of their lives. ("The Teacher's Divine Commission," *Ensign*, Apr. 1979, p. 23.)

MY SUGGESTION, relative to all doctrines and all principles, is that we become students of holy writ, and that we conform our thinking and our beliefs to what is found in the standard works. We need to be less concerned about the views and opinions that others have expressed and drink directly from the fountain the Lord has given us. Then we shall come to a true understanding of the points of his doctrine. And if we pursue such a course, we will soon find that it proceeds in a different direction than the one that the world pursues. We will not be troubled with the intellectual views and expressions of uninspired people. We will soon obtain for ourselves the witness of the Spirit that we are pursuing a course that is pleasing to the Lord, and this knowledge will have a cleansing and sanctifying and edifying influence upon us. ("The Seven Deadly Heresies," in *1980 Devotional Speeches of the Year* [1981], p. 79.)

BECAUSE GOD STANDS revealed or remains forever unknown, and because the things of God are known only by the power of the Spirit, perhaps we should redefine a mystery. In the gospel sense, a mystery is something beyond *carnal* comprehension.
 The saints are in a position to comprehend all mysteries, to understand all doctrine, and eventually to know all things. These high levels of intelligence are reached only through faith and obedience and righteousness. A person who relies on the intellect alone and who does not keep the commandments can never, worlds without end, comprehend the mystery of godliness.
 There is probably more ignorance and confusion as to the mystery of godliness than there is about any other doctrine. As set forth in the three creeds of Christendom—the Nicene, the Apostles', and the Athanasian, which God himself said were an abomination in his sight—and as defined in the articles of religion of the various denominations, this doctrine is a mass of confusion and a mountain of falsity.

Even in the Church, thanks to a lack of knowledge and to intellectuality and the worldly enticement to conform to the general beliefs of an apostate Christendom, there are those who have fallen prey to many false delusions about deity....

The doctrine is what the doctrine is, and the concepts are what the concepts are. It is of no moment whatever that they spread confusion among uninspired worshippers at divers shrines, or among intellectuals whose interest in religion is purely academic and who rely on the power of the mind rather than the power of the Spirit for understanding.

Gospel truths are known and understood only by the power of the Spirit. Eternal life—which is to know God—is such an infinitely great reward that men must study, ponder, and pray, with all their hearts, to gain the needed knowledge.

The Lord gives his truths line upon line and precept upon precept to those who believe and obey. Saving truths come by revelation to prophets, not by reason to false priests or doctors of debate, dissension, and divisiveness. ("The Mystery of Godliness," BYU Fireside Address, 6 Jan. 1985, pp. 49-51.)

WE WOULD LIKE all Latter-day Saint sisters to read all of the Standard Works, to ponder in their hearts the eternal truths that are found in them, and to get on their knees and ask the Lord in sincerity and in faith for understanding and comprehension and guidance. We would like each of you to read them, either by yourself, or with your husband, or with your families, and not simply read the words but ponder and pray about their content so that there will come into your lives the desires for righteousness that grow out of the study of the pure, perfect word of God. We would like the Church to start drinking at the fountain—undiluted—the pure, perfect message that the Lord has given by the mouths of his prophets, the message found in the Standard Works of the Church.

We want to have peace and joy and happiness in this life and be inheritors of eternal life in the world to come. These are the two greatest blessings that it is possible for people to inherit. We can gain them by reading and learning the words of eternal life, here and now, and by keeping the commandments which prepare us for immortal glory in the world to come.

We issue the challenge to all of the women of the Church to join with the brethren of the Church to drink at the fountain; to study the Standard

Works of the Church; to read, ponder, and pray, to ask God for understanding, to get the power of the Holy Spirit into their lives so that each person knows, independent of anyone else, of the truth and divinity of these things, for out of that course comes the joy and satisfaction and peace that the gospel offers. ("Drink from the Fountain," *Ensign*, Apr. 1975, pp. 70, 72.)

Chapter Twenty-Four

Revelation and the Gifts of the Spirit

BY FAITH ALL things can be done. There is nothing too hard for the Lord, and if we have faith, we can do whatever is requisite, according to his mind and will. By faith the worlds were made; by faith the elements can be controlled, rivers turned out of their courses, mountains removed. By faith we can have angels minister to us, see our sick healed, and the dead raised; and what is more important than all this, by faith we can live so as to become the sons of God and be joint heirs with Jesus Christ, entitled to receive and inherit and possess, as he has done before, the fulness of the kingdom of the Father. (Conference Report, Oct. 1953, p. 125.)

WHEN PEOPLE LEARN by the power of the Holy Ghost that the Lord has revealed His Gospel anew, they are obligated, at the peril of losing their inheritance in the Celestial Kingdom, to join the Church by baptism and receive the gift of the Holy Ghost by the laying on of hands....

This gift is bestowed only by the laying on of hands. A legal administrator, who actually represents Deity, promises the newly baptized person that he, on certain terms and conditions, can gain the constant companionship of the Spirit. This gift is reserved for the Saints.

The Holy Ghost may give a flash of revelation to anyone who sincerely seeks truth, a flash comparable to lightning breaking into the darkness of a night storm. But the constant companionship of the Spirit, comparable to walking in the full blaze of the noonday sun, is reserved for those who join the Church and keep the commandments.

Those who enjoy the gift of the Holy Ghost are in the process of sanctifying their lives. The Holy Ghost is a sanctifier; when men receive the baptism of fire, evil and iniquity is burned out of their souls as though by fire. ("What Is Meant by 'The Holy Spirit,'" *Instructor*, Feb. 1965, pp. 56-57.)

AS A PEOPLE, we are in the habit of saying that we believe in latter-day revelation. We announce quite boldly that the heavens have been opened, that God has spoken in our day, that angels have ministered to men, that there have been visions and revelations, and that no gift or grace possessed by the Ancients has been withheld—it has all been revealed anew in our day.

But, ordinarily, when we talk in this way, we are thinking of Joseph Smith, Brigham Young or David O. McKay. We are thinking of apostles and prophets—men who are called, selected or foreordained to hold the positions which they hold and to do the ministerial service that is theirs. We are thinking of them and of the general principle of the Church itself operating by revelation.

Now there is no question at all about this: The organization that we belong to is the Lord's kingdom—it is literally such. As the kingdom of God on earth, it is designed to prepare and qualify us to go to the kingdom of God in heaven which is the celestial kingdom, and this Church *is* guided by revelation. I have sat in meetings with the brethren on several occasions when President McKay, who is the prophet of God on earth, has said in humility and with fervent testimony that the veil is thin, that the Lord is guiding and directing the affairs of the Church, and that it is His Church and He is making His will manifest....

But what I desire to point attention to today is the fact that revelation is not restricted to the prophet of God on earth. The visions of eternity are not reserved for apostles—they are not reserved for the General Authorities. Revelation is something that should be received by every individual. God is no respecter of persons, and every soul, in the ultimate sense, is just as precious in His sight as the souls of those that are called to positions of leadership. Because He operates on principles of eternal, universal and never-deviating law, any individual that abides the law which entitles him to get revelation can know exactly and precisely what President McKay knows, can entertain angels just as well as Joseph Smith entertained them, and can be in tune in full measure with all of the things of the Spirit.

Now for a text I read...these words of the Prophet Joseph Smith. He said: "Reading the experience of others, or the revelation given to *them*, can never give *us* a comprehensive view of our condition and true relation to God. Knowledge of these things can only be obtained by experience through the ordinances of God set forth for that purpose. Could you gaze into heaven five minutes, you would know more than you would by reading all that ever was written on the subject." (*Teachings of the Prophet Joseph Smith*, p. 324.)...

I think our concern is to get personal revelation, to know for ourselves, independent of any other individual...what the mind and the will of the Lord is as pertaining to his Church and as pertaining to us in our individual concerns....

My suggestion is that we need to devote an increasingly large portion of our time in the actual pursuit of knowledge in the spiritual realm. When we deal with spiritual realities, we are not talking about gaining something by reason alone, we are not talking about conveying in some way knowledge to the mind or the spirit that is within us through the senses alone, but we are talking about revelation. We are talking about learning how to come to a knowledge of the things of God by attuning the spirit that we have to the eternal Spirit of God. Such a course, primarily, is the channel and way that revelation comes to an individual....

Now I say that we are *entitled* to revelation. I say that every member of the Church, independent and irrespective of any position that he may hold, is entitled to get revelation from the Holy Ghost; he is entitled to entertain angels; he is entitled to view the visions of eternity; and if we would like to go the full measure, he is entitled to see God the same way that any prophet in literal and actual reality has seen the face of Deity....

We need *religious experience.* we need to become personally involved with God....

What counts in the field of religion is to become a personal participant in it. Instead of reading all that has been written and evaluating all that all the scholars of all the world have said about heaven and hell, we need to do what the Prophet said: gaze five minutes into heaven. As a consequence, we would know more than all that has ever been evaluated and written and analyzed on the subject.

Religion is a matter of getting the Holy Ghost into the life of an individual. We study, of course, and we need to evaluate. And by virtue of our study we come up with some foundations that get us into the frame of mind so that we *can* seek the things of the Spirit. But in the end the result is *getting our souls touched by the Spirit of God.*

Would you like a formula to tell you how to get personal revelation? It might be written in many ways. My formula is simply this: 1. Search the Scriptures. 2. Keep the Commandments. 3. Ask in Faith.

Any person who will do this will get his heart so in tune with the Infinite that there will come into his being, from the "still small voice," the eternal realities of religion. And as he progresses and advances and comes nearer to God, there will be a day when he will entertain angels, when he will see visions, and the final end is to view the face of God.

Religion is a thing of the spirit. Use all your intellectuality to help you, but in the final analysis, you have to get in tune with the Lord....

When a person gets a testimony, he has thereby learned how to get in tune with the Spirit and get revelation. So, repeating the connection—getting in tune anew—he can get knowledge to direct him in his personal affairs. Then ultimately enjoying and progressing in this gift, he can get all revelations of eternity that the Prophet or all the prophets have had in all the ages. (*How to Get Personal Revelation*, [Brigham Young University Speeches of the Year 1966], pp. 1-4, 7-8.)

ABOUT THREE MONTHS ago when we were holding our Priesthood Missionary Committee seminar, Brother Harold B. Lee was speaking and he began his talk by looking at the assembled group of about 40 people, some 30 of them were on the Priesthood Missionary Committee; and he said, "Brethren, there are assembled in this room men of sufficient spiritual stature so that if all the General Authorities were taken and we had to totally reorganize the Church from this group, the Church would continue without missing a heartbeat." That's an accurate substance quotation from his statement....

The opinions and views, even of a prophet, may contain error, unless those opinions and views were inspired by the Spirit. Inspired scripture or statements should be accepted as such. We have this problem however. Paul was one of the greatest theologian-prophets of all the ages, but he had some opinions that weren't in complete accord with the Lord's feelings and he wrote some of them down in his epistles, but being wise and discreet he labeled them as such. He said, "This is what I think": when he got through telling that he said, "Now this is what the Lord thinks." Paul's views, his private opinions, were not very good sometimes.

We even have one of these instances in the Book of Mormon, one where Alma had some personal views on the resurrection. He labeled it as opinion when he wrote it down, and we can stretch and twist and manage to make his personal view conform with what is true, since we have had revelation that tells us what is true on the point. But if we did not have latter-day revelation, it would not be clear, and so we have to conclude that Alma did not have a very good judgment on the particular point that he labeled his opinion.

Brigham Young did the same thing. He said some things on some subjects and they were Brigham Young's idea and they weren't the Lord's idea. A classical story in the Church on this point is that he talked, in the morning session of Conference, and gave a dynamic, fiery speech on a certain subject and then he came back in the afternoon and he said, "This morning you heard what Brigham Young thinks about this subject, and now I would like to tell you what the Lord thinks about it." He reversed himself completely. This is an incident that does not demean or belittle him in any sense. It exalts and ennobles him in the eternal perspective in that he, getting the spirit of inspiration and learning what ought to be presented, in effect getting his errand from the Lord, he was willing to bow to his will and present that philosophy and that suggested procedure to Israel.

Well, the point of this is that prophets are men and that when they act by the spirit of inspiration, what they say is the voice of God; but still they are mortal and they are entitled to and do have private opinions. Unless these are inspired and unless they accord with the revelations, they are just as subject to being in a field by themselves, as anyone else in the Church....

Since "the spirits of the prophets are subject to the prophets" (1 Cor. 14:32), whatever is announced by the Presiding Brethren as they sit in council for the Church, will be the voice of inspiration. But the truth or error of any uninspired statement of an individual will have to be judged by the Standard Works and by the spirit of discernment and inspiration that is in those who actually enjoy the gift of the Holy Ghost....

What [D&C 76:5-11] means, among other things, is that anyone in the Church, who will abide the law that enables him to get in tune with the Lord, can receive the vision of the [three degrees of glory], on the same basis that it was given to Joseph Smith and Sidney Rigdon. Now that means that you and I have a choice. We can read what is in that revelation; we can meditate about it and get some concept and understanding about it. We can get the Spirit to help us as we ponder, and we can thereby learn an appreciable amount about the eternal worlds of glory. Or we can manage ourselves to get in tune to such a degree that we will see, and hear and feel what the Prophet saw and heard and felt. And there are some things that he saw that he didn't write down, except to say with reference to them, that they could only be understood by the power of God and not by written words....

Now you see what this type of doctrine does. This fixes it up so that salvation is not for David O. McKay and the apostles alone. Salvation is for every man in the whole world who will forsake the world and come into the Church and live the law that gets him in tune with the Almighty. This is the reason that we have hands [laid] on our heads and the legal administrator says, "Receive the Holy Ghost."

There is a host of similar revelation we could read and talk about, but what it amounts to is this: Everybody in the Church is entitled to get the inspiration of the Spirit, everybody in the Church is entitled to enjoy the administering of angels, everybody in the Church is entitled to see the face of the Lord. This is written right in the revelations. (D.& C. 93:1.) One of the ancient prophecies talks about a future day when it will no longer be necessary for every man to say to his brother, "Know the Lord, for all shall know me, from the least of them unto the greatest of them." (Jer. 31:34.) In that day people will actually enjoy (and this is millennial) the fulfillment of this promise that they will know the Lord without being taught. They will see him, they will be in communion with him; it will be like it was in the days of Enoch's city. The Lord will appear to them, and they will be qualified as far as spiritual stature goes, for what would be the equivalent of translation and more....

If you and I know how to take the souls that we possess and tune them to the wave band on which the Holy Ghost is revealing truth, and on which the Lord is sending forth the visions of eternity, then we would see the visions and receive the revelations. This is not beyond us. We won't have to sit back and think what a glorious thing it is that we have got prophets and apostles. Now that's true, and nobody can emphasize too strongly the importance of having apostles and prophets, because that establishes affirmatively and positively that there are those on earth who do, in fact, get in communion with the Lord. But that is only part of it. The important part, really, to us...is that we have power as individuals to have revealed to us everything that God told Joseph and the Twelve and so on. We can have revelation. We can get in tune with the Almighty....The Lord is going to leave us to ourselves in large part because this is a probationary estate; we must work out a lot of things for ourselves, but on the other hand, revelation is also available....

The glorious thing to you and me is that we can see and know, because God is no respecter of persons, all that his prophets see and know, if we will just apply the law that is involved." ("Are the General Authorities Human?" Salt Lake Institute of Religion Devotional Address,

28 October 1966, pp. 2-4, 6-7.)

⅃ OUR FAITH CONSISTS of the degree of power and influence we have with God our Father whereby we work works of righteousness and do many miraculous things....

We have a blanket immutable promise that we who are in the Church, who have received the truth, who have already laid the foundations for faith, have the ability to build on those foundations to the point that anything that we will ask of God *which is both good and right*—those two qualifying expressions—we shall obtain. [See 3 Nephi 18:20; Moroni 7:26.)...

There are degrees of faith. We have had faith already to forsake the world and come to Christ. We have had faith already to control some of our appetites, to try to live as becometh saints. We have already got the kind of faith that causes us to pray and petition and fast and plead before the Lord that our loved ones may be healed. We have the degree that causes us to call in the elders of Israel to administer to our sick when necessity arises.

But there isn't a great deal, yet, of the kind of faith in the Church that is saying to a sycamine tree, "be thou plucked up by the root, and be thou planted in the sea." There isn't yet a great deal of the kind of faith that the Brother of Jared had when he said to Mt. Zerin: "Remove—and it was removed." (Ether 12:30.) Nor is there faith of the kind that Enoch had when he caused the rivers to change their courses and the like. (Moses 7:13.) We are working toward that kind of faith. We are trying to perfect and increase and enhance our faith....

This brings us to the matter of personal righteousness. This brings us to the matter of cleansing and perfecting our souls so that we can be in tune with the Holy Spirit, and the Spirit will not dwell in an unclean tabernacle. When we join the Church, we do it because we have acquired an initial quantity of faith. We have come to the knowledge of the truth, and we rejoice beyond what anyone can imagine in the world to think that now we have before us a course that leads to eternal life....

Church membership does not save people. Church membership, baptism, the initiatory ordinances into the kingdom, the initial teachings, *open the door to us* to a course which, if followed, leads eventually to the glorious reward of eternal life. The process of going along this path, which is named "the strait and narrow path," is the process of enduring to the end. It is the process of increasing our faith. It is the process of growing in the things of the Spirit until we have power and influence with God, until we increase within ourselves the ability and the capacity to work and do and perform in temporal concerns and in spiritual concerns. This power and this ability is faith....

Don't go out now and try to cast sycamine trees into the sea. Don't go out and try to move mountains, but go out and start in a small degree to do the thing that you need to do in your life to get what you ought to have temporally and spiritually....

Work on the projects ahead, and when you have taken one step in the acquiring of faith, it will give you the assurance in your soul that you can go forward and take the next step, and by degrees your power or influence will increase until eventually, in this world or in the next, you will say to the Mt. Zerins in your life, "Be thou removed." You will say to whatever encumbers your course of eternal progress, "Depart," and it will be so. (*Lord, Increase Our Faith*, Brigham Young University Speeches of the Year [31 Oct. 1967], pp. 3-4, 6, 9, 11.)

TRUE RELIGION COMES from God, and from no other source.

It is his priesthood that administers the gospel. It is his power that governs his church.

It is at his direction that the gospel is preached and that the gifts of the Spirit are poured out upon the faithful.

His is the power by which miracles are wrought, by which the sick are healed and the dead raised.

He seals men up unto eternal life.

He makes men joint heirs with his Son.

He gives them the fullness of his glory and kingdom.

He is the source of all things, of every true principle, of every saving truth, of revealed religion, and without revelation from him there is no true church, no true religion, and no personal salvation.

God sends apostles and prophets, wise and holy men who have the spiritual talent to commune with him, to receive in their hearts his mind and will, and then to communicate these eternal truths to their fellowmen. Joseph Smith was one of the greatest of these, and we have living apostles and prophets today who make the truths of salvation available to us as a people and to all who will come and join with us.

But people are not saved en masse. Salvation is personal and individual. Religion must come to one man standing alone, independent of all others.

If I am to be saved, I personally must believe and obey the true religion.

I must get religion into my own heart and soul.

What the Prophet Joseph Smith saw and believed and knew will not suffice. True, his revelations make salvation available to me; they open the door. But I must see and believe and know for myself.

I must know God.

I must learn the truths of salvation.

I must feel the power of his priesthood.

I must receive the gifts of his Spirit.

I must be born again.

I must receive revelation.

No man can be saved unless and until he receives revelation....

Accordingly, those who are saints indeed, those who have been born again, those who are so living as to be in tune with the Spirit—they are they who receive revelation, personal revelation, revelation which is the mind and will of God to them as individuals. They know there are apostles and prophets directing the kingdom who receive revelation for the Church and the world. But they as individuals receive personal revelation in their own affairs.

And there are no restrictions placed upon them; there are no limitations as to what they may see and know and comprehend. No eternal truths will be withheld, if they obey the laws entitling them to receive such truths.

Joseph Smith and the prophets had revelation. They saw God, viewed the visions of eternity, entertained angels, came upon Mount Zion, stood in heavenly places, and had communion with the general assembly and Church of the Firstborn....

We learn that any man who obeys the law entitling him to receive revelation shall see and hear and know for himself. Revelation for the Church comes through those who are prophets, seers, and revelators to the Church, but personal revelation, revelation for the guidance of the individual, revelation which says to a man and a woman, "Son, daughter, thou shalt be exalted; thou shalt have part and lot in my kingdom," this revelation comes to them as individuals, alone and apart from all others....

There are no limitations placed upon any of us. Revelations are not reserved for a limited few or for those called to positions of importance in the Church. It is not position in the Church that confers spiritual gifts. It is not being a bishop, a stake president, or an apostle that makes revelation and salvation available. These are high and holy callings which open the door to the privilege of great service among men. But it is not a call to a special office that opens the windows of revelation to a truth seeker. Rather it is personal righteousness; it is keeping the commandments; it is seeking the Lord while he may be found.

God is no respecter of persons. He will give revelation to me and to you on the same terms and conditions. I can see what Joseph Smith and Sidney Rigdon saw in the vision of the degrees of glory—and so can you. I can entertain angels and see God, I can receive an outpouring of the gifts of the Spirit—and so can you....

I know man can receive revelations, because I have received them. God has spoken to me, not for the guidance of the Church, not for your benefit, but for mine. The same thing has or can or should happen in the life of every member of his kingdom.

God be praised that, unworthy though we are, he stands ready to and does in fact reveal himself to those of us who are sons and daughters in his kingdom. ("The Rock of Salvation," *Improvement Era*, Dec. 1969, pp. 84-85.)

I SHALL SAY something about how we can seek and gain the Spirit of the Lord.

I think it goes without saying that if we manage to do this, then everything else in our lives will fall into a perfect pattern. We will marry right; we will keep the commandments; we will devote ourselves to the Lord's affairs; we will somehow or other manage to prosper temporally; and we will get along in that course that leads to eventual eternal life in our Father's Kingdom.

In my judgment, the greatest gift that anyone can receive in mortality is the actual enjoyment of the Gift of the Holy Ghost. The greatest thing that anyone can have in eternity, of course, is eternal life, which means that we receive the kind of life that God our Father lives. When we come into the Church through the waters of baptism, a legal administrator places his hands on our heads and says, "Receive the Holy Ghost," which gives us the Gift of the Holy Ghost, or in other words the right to the constant companionship of that member of the Godhead, based on faithfulness.

Now, the actual enjoyment of the Gift, the actual receipt of revelation from the Holy Spirit, is conditioned upon obedience, conformity, and personal righteousness. The Spirit will not dwell in an unclean tabernacle. There are hosts of people in the Church who have received the Gift, meaning they have the right to the companionship of the Spirit, but who never in fact are born again. They never in reality become new creatures of the Holy Ghost; they do not get the enlightenment from on high that impels them forward on the course that leads to Eternal Life.

I think there is no better way to express our goal and objective in life than to say that we ought to seek with all our power, might, and strength, to be guided by the Spirit of the Lord. The Holy Ghost is a personage of Spirit, a spirit entity, a spirit individual. He is a member of the Godhead. He has assigned to him a particular and express responsibility associated with the salvation of men. Joseph Smith said, "The Holy Ghost is a revelator and any man who has received the Holy Ghost has received revelation." In other words, the Holy Ghost is broadcasting truth into all immensity. It is available for us to receive if we can learn how to get in tune, if we can learn what we have to do to be guided in our lives by the Holy Spirit....

Now, we are assembled here in this room at the Institute. This room is full of language that none of us are hearing, and full of scenes that none of us are viewing. But if somebody brought a radio in here and tuned it into the right wave band, we would hear...the announcements that are being proclaimed. Or, if somebody got a television set in here and tuned it to the right wave band, we would see the pictures that are being projected, the plays and the dramas and so on.

This room also is full of the revelations of eternity. This room is full of the visions of eternity. Here in this room, at this moment, there is everything that Joseph Smith and Sidney Rigdon saw, as recorded in Section 76 of the Doctrine and Covenants. There is a view of the Celestial Kingdom; there is a view of things that are so glorious spiritually that it is not lawful for man to utter them. But I suppose that none of us are hearing these revelations or seeing these visions. I think we are all centering our attention on what is going on in the meeting.

The Holy Ghost is a revelator. The Holy Ghost is broadcasting truth. He is broadcasting visions. The receiving set, in this instance, is the human soul. Now, I have a human soul, and if I know how to tune the wave band of my soul to the revelations that are being broadcast, then I would hear the mind and will and voice of God, and there would come into my mind whatever eternal truths I managed to come in contact with. I would hear the voice of God. Similarly, if I knew how to tune my soul to the spiritual wave bands involved, I would see the things of eternity.

They are here; they are available.

Joseph Smith, in one of his greatest sermons, said, "God has not revealed anything to Joseph that He will not reveal to the Twelve and to the least and last saint as soon as he is able to bear it." That is, God is no respecter of persons. Any revelations that the President of the Church can get, I can get, as far as the doctrines of eternal truth are concerned. The Lord may tell him something for the governing of the Church, because that is his business and his affair, but as far as eternal truth is concerned, as far as the principles that I have to live in order to conform my life perfectly to the Lord's law and thereby gain eternal life, I can get every one of those by independent, personal revelation simply because God is no respecter of persons. The ultimate millennial destiny of the Church is for all the members to arrive at a state and degree of perfection and righteousness where it will no longer be necessary for every man to say to his neighbor, "Know the Lord, because all will know him," meaning from personal revelation, from the greatest to the least, as the Prophet explained in using that quotation from the Old Testament.

There are [billions of] people on earth today; and the laws exist—they are everywhere, they are universal in application—whereby any of these [billions of] people can get in tune with the Spirit of the Lord and receive revelation. The reality of the situation is, that just a little cluster of people, just a little handful of Latter-day Saints, just a few people who are sincerely and devoutly seeking to know the truth of the restoration, manage to get their souls in tune so that they receive revelation and so that they see visions. As a matter of fact, there are not too many even of the Latter-day Saints who have progressed in the things of the Spirit to the point where they see angels, where they see people from the other worlds, where they see visions of what is going on in the Paradise of God, and the like. It is a matter of obedience to the law, conformity to the laws upon which receipt of the blessings are predicated. I think there is absolutely no question at all that we are entitled to seek revelation, and we are able to gain revelation just as soon as we learn the laws and live the laws that enable us to tune our souls to the wave band on which the Holy Spirit is broadcasting....

The intelligent part of the human personality is the spirit that is within. As far as this body is concerned, it does not know a thing, but my spirit knows whatever it is I happen to know. As the Prophet said, "The mind of man is in the spirit." So any knowledge or any intelligence or any revelation that I receive has to be lodged in the spirit. Well, I can get knowledge to my mind, or my spirit, through my senses, through touch and taste and smell, etc. Or, I can get knowledge to my spirit through my reason, through the ability to evaluate and sort things out. My senses—my touch and my taste and my smell—can be deceived. One thing can be involved and I can think it is something else. My reason can be deluded; I can be in error in the conclusions that I reach. But there is one provision that is made for getting knowledge to the mind of man which cannot be deceived, and that is to get it by revelation from the Holy Spirit. The Holy Spirit is a personage of Spirit, and the intelligent, sentient, believing, understanding part of me is a spirit entity, a child of God, to whom the Holy Spirit can speak....

I do not know how the Holy Ghost, being a personage of spirit, is able to convey truth to the spirit that is within me and to do it with absolute certainty. All I know is that [it does] happen. There are some laws that are ordained and some provisions that are made whereby the spirit that is within man can absorb truth from the Holy Spirit with absolute certainty. Doubt and question are totally and completely removed....

I happen to be tone deaf, or virtually so, but I can talk about music. Such is no problem at all. I can talk for hours about music. That is not the issue; it does not make me a musician. And similarly it is not talking *about* religion that identifies spiritual people. The only way that you identify spiritually endowed people is to get them involved in a spiritual experience. Something has to happen in their lives. They have to be fed spiritually. You are fed spiritually when you hear testimonies, when you pray, when you worship, when you do a great variety of things that the Church provides, things that enable you to get in tune with the mind and will of the Lord. We bear testimony, and we counsel the people to do this and this and this, to have the Spirit of the Lord as a companion.

You must get a spiritual experience; you must get revelation. Nobody really gets a spiritual experience of any magnitude until he gets a revelation from the Holy Spirit. And, if you have had a revelation, then you have had a spiritual experience. If you have not had a revelation, you need to follow the formula and the pattern that the Lord has provided so that you get a spiritual experience. Once you get a spiritual experience and follow the pattern and you know what to do, then you apply those same rules and regulations and pursue that same course, and you can get revelation on added things. That, of course, is what Joseph Smith did. He grew in the things of the Spirit. At first he used the Urim and Thummim; later he did not have to use it. He first got revelation with great effort and great labor and, pretty soon, he had the spiritual stature when things came much easier to him. We can grow in this knowledge....

It is through experience in the things of the Spirit that you identify the voice and mind and will of the purposes of the Lord. This is the beginning of the attaining of revelation, and then you have power to grow in grace and understanding. The ultimate objective is to gain all things by the power of the Holy Ghost so that ye may know the truth of all things. Eventually, you can get all light and all knowledge and all understanding and you can become like Christ, and this means you gain eternal life in his kingdom. I do not think there is any counsel that is more embracing, more all-inclusive, than the counsel to seek the Spirit; and if we gain the Spirit and endure to the end, our reward is one of peace and joy in this life and eternal life in the world to come. This is our aim and our objective....

I came here today and it does not make one particle of difference to me what I say; it is totally and completely immaterial to me what I say in this meeting. Meaning: I have no message of my own. I did not create any doctrine. I did not establish any truth that needs to be proclaimed. I come here as the Lord's representative, as an Elder in Israel who is an agent of Christ; and my sole purpose and my sole mission is to get in tune with the Holy Spirit so that what I say on this occasion will be the mind and the voice of the Lord and as a consequence will be the right thing. If I get in tune with the Lord—perfect. If I do not, I have failed.

The other half of it is that you come here to hear. It really should not make a particle of difference to you what you hear. You do not come with any predisposition that some particular thing should be taught or that some viewpoint should be endorsed. You come here to hear the voice of the Lord. If you get in tune with the same Spirit that I get in tune with, then what I say is true and right, and as you hear it, it finds lodgment in your heart, and our revelation says then we are mutually edified. (Salt Lake Institute of Religion Devotional Address, Lectures in Theology: "Last Message Series," 22 January 1971, pp. 2-8.)

I ASK, "Are we walking in the path that Joseph Smith trod? Are we receiving the revelations and visions and working the miracles—doing the things that he did?" If we are not, to the full measure that we should, well might we ask ourselves, "Where is the Lord God of Joseph Smith?"

Now I do not want to be understood to indicate that miracles and signs have ceased. They are with us. This is God's kingdom. There is not the slightest question or doubt about that. The sick are healed, and the dead are raised. The eyes of the blind are opened as much today as they were during the ministry of Joseph Smith. But I do think that this is more limited, in the sense that it has not spread among the generality of people in the Church as fully as it should. (*The Lord God of Joseph Smith*, Brigham Young University Speeches of the Year [4 Jan. 1972], p. 2.)

WHEN WE DWELT in the presence of God our Heavenly Father, we were endowed with agency. This gave us the opportunity, the privilege, to choose what we would do—to make a free, untrammeled choice. When Father Adam was placed in the Garden of Eden, he was given this same power, and we now possess it. We're expected to use the gifts and talents and abilities, the sense and judgment and agency with which we are endowed.

But on the other hand, we're commanded to seek the Lord, to desire his Spirit, to get the spirit of revelation and inspiration in our lives. We come into the Church and a legal administrator places his hands upon our head and says, "Receive the Holy Ghost." This gives us the gift of the Holy Ghost, which is the right to the constant companionship of that member of the Godhead, based on faithfulness.

And so we're faced with two propositions. One is that we ought to be guided by the spirit of inspiration, the spirit of revelation. The other is that we're here under a direction to use our agency, to determine what we ought to do on our own; and we need to strike a fine balance between these two, if we're going to pursue a course that will give us joy and satisfaction and peace in this life and lead to eternal reward in our Father's kingdom....

Implicit in asking in faith is the precedent requirement that we do everything in our power to accomplish the goal that we seek. We use the agency with which we have been endowed. We use every faculty and capacity and ability that we possess to bring about the eventuality that may be involved. Now this is translating the Book of Mormon, it's choosing a wife, it's choosing employment, it's doing any one of ten thousand important things that arise in our lives....

There's a fine balance between agency and inspiration. We're expected to do everything in our power that we can, and then to seek an answer from the Lord, a confirming seal that we've reached the right conclusion; and sometimes, happily, in addition, we get added truths and knowledge that we hadn't even supposed....

Well, do you want a wife? Do you want anything that's right and proper? You go to work and you use the agency and power and ability that God has given you. You use every faculty, you get all the judgment that you can centered on the problem, you make up your own mind, and then, to be sure that you don't err, you counsel with the Lord. You talk it over. You say, "This is what I think; what do you think?" And if you get the calm, sweet surety that comes only from the Holy Spirit, you know you've reached the right conclusion; but if there's anxiety and uncertainty in your heart, then you'd better start over, because the Lord's hand is not in it, and you're not getting the ratifying seal that, as a member of the Church who has the gift of the Holy Ghost, you are entitled to receive....

If you learn how to use the agency that God has given you,...and if you reach conclusions that are sound and right, and you counsel with the Lord and get his ratifying seal of approval upon the conclusions you've reached, than you've received revelation, for one thing; and for another thing, you're going to have the great reward of eternal life, be lifted up at the last day. Now, we're not all equal by any means, some have one talent and capacity and some another. But if we use the talents we have, somehow we'll come out all right....

It's a literal fact that we have the gift and power of the Holy Ghost. We have the spirit of revelation, the spirit of testimony, the spirit of prophecy. These things must be, or else we're not the church and kingdom of God; we're not the Lord's people.

Now, the fact is that we do have them; revelation works. Don't shy away from getting revelation....We're entitled to the spirit of revelation. But what I'm attempting to teach this morning is that there's a how and a procedure, and there are conditions precedent, and it is our obligation to go to work on our problems and then counsel with the Lord and get the ratifying seal of the Holy Spirit on the conclusions that we've reached; and that ratifying seal is the spirit of revelation. ("Agency or Inspiration—Which?" in *Speeches of the Year 1973* [1974], pp. 108-117.)

WE HAVE THE PROMISE that if we seek him with full purpose of heart, keeping his commandments and walking uprightly before him, we shall indeed see his face and eventually be inheritors with him of eternal life in his Father's kingdom. ("Think on These Things," *Ensign*, Jan. 1974, p. 48.)

OTHER ETERNAL VERITIES are these—that God has spoken in our day;...that the church and kingdom of God has been set up on earth anew; that it administers the gospel by the power of the holy priesthood; and that there are had among us the gifts, signs, miracles, and all the wonders, blessings, and graces that were ever had in any day when the Lord had a people on earth. ("The Ten Commandments of a Peculiar People," in *Speeches of the Year 1975* [1976], p. 37.)

BECAUSE HE IS no respecter of persons and chooses to honor and bless all those who love and serve him, the Lord pours out revelations and gives glorious visions to all those who obey the laws upon which the receipt of these spiritual gifts is predicated. Their receipt is not limited to prophets and apostles. All are alike unto God where the outpouring of his gifts is concerned. ("A New Commandment—Save Thyself and Thy Kindred!" *Ensign*, Aug. 1976, p. 7.)

THERE IS MORE revelation to come relative to salvation for the dead and all other things. The last word has not been spoken on any subject. Streams of living water shall yet flow from the Eternal Spring who is the source of all truth. There are more things we do not know about the doctrines of salvation than there are things we do know.

When we as a people believe and conform to all of the truths we have received, we shall receive more of the mind and will and voice of the Lord. What we receive and when it comes are in large measure up to us. The Lord has many things he wants to tell us, but so far we have not attained that unity and spiritual stature which will enable us to pull down knowledge from heaven upon us. ("A New Commandment—Save Thyself and Thy Kindred!" *Ensign*, Aug. 1976, p. 11.)

WE ARE A KINGDOM of brethren, a congregation of equals, all of whom are entitled to receive all of the blessings of the priesthood. There are no blessings reserved for apostles that are not freely available to all the elders of the kingdom; blessings come because of obedience and personal righteousness, not because of administrative positions....

The gift of the Holy Ghost is the right to the constant companionship of that member of the Godhead based on faithfulness. It is the right to receive revelation, to see visions, to be in tune with the Infinite.

John, who held the Priesthood of Aaron, baptized with water for the remission of sins. Jesus, who was an high priest forever after the order of

Melchizedek, baptized with the Holy Ghost and with fire.

The Holy Ghost is a revelator; he bears witness of the Father and the Son, those Holy Beings whom to know is eternal life. Thus it is that "this greater priesthood...holdeth the key of the mysteries of the kingdom, even the key of the knowledge of God." (D&C 84:19.)

The spiritual gifts are the signs which follow those that believe; they are the miracles and healings performed in the name of the Lord Jesus; they include marvelous outpourings of truth and light and revelation from God in heaven to man on earth. ("The Ten Blessings of the Priesthood," *Ensign*, Nov. 1977, p. 33.)

IT IS HIS WILL that we gain testimonies, that we seek revelation, that we covet to prophesy, that we desire spiritual gifts, and that we seek the face of the Lord.

The Lord wants all his children to gain light and truth and knowledge from on high. It is his will that we pierce the veil and rend the heavens and see the visions of eternity....

Such is his promise [D&C 93:1] to us here and now while we yet dwell as mortals in a world of sorrow and sin. It is our privilege even now—the privilege of all who hold the holy priesthood—if we will strip ourselves from jealousies and fears and humble ourselves before him, as he has said, to have the veil rent and see him and know that he is. ("'Thou Shalt Receive Revelation'," *Ensign*, Nov. 1978, p. 61.)

WE'RE GOING TO be judged in the spiritual realm by how many of the gifts of the spirit we manage to get into our lives. ("The Probationary Test of Mortality," Salt Lake Institute of Religion Devotional Address, 10 January 1982, p. 10.)

THANKS BE TO GOD that the heavens have been rent, that the Father and the Son appeared to Joseph Smith, that revelation and visions and gifts and miracles abound among the true Saints.

Thanks be to God that in our day many have seen the face of his Son and that he has poured out the gift of his Spirit upon an even greater number. ("The Seven Christs," *Ensign*, Nov. 1982, p. 34.)

WE HAVE NOT received, by any means, all of the word of the Lord. I think we have received most of the word of the Lord that is required until the day of the Second Coming. The Lord has given all that people in the world have the spiritual capacity to receive at this time. There is going to be another great dispensation, that is, another great period of enlightenment, when he comes; and at that time he will reveal all things, such as the sealed portion of the Book of Mormon. He will not reveal the sealed portion of the Book of Mormon now, and let us publish it to the world, because what it contains is so far beyond the spiritual capacity of men that it would drive people away from the truth rather than lead them to the truth. Actually, it is an act of mercy for the Lord to limit, to a particular people, the amount of revelation they receive, because if more were offered than they are capable of receiving, it would be a barrier to spiritual progression. The sealed portion of the Book of Mormon falls in that category.

We are now in a glorious dispensation in which we have received substantially all of the revelations we are able to bear; it is true, however, that if we were able to unite and have faith, we would get more. That is one of the things that was involved when President Kimball received the revelation that the gospel and all of its blessings (the priesthood and the ordinances of the House of the Lord) were now to go to those of every race and kindred and tongue without any reservation except that people live in righteousness and be worthy to receive what is offered to them. That new revelation came in large measure because the prophet of God and those associated with him united in faith and in prayer and in desire and sought for an answer from the Lord. There are added revelations we could receive, and I hope will receive as we manage to get in tune with the Spirit. But the great reservoir of revelation for our dispensation, meaning the things that we need to know to govern our conduct, in order to gain an eternal life, these things have already been given. And there will not be great added reservoirs of substantive revelation that will come before the Second Coming because of the wickedness of the world. Some of that wickedness spills over, and prevails among the Latter-day Saints. But, eventually, there will be a day of great added revelation. ("This Generation Shall Have My Word Through You," *Hearken O Ye People: Discourses on the Doctrine and Covenants* [Sandy, Utah: Randall Book, 1984], pp. 11-12.)

WHAT I AM SAYING is that the ultimate end of spiritual progression is, not only to know that the revelations are true, but to see visions and feel the Spirit and get the added light and knowledge which it is not lawful to utter and which was not recorded in the revealed record. What a glorious dispensation we live in. We live in a day when the Lord desires to confirm his word in the hearts of all who will heed his voice, and it is our privilege so to obtain. ("This Generation Shall Have My Word Through You," *Hearken O Ye People: Discourses on the Doctrine and Covenants* [Sandy, Utah: Randall Book, 1984], p. 14.)

THEN JESUS CAME, journeying from Galilee to the Jordan near Jerusalem. He asked for baptism. In awe, overwhelmed that the very Son of God himself should seek baptism at his hand, and yet knowing before that such would be the case, John said: "I have need to be baptized of thee, and comest thou to me?" Jesus replied: "Suffer it to be so now: for thus it becometh us to fulfil all righteousness."

John acceded to his cousin's wish. Solemnly, with dignity, in the power and authority of the priesthood of Aaron—by which authority the Levites had baptized through the centuries—he immersed the Lord Jesus in the murky waters of the Jordan.

Then came the miracle—the heavens were opened and John saw the Holy Ghost descending in peace and serenity, like a dove, to be and abide with the Lamb of God forever. This is one of possibly two occasions in all history, of which we have record, in which the personage of the Holy Ghost was seen by mortal man. And yet there was more to come. A voice spoke, a voice from heaven, the voice of the Father of us all. It said in words of glorious majesty: "This is my beloved Son, in whom I am well pleased." (See Matt. 3:11-17.) ("A Man Called John," *New Era*, May 1984, p. 6.)

IS IT PROPER to seek for spiritual gifts? Should we plead with the Lord for the gift of prophecy, or of revelation, or of tongues? Is it fitting and right to pray for the soul-sanctifying privilege of seeing the face of the Lord Jesus while we yet dwell as mortals in a sin-filled world? Does the Lord expect us to desire and seek for spiritual experiences, or do the divine proprieties call for us simply to love the Lord and keep his commandments, knowing that if and when he deems it proper he will grant special gifts and privileges to us?

By way of answer, it almost suffices to ask such questions as these: Are we not expected to seek salvation, the greatest of all the gifts of God? Why, then, should we not prepare ourselves for this greatest of all boons by seeking the enjoyment of the lesser ones? If we are to see his face in that eternal realm, where the same sociality that exists among us here, then coupled with eternal glory, shall endure everlastingly, can we go amiss by seeking to establish that sociality here and now? Are we not commanded: Ask and ye shall receive; seek and ye shall find; knock and it shall be opened? Why, then, should we smother a desire to heal the sick or raise the dead or commune with friends beyond the veil?

Also by way of answer to the queries at hand, we might with propriety reason along this line: If spiritual gifts are interwoven with and form part of the very gospel of salvation itself, can we enjoy the fulness of that gospel without possessing the gifts that are part of it? If gifts and miracles shall—inevitably, always, and everlastingly—follow those who believe, how can we be true believers without them? And if we are to seek the gospel, if we are to hunger and thirst after righteousness, if our whole souls must cry out for the goodness of God and his everlasting association, how can we exempt ourselves from seeking the gifts of the Spirit that come from and prepare us for his presence? (*A New Witness for the Articles of Faith* [Salt Lake City: Deseret Book, 1985], pp. 368-69.)

Chapter Twenty-Five

Prayer

WE ARE A PRAYING PEOPLE—not giving lip service only, not reciting mere words, not repeating memorized phrases—but praying with all the energy and power we possess, praying until the heavens open and the Lord rains down righteousness upon us. No one can pray with perfect faith unless he keeps the commandments. An immoral man can never generate the faith to raise the dead. A person who does not keep the Word of Wisdom will be hindered in healing the sick, and so on right down to the dress and grooming standards. ("The Ten Commandments of a Peculiar People," in *Speeches of the Year 1975* [1976], p. 38.)

IT IS CLEAR that we should pray for all that in wisdom and righteousness we should have. Certainly we should seek for a testimony, for revelations, for all of the gifts of the Spirit, including the fulfillment of the promise in Doctrine and Covenants 93:1 of seeing the face of the Lord. But above all our other petitions, we should plead for the companionship of the Holy Ghost in this life and for eternal life in the world to come. ("Why the Lord Ordained Prayer," *Ensign*, Jan. 1976, p. 10.)

IN PRAYER WE speak to the Lord, and he speaks to us. It is our privilege to have our voices heard in the courts above and to hear the answering voice of the Lord conveyed by the power of his Spirit.

Prayer changes our lives. Through it we draw near to the Lord, and he reaches out his finger and touches us, so we never again are the same.

Prayer is a great tower of strength, a pillar of unending righteousness, a mighty force that moves mountains and saves souls. Through it the sick are healed, the dead are raised, and the Holy Spirit is poured out without measure upon the faithful.

In prayer we bind ourselves by solemn covenants to love and serve the

Lord all our days. In it we pay our devotions and offer our sacraments to the Most High.

Now, there are special prayers reserved and offered for those who drink the still waters and lie down in green pastures, prayers which are not uttered for those who yet dwell in the deserts of sin.

With these things in mind, may I tell you some of the prayers in my heart, prayers that I think will join with like feelings in your hearts, and will unite in one mighty chorus of praise and petition, of adoration and thanksgiving, as they ascend and are heard in the courts above....

Father, we ask thee, in the name of Jesus Christ, to hear the words of our mouth, to discern with thy all-seeing eye the thoughts and intents of our heart, and to grant us our righteous desires.

We feel it is a great privilege to come into thy presence, to bow before thy throne, to address thee as Father; and we know thou wilt hear our cries. May we speak by the power of the Holy Ghost....

Father, thou hast given us the word of reconciliation and hast poured out revelations and visions upon us. We are thy people, and we desire to be worthy of the calling and election that is ours.

Thou hast wrought miracles in our midst; given us the holy scriptures, particularly thy word manifest in our day; conferred upon us the gift of the Holy Ghost by which we are guided into all truth, and by which our souls are sanctified.

For all these things we are grateful beyond any measure of expression, and because of them we shall praise thy holy name forever.

We confess our sins before thee and seek remission thereof, lest anything stand between us and thee in receiving a free flow of thy Spirit....

O Father, there are those among us, not a few in number, who desire and are worthy to have eternal companions. Wilt thou prepare the way before them that they may have the desires of their hearts in righteousness....

O Lord, increase our faith, and let the sick be healed and the dead raised even in greater numbers than at present.

But above this, O thou God of healing, wilt thou cause him who came with healing in his wings also to heal us spiritually.

We would be clean;...we desire and seek above all, the companionship of thy Holy Spirit. We pray, as did they of old, that we might receive the Holy Ghost.

O Father, we rejoice in the gifts of the Spirit and seek them in greater abundance. Let testimony and revelation and visions and miracles multiply among us.

Let us know the wonders of eternity, even those things which eye has not seen, nor ear heard, nor have yet entered into the heart of man....

Let us see the face of thy Son while we dwell here as mortals. Let us hear him say: Come ye blessed of my Father; ye shall enter into the joy of thy Lord; thy calling and election has been made sure; thou art a joint-heir with me, and shall yet receive, possess, and inherit all that my Father hath. ("Patterns of Prayer," *Ensign*, May 1984, pp. 32-34.)

Chapter Twenty-Six

Priesthood and the
Keys of the Kingdom

WE NEED TO REMIND ourselves of the standard definition of priesthood. Priesthood is the power and authority of God delegated to man on earth to act in all things for the salvation of men....

Keys, as we use them when we are associating them with rule in the priesthood, mean the right of presidency.

...It takes two things if an ordinance is going to be performed, or if the gospel is going to be preached, or anything is going to be done with proper authorization so that it will be of effect here and binding in eternity. It takes priesthood, which is power and authority, and keys, which is the right to authorize the authority to be used.

If all we had was priesthood, then we could not do anything. We could not use our priesthood. All of us have priesthood that we do not use for a multitude of purposes; but all of us could use that priesthood for this very multitude of purposes if someone who held the keys authorized us to use it for those purposes.

So keys are the right of presidency. And as all of us know they are exercised in their fullness, in their totality, by one man on earth at a time. That necessarily must be because there has to be one man who presides over all others, and that man, of course, is the senior apostle on earth who at all times is the President of the Church, the presiding high priest, the one holding the keys of the kingdom.

...We have keys authorizing us to use the priesthood for this purpose or that or some other. As a matter of fact, there are purposes for which the priesthood is designed to be used but for which we cannot use it because the keys of that particular thing have not been given. For instance, "by the power of the priesthood men will be resurrected." But none of us yet in mortality have the keys of the resurrection and so we cannot use the authority which the priesthood has in that field because no one can authorize us to use it. That key is not had. ("The Keys of the Kingdom," unpublished address given to the Wilford Stake priesthood meeting, 21 February 1955, pp. 1-2; copy available in LDS Historical Department, Salt Lake City, Utah.)

WHAT ARE KEYS? Keys, as used in connection with priesthood and the Church and the kingdom, are the right of presidency; that is, they are the directing power, the ability to designate how and under what circumstances the priesthood will be used, and to regulate and govern all of the affairs of the Church which is the kingdom. (*Keys of the Kingdom*, Brigham Young University Speeches of the Year [23 Apr. 1957], p. 2.)

ONCE THE KEYS were given, once all of the powers and authorities had been restored, we had what is called the fulness of the gospel. The fulness of the gospel does not necessarily consist in having the fulness of knowledge, in knowing all things or having all doctrine revealed or interpreted to us. But the fulness of the gospel in its nature and by definition consists in having all of the keys and all of the power and all of the authority that are necessary to seal men up so that they may inherit a fulness of reward, meaning exaltation in the kingdom hereafter. (*Keys of the Kingdom*, Brigham Young University Speeches of the Year [23 April 1957], p. 5.)

ALL THOSE WHO receive the Melchizedek Priesthood enter into a covenant with the Lord. Each such person solemnly promises:
I covenant to receive the priesthood;
I covenant to magnify my calling in the priesthood; and
I covenant to keep the commandments, to "live by every word that proceedeth forth from the mouth of God." (D&C 84:44.)
The Lord on his part covenants to give such faithful persons "all that my Father hath," which is eternal life in the kingdom of God. (D&C 84:38; see also 84:33-44.)
Then the Lord—to show the binding nature of his promise—swears with an oath that the promised reward shall be obtained.
This oath, as it pertained to the Son of God himself, is spoken of in these words: "The Lord hath sworn, and will not repent, Thou art a priest for ever after the order of Melchizedek." (Ps. 110:4.) ("The Ten Blessings of the Priesthood," *Ensign*, Nov. 1977, p. 34.)

PRIESTHOOD IS POWER like none other on earth or in heaven. It is the very power of God himself, the power by which the worlds were made, the power by which all things are regulated, upheld, and preserved.

It is the power of faith, the faith by which the Father creates and governs. God is God because he is the embodiment of all faith and all power and all priesthood. The life he lives is named eternal life....

Faith and priesthood go hand in hand. Faith is power and power is priesthood. After we gain faith, we receive the priesthood. Then, through the priesthood, we grow in faith until, having all power, we become like our Lord....

We received the priesthood first in the premortal existence and then again as mortals. Adam held the keys and used the priesthood when he participated in the creation of the earth. After his baptism he received the priesthood again, and he now stands as the presiding High Priest over all the earth.

All of us who have calls to minister in the holy priesthood were foreordained to be ministers of Christ, and to come here in our appointed days, and to labor on his errand.

The holy priesthood did more to perfect men in the days of Enoch than at any other time. Known then as the order of Enoch (see D&C 76:57), it was the power by which he and his people were translated. And they were translated because they had faith and exercised the power of the priesthood.

It was with Enoch that the Lord made an eternal covenant that all who received the priesthood would have power, through faith, to govern and control all things on earth, to put at defiance the armies of nations, and to stand in glory and exaltation before the Lord.

Melchizedek was a man of like faith, "and his people wrought righteousness, and obtained heaven, and sought for the city of Enoch." (JST Gen. 14:34.) Since his day the priesthood has been called after his name.

There are in the Church two priesthoods: the Aaronic or Levitical, and the Melchizedek. The Aaronic Priesthood is a preparatory priesthood, a schooling priesthood, a lesser priesthood, a divine system that prepares men to receive the Melchizedek Priesthood.

The Melchizedek Priesthood is the highest and holiest order ever given to men on earth. It is the power and authority to do all that is necessary to save and exalt the children of men. It is the very priesthood held by the Lord Jesus Christ himself and by virtue of which he was able to gain eternal life in the kingdom of his Father.

Both of these priesthoods are given by covenant. (See D&C 84:33-41.) Both of them surpass any earthly power; both of them prepare men for salvation....

Those who receive the Melchizedek Priesthood covenant and promise, before God and angels, to magnify their callings, to "live by every word which proceedeth forth from the mouth of God" (D&C 84:44), to marry for time and all eternity in the patriarchal order, and to live and serve as the Lord Jesus did in his life and ministry.

In return the Lord covenants and promises to give them all that his Father hath, meaning eternal life, which is exaltation and godhood in that eternal realm where alone the family unit continues in eternity.

In return the Lord admits them to his eternal patriarchal order, an order that prevails in the highest heaven of the celestial world, an order that assures its members of eternal increase, or in other words of spirit children in the resurrection. (See D&C 131:1-4.)

These are the most glorious promises given to men. There neither is nor can be anything as wondrous and great. And so the Lord uses the most powerful and emphatic language known to the human tongue to show their importance and immutability. That is to say, the Lord swears with an oath in his own name, because he can swear by no greater, that everyone who keeps the covenant made in connection with the Melchizedek Priesthood shall inherit, receive, and possess all things in his everlasting kingdom, and shall be a joint-heir with that Lord who is his Only Begotten.

God swore with an oath that Christ would be exalted, and he swears anew, at the time each of us receives the Melchizedek Priesthood, that we will have a like exaltation if we are true and faithful in all things....

Truly, there is power in the priesthood—power to do all things!

If the world itself was created by the power of the priesthood, surely that same power can move mountains and control the elements.

If one-third of the hosts of heaven were cast down to earth by the power of the priesthood, surely that same power can put at defiance the armies of nations or stay the fall of atomic bombs.

If all men shall be raised from mortality to immortality by the power of the priesthood, surely that same power can cure the diseased and the dying and raise the dead. ("The Doctrine of the Priesthood," *Ensign*, May 1982, pp. 32-34.)

IN OUR DISPENSATION the Melchizedek Priesthood came in 1829; men were ordained to the holy apostleship in February of 1835; various keys were given at divers times, chiefly on April 3, 1836; and this continued until all the rivers of the past had flown into the ocean of the present, and mortal men possessed all of the keys and powers ever vested in men in any age from Adam to the present.

By way of climax, all of the keys of the kingdom were given to the Twelve in the winter of 1844. They then received what the revelations call the fulness of the priesthood, together with the power to confer that eternal fulness upon others....

...The keys of the kingdom of God—the right and power of eternal presidency by which the earthly kingdom is governed—these keys, having first been revealed from heaven, are given by the spirit of revelation to each man who is both ordained an Apostle and set apart as a member of the Council of the Twelve.

But since keys are the right of presidency, they can only be exercised in their fulness by one man on earth at a time. He is always the senior Apostle, the presiding Apostle, the presiding high priest, the presiding elder. He alone can give direction to all others, direction from which none is exempt.

Thus, the keys, though vested in all of the Twelve, are used by any one of them to a limited degree only, unless and until one of them attains that seniority which makes him the Lord's anointed on earth....

We need not fear for the future. This is the Lord's work; it is his kingdom; and he governs its affairs as he chooses. The keys, having been committed to man on earth, are now vested in those of his own choosing. ("The Keys of the Kingdom," *Ensign*, May 1983, p. 23.)

Chapter Twenty-Seven

Succession in the Presidency

JOSEPH AND HYRUM did go to a martyr's grave and did seal their testimony with their blood. When that took place the Twelve were off on missions in various parts of the United States.[9] It would appear that the Lord had them off on these missions so that they would be away from the turmoil and the persecution of Nauvoo at the time and be preserved. ("The Keys of the Kingdom," unpublished address given to the Wilford Stake priesthood meeting, 21 February 1955, p. 7; copy available in LDS Historical Department, Salt Lake City, Utah.)

THE MEETING...took place in due course in the forepart of August in 1844. Now that was the occasion when the saints were assembled to decide the leadership of the Church. This is the story again that all of us know. Sidney Rigdon spoke at great length, without inspiration. The longer he talked the more evident it was to the assembled hosts of Israel that he did not have the Lord with him. His spirit was not present.

Brigham Young, you know, had said during that interval that he did not care who led the Church. All he wanted to know was what the Lord thought about it. Well, on that occasion Brigham Young got up to address the people after Sidney Rigdon had spoken. Then a very marvelous event transpired. What they saw was the Prophet Joseph Smith standing before them and the voice that they heard was the voice of Joseph. In other words, Brigham Young was transfigured before the congregation, thousands of them, and the Lord visibly manifest that the mantle of the Prophet had fallen on Brigham Young. Immediately, or soon thereafter, the vote was taken and the Church voted in accordance

---

9. These missions were for the purpose of promoting the Prophet Joseph Smith's candidacy in his short-lived campaign for president of the United States.

with this law of common consent to accept the Twelve as their leadership and follow them.

Now there were a few dissident persons. But there were not any negative votes that amounted to anything as far as numbers are concerned. We have let ourselves be led astray in believing that there was a great apostasy in that day. There was an apostasy, but there most assuredly was not a great apostasy. At least 95% of the Latter-day Saints in the city of Nauvoo and its environs not only stayed with the Church but came with the Church to the Rocky Mountains. There were a few that were sloughed off, but it was 1896 before the "Reorganized Church"—this is more than 50 years after the death of the Prophet—it was 1896 before they could even gather together a thousand people who ever in their lifetime had belonged to the Church the Prophet headed.

So there was an apostasy, there were people who fell away but it did not amount to much. It did not amount to anything more than a lot of these apostate cults that break off in our day and in the end it won't amount to anything more. Well, Brigham Young and the apostles led the Church. They led the Church west. The Church was under the direction of the Twelve. The Twelve acted as the First Presidency from that time in 1844 until December of 1847, after Brigham Young had come to the West and after they had gone back to Winter Quarters. Then back there at Winter Quarters in a conference of the Church, Brigham Young was sustained as the President of the Church and as I recall he took Heber C. Kimball and Willard Richards as his counselors and other brethren were chosen to come in and fill the vacancies in the Twelve. ("The Keys of the Kingdom," unpublished address given to the Wilford Stake priesthood meeting, 21 February 1955, pp. 7-8; copy available in LDS Historical Department, Salt Lake City, Utah.)

I WOULD LIKE...to talk...about succession in the presidency and to let you have a feeling and an understanding of what is involved when the Lord calls a prophet to other spheres of activity....

For reasons that are not wholly and completely known to us, although we do have some vision and understanding of what is involved, on Wednesday, December 26, 1973, the Lord reached forth his hand and touched his servant, President Harold B. Lee. President Lee had been in good health; he had been vigorous and active up to that point in his life. But on that day the Lord said to him: "Come hither. I have other work for you to do in another sphere. I have greater labors and a greater work for you here than you've been doing in mortality."...

When President Lee passed he was attended by President Marion G. Romney, his second counselor, and President Spencer W. Kimball, the President of the Council of the Twelve. President N. Eldon Tanner was in Arizona at the time. Brother Romney, as the representative of and counselor to President Lee, was in complete and total charge at the hospital. He gave President Lee a blessing. He felt the spirit of peace and satisfaction, the calm assurance that whatever eventuated would be right. He did not promise President Lee that he would be healed. The President had become ill very rapidly, just in a matter of hours or moments. Shortly after this blessing, he passed away. At the moment he passed, Brother Romney, in harmony with the system and the established tradition and custom of the Church, stepped aside, and President Spencer W. Kimball was then in complete charge and had total direction. President Kimball was at that moment the senior apostle of God on earth. And as the last heartbeat of President Lee ceased, the mantle of leadership passed to President Kimball, whose next heartbeat was that of the living oracle and presiding authority of God on earth. From that moment the Church continued under the direction of President Kimball....

When the President of the Church passes on, the First Presidency is disorganized, and the mantle of leadership—the reins of presidency—go to the senior man left and to the Council of the Twelve as a body; in effect the Council of the Twelve then becomes the First Presidency of the Church and so continues unless and until a formal reorganization takes place....

The Council of the Twelve met in the upper room of the Salt Lake Temple on Sunday, December 30 [1973], at 3:00 P.M. for the purpose of reorganizing the First Presidency of the Church. Normally in that upper room there are three chairs occupied by the First Presidency and twelve chairs in a semicircle in front of them occupied by the members of the Council of the Twelve. On this occasion, however, there were fourteen chairs in the semicircle, because there were fourteen Brethren present who had been sustained and ordained and set apart as members of the Council of the Twelve.

We took our places in those chairs, and President Kimball presided in the meeting, which lasted for about 3½ hours. In the course of this meeting President Kimball explained the business to be transacted, the things that might be done if the Brethren felt so guided and led....

He expressed himself as to what should be done, and he said that the proposition to be first considered was whether the First Presidency should then be reorganized or whether the Church should continue to function with the Council of the Twelve as its presiding officers. He then invited each member of the Twelve, commencing with Elder Ezra Taft Benson and continuing around the circle to me, to arise in turn and express himself frankly and fully and freely as to what ought to be done. I'll tell you what in thought-content and substance was said by all of the Brethren on that occasion....

Each member of the Council in turn, specifically and pointedly, expressed himself to the effect that now was the time to reorganize the First Presidency of the Church, that there should not be further delay, that the effective and proper operation of this great organization that we have from the Lord needed this administrative arrangement. Each one in turn expressed himself that President Spencer W. Kimball was the man whom the Lord wanted to preside over the Church; there was no question whatever about that. There was total and complete unity and harmony....

And so after there had been full expression and consideration, Elder Ezra Taft Benson, the next one in seniority to President Kimball, made the formal motion that the First Presidency of the Church be reorganized; that President Spencer W. Kimball be sustained, ordained, and set apart as the President of the Church; as the prophet, seer, and revelator to the Church; and as the Trustee-in-Trust. This motion was adopted unanimously....

At this point, he chose his first counselor, President N. Eldon Tanner, who responded appropriately and sweetly; he then chose President Marion G. Romney to be the second, who similarly responded. Following these appointments, Brother Benson was sustained as the President of the Council of the Twelve. And then all those present placed their hands upon the head of President Kimball, and he was ordained and set apart with President Benson being mouth, to serve as President of the Church and as the prophet, seer, and revelator for this time and this season.

Now, President Lee has passed away. He was a great spiritual giant, a prince in Israel, someone to whom we looked with unbounded admiration. Few men have lived in our day who have had more direct contact with the Lord, who have felt the spirit of inspiration and who have been able to convey the mind and will of the Lord to his people as well as President Lee has done. We had supposed, not knowing the providences of the Lord, that President Lee would be with us for a long time. But there are two things we should note in his call to go elsewhere. One is that the Lord has another work for him to do, and it is a greater and more extensive work than what he was presently assigned to do. The Lord, in his infinite wisdom and goodness, knows what ought to be done with his servants. The other thing to note is that when the Lord calls a new prophet he does it because he has a work and a labor and a mission for the new man to perform.

I can suppose that when the Prophet Joseph Smith was taken from this life the Saints felt themselves in the depths of despair. To think that a leader of such spiritual magnitude had been taken from them!...We do not have language or capacity or ability to extol the greatness and the glory of the ministry and mission of the Prophet Joseph Smith. And yet when he was taken the Lord had Brigham Young. Brigham Young stepped forth and wore the mantle of leadership. With all respect and admiration and every accolade of praise resting upon the Prophet Joseph, still Brigham Young came forward and did things that then had to be done in a better way than the Prophet Joseph himself could have done them.

Now, no one can say too emphatically or too strongly or praise too highly the leadership of President Lee, but this is a forward-looking Church. We do not look backward. We do not do other than go forward and onward. Our destiny is to proclaim the everlasting gospel into every ear. This Church will roll on until the knowledge of God covers the earth as the waters cover the sea. And so we look to the future. We now look to a new prophet who will wear the mantle of leadership and who will, with dignity and honor and inspiration and with the guidance of heaven, do things that are appointed for his time and his season that no one else could have done. The Lord's hand is in the work, and Spencer Kimball is the prophet of God, the mouthpiece of the Almighty for the time and the season that are appointed ahead. ("Succession in the Presidency," in *Speeches of the Year 1974* [1975], pp. 17-25.)

Chapter Twenty-Eight

Temple Ordinances

ACCORDING TO THE revelations which we have received, the fulness of the priesthood, meaning, I suppose, the fulness of the blessings of the priesthood, is had only in the temples of God. (Conference Report, Oct. 1950, p. 15.)

THE ORDINANCES THAT are performed in the temples are the ordinances of exaltation; they open the door to us to an inheritance of sonship; they open the door to us so that we may become sons and daughters, members of the household of God in eternity. If we go to the temples with an honest heart and a contrite spirit, having prepared ourselves by personal righteousness and worthiness and proper living, then in those houses we receive the ordinances and the instructions which enable us, if we thereafter continue faithful, to receive eventually the fulness of the Father.

The temple ordinances open the door to gaining all power and all wisdom and all knowledge. Temple ordinances open up the way to membership in the Church of the Firstborn. They open the door to becoming kings and priests and inheriting all things. (Conference Report, Oct. 1955, pp. 12-13.)

WE ARE LATTER-DAY Israel; we are part of the seed of Abraham; we hold the power and authority of this priesthood; we are a light to the gentile nations, and as a result we are under command to carry the message of salvation to them. But we are also chosen and appointed to be saviors to Israel itself, to the seed of Abraham—to the whole kingdom and nation of people of the chosen lineage, who have lived in all the days since Abraham—whether they lived when the gospel was here or whether they did not.

May I now show how these principles work by using myself as the illustration. I have received the gospel; I have been baptized under the hands of a legal administrator; I have received the gift of the Holy Ghost—all of which has put me on a path leading to an inheritance of salvation in the celestial world. Also, I have gone to the temple and been sealed to one of God's choicest handmaidens and have thereby obtained a place on the path leading to an inheritance of eternal life in the highest heaven of the celestial world. By obedience I have power to press forward and obtain these great rewards.

Because I have some understanding and realization of the glory, importance, and worth of these gospel blessings, there has come into my heart a great desire to have my children after me become inheritors of the same identical blessings that I have received, and so I strive to bring up my children in light and truth. Next to my own salvation and that of my wife, there is nothing so important to me as the salvation of my children.

Further, because I know the priceless worth of the gospel and the blessings that flow from it, I have a desire that my ancestors—those who lived when the gospel was not on earth and who have not had the privileges which are mine—I have a great desire that they also should be inheritors of these blessings. In other words, the promises made to the fathers have been planted in my heart, and I am obligated to act as a minister for the salvation of those in my line who have lived and died without having the gospel preached to them. ("Salvation: A Family Affair," *Improvement Era*, April 1959, p. 474.)

I THINK IT IS perfectly clear that the Lord expects far more of us than we sometimes render in response. We are not as other men. We are the saints of God and have the revelations of heaven. Where much is given much is expected. We are to put first in our lives the things of his kingdom.

We are commanded to live in harmony with the Lord's laws, to keep all his commandments, to sacrifice all things if need be for his name's sake, to conform to the terms and conditions of the law of consecration.

We have made covenants so to do—solemn, sacred, holy covenants, pledging ourselves before gods and angels.

We are under covenant to live the law of obedience.

We are under covenant to live the law of sacrifice.

We are under covenant to live the law of consecration.

With this in mind, hear this word from the Lord: "If you will that I give unto you a place in the celestial world, you must prepare yourselves by doing the things which I have commanded you and required of you." (D&C 78:7.)

It is our privilege to consecrate our time, talents, and means to build up his kingdom. We are called upon to sacrifice, in one degree or another, for the furtherance of his work. Obedience is essential to salvation; so, also, is service; and so, also, are consecration and sacrifice.

It is our privilege to raise the warning voice to our neighbors and to go on missions and offer the truths of salvation to our Father's other children everywhere. We can respond to calls to serve as bishops, as Relief Society presidents, as home teachers, and in any of hundreds of positions of responsibility in our various church organizations. We can labor on welfare projects, engage in genealogical research, perform vicarious ordinances in the temples.

We can pay an honest tithing and contribute to our fast offering, welfare, budget, building, and missionary funds. We can bequeath portions of our assets and devise portions of our properties to the Church when we pass on to other spheres.

We can consecrate a portion of our time to systematic study, to becoming gospel scholars, to treasuring up the revealed truths which guide us in paths of truth and righteousness....

We know full well that the laborer is worthy of his hire, and that those who devote all their time to the building up of the kingdom must be provided with food, clothing, shelter, and the necessaries of life. We must employ teachers in our schools, architects to design our temples, contractors to build our synagogues, and managers to run our businesses. But those so employed, along with the whole membership of the Church, participate also on a freewill and voluntary basis in otherwise furthering the Lord's work. Bank presidents work on welfare projects. Architects leave their drafting boards to go on missions. Contractors lay down their tools to serve as home teachers or bishops. Lawyers put aside *Corpus Juris* and the Civil Code to act as guides on Temple Square. Teachers leave the classroom to visit the fatherless and widows in their afflictions. Musicians who make their livelihood from their artistry willingly direct church choirs and perform in church gatherings. Artists who paint for a living are pleased to volunteer their services freely....

And every member of his church has this promise: That if he remains true and faithful—obeying, serving, consecrating, sacrificing, as required by the gospel—he shall be repaid in eternity a thousandfold and shall have eternal life. What more can we ask? ("Obedience, Consecration, and

Sacrifice," *Ensign*, May 1975, pp. 51-52.)

WHAT IS A TEMPLE? It is the House of the Lord; it is a holy sanctuary. That word is used in the Old Testament with reference to the temple.... A sanctuary is a place set apart from the world, a place reserved for spiritual things. It is in the temple that the veil is parted. It is in the temple that the veil is lifted, the veil between this life and the next realm of existence.

The veil is thin; the temple is the place where time and eternity link hands and are joined together and the foundations are laid for eternal joy, eternal felicity, and eternal happiness in the realms that are ahead.

We know that God is no respecter of persons, that he deals with every individual solely on the basis of personal righteousness. He has given a blanket promise in the revelations that spiritual gifts will flow to the faithful, even to the point, the promise so stipulates, that every faithful person will see the face of the Lord....The temple is the House of the Lord, and if the Lord has occasion to visit any particular part of his kingdom, the place where he will come will be the sanctuary that is appointed, the house that has been dedicated to him, the house that is his. ...Because all faithful people stand on a footing of total and complete equality, because all receive blessings as a result of righteousness and not of church position or some other eminence, all who are entitled to see the face of the Lord will receive that blessing in the House of the Lord....I state these things to help us gain a perspective of the spiritual worth of what is involved in a House of the Lord. ("The Promises Made to the Fathers," *Studies in Scripture, The Old Testament*, vol. 3, Kent P. Jackson and Robert L. Millet eds. [Randall Book: Salt Lake City, 1985], pp. 47-48.)

Chapter Twenty-Nine

Eternal Marriage

IT IS A DOCTRINE of the gospel that we should love our husbands and our wives with deep and abundant affection. The Lord said in our day through Joseph Smith: "Thou shalt love thy wife with all thy heart, and shalt cleave unto her and none else." (Doctrine & Covenants 42:22.) And he might have continued with equal verity in this revelation and said, "Thou shalt love thy husband with all thy heart and shalt cleave unto him and none else."

How much do you love your husband or your wife? How much deep and abiding affection do you in reality have for the young man or the young woman whom you expect to marry? I suppose, in order to understand what is involved here, we should look at the doctrine of celestial marriage as it has been revealed in this day. We cannot truly comprehend the principle of eternal love without an understanding of the doctrine of eternal marriage.

There are, of course, two orders or systems of matrimony in the Church. One we call civil marriage, a marriage "until death us do part," a marriage performed by the authority of the state, a marriage which has in effect a built-in divorce decree, because it is specified in the marriage itself that it will have an end.

On the other hand, we have celestial marriage, temple marriage, a marriage performed both by the authority of the state and also by virtue of the binding and sealing keys restored by Elijah the prophet in this dispensation, a marriage (if all goes well with it and the participating parties keep the covenant) that will endure in time and in eternity.

Eternal marriage is directly and intimately associated with the doctrine of exaltation. It is intimately connected with obtaining eternal life in the kingdom of God. It plays as vital and important a part as any of our acts can play in the eternal plan of salvation. If we can view it in its relationship to obtaining eternal life, then we can comprehend its eternal

Bruce R. McConkie: Highlights From His Life & Teachings

importance to us....

Our revelation says that in the celestial glory there are three heavens or degrees, and that in order to obtain the highest, a man must enter into this order of marriage of which I speak, celestial marriage, and that, if he does not, he cannot obtain it. He may enter into a lesser kingdom but that is the end of his progression in the highest eternal sense. He cannot have an increase, an eternal increase, the increase which is the glory of exalted beings in the celestial world.

We understand from the revelations that those who come up in immortality as husband and wife will grow, enlarge, advance, and progress until they inherit what is termed the "fulness of the Father." Then no power, no dominion, no truth will be withheld from them. But those who do not so inherit will come up in immortality, separately and singly, that is unmarried, without exaltation, in whatever degree of reward they merit, but forever denied the eternal fulness.

Thus celestial marriage is the gate to exaltation. It opens the door. Those who have a continuation of the family unit in eternity have exaltation. If the family unit does not continue in eternity, there is no exaltation, or in other words, there is no eternal life. By definition, eternal life is God's life. It is the type, kind, status, and quality of existence which he enjoys as an exalted being....

Now there is not anything which is good and wholesome that is withheld from a couple because of a celestial marriage. I was married to my wife in the temple; it is a celestial marriage. I can have everything in that marriage, which is wholesome and good and pure, that anyone can have in any type of marriage; and, in addition, I can have much more. Through faith, devotion, and conformity to the covenant that goes with celestial marriage, I can have the sanctifying influence of the love of Christ in my home, and I can have the hope of eternal union and eternal companionship hereafter. Nothing is denied a person through celestial marriage. Everything that is right and good is available and then much, much more in addition....

So I say, how much do you love your husband or your wife? Well you love her proportionately as you conform to the standards of the Church, proportionately as you do those things that will get a temple recommend, as you do those things that will keep in binding and sealing force the covenant of marriage that is made in the temple.

Suppose you cannot get a temple recommend because you do not keep the Word of Wisdom. Well, you are saying in a very realistic sense (it may seem a blunt expression) but quite realistically you are saying, "I love this cigarette more than I love my wife and the hope of eternal companionship with her. I love this cup of coffee or this cocktail more than I love the girl I expect to make my wife." Suppose you cannot get a temple recommend because you do not pay an honest tithing. Well, you are saying quite realistically, "I love one-tenth of my interest annually more than I love the hope of eternal life with this woman in the mansions that are prepared."

If you have already been married in the temple and you do not abide the covenant and do not walk uprightly as you should, you are saying in effect, "I love the things of this world more than I love the person I have made my eternal companion or more than the person I want to take as my eternal companion," because the eternal reward does not come unless the law is obeyed and complied with in the full. (*The New and Everlasting Covenant of Marriage*, Brigham Young University Speeches of the Year [20 Apr. 1960], pp. 2-6.)

"THE MOST IMPORTANT single thing that any Latter-day Saint ever does in this world is to marry the *right* person in the *right* place by the *right* authority."...

...Let us single out that thing which is more important than any other, that which should be preeminent and paramount in our lives.

I suggest to you that this is celestial marriage. Our hope and aim, our goal and desire is to receive this reward—to become like Him, to become like our Father. If we do this, we gain glory and honor, dignity, power and might such as He has. In addition to that, we exist and dwell in an eternal family unit, being husband and wife, mother and daughter, father and son.

The gospel plan which we have received is designed to prepare us to become like Him. It is a schooling process. And as we go through this schooling system we come to a point of advancement and progression where we qualify to take the particular course, the one singled out from all other courses of education in spiritual realms, the course that will enable us to gain exaltation and become like our Father. The name of that course is celestial marriage. Celestial marriage opens the gate that puts people on the path leading to exaltation and glory and to a continuation of the family unit in eternity....

...I suggest that the test which governs, which controls, which regulates, which indicates to us the course which we should pursue where marriage is concerned, is this matter of how much we love our husbands and our wives.

This matter of love is an abstract thing. In order to make it somewhat specific and concrete, I suggest to you that the measuring rod, the standard, by which it may be determined, the thing which weighs how much love is involved in the family unit, is time—how long you would like the marriage union to last. Do you want it to be a worldly or civil marriage that goes until death us do part? Or would you like it to be an association that endures in time and in eternity?

Let me suppose for you this situation. You are a young woman. You are attending the Brigham Young University. You are enjoying the social, cultural and other advantages that accrue from this great institution. A young man is courting you. You have a good idea what his aim is. Finally he says, "Mary, I love you. I would like you to be my wife. I love you so much that I would like you to be my wife for 17 days!" That is almost three weeks! Mary says, "I think I had better find some other companion."

I saw on the front page of the *Deseret News* some years back the picture of a lovely-appearing young woman, who had been killed in an automobile accident. She was from a prominent family, hence the front page location for the story. I read the account. It said she had been working in Salt Lake City, that she had gone to New York City and met her fiance who was working there. They had been married there and were on a honeymoon. Traveling on a turnpike in Pennsylvania there was an automobile accident. He was in the hospital and her life was taken.

Nobody pretends that when he said, "Mary, will you marry me?" he added, "for 17 days." But no one reads the future, and the marriage that was performed in New York, where there are no temples, was until death us do part. So, for all practical purposes, in deed though not in words, he had said, "Will you marry me for 17 days?" The marriage was over. They had 17 days' worth of love.

Someone says to you, "Mary, will you marry me and divorce me today?" That is unthinkable, of course; but for all practical purposes and from a realistic view of things, that is what happens when a civil marriage is performed. That is to say, inherent in, implicit in, as part of the marriage ceremony, there is also a divorce decree.

...If somebody gets married by a civil ceremony, that marriage is going to be final at some unspecified time—at the time of death.

We want eternal family units. This particular period of time when we attend college is normally the period when we choose a husband or a wife, and, hence, one of the great advantages of coming to the Brigham Young University is to find other people with like ideals—modest and lovely and wholesome young women, upright and outstanding young men....

...We want someone who in due course will be qualified and ready and worthy to take us to the temple of God, to the one place where an eternal marriage can be performed; someone who will love us more than he loves a cigarette, which if he takes he cannot get a temple recommend; someone who will love us more than a cocktail, which if he takes he cannot be worthy to go to the temple and have these blessings.

I think there is no concept known to the human mind as edifying and as noble and as glorious as the concept that the family unit continues. I don't think it makes any difference what church a person belongs to, what philosophy of life he has, what view of eternity possesses his soul and thinking, in his sober and reflective moments, the thing that he would rather have than anything else of enduring nature is the continued association of the members of his family. This is the heart and the center of revealed religion, and everything that we have in the Church, bar nothing, is preparatory to celestial marriage; it is to qualify and train and get people in a frame of mind where they will desire and will, in fact, enter into that order. And then everything that we have in the Church, from the day that a person enters into this system of marriage until he passes on into eternity—everything that we have looks back to that system of marriage and is designed to enable and help us to keep the covenant that we make in connection with it, so that all the terms and conditions will be everlastingly in force....

Celestial marriage—this is the glorious concept of the gospel. Having before us, then, the Lord's eternal perspective of life, I come back to the text statement that I quoted, and I repeat it with emphasis: "The most important single thing that any Latter-day Saint ever does in this world is to marry the *right* person in the *right* place by the *right* authority." Such opens the door to the fulness of all good things in this life and to eternal exaltation in the life to come. (*Choose an Eternal Companion*, Brigham Young University Speeches of the Year [3 May 1966], pp. 2-6.)

WHEN WE AS Latter-day Saints talk about marriage we are talking about a holy celestial order. We are talking about a system out of which can grow the greatest love, joy, peace, happiness, and serenity known to humankind. We are talking about creating a family unit that has the potential of being everlasting and eternal, a family unit where a man and a wife can go on in that relationship to all eternity, and where mother and daughter and father and son are bound by eternal ties that will never be severed. We are talking about creating a unit more important than the Church, more important than any organization that exists on earth or in heaven, a unit out of which exaltation and eternal life grow; and when we talk about eternal life, we are talking about the kind of life that God our Heavenly Father lives....

"The new and everlasting covenant" is the fulness of the gospel, and the gospel is the covenant of salvation that the Lord makes with men. It is new because it has been revealed anew in our day; it is everlasting because it has always been had by faithful people, not only on this earth but on all the earths inhabited by the children of our Father....

...We have power, as mortals, to make between ourselves any arrangements that we choose to make and that are legal in the society where we live, and they will bind us as long as we agree to be bound, even until death takes us. But we do not have power, as mortals, to bind ourselves after death. Neither you nor I can enter a contract to buy or sell or go or come or paint or perform or do any act in the sphere that is ahead. God has given us our agency here and now as pertaining to mortality.

We are mortal; this is a temporal sphere, a time-bound sphere. And if we are going to do anything here and now that bridges the gulf of death,...anything that remains with us in the resurrection, we have to do it by a power that is beyond the power of man—it has to be the power of God. Man is mortal and his acts are limited to mortality; God is eternal and his acts have no end....

...This matter of being sealed by the Holy Spirit of promise applies to every ordinance and every covenant and all things that there are in the Church. Do not talk about marriage and the Holy Spirit of promise unless and until you understand first the concept and the principle and its universal application.

One of our revelations speaks of "the Holy Spirit of promise, which the Father sheds forth upon all those who are just and true" (D&C 76:53), meaning that every person who walks uprightly, does the best that he can, overcomes the world, rises above carnality, and walks in paths of righteousness will have his acts and his deeds sealed and approved by the Holy Spirit. He will be, as Paul would have expressed it, "justified by the Spirit" (see 1 Corinthians 6:11). Therefore, if a man is going to be married and wants a marriage that lasts for a week, or three weeks, or three months, or as long as Hollywood prescribes, or even "until death us do part," he can be married by the power of man within the parameters and the limits that are set; he has that prerogative by the agency that the Lord has given him. But if he wants a wife to be his in the realms ahead, he had better find someone who has power to bind on earth and seal in heaven.

In order to get a proper marriage one must do this: first, search for and seek out celestial marriage—find the right ordinance; second, look for a legal administrator, someone who holds the sealing power—and that power is exercised only in the temples that the Lord has had built by the tithing and sacrifice of his people in our day; and third, so live in righteousness, uprightness, integrity, virtue, and morality that he is entitled to have the Holy Spirit of God ratify and seal and justify and approve, and in that event his marriage is sealed by the Holy Spirit of promise and is binding in time and in eternity.

So we Latter-day Saints struggle and labor and work to be worthy to get a recommend to go to the temple, for the spirit will not dwell in an unclean tabernacle. We struggle and labor to get our tabernacles clean, to be pure and refined and cultured, to have the Spirit as our companion; and when we get in that state our bishop and our stake president give us a "recommend" to go to the temple. We go there and make solemn and sober covenants, and having so done we then labor and struggle and work with all our power to continue in the light of the Spirit so that the agreement we have made will not be broken. If we do that, we have the assurance of eternal life. We do not need to tremble and fear; we do not need to have anxiety or worry if we are laboring and working and struggling to the best of our abilities. Though we do not become perfect, though we do not overcome all things, if our hearts are right and we are charting a course to eternal life in the manner I indicate, our marriages will continue in the realms that are ahead. We shall get into the paradise of God and we shall be husband and wife. We shall come up in the resurrection and we shall be husband and wife.

Anyone who comes up in the resurrection in the marriage state has the absolute guarantee of eternal life, but he will not then be a possessor and inheritor of all things—there is a great deal of progress and advancement to be made after the grave and after the resurrection. But he will be in the course where he will go on in the schooling and preparing processes until eventually he knows all things and becomes like God our Heavenly Father, meaning that he becomes an inheritor of eternal life....

...Eventually there will be a great patriarchal chain of exalted beings from Adam to the last man, with any links left out being individuals who are not qualified and worthy to inherit, possess, and receive along the indicated line.

I am talking now to people who have opportunity to live the law. Anyone who has the opportunity is required to do so; it is mandatory. I am perfectly well aware that there are people who did not have the opportunity but who would have lived the law had the opportunity been afforded; and those individuals will be judged in the providences and mercy of a gracious God according to the intents and desires of their hearts. That is the principle of salvation and exaltation for the dead.

I have talked only in general terms; I have deliberately not been specific. I have designed to set forth true principles....I have desired and designed to set forth the general concept that is involved with the hope that, having the concept before us, each of us will then determine for ourselves the courses that we have to pursue as individuals to obtain the indicated rewards. ("Celestial Marriage," in *1977 Devotional Speeches of the Year* [1978], pp. 170-74.)

THERE ARE THOSE who say that temple marriage assures us of an eventual exaltation. Some have supposed that couples married in the temple who commit all manner of sin, and who then pay the penalty, will gain their exaltation eventually.

This notion is contrary to the whole system and plan that the Lord has ordained, a system under which we are privileged to work out our salvation with fear and trembling before him. If we believe and obey, if we enter the waters of baptism and make solemn covenants with the Lord to keep his commandments, we thereby get on a strait and narrow path that leads from the gate of repentance and baptism to a reward that is called eternal life. And if we traverse the length of the path going upward and forward and onward, keeping the commandments, loving the Lord, and doing all that we ought to do, eventually we will be inheritors of that reward.

And in exactly and precisely the same sense, celestial marriage is a gate that puts us on a path leading to exaltation in the highest heaven of the celestial world. It is in that highest realm of glory and dignity and honor hereafter that the family unit continues. Those who inherit a place in the highest heaven receive the reward that is named eternal life. Baptism is a gate; celestial marriage is a gate. When we get on the paths of which I speak, we are then obligated to keep the commandments. My suggestion in this field is that you go to the temple and listen to a ceremony of celestial marriage, paying particular and especial attention to the words, and learn what the promises are that are given. And you will learn that all of the promises given are conditioned upon subsequent compliance with all of the terms and conditions of that order of matrimony. ("The Seven Deadly Heresies," in *1980 Devotional Speeches of the Year* [1981], p. 77.)

Chapter Thirty

The Reward of the Faithful

I THINK THERE is no occasion for any person in this Church to fear for the destiny of the kingdom. We do not need to steady the ark, but we do need to have in our hearts a fear that we may not make ourselves worthy, that we may not hew to the line of righteousness and keep the commandments of God with that degree of valiance which will give us our exaltation in the eternal worlds. (Conference Report, Oct. 1947, p. 62.)

PETER TALKS ABOUT making our calling and election sure, and all in the world that means is that we pursue the appointed course to the point that we get a guarantee that we will receive the things to which we have been called—that we will inherit the promised foreordained blessings. And so, what is involved is three things: one is baptism, two is celestial marriage, and three is then so living that in fact our calling and election does become sure....

What Peter announces is that there is such a thing as making these conditional promises absolute. Obviously any person who gains exaltation, in the ultimate and in the end, has made his calling and election sure. So in one manner of speaking, no one will ever gain exaltation, no one will ever have the family unit continue in eternity unless his calling and his election has been made sure, or in other words, unless he has gained the promise that he shall inherit eternal life.

But, on the other hand, when we talk about this, what we ordinarily mean is that for some individuals who pursue a course of righteousness and devotion, the day of judgment is in effect advanced so that sometime along the line, as they are pursuing the course leading to exaltation, the Lord says to them: "Son, thou shalt be exalted." And at that time, they then have their calling and election made sure; they have for all practical purposes worked out their salvation; they have the assurance of eternal life in the kingdom of God.

...Making one's calling and election sure grows out of baptism for one thing, and it grows out of celestial marriage for another. There is no such thing as gaining exaltation and eternal life except in and through the continuation of the family unit in eternity. Since making one's calling and election sure grows out of celestial marriage, the Lord took occasion to reveal the doctrine relative to it in connection with the revelation on marriage. If we enter in at this gate of marriage and then pursue a steadfast course, we gain eternal life. Making our calling and election sure is thus a matter of being married in the temple and of keeping the terms and conditions of this new and everlasting covenant of marriage. After entering in at the gate of celestial marriage, if we keep the commandments, then at some subsequent time, after great devotion and righteousness, after the Lord has proved us at all hazards, then he says: "Ye shall come forth in the first resurrection:...and shall inherit thrones, kingdoms, principalities, and powers, dominions, all heights and depths." (D&C 132:19.)

In other words God, by revelation, tells us that our calling and election is made sure, that we are sealed up unto eternal life....

They have eternal life; they have exaltation, and exaltation consists in being like God our Father. The whole purpose of our creation is to progress from our first spirit estate to the final glorious dominion and exaltation that God our Father has so that we become like him. This is what life is about....

This, then, without amplifying, without saying more, is the doctrine that is involved. It is not something that is beyond us; it is not outside the realm of our capabilities. The Lord would not offer baptism to a people and say, "Be baptized and you can be saved in my kingdom," unless he knew that the people had it within their power to enter into baptism and to do the things that will result in the promised salvation. And the Lord would not offer to a people celestial marriage and say to them, "Now enter this order of matrimony and keep the covenant and you will have eternal life," unless he knew that the people had the talent and the spiritual capacity and ability to gain the promised reward. And the same thing applies to making our calling and election sure. The Lord would not say to us, "Make your calling and election sure," unless he knew it was within our spiritual potential—unless we had the capacity and ability to press forward in steadfastness and devotion until that desired eventuality occurred.

Now, I am suggesting that this is within the realm of possibility and of probability for the members of the Church today. Many in this dispensation have obtained such a status. This ought to cause us to make a firm and unshakable determination to gain the blessings and benefits of baptism; to gain the blessings and benefits of celestial marriage; and in each instance those blessings accrue on condition that we keep the covenants that we make in connection with those holy ordinances. And then we ought to press forward with a steadfastness in Christ, keeping the commandments and living by every word that proceedeth forth from the mouth of God, so that our calling and election shall be made sure. (*Making Our Calling and Election Sure*, Brigham Young Univeristy Speeches of the Year [25 Mar. 1969], pp. 7-10.)

WE ARE BORN again when we die as pertaining to unrighteousness and when we live as pertaining to the things of the Spirit. But that doesn't happen in an instant, suddenly. That also is a process. Being born again is a gradual thing, except in a few isolated instances that are so miraculous they get written up in the scriptures. As far as the generality of the members of the Church are concerned, we are born again by degrees, and we are born again to added light and added knowledge and added desires for righteousness as we keep the commandments.

The same thing is true of being sanctified. Those who go to the celestial kingdom of heaven have to be sanctified, meaning that they become clean and pure and spotless. They've had evil and sin and iniquity burned out of their souls as though by fire, and the figurative expression there is "the baptism of fire." Here again it is a *process*. Nobody is sanctified in an instant, suddenly. But if we keep the commandments and press forward with steadfastness after baptism, then degree by degree and step by step we sanctify our souls until that glorious day when we're qualified to go where God and angels are.

So it is with the plan of salvation. We have to become perfect to be saved in the celestial kingdom. But nobody becomes perfect in this life. Only the Lord Jesus attained that state, and he had an advantage that none of us has. He was the Son of God, and he came into this life with a spiritual capacity and a talent and an inheritance that exceeded beyond all comprehension what any of the rest of us was born with. Our revelations say that he was like unto God in the premortal life and he was, under the Father, the creator of worlds without number. That Holy Being was the Holy One of Israel anciently and he was the Sinless One in mortality. He lived a perfect life, and he set an ideal example. This shows that we can strive and go forward toward that goal, but no other mortal—not the greatest prophets nor the mightiest apostles nor any of the righteous saints of any of the ages—has ever been perfect, but we must become perfect to gain a celestial inheritance. As it is with being born again, and as it is with sanctifying our souls, so becoming perfect in Christ is a process.

We begin to keep the commandments today, and we keep more of them tomorrow, and we go from grace to grace, up the steps of the ladder, and we thus improve and perfect our souls. We can become perfect in some minor things. We can be perfect in the payment of tithing. If we pay one-tenth of our interest annually into the tithing funds of the Church, if we do it year in and year out, and desire to do it, and have no intent to withhold, and if we would do it regardless of what arose in our lives, then in that thing we are perfect. And in that thing and to that extent we are living the law as well as Moroni or the angels from heaven could live it. And so degree by degree and step by step we start out on the course to perfection with the objective of becoming perfect as God our Heavenly Father is perfect, in which eventuality we become inheritors of eternal life in his kingdom.

As members of the Church, if we chart a course leading to eternal life; if we begin the processes of spiritual rebirth, and are going in the right direction; if we chart a course of sanctifying our souls, and degree by degree are going in that direction; and if we chart a course of becoming perfect, and, step by step and phase by phase, are perfecting our souls by overcoming the world, then it is absolutely guaranteed—there is no question whatever about it—we shall gain eternal life. Even though we have spiritual rebirth ahead of us, perfection ahead of us, the full degree of sanctification ahead of us, if we chart a course and follow it to the best of our ability in this life, then when we go out of this life we'll continue in exactly that same course. We'll no longer be subject to the passions and the appetites of the flesh. We will have passed successfully the tests of this mortal probation and in due course we'll get the fulness of our Father's kingdom—and that means eternal life in his everlasting presence.

The Prophet told us that there are many things that people have to do, even after the grave, to work out their salvation. We're not going to be perfect the minute we die. But if we've charted a course, if our desires are right, if our appetites are curtailed and bridled, and if we believe in the Lord and are doing to the very best of our abilities what we ought to do, we'll go on to everlasting salvation, which is the fulness of eternal reward in our Father's kingdom.

I think we ought to have hope; I think we ought to have rejoicing. We can talk about the principles of salvation and say how many there are and how people have to meet these standards. And it may thereby seem hard and difficult and beyond the capacity of mortals so to obtain. But we need not take that approach. We ought to realize that we have the same appetites and passions that all of the saints and righteous people had in the dispensations that have gone before. They were no different than we are. They overcame the flesh. They gained the knowledge of God. They understood about Christ and salvation. They had the revelations of the Holy Spirit to their souls certifying of the divine sonship and of the prophetic ministry of whatever prophets ministered among them. And as a consequence they worked out their salvation.

Occasionally in the overall perspective someone came along who so lived that he was translated, but that's not particularly for our day and generation. When we die our obligation is to go into the spirit world and continue to preach the gospel there. So, as far as people now living are concerned, our obligation is to believe the truth, and live the truth, and chart a course to eternal life. And if we do it, we get peace and joy and happiness in this life; and, when we go into the eternal realms ahead, we continue there to work in the cause of righteousness. And we will not fail! We will go on to eternal reward.

The Prophet Joseph Smith said that no man can commit the unpardonable sin after he departs this life. Of course he can't; that's part of the testing of this mortal probation. And on that same basis, anybody who is living uprightly and has integrity and devotion, if he's doing all that he can here, then when he leaves this sphere he's going to go into the paradise of God and have rest and peace—that is, rest and peace as far as the troubles and turmoils and vicissitudes and anxieties of this life are concerned. But he'll continue to labor and work on the Lord's errand, and eventually he'll come up in the Resurrection of the Just. He'll get an immortal body, meaning that body and spirit will be inseparably connected. That soul will never again see corruption. Never again will there be death, but what is equally as glorious, or more so, that soul will go on to eternal life in the kingdom of God. And eternal life means the continuation of the family unit. Eternal life means inheriting, receiving, and possessing the fulness of the Father, the power and might and creative ability and all that he has that enabled him to create worlds without number and to be the progenitor of an infinite number of spirit progeny. ("Jesus Christ and Him Crucified," in *1976 Devotional Speeches of the Year* [1977], pp. 399-402.)

MAY I SAY that this life never was intended to be easy. It is a probationary estate in which we are tested physically, mentally, morally, and spiritually. We are subject to disease and decay. We are attacked by cancer, leprosy, and contagious diseases. We suffer pain and sorrow and afflictions. Disasters strike; floods sweep away our homes; famines destroy our food; plagues and wars fill our graves with dead bodies and broken homes with sorrow.

We are called upon to choose between the revealed word of God and the soul-destroying postulates of the theoretical sciences. Temptations, the lusts of the flesh, evils of every sort—all these are part of the plan, and must be faced by every person privileged to undergo the experiences of mortality.

The testing processes of mortality are for all men, saints and sinners alike. Sometimes the tests and trials of those who have received the gospel far exceed any imposed upon worldly people. Abraham was called upon to sacrifice his only son. Lehi and his family left their lands and wealth to live in a wilderness. Saints in all ages have been commanded to lay all that they have upon the altar, sometimes even their very lives.

As to the individual trials and problems that befall any of us, all we need say is that in the wisdom of Him who knows all things, and who does all things well, all of us are given the particular and specific tests that we need in our personal situations....

Where the true Saints are concerned there is no sorrow in death except that which attends a temporary separation from loved ones. Birth and death are both essential steps in the unfolding drama of eternity....

There is no equivocation, no doubt, no uncertainty in our minds. Those who have been true and faithful in this life will not fall by the wayside in the life to come. If they keep their covenants here and now and depart this life firm and true in the testimony of our blessed Lord, they shall come forth with an inheritance of eternal life.

We do not mean to say that those who die in the Lord, and who are true and faithful in this life, must be perfect in all things when they go into the next sphere of existence. There was only one perfect man—the Lord

Jesus whose Father was God.

There have been many righteous souls who have attained relative degrees of perfection, and there have been great hosts of faithful people who have kept the faith, and lived the law, and departed this life with the full assurance of an eventual inheritance of eternal life.

There are many things they will do and must do, even beyond the grave, to merit the fulness of the Father's kingdom that final glorious day when the great King shall say unto them, "Come, ye blessed of my Father, inherit the kingdom prepared for you from the foundation of the world." (Matt. 25:34.)

But what we are saying is that when the saints of God chart a course of righteousness, when they gain sure testimonies of the truth and divinity of the Lord's work, when they keep the commandments, when they overcome the world, when they put first in their lives the things of God's kingdom: when they do all these things, and then depart this life—though they have not yet become perfect—they shall nonetheless gain eternal life in our Father's kingdom; and eventually they shall be perfect as God their Father and Christ His Son are perfect....

Sometimes the Lord's people are hounded and persecuted. Sometimes He deliberately lets His faithful saints linger and suffer, in both body and spirit, to prove them in all things, and to see if they will abide in His covenant, even unto death, that they may be found worthy of eternal life. If such be the lot of any of us, so be it.

But come what may, anything that befalls us here in mortality is but for a small moment, and if we are true and faithful God will eventually exalt us on high. All our losses and sufferings will be made up to us in the resurrection. ("The Dead Who Die in the Lord," *Ensign,* Nov. 1976, pp. 106-8.)

THERE ARE THOSE who believe we must be perfect to gain salvation.

This is...a doctrinal misunderstanding that I mention...to turn our attention from negative to positive things. If we keep two principles in mind we will thereby know that good and faithful members of the Church will be saved even though they are far from perfect in this life.

These two principles are (1) that this life is the appointed time for men to prepare to meet God—this life is the day of our probation; and (2) that the same spirit which possesses our bodies at the time we go out of this mortal life shall have power to possess our bodies in that eternal world.

What we are doing as members of the Church is charting a course leading to eternal life. There was only one perfect being, the Lord Jesus. If men had to be perfect and live all of the law strictly, wholly, and completely, there would be only one saved person in eternity. The prophet taught that there are many things to be done, even beyond the grave, in working out our salvation.

And so what we do in this life is chart a course leading to eternal life. That course begins here and now and continues in the realms ahead. We must determine in our hearts and in our souls, with all the power and ability we have, that from this time forward we will press on in righteousness; by so doing we can go where God and Christ are. If we make that firm determination, and are in the course of our duty when this life is over, we will continue in that course in eternity. That same spirit that possesses our bodies at the time we depart from this mortal life will have power to possess our bodies in the eternal world. If we go out of this life loving the Lord, desiring righteousness, and seeking to acquire the attributes of godliness, we will have that same spirit in the eternal world, and we will then continue to advance and progress until an ultimate, destined day when we will possess, receive, and inherit all things. (The Seven Deadly Heresies," in *1980 Devotional Speeches of the Year* [1981], pp. 78-79.)

YOU COULD TAKE the expressions that I've made and say they're a little severe, or they're harsh or difficult, and hence, it's hard to gain eternal salvation. I'd like to append to them the fact—and this is a true gospel verity—that everyone in the Church who is on the straight and narrow path, who is striving and struggling and desiring to do what is right, though is far from perfect in this life; if he passes out of this life while he's on the straight and narrow, he's going to go on to eternal reward in his Father's kingdom.

We don't need to get a complex or get a feeling that you have to be perfect to be saved. You don't. There's only been one perfect person, and that's the Lord Jesus, but in order to be saved in the Kingdom of God and in order to pass the test of mortality, what you have to do is get on the straight and narrow path—thus charting a course leading to eternal life—and then, being on that path, pass out of this life in full fellowship. I'm not saying that you don't have to keep the commandments. I'm saying you don't have to be perfect to be saved. If you did, no one would be saved. The way it operates is this: you get on the path that's named the "straight and narrow." You do it by entering the gate of repentance and baptism. The straight and narrow path leads from the gate of repentance and baptism, a very great distance, to a reward that's called eternal life. If you're on that path and pressing forward, and you die, you'll never get off the path. There is no such thing as falling off the straight and narrow path in the life to come, and the reason is that this life is the time that is given to men to prepare for eternity. Now is the time and the day of your salvation, so if you're working zealously in this life—though you haven't fully overcome the world and you haven't done all you hoped you might do—you're still going to be saved. You don't have to do what Jacob said, "Go beyond the mark." You don't have to live a life that's truer than true. You don't have to have an excessive zeal that becomes fanatical and becomes unbalancing. What you have to do is stay in the mainstream of the Church and live as upright and decent people live in the Church—keeping the commandments, paying your tithing, serving in the organizations of the Church, loving the Lord, staying on the straight and narrow path. If you're on that path when death comes—because this is the time and the day appointed, this is the probationary estate—you'll never fall off from it, and, for all practical purposes, your calling and election is made sure. Now, that isn't the definition of that term, but the end result will be the same. ("The Probationary Test of Mortality," Salt Lake Institute of Religion Devotional Address, 10 Jan. 1982, pp. 12-13.)

Chapter Thirty-One

The Second Chance Theory

ONE OF THE DOCTRINES of this kingdom, in which there is great comfort for the Saints, is that of salvation for the dead. We know that in the mercy of God our worthy ancestors may become joint heirs with us of the riches of eternity—and this because our God is no respecter of persons. Joseph Smith said that the greatest responsibility in this world that God has laid upon us—speaking to the Latter-day Saints of their individual responsibility—is to seek after our dead. We know that we, without them, cannot be made perfect; neither can they, without us.

But at the same time, in this glorious doctrine of salvation for the dead, there is a warning to the Latter-day Saints. This warning arises because the doctrine is limited to those who die without a knowledge of the gospel. It has no application to us. As far as I am concerned, as far as you are concerned, as far as all the people are concerned who have a knowledge of the gospel, now is the time and the day of our salvation....

There is no promise—that I know anything about—that those who reject the gospel in this life will be heirs of the celestial kingdom in the world to come.

These revelations [D&C 128:5; Alma 34:31-33; 3 Ne. 28:34-35; 2 Ne. 9:27; D&C 82:3; 3 Ne. 12:20] divide the heirs of salvation into two classes: first, those who have opportunity to accept and live the gospel in this life—this means all of the Latter-day Saints and all others who have a sufficient witness of Christ borne to them—all of them are under obligation to accept the truth here and now, to hearken to the counsels of the living oracles, and to live according to the best light and knowledge that God gives them. If they do this they work out their salvation.

The other class of people who will be heirs of the celestial kingdom are those who would have accepted the gospel with all their hearts, had they had opportunity to accept it here. For them, the ordinances of salvation will be performed and they will be heirs of the kingdom, and with the righteous and faithful of this life, will go into our Father's kingdom and have eternal rest....

Now the question naturally arises, in the light of these principles and doctrines, "What happens to those who have an opportunity to accept the truth in this life, but who fail or neglect to do it, and who hereafter accept it in the spirit world?" The Lord has given us answer by revelation. [D&C 76:73-74.]

I do not sit in judgment. Judgment is the Lord's and he will repay. But at the same time since these doctrines have come to us in such great plainness in this day, we are bound to know them, to live in accordance with them—and failing such, we will merit the penalty which a just God has decreed for our disobedience, for our sinning against the light....

As far as you and I are concerned, at this time, this life is the most important part of all eternity. (Conference Report, Apr. 1948, p. 48-51.)

THERE ARE THOSE who believe that the doctrine of salvation for the dead offers men a second chance for salvation.

I knew a man, now deceased, not a member of the Church, who was a degenerate old reprobate who found pleasure, as he supposed, in living after the manner of the world. A cigarette dangled from his lips, alcohol stenched his breath, and profane and bawdy stories defiled his lips. His moral status left much to be desired.

His wife was a member of the Church, as faithful as she could be under the circumstances. One day she said to him, "You know the Church is true; why won't you be baptized?" He replied, "Of course I know the Church is true, but I have no intention of changing my habits in order to join it. I prefer to live the way I do. But that doesn't worry me in the slightest. I know that as soon as I die, you will have someone go to the temple and do the work for me and everything will come out all right in the end anyway."

He died and she had the work done in the temple. We do not sit in judgment and deny vicarious ordinances to people. But what will it profit him?[10]

---

10. This particular line was revised by Elder McConkie before publication by BYU. Originally it read, "He died, and she did, and it was a total and complete waste of time." (Transcript from sound recording of *Seven Deadly Heresies.*)

There is no such thing as a second chance to gain salvation. This life is the time and the day of our probation. After this day of life, which is given us to prepare for eternity, then cometh the night of darkness wherein there can be no labor performed.

For those who do not have an opportunity to believe and obey the holy word in this life, the first chance to gain salvation will come in the spirit world. If those who hear the word for the first time in the realms ahead are the kind of people who would have accepted the gospel here, had the opportunity been afforded them, they will accept it there. Salvation for the dead is for those whose first chance to gain salvation is in the spirit world. ("The Seven Deadly Heresies," in *1980 Devotional Speeches of the Year* [1981], p. 77.)

Chapter Thirty-Two

The Preexistence and Intelligence

[This chapter contains some of Elder McConkie's most intriguing doctrinal teachings. He understood the importance of the preexistence and the logic of it within the plan of salvation. Since there is not a great deal of revealed information on some aspects of this doctrine, he was always careful to support his teachings on these matters with scripture or statements from the Prophet Joseph Smith. If he could not do so, and he ventured an opinion, he cautioned that it was then in the realm of "pure speculation." The following chapter contains excerpts from several different sources, highlighting Elder McConkie's teachings on some of the more interesting and significant concepts within the doctrine of preexistence. The first item is from a *typescript* of a lecture given in the summer of 1967 to graduate students, CES teachers, and others at Brigham Young University. Because of the nature of the classroom presentation, including questions and answers, the material is not as organized and formal as it would have been if prepared first in book form. This format serves to give the reader a sense of Elder McConkie's engaging classroom style, not commonly experienced.]

TODAY WE ARE going to take the subject of preexistence....This is one of the things that is unique and distinctive to us. There are no people in the world, as far as I know, at least none of any substance or size, that have a concept of a doctrine like this, preexistence....

I say this is an obvious and simple thing, and yet we immediately get into a field where there is a lot of speculation, a lot of uncertainty and a lot of ambiguity, and I'm not going to pretend to answer all of the questions today in the field that we discuss, but I am hopefully going to open up one of these avenues of investigation and make some suggestions as to what is seemingly founded and certain and absolute as far as revelation is concerned, and other things that seemingly get off into somewhat a realm of speculation and uncertainty. We are not going to say categorically that this is true or this is false. But I will suggest that some of the things that are said in the church are in the realm of speculation and can't be definitely and categorically known as far as the revelations are concerned....

When we get talking about preexistence, we are talking about where the human personality, the ego, the thing that is the living sensitive part of the human personality, where it came from. The preexistence, as I view it, has a very definite meaning to us. Now we're concerned in this connection with the problem, "What is a spirit?" And in answer to that I simply refer to such things as this: The 24th chapter of Luke where the man Jesus, resurrected, appeared to the disciples in the upper room and the record says they thought they had seen a spirit. He was a man in all respects, indicating that they understood that a spirit was a man. The same thing is true when he walked on the water, they thought it was a spirit. In other words, a spirit is a man. The same thing is true in this account in the book of Ether where the Lord, Jesus, appears and says, "this body ye now behold is the body of my spirit, even as I appear unto thee in the spirit will I appear unto my people in the flesh." When we talk about a spirit now, what we're talking about is an entity....

We're not talking about some ethereal essence, fluid or something else that fills immensity, we're talking about spiritual men and women as the offspring of God and this brings us to the next consideration. The foundation upon which preexistence rests. There are certain things that have to be known and have to be understood in order to be capable of believing in preexistence. And one of these things is the eternity of matter. You can't believe in the doctrine of preexistence unless you believe that all things exist everlastingly. If you believe what the heresies of the sectarian world, particularly in the past, have been; that God created things out of nothing, you'd have a problem with this.

Let's read...[D&C 93:29]. "Man was also in the beginning with God." Previously in this section he said that he was the First Born and that he was in the beginning with the Father. Now he is coming to the added thing that "man was also in the beginning with God." We'll have a real problem of interpretation here. That said MAN; now the next sentence says, "intelligence or the light of truth, was not created or made, neither indeed can be." Now here is something that is called intelligence. This is not intelligence in the sense that we use the word when we talk of intellectual things and native endowments and capacities, at least not strictly that. This is intelligence, or in other words, light and truth....

It always existed, it was not created, it wasn't made, neither indeed can be. So here is something that has always existed, it fills all immensity, it is everywhere present, it has a name, intelligence. It seemingly is the best name that the Lord can give it as far as we are concerned to get the concept over....

The third chapter [of Abraham] beginning with verse 22:

> Now the Lord had shown unto me, Abraham, the intelligences that were organized before the world was; and among all these there were many of the noble and great ones;
> And God saw these souls that they were good, and he stood in the midst of them, and he said: These I will make my rulers; for he stood among those that were spirits, and he saw that they were good; and he said unto me: Abraham, thou art one of them; thou wast chosen before thou wast born.

Intelligence is something that is everlasting and everywhere, it cannot start and it cannot stop, it just is. Now this is beyond our capacity to comprehend. Just like life itself is beyond our capacity to comprehend. We have to have a starting point and so we start here. Now Abraham sees something in vision, and what he sees is called intelligences and he's added an "s" to this word "intelligence." He says "the intelligences that were organized," so there is something involved here in the way of organization. And then he continues down in the account, he equates intelligences with spirits. He has then as near as I can read what he's saying here are synonymous, intelligences and spirits....

But what concerns us right now is seemingly Abraham equates intelligences with spirits. And we've got something over here [in D&C 93:29] that is called intelligence which is an ever existing matter. Now, look at Section 131 and let's take our standard statement about matter. Section 131, we're concerned with verses 7 and 8. "There is no such thing as immaterial matter." That is, everything's got substance. These spirit beings from preexistence have some substance. "All spirit is matter, but it is more fine or pure, and can only be discerned by purer eyes; we cannot see it; but when our bodies are purified we shall see that it is all matter." Spirit is matter. Now suppose I write, based on that phrase, this statement, "Spirit matter" (leaving off 'is' so that we can have something we can use as a word to give a concept to it). Well, I think really that does it. Intelligence and spirit matter, spirit matter and spirits, well, what is preexistence? Now you talk about us being the sons and daughters of God. Well, how did you get to be a son or daughter of God? You were born, weren't you. There is a definite specific time in existence when each of us was born as the offspring of Deity. Christ is the First Born. What does it mean for Christ to be born as the offspring of Deity? Or think of an eternity ahead in terms of somebody in this life who gains exaltation. He has eternal increase. He has, in Joseph Smith's language, spirit children in the resurrection. So there is going to be a specific time if you gain exaltation where spirits will be born to you as Christ was born of the Father. If I evaluate this correctly, this spirit matter or spirit element, the revelation used the word "matter," it would be in effect the equivalent of elements as we use the terms, and we are just trying to get words to get the concepts over. This spirit element was born as a spirit being or offspring. Or in other words, this thing that is called intelligence was organized into intelligences who are spirits. Now you think about this life. You get married and you have children. Well, you organize temporal elements into a mortal soul, or in other words, a temporal element is born into a mortal body, formed or framed. Our bodies are created from the dust of the earth, meaning that they come from the elements that surround us. This by analysis is the same process as we understand it, that went on in preexistence. Now what I'm saying is that the intelligence and spirit matter seem to be equated as the same thing, and that intelligences and spirits seem to be the same thing, and that the organization of intelligence is into intelligences, and the birth of spirit matter, which is the same thing, is a birth into a state of spirits. When we begin our preexistence life, now, this, as I understand it, is as far as we can prove and establish and go from the revelation.

But what is not a bit uncommon in the church is for people, and you hear it everywhere and I don't say it's false, I just say it is in the realm of speculation, you find them going one step farther than this....

People say here is preexistence, and they say there is something before preexistence. Well, this is true, in my judgment if you get it right. Now here is spirit matter, as we have been saying, and this spirit matter is born as an entity. So the problem becomes one of what is involved before the state that we talked of as preexistence, the way we are defining it this morning. As far as I can evaluate it is just a matter of spirit matter.

[D&C 93:30] "All truth is independent in that sphere in which God has placed it, [now notice] to act for itself, as all intelligence also; otherwise there is no existence." Now this is an extremely interesting verse. Remember that light and truth [are] equated here as synonyms for intelligence. Now it seems to say that intelligence is independent in that sphere in which God has placed it; I don't think that's too far of a conclusion to draw, taking 29 and 30 together. To act for itself, well it says it has all intelligence also, otherwise there is no existence and our problem revolves around those five words, "otherwise there is no existence." Well, you read that and you get an assumption immediately, or at least it is logical to get an assumption from it. But over here is something that is called intelligence that has always existed and that this intelligence is independent in its sphere and then this phrase, otherwise there is no existence. Well, if it is independent in its sphere it sounds like there is some kind of agency involved that causes portions of this intelligence to get itself organized into intelligences. Now I'm saying that's what it sounds like. I don't think that is really what it's saying. But it sounds like it's saying that, and this theory that says there is something that precedes preexistence as far as I know was created by B. H. Roberts years ago. And when he created it he invented a new word that isn't in the English language in order to describe what he was thinking about, what he was saying. And the word that he invented was this: Intelligencies, and he speculated, if I may so term it, that there were these things, intelligencies, and they were the things that were born as spirit children. Well, our scripture now has said, that "otherwise there is no existence," that is if there wasn't agency involved. Now, I'll take one more passage and then we'll discuss a little of what is involved....

There are some things in the Book of Mormon that are quite deep and quite philosophical and this is one of them. Talk about philosophy, if you want some mental exercise in spiritual things here's a sample of it. Lehi is talking to Jacob, and let's follow his reasoning now. "If ye shall say there is no law, ye shall also say there is no sin." Now notice [his reasoning:] No law, well then there is no sin. Now the next step. "If ye shall say there is no sin, ye shall also say there is no righteousness." No sin, no righteousness, now that is clear. "And if there be no righteousness there be no happiness." And I think that is clear. "And if there be no righteousness nor happiness, there be no punishment nor misery. And if these things are not there is no God." Now, you want some philosophical reasoning, syllogisms, "If these things are not there is no God," Now he's talking about agency. Agency is the ability to choose to go one direction or another. "If these things are not there is no God. And if there is no God we are not, neither the earth; for there could have been no creation of things [now notice his language] neither to act nor to be acted upon; wherefore, all things must have vanished away." If there were no agency all things must have vanished away. Now this is impossible, this is just totally beyond possibility, but this is a tremendous argument. He is arguing that because things exist (and this is a philosophical thing), therefore there is agency. If there were no agency, there would be no existence. That's the effect of this. You have opposite, which means agency, and opposition in all things, two sides, so the fact that things exist, that we are, proves that there's opposite, otherwise philosophically we would not exist and all things would have vanished away.

Now with that in mind, this is 2nd Nephi beginning there, with that in mind, go back to this verse in section 93. "All truth is independent in that sphere in which God has placed it, to act for itself, [agency] as all intelligence also; [now I'm going to twist this scripture a little]: [otherwise all things have vanished away] (Do you follow me?) otherwise there is no existence." Otherwise all things have vanished away. I wonder if these two things aren't equated. I wonder if they don't mean the same thing. Seems to me they do. Lehi makes some marvelous arguments here and when the Lord gets to talking about it, he doesn't bother to argue the case, he just draws the conclusion that there is no existence with anything unless there is agency, unless there is a choice to go one way or the other there is no existence. If it's not hot on one hand and cold on the other there is nothing. There is no middle ground. Unless there is darkness on one hand and light on the other, there is nothing, because you have to have opposites to have existence. That is the philosophical argument. If there is no sin there is no righteousness, and the ultimate argument is there is no man, no God, no earth or anything and all things would vanish away; and so in [D&C 93:30] intelligence and truth, which is back here [before spirit birth], can act for itself, otherwise there is no existence. Now you tell me what that means. Does that mean that this [pre-spirit birth matter] has some power to elect to be born as the offspring of God or to be born as a spirit rabbit, or something else, because everything existed in the spirit because animals have spirits as well. Now I don't think it means that....

Agency exists among intelligent beings and we are endowed with agency when we're born the offspring of God, and some things have power to act, and the things that have power to act are those that are endowed with the power [to act], and some things have power to be acted upon. We read those two phrases didn't we? And the things that are acted upon are the inert things, the things that have no life of the kind we are talking about when we say spirits. Now there is a sense in which there is life in everything, even though we consider it to be dead. Well, I throw that out to you now, and the only conclusion that I'm drawing which I think is fully substantiated (in my mind) is that the revelations say there is this which becomes this which in due part is born into mortality, and that if we go farther than that we are in the realm of speculation. Now to my personal knowledge, there have been at least a dozen times since I have been [a General Authority], more times than that maybe, when the brethren have taken out of either priesthood or gospel doctrine lessons any concept that there was agency and power and the ability in this to choose to be born....But this is the way that I understand the doctrine of preexistence, and beyond this seems to me to be speculation.

Question: Did we choose to be a male or female?

No, I don't think we choose to be male or female. I think God chose that. Now if by that you mean that some of this intelligence back here chose to be born a female spirit,...you see you just get off into the realm of pure speculation....

We have some extremely interesting concepts and some of them (and they're only revealed in part), and some of them are beyond our ability to understand, things just go on everlastingly. Here is preexistence, meaning spirit children, the way we're defining things. Now following this is mortality. And that's where we are now, and following mortality leading out to the spirit world are kingdoms of glory, three of them: terrestrial, telestial, and celestial, and in the celestial, the highest heaven, the marriage union continues, and people who get exalted through marriage and are in this union have spirit children and so we have come to a point where there is preexistence all over again because here are exalted beings who have children and you have duplicated what went before. And these spirit children have a mortality and a limited few of them gain exaltation and so you have got preexistence all over again and so you just go on everlastingly and we have this phrase in the scriptures that says Christ is from everlasting to everlasting. Christ is from everlasting to everlasting, to everlasting to everlasting the same. ("The Preexistence of Man," typescript of summer 1967 class lecture given at BYU; original audio tape in BYU Religious Instruction Audiovisual Materials. The compiler has edited the quoted portions from the full text.)

THIS MATTER OF being born and having a family relationship is purely a matter of definition. We were born first as the spirit children of God, our Heavenly Father. We lived with him for an infinite period. Our lives did not commence when we started out this mortal existence. This mortal sphere is simply a change of status for the eternal spirit that had lived for an infinite period in the presence of God, our Heavenly Father. Birth is a change of status. It is a new way of living. (*Households of Faith*, Brigham Young University Speeches of the Year [1 Dec. 1970], p. 4.)

THERE IS A STATEMENT in our literature that says that the Prophet and his associates learned, by translating the papyrus received from the catacombs of Egypt, that life had been going on in this system for 2,555,000,000 years. (Brigham Young University Speeches of the Year [4 Jan. 1972], p. 7.)

PREEXISTENCE IS NOT some remote and mysterious place. All of us are but a few years removed from the Eternal Presence, from him whose children we are and in whose house we dwelt. All of us are separated by a thin veil only from the friends and fellow laborers with whom we served on the Lord's errand before our eternal spirits took up their abodes in tabernacles of clay.

True, a curtain has been drawn so we do not recall our associations there. But we do know that our Eternal Father has all power, all might, all dominion, and all truth and that he lives in the family unit. We do know that we are his children, created in his image, endowed with power and ability to become like him. We know he gave us our agency and ordained the laws by obedience to which we can obtain eternal life. We know we had friends and associates there. We know we were schooled and trained and taught in the most perfect educational system ever devised, and that by obedience to his eternal laws we developed infinite varieties and degrees of talents. ("God Foreordains His Prophets and His People," *Ensign,* May 1974, p. 73.)

YOU ASKED: "Is it official church doctrine, affirmed by the Living Prophet and all of the presiding brethren, that we had no identity, that we were not individual intelligent entities before we were born into the spirit world?"

In answer I can do only two things: 1. Tell you what I understand the doctrine of the Church is, and 2. Give you a little background which may interest you as to the reaction the Brethren have had to this point when it has been raised in recent years.

As to official Church pronouncements on doctrinal points, they are almost nonexistent. The Brethren made one in 1916 entitled, "The Father and the Son, A Doctrinal Exposition." The First Presidency made another in 1913 on the subject of evolution....

As far as official doctrinal pronouncements are concerned, about all the Brethren ever do is say here are the Standard Works, get the spirit of inspiration and figure out what the doctrines are. Those with extensive backgrounds of study in the Church are aware that differing opinions have been expressed by various of the Brethren on certain points over the years. This, of course, is of no great moment. All the opinions cannot be true, but the marvel is that there are so few differences in views and that there is so great harmony on the basics of the gospel.

As far as I know there is no official pronouncement on the subject at hand, but that applies also to a thousand other subjects, all of which are equally or more basic to an understanding of the plan of salvation.

In my judgment, spirit element exists and it was organized into spirit beings, or in other words intelligence exists and it became the intelligences that were organized. In my judgment there was no agency prior to spirit birth and we did not exist as entities until that time. I do know that this matter has arisen perhaps six or eight times in the years that I have been here and have been involved in reading and approving priesthood or auxiliary lessons. In each of these instances, the matter was ordered deleted from the lesson. In each case it was expressly stated that we have no knowledge of any existence earlier than our existence as the spirit children of God. The views in this field were described as pure speculation. President Joseph Fielding Smith personally, on more than one occasion directed this material not be published and said that he did not believe it, and of course, as you have indicated I do not believe it either.

As far as I know the ideas in this field originated with B. H. Roberts who wrote the first series of lessons ever used on a church-wide basis for priesthood quorums. In these lessons he came up with the idea that there were intelligencies, a word which he created for the purpose of describing the entities that supposedly existed as such before they were clothed with spirit bodies. This was pure fantasy and pure speculation. It caught on and has been bobbing to the top now and then ever since, except that the word that he created is no longer used. It is this doctrine that the

Brethren have described as pure speculation. In my judgment there is no revelation which sustains and supports it. The one used primarily is the passage in the 93rd Section of the Doctrine and Covenants which talks about all truth being independent in the sphere in which God has placed it, to act for itself as all intelligence also, with this phrase added, "otherwise there is no existence." From this some have inferred that there was agency inherent in some entity prior to the birth of spirit children. In my judgment this is simply a summary statement of what Lehi is talking about in the second chapter of 2 Nephi where he presents an argument, that if such and such does not exist then something else does not and finally reaches the conclusion for argument's sake, that "all things must have vanished away." This, of course, is merely a form of reasoning and not intended to mean that all things have or could vanish away. It is the amplified explanation of what is meant by the statement in Section 93.

I don't remember discussing this matter with any of the Brethren except that I know several of them have been present when President Joseph Fielding Smith expressed his views on the matter, and I assume that those present were in accord with President Smith's expressions, at least I was. (Correspondence from Elder Bruce R. McConkie to Walter M. Horne, 2 October 1974; original letter in author's possession.)

HOW LONG DID Adam and Abraham and Jeremiah (and all men!) spend in preparing to take the test of a mortal probation? What ages and eons and eternities passed away while Christ dwelt in the Eternal Presence and did the work then assigned him? How can we measure infinite duration in finite terms? To such questions we have no definite answers. Suffice it to say, the passage of time was infinite from man's viewpoint. We have an authentic account, which can be accepted as true, that life has been going on in this system for almost 2,555,000,000 years. Presumably this system is the universe (or whatever scientific term is applicable) created by the Father through the instrumentality of the Son.

[Note: The following information is contained in an endnote referring to the above paragraph.] All of the prophets who have seen within the veil have known many things that were never preserved and passed on to their posterity and to the residue of men. Joseph Smith and the early brethren in this dispensation knew much that we do not know and will not know until we attain the same spiritual stature that was theirs. This matter of how long eternity has been going on in our portion of created things is one of these matters. The sliver of information that has been preserved for us is found in an epistle of W. W. Phelps, written on Christmas day, 1844, and published to the Church in the *Times and Seasons.* Brother Phelps speaks of, "Jesus Christ, whose goings forth, as the prophets said, have been from of old, from eternity."...Then, in an interpolative explanation of what is meant by "from eternity," or "from everlasting," Brother Phelps says, "And that eternity [the one during which Christ's doings have been known], agreeable to the records found in the catacombs of Egypt, has been going on in this system [not this world], almost two thousand five hundred and fifty-five millions of years." (*Times and Seasons* 5:758.) That is to say, the papyrus from which the Prophet Joseph translated the Book of Abraham, to whom the Lord gave a knowledge of his infinite creations, also contained this expression relative to what apparently is the universe in which we live, which universe has been created by the Father through the instrumentality of the Son. The time mentioned has no reference, as some have falsely supposed, to the period of this earth's existence. (*The Mortal Messiah,* Book 1 [Salt Lake City: Deseret Book, 1979], pp. 29, 32-33n.)

AFTER HE HAD begotten us as his spirit children, he gave us our agency, which is the power and ability to choose; he also gave us laws and allowed us to obey or disobey, in consequence of which we can and did develop talents, abilities, aptitudes, and characteristics of diverse sorts. He ordained and established a plan of salvation. It was named the gospel of God, meaning God our Heavenly Father, and it consisted of all of the laws, powers, and rights, all of the experiences, all of the gifts and graces needed to take us, his spirit sons and daughters, from our then-spirit state of low intelligence to the high, exalted state where we would be like him. ("Celestial Marriage," in *1977 Devotional Speeches of the Year* [1978], p. 170.)

THESE WORDS [3 Nephi. 1:12-14] spoken in the name of the Lord Jesus, are sometimes used, erroneously, as an argument that the Spirit Christ was not in the body being prepared in Mary's womb, and that therefore the spirit does not enter the body until the moment of birth, when the mother's offspring first breathes the breath of life. This is not true.

As amply attested by the writings and teachings of President Brigham Young and others, the spirit enters the body at the time of quickening, whenever that is, and remains in the developing body until the time of birth. In a formal doctrinal statement the First Presidency of the Church (Joseph F. Smith, Anthon H. Lund, and John R. Winder) have said: "The body of man enters upon its career as a tiny germ or embryo, which becomes an infant, quickened at a certain stage by the spirit whose tabernacle it is, and the child, after being born, develops into a man.".…

With reference to the words here spoken by the Lord Jesus on the night of his birth, we must understand that someone else, speaking by what is called divine investiture of authority, is speaking the words in the first person as though he were the Lord, when in fact he is only speaking in the Lord's name. In many revelations the Son speaks in this same way as though he were the Father. (*The Mortal Messiah,* Book 1 [Salt Lake City: Deseret Book, 1979], p. 349, note 1.)

IN THE PREEXISTENCE we lived in the presence of God. All of us have seen God, our Father. No person on earth lives who, back in that sphere, did not see the face of God, and we knew that all of the teaching that came from Him was His, that it originated with Him, that He was our Father. We were taught, obviously, by other people in preexistence who represented Him in various schools, as it were, that we attended. But all of the truths were His, and we knew it. That kind of a life is described as "walking by sight." Please note—we walked by sight because we knew the source of the teaching, and we were spirit beings.

We don't understand everything about a spirit. We know a spirit is a man or a woman. We do know this: When we came down here into mortality, we came under circumstances where the curtain was drawn and we wouldn't remember preexistence, and instead of walking by sight, we would walk by faith.…

…We no longer have the personal knowledge that the truths are coming from God. Back there we were tried and examined and on probation as spirit beings.…

…It's unavoidable to reach the conclusion that we lived there for an infinite period of time. We've heard some of the early brethren talk in terms of millions of years. It certainly was that. I would suppose that we can get some vision and understanding of how long we lived in the premortal life by just reciting some of the things that happened. We know that here's a being who is called the Firstborn Spirit, who is the Lord Jesus, and that He lived there long enough to advance and progress to become like God and to become, under the Father, the Creator of worlds without number. It's implicit in that kind of a concept that long periods of time—totally beyond mortal conception—were involved. That means that we prepared, for what we would designate as an infinite duration of time, for the privilege and opportunity of coming down here and taking the test of mortality, and so this mortal life becomes the final examination for all of the life that we lived back there. We prepared and went to school. ("The Probationary Test of Mortality," Salt Lake Institute of Religion Devotional Speech, 10 Jan. 1982, pp. 7-8.)

SCHOOLING IS NOTHING new to us here. We went to school in preexistence. There were occasions where Adam taught the classes, and when Abraham taught the classes, and when Joseph Smith did. And the classes were so numerous and so extensive that the whole house of Israel—that group of spirits who were foreordained to become Israelites—were teachers; and they taught classes. And the witness of truth was borne and we were given the opportunity to advance and progress. When the time came for us to come down to mortality, we ended a course of instruction that had been going on for an infinitely long period of time and commenced a new course of instruction—a mortal course. In effect, this mortal course is the final examination for all of the life that we lived through in this infinite premortal period. (As cited in *Doctrines of the Restoration,* ed. Mark L. McConkie [Salt Lake City: Bookcraft, 1989], pp. 340-41.)

Chapter Thirty-Three

The Virgin Birth

WE BELIEVE THAT he came into the world, born of Mary, literally and actually, as we are born of our mothers; that he came into the world, born of God the Eternal Father, the Almighty Elohim, literally and actually, as we are born of our earthly fathers. (Conference Report, Oct. 1951, p. 146.)

OUR PROCLAMATION IS that he came into the world to ransom men from the temporal and spiritual death brought upon them through the fall of Adam; that he was born of Mary, inheriting from her the power of mortality, which is the power to die; that he is literally the Son of God, in the same sense in which all men are the offspring of mortal fathers; and that he inherited from his Father the power of immortality, which is the power to live. ("Our Belief in Christ," *Improvement Era*, Dec. 1970, p. 113.)

WHERE THEN SHALL he be born? On which of all the worlds of his creating shall he dwell? Where shall he come to bow neath an infinite burden in a self-chosen Gethsemane? And where shall he find his Calvary where he can be crucified by sinful men?

For his own purposes the Eternal Father, who knoweth all things and doeth all things well, chose planet earth as the place for the birth, and for the ministry, and for that atoning sacrifice of the One who was his Beloved and Chosen from the beginning.

Why? Why this earth rather than any other? We are left to wonder. We know that among all the workmanship of the Father's hands there has not been so great wickedness as among the inhabitants of this particular earth. We know that Christ came among "the more wicked part of the world," and that there was "none other nation on earth that would crucify their God. For," as the scripture saith, "should the mighty miracles be wrought among other nations they would repent, and know that he be their God." (2 Ne. 10:3-5.)

Could it be that planet earth was chosen as the place for the birth of a God because we on this earth are in greater need for direct and personal guidance than those who live on other earths? Could it be that a gracious Father arranged to tie the birth of his Son in with the history of Israel and with the house of David as a special favor to people here, to people who need to feel a closeness and a kinship to the Eternal One? Could it be that our knowledge of his life and ministry has come to us because we, above all peoples, need the enlightenment and encouragement found in the gospel accounts?

Whatever the reasons the decree went forth from the Father that his Beloved and Chosen One should find mortal habitation among us, among some of the lowest and weakest of his eternal children. And because he so decreed, we have great reason to rejoice. Our Lord's life here, in a setting familiar to us and under circumstances with which we can equate, gives us great encouragement. What he did here is an ever present beacon guiding us in the way to perfection.

The birth of a God—when should it be? It was programmed into the eternal scheme of things so as to take place in the meridian of time. The meridian of time, the mid-point in time! It was to be four thousand years after the birth of the first man and, as we suppose, four thousand years before the great winding up scene when this earth shall become a celestial sphere.

The meridian of time, the high point in time! The high point, indeed—it was to be the one and only time in all eternity when a God would make flesh his tabernacle. It was to be the age of atonement, the age when the ransom would be paid, the age in which death would be swallowed up in victory. It was to be the age in which the crumbling dust in ten thousand tombs would cleave together and the saints of God would come forth from their graves in glorious immortality and be crowned with eternal life on the right hand of Him whose servants they had been.

The birth of a God—to whom would he be born? To the most blessed and favored one of all womankind; to the one prepared and foreordained for this signal honor from all eternity; to Mary of Nazareth of Galilee—she was chosen to be the mother of the Son of God.

And since God was to be the Father of his own Son, the Messianic word acclaimed: "Behold, a virgin shall conceive, and bear a son, and shall call his name Immanuel" (Isa. 7:14), Immanuel, meaning God with us!

Nephi bears this concordant testimony: "I beheld the city of Nazareth," he says, "and in the city of Nazareth I beheld a virgin, and she was exceedingly fair and white,...a virgin, most beautiful and fair above all other virgins." And from the lips of an angel he heard these words: "Behold, the virgin whom thou seest is the mother of the Son of God, after the manner of the flesh."

Then Nephi said: "And it came to pass that I beheld that she was carried away in the Spirit; and after she had been carried away in the Spirit for the space of a time the angel spake unto me, saying: Look! And I looked and beheld the virgin again, bearing a child in her arms. And the angel said unto me: Behold the Lamb of God, yea, even the Son of the Eternal Father!" (1 Ne. 11:13-21.)

What is more fitting than for the Holy One of Israel, whose mortal life was to be one without sin, what accords more perfectly with the whole nature of his life than that he should be born of a virgin, of the fairest and most gracious of all the virgins on earth. Indeed, how could it be otherwise for a Child whose Father was God?

And what is more fitting for the Promised Messiah, who is to be Lord and King over all the earth, what accords better with the concept that he shall rule and reign forever in the house of Israel, than to have him come into mortality as the Son of Israel's greatest king?...

According to the marriage discipline then prevailing among the Jews, Joseph a Jew and Mary a Jewess were espoused and considered to be husband and wife, although they could not properly live in the conjugal relationship until after a second marriage ceremony was performed, nor could Mary properly live with any other man. We can imagine Joseph's sorrows and feel the sadness of his tears when he learned that his beloved wife—for such she was considered to be—was with Child by Another.

As his sorrows weighed in upon him, "the angel of the Lord"—we suppose it was Gabriel—"appeared unto him in a dream, saying, "Joseph, thou son of David, fear not to take unto thee Mary thy wife: for that which is conceived in her is of the Holy Ghost." That is to say, Mary had been overshadowed, as Luke recorded, and had conceived by the power of the Holy Ghost, and the Son of the Highest, who is God above all, was then in her womb....

The birth of a God—where shall it take place? If the Lord of the Universe is to take upon himself the form of a man, in what setting shall such a transcendent event unfold? Is there a place on earth worthy of such a birth? Or does the very universe itself contain a site of sufficient renown and eminence to be a fit place for the birth of its Eternal Creator? Can it take place anywhere but on Kolob itself?

Rome rules the world. Shall the Lord be born in Caesar's palace in the Eternal City? Herod is king in the land Jehovah promised to Abraham and his seed, of whom Christ is part. Is his palace an appropriate place for the birth of Israel's King? The Temple of Jehovah graces the Holy City. The walls around its courts are nearly a mile in length. The stones of its chief building are of majestic marble covered with solid gold. The great altar, the holy of holies (into which the high priest enters on the day of atonement to pronounce the ineffable Name and atone for the sins of the people) and the veil of the temple—all are there. Is this a proper place for the High Priest of our Profession to begin his mortal life?...

Let not Christ be born under the roof of Augustus where all the intrigue and sins of the world center. Let him stay far from the home of Herod who soon will slaughter the Innocents in Bethlehem as he thirsts for the blood of the newborn King. Let him not be in subjection to the ancient law administered in the Temple. Though it be his Father's house, those who administer its ordinances and regulate its affairs have made it a den of thieves. But let Christ be born and let him live as the Messianic word promises.

And so we find Joseph and Mary in Nazareth. The time for the birth of births is near, and Bethlehem is some eighty miles away by the closest route. Whether the married couple were even aware that "their" Son, as the world would assume him to be, must be born in Bethlehem we do not know. But at this point a divine providence began regulating the affairs of all concerned.

Caesar Augustus decreed "that all the world should be taxed," meaning that the citizens and subjects of his empire should be counted with each one paying a head tax. It was totally immaterial to him how and under what circumstances the counts were made. Herod who, under Caesar, was king of the Jews was an able and astute political leader. However much his reign reeked with evil and immorality and murder—he had ten wives and spent his life in debauchery and intrigue—however vile he was as a man, he had the political instinct to know that the Jews should be counted and taxed in the cities of their ancestors. Indeed, Herod himself was half Jew and half Idumean, and he is the one who ordered the journey that took Joseph and Mary—willingly or unwillingly—to Bethlehem, because Joseph "was of the house and lineage of David," and

Bethlehem was the City of David.

The scriptures say only that Joseph and Mary went to Bethlehem. We know from other sources, however, how people travelled in that day, and we can picture with almost certainty the things they did. It is quite unlikely that they went through Samaria because of the animosities that existed between the two peoples. Probably their route led them through Perea, and certainly, having Mary's condition in mind, they would have spent a full week en route. To travel alone was unheard of; friends and relatives always banded together for their own protection and for the pleasant conversations that were a way of life in their religion-oriented society.

They used donkeys and oxen, sometimes camels, and they carried their own food and bedding. At night they camped at the everywhere present caravanserais. These established places of repose and sleep were all built to a common pattern. They consisted of a series of rooms of wood or stone, built in a square or rectangle, surrounding an open court, with the only doors opening onto the court. They were commonly built on a platform which was a foot or two higher than the courtyard. The courtyard was the stable. It was there they tethered their animals. One would expect to find donkeys and oxen, sometimes camels, and occasionally sheep and goats in these enclosures.

It was to one of these caravanserais, in the environs of Bethlehem, that Joseph and Mary and their party came on the night appointed for the birth of a God. The travel of the day must have been restricted because of Mary's condition. In any event when they arrived all of the rooms were filled. These rooms in Hebrew are called katalyma, which word appears only twice in the New Testament. It has no English equivalent, the nearest meaning probably being hostel. In one New Testament instance the meaning is given as guestchamber. In the passage concerning our Lord's birth it is translated inn, which is corrected by the Prophet in the Inspired Version to read inns in the plural. Thus the statement, "There was no room for them in the inns," simply means that the rooms at the caravanserais were filled and they must of necessity sleep in the open air.

Joseph made the choice to sleep in the courtyard with the animals, in the stable if you will. And we cannot think other than that there was a divine providence in this. The great God, the Father of us all, intended that his Only Begotten Son should be born in the lowest of circumstances and subject to the most demeaning of surroundings.

There amid the lowing of cattle and the bleating of sheep; there where the calm of the night was filled with the sounds of braying asses and yelping dogs; there where the stench of urine and the stink of dung fouled the nostrils of delicate souls—there in a stable the Son of God was born. There the King of Heaven was wrapped in swaddling clothes and laid in a manger. That there were loving kinswomen who acted as midwives, we cannot doubt. And that a divine providence guided each step taken by all the participants is even more certain.

...Why was this night of nights different from all the others that ever have been or ever will be? Truly it was the night upon which a God was born. And his birth, demeaning and low and seemingly insignificant, was but a harbinger of his death. He was born in a stable and he died on a cross—all because his Father willed it so....

Why was this night different from all others? Because on it One was born who was different from all others. A God was born. He came in to this world inheriting from his Father the power of immortality and from his mother the power of mortality. His birth enabled him to work out the infinite and eternal atonement, than which there neither has been nor will be an event of such magnitude and import.

We testify that a God was born some two thousand years ago and that if we follow the course he charted for us and for all men, we will have peace and joy in this life and be inheritors of eternal life in the world to come. (From unpublished address, "A God Is Born," Christmas Devotional, Salt Lake Tabernacle, 11 Dec. 1980; available in LDS Historical Dept. Archives.)

Chapter Thirty-Four

The Book of Mormon

I HAVE READ the Book of Mormon, prayerfully and carefully, more times than I have fingers; I believe it, sincerely and wholeheartedly. I know that it is a true witness of Christ and an accurate revealer of the Doctrines of Christ. (In Conference Report, April 1949, p. 91.)

IT IS EASIER to convert people to the Book of Mormon than it is to convince them of what the Bible is really saying. (Personal recollection of Joseph Fielding McConkie [1983], son of Bruce R. McConkie, cited in Joseph Fielding Smith, *Here We Stand* [Salt Lake City: Deseret Book, 1995, p. 88.)

TWO MINISTERS OF one of the largest and most powerful Protestant denominations came to a Latter-day Saint conference to hear me preach.

After the meeting I had a private conversation with them, in which I said they could each gain a testimony that Joseph Smith was the prophet through whom the Lord had restored the fulness of the gospel for our day and for our time.

I told them they should read the Book of Mormon, ponder its great and eternal truths, and pray to the Father in the name of Christ, in faith, and he would reveal the truth of the book to them by the power of the Holy Ghost....

All of this I explained to my two Protestant friends. One of them, a congenial and decent sort of fellow, said somewhat casually that he would read the Book of Mormon. The other minister, manifesting a bitter spirit, said: "I won't read it. We have experts who have read the Book of Mormon, and I have read what our experts have to say about it."...

Shortly after my experience with these two ministers, two other ministers from the same denomination came to another of our conferences to hear me preach. And, once again, after the meeting I had a private discussion with them.

My message was the same. Taking the Book of Mormon as their guide, they must read, ponder, and pray in order to gain a witness from the Spirit as to the truth and divinity of this great latter-day work.

I told them of my prior experience with their two colleagues and how one of them had refused to read the Book of Mormon, saying that they had experts who had read the book and he had read what their experts had said.

I then said, "What is it going to take to get you gentlemen to read the Book of Mormon and find out for yourselves what is involved, rather than relying on the views of your experts?"

One of these ministers, holding my copy of the Book of Mormon in his hands, let the pages flip past his eyes in a matter of seconds. As he did so, he said, "Oh, I've read the Book of Mormon."

I had a momentary flash of spiritual insight that let me know that his reading had been about as extensive as the way he had just flipped the pages. In his reading he had done no more than scan a few of the headings and read an isolated verse or two.

A lovely young lady, a convert to the Church whose father was a minister of the same denomination as my four Protestant friends, was listening to my conversation with the second two. At this point she spoke up and said, "But Reverend, you have to pray about it."

He replied, "Oh, I prayed about it. I said, 'O God, if the Book of Mormon is true, strike me dead'; and here I am."

My unspoken impulse was to give this rejoinder: "But Reverend, you have to pray in faith!"

May I be so bold as to propose a test and issue a challenge. It is hoped that all who take this test will have a knowledge of the Holy Bible, because the more people know about the Bible, the greater their appreciation will be of the Book of Mormon.

This test is for saint and sinner alike; it is for Jew and Gentile, for bond and free, for black and white, for all of our Father's children. We have all been commanded to search the scriptures, to treasure up the Lord's word, to live by every word that proceedeth forth from the mouth of God. . . . This, then, is the test:

Let every person make a list of from one hundred to two hundred doctrinal subjects, making a conscious effort to cover the whole field of gospel knowledge. The number of subjects chosen will depend on personal inclination and upon how broad the spectrum will be under each subject.

Then write each subject on a blank piece of paper. Divide the paper into two columns; at the top of one, write "Book of Mormon," and at the top of the other, "Bible."

Then start with the first verse and phrase of the Book of Mormon, and continuing verse by verse and thought by thought, put the substance of each verse under its proper heading. Find the same doctrine in the Old and New Testaments, and place it in the parallel columns.

Ponder the truths you learn, and it will not be long before you know that Lehi and Jacob excel Paul in teaching the Atonement; that Alma's sermons on faith and on being born again surpass anything in the Bible; that Nephi makes a better exposition of the scattering and gathering of Israel than do Isaiah, Jeremiah, and Ezekiel combined; that Mormon's words about faith, hope, and charity have a clarity, a breadth, and a power of expression that even Paul did not attain; and so on and so on.

There is another and simpler test that all who seek to know the truth might well take. It calls for us simply to read, ponder, and pray—all in the spirit of faith and with an open mind. To keep ourselves alert to the issues at hand—as we do read, ponder, and pray—we should ask ourselves a thousand times, "Could any man have written this book?"

And it is absolutely guaranteed that sometime between the first and thousandth time this question is asked, every sincere and genuine truth seeker will come to know by the power of the Spirit that the Book or Mormon is true, that it is the mind and will and voice of the Lord to the whole world in our day. ("What Think Ye of the Book of Mormon?" *Ensign*, Nov. 1983, pp. 72-74.)

LET ME SPEAK plainly. Satan hates and spurns the scriptures. The less scripture there is, and the more it is twisted and perverted, the greater is the rejoicing in the courts of hell.

There has never been a book—not even the Book of Mormon—that has been so maligned and cursed and abused as the Bible.

There is not much the world can do about the Book of Mormon. It is here and it is what it is. It cannot be modified or changed. Men have no choice but to believe or disbelieve it. If they disbelieve they can talk about Solomon Spaulding or any other figments of their imaginations that suits their fancies of the moment.

But the Book of Mormon remains secure, unchanged and unchangeable, a firm and steady witness of Christ and his doctrine. The

Book of Mormon has been, is now, and will forever remain secure in the hands of the servants of the Lord, for which we are immeasurably grateful.

But with the Bible it was not and is not so. It is now in the hands of intellectuals and unbelievers and ministers whose delight it is to twist and pervert its doctrines and to spiritualize away the plain meanings of all its important parts. And it once was in the sole and exclusive care and custody of an abominable organization, founded by the devil himself, likened prophetically unto a great whore, whose great aim and purpose was to destroy the souls of men in the name of religion....

I am clear in my mind that the sealed portion of the Book of Mormon will not come forth until the Millennium. The same thing is undoubtedly true of the fulness of the Bible, though some additions could well be made before that time. ("The Doctrinal Restoration," *The Joseph Smith Translation: The Restoration of Plain and Precious Things*, Monte S. Nyman and Robert L. Millet, eds. [Provo, Utah: BYU Religious Studies Center, 1985], pp. 12, 15.)

Chapter Thirty-Five

The Prophet Joseph Smith

JOSEPH SMITH SAT with Father Abraham in the councils of eternity, and Joseph Smith was ordained as Abraham was ordained to come down and be the head of a gospel dispensation here. He had ascended by virtue of obedience, intelligence, progression, and righteousness to a high state of spiritual perfection in that world. When he came here, he brought with him the talents and abilities, the deep spirituality, and the innate righteousness that he developed back there under the tutelage of God the Father....

The spirit men who were associated with Christ and with Adam in the pre-existent eternities, and who were more valiant than all their fellows, were the ones chosen to head the various dispensations of the gospel. One of these was the Prophet Joseph Smith. It doesn't take much reflection then, it seems to me, for us to know that Joseph Smith was one of the dozen greatest spirits that God the Eternal Father had in all the councils of eternity; that he came so as to be here at the appointed time and at the express hour and at the very moment that the Lord designed to open this dispensation. He was here to take his part in that event.

I do not think that the Father and the Son would have appeared to an ordinary fourteen-and-a-half-year-old boy, if he had gone out into that grove of trees to ask the Lord which of all the churches was right. I think the Lord had been preparing Joseph Smith for that event from all eternity; that Joseph Smith had the spiritual stature, the strength for righteousness that enabled him to endure the vision; that he had the talent and ability to press forward in righteousness in the kingdom of God on earth: first, to establish it; and then, somewhat, to perfect its organization before he was taken home, before he sealed his testimony with his blood. (In Conference Report, Oct. 1951, pp. 148-49.)

I SUGGEST THAT the greatest question in the spiritual realm today is this: Was Joseph Smith called of God? Did he in fact receive the revelations which we certify were given to him? If he was called of God, if the Father and the Son appeared to him, if the heavens have been opened and the Church and kingdom of God has been set up again on earth through his instrumentality, then all men everywhere can find salvation by coming to this kingdom, by learning for themselves of the divinity of the work, and by hearkening to the precepts that are taught here. ("The Divine Mission of Joseph Smith," *Improvement Era*, Dec. 1962, p. 908.)

THE PRONOUNCEMENTS, the vision, the glory, the truth, revealed in the First Vision, are in effect, by way of illustration, giving us some arithmetic. It is teaching us some basic, fundamental things. When we come to these crowning, concluding weeks of the Prophet's life, the knowledge that he gives us about God is in the realm of calculus. Our problem is that we take this calculus, and with a slight and restricted view about it, which sometimes gets us out of perspective, we do not recognize, understand, and know the importance of all the algebra, geometry, and fundamental principles that intervened and were taught between the time of the First Vision and the crowning pronouncements. (*The Lord God of Joseph Smith*, Brigham Young University Speeches of the Year [4 Jan. 1972], p. 3.)

I SUPPOSE THAT Joseph Smith excepted, there isn't anyone who hasn't slipped and erred on some doctrinal point or another. (Unpublished letter from Bruce R. McConkie to Walter M. Horne, 2 Oct. 1974, p. 2; original in author's file.)

AS TO THIS man, Joseph Smith, let us say—
Here is a man who was chosen before he was born, who was numbered with the noble and great in the councils of eternity before the foundations of this world were laid.
Along with Adam and Enoch and Noah and Abraham, he sat in council with the Gods when the plans were made to create an earth whereon the hosts of our Father's children might dwell.
Under the direction of the Holy One and of Michael, who became the first man, he participated in the creative enterprises of the Father.
In his premortal state he grew in light and knowledge and intelligence,

attained a spiritual stature which few could equal, and was then foreordained to preside over the greatest of all gospel dispensations.

Here is a man who was called of God as were the prophets of old.

Born among mortals with the talents and spiritual capacity earned in preexistence, he was ready at the appointed time to perform the work to which he had been foreordained.

In the spring of 1820 the Supreme Rulers of the universe rent the veil of darkness which for long ages had shrouded the earth. Choosing the time and the place and the person, they came down from their celestial home to a grove of trees near Palmyra, New York. Calling young Joseph by name, they then told him that pure and perfect religion was no longer found among men and that he would be the instrument in their hands of restoring the fulness of their everlasting gospel....

Here is a man to whom the heavens were an open book, who received revelations, saw visions, and understood the deep and hidden mysteries of the kingdom by the power of the Holy Ghost....

His vision of the degrees of glory is the most complete and wondrous account of that which is beyond the veil which has come to us from the pen of any prophet. His numerous revelations, given in the name of the Lord, set forth the wonders of eternity and the glories of the gospel as plainly and persuasively as do those of the apostles and prophets of old.

Here is a man who has given to our present world more holy scripture than any single prophet who ever lived; indeed, he has preserved for us more of the mind and will and voice of the Lord than the total of the dozen most prolific prophetic penmen of the past.

He translated the Book of Mormon by the gift and power of God, which book is comparable to the Bible itself; is an account of God's dealings with the ancient inhabitants of the American world; and contains the fulness of the everlasting gospel....

His sayings and doings, his goings and comings, the details of his daily life, are well-known. His journal, covering primarily the period from the organization of the Church in Fayette to his death in Carthage, is now published by the Church in six volumes totaling 3,295 pages. Here is a man who, like the Master, whose servant he was, cast out devils and healed the sick....

Here is a man who was persecuted, hounded, driven, and finally slain for the witness he bore and the testimony of Jesus that was his....

Here is a man whose greatness lies in the fact that he was a witness of that same Lord for whom his fellow prophets in days long past had laid down their lives....

Here is a man who was a prophet in the full and complete and literal sense of the word, as all who hearken to the voice of the Spirit shall know. ("Joseph Smith—The Mighty Prophet of the Restoration," *Ensign*, May 1976, pp. 94-97.)

THERE IS A LIMITED number of mighty, noble spirits who headed the respective dispensations. How many we do not know; perhaps there were eight or ten or twenty, but the number does not matter. At any rate, we soon have a small group of select individuals who stand in intelligence and power and might next to the Lord Jehovah. In the same sense that he was like unto God, these chosen and select individuals who were destined to head his work for these long ages were like unto Christ.

When sifting out the relative importance of individuals, without knowing the details, we can conclude that a man born in modern times to head this dispensation was like unto Adam, like unto Moses, like unto Abraham, like unto Christ—in other words, was one of the ten or twenty noblest and greatest spirits who, up to this time, have been born into mortality. He and hosts with him performed their labors and their work in the creative enterprises that brought this earth rolling into existence, and he and his associates headed the periods of time when eternal truth went out to the sons of men.

That is how we rank and place the prophet Joseph Smith: he is one of the great dispensation heads, and a dispensation head is a revealer for his age and his period of the knowledge of Christ and of salvation. Thus, the other prophets of the dispensation who are associated with him and who come after him, who sustain his work and bear record of him, become witnesses that he—the chief prophet of their age—revealed the Lord Jesus and hence made salvation available....

With those principles in mind, let us be vividly and acutely aware of their application to Joseph Smith. One of our revelations says—in the words of the Lord Jesus, speaking to Joseph Smith—"This generation shall have my word through you" (D&C 5:10). I think He made that statement, either in those verbatim words or in thought content, to every dispensation head there has been, I think he said it to Enoch, Moses, Abraham, and in principle to all: "This generation shall have my word through you." Someone has to reveal eternal truth, and these brethren whom I have mentioned are the ones to whom the Lord gave that obligation....

What is the measure of our discipleship? How do we measure and test how firmly we are rooted in the restored faith? I think one of the great tests is the degree and the extent, the fervor and sincerity, the devotion and true belief that we give to the words that come from the Prophet Joseph Smith. ("Joseph Smith: A Revealer of Christ," in *1978 Devotional Speeches of the Year* [1979], pp. 117-19.)

IT IS...FASHIONABLE in some quarters to contend that we Mormons esteem the Prophet Joseph Smith so highly that even the Lord Jesus takes a secondary position.

It is true that Joseph Smith is one of a dozen or a score of those prophets who stand preeminent above all men in greatness and spiritual stature. It is true that his place in the heavenly hierarchy makes him a prophet of prophets and a seer of seers. He ranks with Enoch and Abraham and Moses. But salvation is in Christ, not in Abraham, not in Moses, not in Joseph Smith. ("'Who Hath Believed Our Report?'" *Ensign*, Nov. 1981, p. 47.)

WE ALL KNOW that salvation is in Christ. He is the Firstborn of the Father. He was like unto God in the premortal life, and he became, under the Father, the Creator of all things. We look to him; our faith centers in him, and through him, in the Father.

Next to Christ stands that great spirit person Michael, who led the armies and hosts of heaven when there was war and rebellion in heaven, and who, being foreordained so to do, came here as the first man of all men and became the presiding High Priest over the earth. The second person in this hierarchy is Gabriel who came into this life as Noah. After that we do not know the order of priority, except that singled out from among the hosts of heaven were certain who were foreordained to be the heads of dispensations.

Dispensations are those periods of time when the plan of salvation, the Word—the Eternal Word—is dispensed to men on earth. How many there have been we do not know. I suppose there have been 10; maybe there have been 20; there could have been more. I am speaking now—not of what sometimes are called dispensations, in the sense that John the Baptist and Paul and some of the other prophets had special appointments—I am speaking of those great eras or periods, of those designated portions of the earth's history when the Lord, through one man, gives his word to the whole world and makes all the prophets, and all the seers, and all the administrators, and all the apostles of that period subject to, and exponents of, what came through that individual. What this means is that the head of a gospel dispensation, a dispensation of the sort that we are now mentioning, stands as one of the 10 or 20 greatest spirits who have so far been born on earth.

We know very little about the calibre of men who will be born during the Millennium. There will be many great spirits come then. It seems reasonable to suppose, however, that the Lord has singled out certain ones who had special spiritual talents and capabilities to come to earth in periods of turmoil and wickedness and rebellion and evil, to be lights and guides to the world. This gives us a little perspective of what is involved in the life and in the status and position of Joseph Smith.

You start out with the Lord Jesus, and then you have Adam and Noah. Thereafter come the dispensation heads. Then you step down, appreciably, and come to prophets and apostles, to the elders of Israel, and to wise and good and sagacious men who have the spirit of light and understanding. Every prophet is a witness of Christ; every dispensation head is a revealer of Christ for his day; and every other prophet or apostle who comes is a reflection and an echo and an exponent of the dispensation head. All such come to echo to the world and to expound and unfold what God has revealed through the man who was appointed for that era to give his eternal word to the world. Such is the dispensation concept....

When Joseph Smith spoke by the power of the Holy Ghost, it was as though the Lord Jesus himself was saying the words. The Prophet's voice was the voice of the Lord; he was not perfect; Christ only was free from sin and evil. But he was as near perfection as mortals can get without being translated. He was a man of such spiritual stature that he reflected the image of the Lord Jesus to the people. His voice was the voice of the Lord....

...The test of discipleship is how totally and completely and fully we believe the word that was revealed through Joseph Smith, and how effectively we echo or proclaim that word to the world.

The word is found in the visions and revelations and inspired utterances of Joseph Smith. Many of these are recorded in the *History of the Church*. The account of the First Vision is also in the Pearl of Great Price. The Wentworth letter is the equal and equivalent of what is already in the Pearl of Great Price; it is scripture, except that we have not presented it to the Church and bound ourselves to accept it and proclaim it to the world. There are many things of equal validity, truth, and literary excellence to those that have formally been placed in our scriptural accounts....

Joseph Smith had, as no other man in our dispensation, the ability to be in tune with the Comforter and to speak forth things that were the mind and voice of the Lord, including things that are not in the Standard Works. I suppose the most notable of all that he did in this respect was the King Follet sermon, said to be the greatest sermon of his entire ministry. I suppose there isn't anything that surpasses the sermon he gave on the Second Comforter. It was as though God spoke when he spoke. ("This Generation Shall Have My Word Through You," *Hearken O Ye People: Discourses on the Doctrine and Covenants* [Sandy, Utah: Randall Book, 1984], pp. 3-7, 10.)

ONCE OR TWICE in a thousand years, sometimes as often as every hundred years or so, always at irregular intervals, always when the divine purpose calls for such an event—a man of near divine stature comes to earth. Abraham was one; Moses another. Joseph Smith is the one for our day. ("A Man Called John," *New Era*, May 1984, p. 4.)

Chapter Thirty-Six

Prophets

FROM THE BEGINNING, from the days of the Prophet Joseph to this moment, the men who have been living oracles, witnesses of the truth of these things, have been sound, stable, great, intelligent, competent men. We have not been led by people who are unstable or fanatical or unbalanced in any sense of the word. We have had men who have been educators and bankers, presidents of insurance companies, people who have sat in the halls of Congress and in Cabinets with Presidents, the most stable, mature, and sensible men, industrialists and otherwise, that any one could expect to find.

Now it would seem to me that when men of the highest, soundest caliber—I mean the living oracles, the Presidency and the Twelve, from the beginning to now—stand up as we have heard it done here this morning, and bear fervent witness to the divinity of these things, and certify that they know as they know that they live, that God has spoken in this day, it seems to me that any person in the world who has spiritual inclination ought to stay himself and wonder, and be willing to search and make inquiry, and find whether these glorious and marvelous things are true, or whether they are not.

I had a man tell me how it came about that he was converted to the Church in his later years, past sixty. He said that he chanced to be on Temple Square. He walked into this building when President J. Reuben Clark was addressing a civic organization on a civil or political subject. At the end of his talk, this man told me, President Clark said in substance, "Now, I am going to bear you my testimony about Joseph Smith and the restoration of the gospel," which he did with the power that few can equal. The convert then said, "I had never before heard of Joseph Smith, but I did know who J. Reuben Clark was, and I figured that if a man of that caliber would tell me in the sincerity with which he spoke that this great truth was available, that I ought to make inquiry and find out," and he investigated and joined the Church. That is a very sensible attitude. ("Testimony of the Restoration," *Improvement Era*, Dec. 1956, p. 953.)

THE WORLD NEEDS prophets today as much as it ever did—prophets who are the Lord's agents, who stand as legal administrators with power like Peter's to bind on earth and have their acts sealed eternally in the heavens; prophets who speak for God, who reveal his mind and his will to the people; prophets who reveal and interpret the truths about Christ our Lord and his gospel.

And thanks be to God, for through his grace and goodness, prophets have again been called to reveal anew, with power and conviction, the truths about Christ and salvation. As foretold and promised by the prophets of old, the great era of restoration has commenced. Christ has again revealed himself from heaven; priesthood and keys have again been conferred upon living Apostles; revelation, visions, miracles, and all the gifts and graces enjoyed by the faithful of old are again offered to those who will come unto Christ, confess his holy name before men, and believe in their hearts that God has raised him from the dead and made him both Lord and King. ("Come unto Christ," *Improvement Era*, Dec. 1964, p. 1061.)

I CERTIFY TO YOU that I know just as well as I know anything in this world that this work is true; that God's hand is in it; that Jesus is the Lord; that there are living prophets on earth today to whom the veil is open—the veil is not drawn to them. Accordingly, they give the mind and the will and the voice of God to the world today. This thing is true. God's hand is in it. Truth will prevail. The ultimate destiny of this Church is to fill the whole earth and bring righteousness and peace into the hearts of all men, which of course is the millennial destiny.

I know of myself that these things are true. I feel that I am in tune and as a consequence if you are in tune, you know in your heart that what I say is true—that Jesus is the Lord and that God's hand is in this work. (*Ye Are My Witnesses*, Brigham Young University Speeches of the Year [14 March 1967], p. 10.)

I BELIEVE THAT Spencer W. Kimball was foreordained to be the president of The Church of Jesus Christ of Latter-day Saints; to be the prophet, seer, and revelator to the Lord's people; and to be the mouthpiece of God on earth for the time and season that lies ahead.

I know he was called and chosen and ordained to this ministry by the spirit of prophecy and revelation and was present when the Spirit of the Lord testified to each member of the Council of the Twelve that it was the mind and will of him whose witnesses we are, and on whose errand we serve, that President Kimball should now step forward and lead his people.

It was as though the Lord by his own voice said: "My servant President Harold B. Lee was true and faithful in all things that I appointed him to do; his ministry among you is completed; and I have called him to other and greater labors in my eternal vineyard. And I, the Lord, now call my servant President Spencer W. Kimball to lead my people and to continue the work of preparing them for that great day when I shall come to reign personally upon the earth...."

It seems easy to believe in the prophets who have passed on and to suppose that we believe and follow the counsel they gave under different circumstances and to other people. But the great test that confronts us, as in every age when the Lord has a people on earth, is whether we will give heed to the words of his living oracles and follow the counsel and direction they give for our day and time....

Accordingly it is my desire to lay before us the plain fact that these humble men who preside over the church and kingdom of God on earth in our day are like unto the prophets and apostles of old and are the ones whom God hath chosen to lead and direct his earthly kingdom in these last days. Those of us who sit almost daily at the feet of Presidents Spencer W. Kimball, N. Eldon Tanner, and Marion G. Romney marvel at the wisdom and judgment that attend their decisions and recognize them as preachers of righteousness of the same stature as Peter, James, and John, who were the First Presidency of the church in their day.

May I say that there is no chance in the call of these brethren to direct the Lord's work on earth. His hand is in it. He knows the end from the beginning. He ordained and established the plan of salvation and decreed that his everlasting gospel should be revealed to man in a series of dispensations commencing with Adam and continuing to Joseph Smith. And he—the Almighty—chooses the prophets and apostles who minister in his name and present his message to the world in every age and dispensation. He selects and foreordains his ministers; he sends them to earth at the times before appointed; he guides and directs their continuing mortal preparations; and he then calls them to those positions they were foreordained to receive from before the foundations of the earth....

By obedience, by conformity, by personal righteousness, because he elected to follow in the path of the Chosen and Beloved Son, Spencer W. Kimball was noble and great in the preexistence. Above all his other talents, he developed the talent for spirituality—the talent to believe and accept the truth, the talent to desire righteousness.

He knew and worshiped the Lord Jehovah, who was "like unto God." (Abr. 3:24.) He was a friend of Adam and Enoch. He took counsel from Noah and Abraham. He sat in meetings with Isaiah and Nephi. He served in the heavenly kingdom with Joseph Smith and Brigham Young. ("God Foreordains His Prophets and His People," *Ensign*, May 1974, pp. 71-73.)

WE HAVE COMPETENT and able leadership in the Church today. There is great inspiration at the head. President Kimball is a mighty, a valiant, and a courageous prophet. The Lord has sent some people to earth in our day who have the spiritual stature of Peter, James, and John, and of Moses and Abraham, and some of the ancients. We speak particularly of the Prophet Joseph Smith, who is of such a caliber that he ranks with Enoch and Abraham and Moses. And then we speak of those who have succeeded him, whose spiritual stature is like that of the prophets in ancient Israel. What a wondrous and marvelous thing it is to belong to a church that is true, and to know in our hearts of its truth and divinity, and to be privileged to drink of the fountains of living water that flow from the prophets and wise men that God has sent to minister among us. ("The Foolishness of Teaching," address to seminary and institute personnel, [Salt Lake City: The Church of Jesus Christ of Latter-day Saints, 1981], p. 1.)

Chapter Thirty-Seven

Prophecy

[This chapter is not so much teachings about the doctrine of prophecy as it is selections from some of the actual prophecies uttered by Elder McConkie.]

WE LIVE IN a perilous world situation. Things are not going to get better. They are going to get worse until the day of the coming of the Son of Man. And the tests that are being given to the members of the Lord's Church will, in my judgment, increase in severity and intensity. ("Charity Which Never Faileth," *Relief Society Magazine*, March 1970, p. 168.)

I DON'T PRETEND to be able to read the future, but I have a very strong feeling that conditions in the world are not going to get better. They are going to get worse until the coming of the Son of Man, which is the end of the world, when the wicked will be destroyed.

I think the world is going to get worse, and the faithful portion of the Church, at least, is going to get better. The day is coming, more than ever has been the case in the past, when we will be under the obligation of making a choice, of standing up for the Church, of adhering to its precepts and teachings and principles, of taking the counsel that comes from the apostles and prophets whom God has placed to teach the doctrine and bear witness to the world. The day is coming when this will be more necessary than has ever been the case in our day or at any time in our dispensation. ("Be Valiant in the Fight of Faith," *Ensign*, Nov. 1974, p. 35.)

I SHALL TELL you the vision that I have for the people of Chile. I foresee the day when the seven stakes here will be seven times seventy.

I foresee the day when the two hundred and fifty native Chilean missionaries will be numbered in the thousands. I foresee the day when the thirty thousand members of the Church in this great nation will become the ten thousands of Ephraim and the thousands of Manasseh of whom the scriptures speak. (See Deuteronomy 33:17.) I foresee the day when The Church of Jesus Christ of Latter-day Saints will be the most powerful influencing leaven in this whole nation. I foresee the day when the Lord will pour out his blessings abundantly upon Chile as a nation because of the great number of righteous members of the Church of Jesus Christ who live here. (Santiago Chile Area Conference, Santiago, Chile, 1977, p. 23.)

FOR THE MOMENT we live in a day of peace and prosperity but it shall not ever be thus. Great trials lie ahead. All of the sorrows and perils of the past are but a foretaste of what is yet to be. And we must prepare ourselves temporally and spiritually.

Our spiritual preparation consists in keeping the commandments of God, and taking the Holy Spirit for our guide, so that when this life is over we shall find rest and peace in paradise and an ultimate inheritance of glory and honor in the celestial kingdom.

Our temporal preparation consists in using the good earth in the way the Lord designed and intended so as to supply all our just wants and needs. It is his purpose to provide for his Saints for all things are his, but, he says, it must needs be done in his own way....

Be it remembered that tribulations lie ahead. There will be wars in one nation and kingdom after another until war is poured out upon all nations and two hundred million men of war mass their armaments at Armageddon. Peace has been taken from the earth, the angels of destruction have begun their work, and their swords shall not be sheathed until the Prince of Peace comes to destroy the wicked and usher in the great Millennium.

There will be earthquakes and floods and famines. The waves of the sea shall heave themselves beyond their bounds, the clouds shall withhold their rain, and the crops of the earth shall wither and die.

There will be plagues and pestilence and disease and death. An overflowing scourge shall cover the earth and a desolating sickness shall sweep the land. Flies shall take hold of the inhabitants of the earth, and maggots shall come in upon them. (See D&C 29:14-20.)...

Bands of Gadianton robbers will infest every nation, immorality and murder and crime will increase, and it will seem as though every man's hand is against his brother.

We need not dwell more upon these things. We are commanded to search the scriptures where they are recounted with force and fervor, and they shall surely come to pass.

It is one of the sad heresies of our time that peace will be gained by weary diplomats as they prepare treaties of compromise, or that the Millennium will be ushered in because men will learn to live in peace and to keep the commandments, or that the predicted plagues and promised desolations of latter days can in some way be avoided.

We must do all we can to proclaim peace, to avoid war, to heal disease, to prepare for natural disasters—but with it all, that which is to be shall be.

Knowing what we know, and having the light and understanding that has come to us, we must—as individuals and as a Church—use our talents, strengths, energies, abilities, and means to prepare for whatever may befall us and our children.

We know that the world will go on in wickedness until the end of the world, which is the destruction of the wicked. We shall continue to live in the world, but with the Lord's help we shall not be of the world. We shall strive to overcome carnality and worldliness of every sort and shall invite all men to flee from Babylon, join with us, and live as becometh Saints....

We do not know when the calamities and troubles of the last days will fall upon any of us as individuals or upon bodies of the Saints. The Lord deliberately withholds from us the day and hour of his coming and of the tribulations which shall precede it—all as part of the testing and probationary experiences of mortality. He simply tells us to watch and be ready.

We can rest assured that if we have done all in our power to prepare for whatever lies ahead, he will then help us with whatever else we need....

We do not say that all of the Saints will be spared and saved from the coming day of desolation. But we do say there is no promise of safety and no promise of security except for those who love the Lord and who are seeking to do all that he commands.

It may be, for instance, that nothing except the power of faith and the authority of the priesthood can save individuals and congregations from the atomic holocausts that surely shall be.

And so we raise the warning voice and say: Take heed; prepare; watch and be ready. There is no security in any course except the course of obedience and conformity and righteousness. ("Stand Independent above All Other Creatures," *Ensign*, May 1979, pp. 92-93.)

WE PROPHESY—it is my voice you hear, but it is the united voice of all my Brethren which speaks—we prophesy that this great latter-day work will come off triumphant, that the great God will guide the destinies of his people, that this kingdom of God now set up on earth will roll forth until the kingdom of heaven shall come, until the Lord Jesus Christ shall come again in the clouds of heaven to reign gloriously among his Latter-day Saints. ("The Mystery of Mormonism," *Ensign*, Nov. 1979, p. 55.)

AS TO THE DESOLATIONS, upheavals, and trials of the latter days—
We shall see more of these than at any time in the history of the earth. There will be earthquakes, floods, plagues, and famines in all parts of the earth. There will be wars, desolation, destruction, and death in every nation and among every people. Gadianton bands will prey upon their fellows; crime and degeneracy and wickedness will increase on every hand. Lust and immorality and perversions and all the evils of Sodom and Gomorrah will sweep the earth as with a flood. The dispensation of the fulness of times is the one in which the Lord is preparing the vineyard to be burned; it is the day when every corruptible thing will be destroyed; it is destined to be a day of vengeance and destruction where the wicked are concerned. As it was in the days of Noah so shall it be in the day of the coming of the Son of Man.
In the midst of all this the Lord's Saints are commanded to stand in holy places and be not moved. The tests coming to them as individuals will be no different than those poured out upon people in ages past. Testing and trials are the common lot of all mankind in all ages. We are here to see if we will bridle our passions and overcome the evils of the world in spite of earth and hell. Life never was intended to be easy. What though some suffer and die, what though they lay down their lives for the testimony of Jesus and the hope of eternal life—so be it—all these things have prevailed from Adam's day to ours. They are all part of the eternal plan; and those who give their "all" in the gospel cause shall receive the Lord's "all" in the mansions which are prepared.
What, then, lies ahead for us as the Saints of the Most High?
Ours is the most glorious of all dispensations. In it will come to pass

the destruction of evil and the triumph of truth. So far the foundation has been laid. We are now building the house of the Lord upon that foundation. We have many things yet to do.

We have yet to gain that full knowledge and understanding of the doctrines of salvation and the mysteries of the kingdom that were possessed by many of the ancient Saints. O that we knew what Enoch and his people knew! Or that we had the sealed portion of the Book of Mormon, as did certain of the Jaredites and Nephites! How can we ever gain these added truths until we believe in full what the Lord has already given us in the Book of Mormon, in the Doctrine and Covenants, and in the inspired changes made by Joseph Smith in the Bible? Will the Lord give us the full and revealed account of the creation as long as we believe in the theories of evolution? Will he give us more guidance in governmental affairs as long as we choose socialistic ways which lead to the overthrow of freedom?

We have yet to attain that degree of obedience and personal righteousness which will give us faith like the ancients: faith to multiply miracles, move mountains, and put at defiance the armies of nations; faith to quench the violence of fire, divide seas and stop the mouths of lions; faith to break every band and to stand in the presence of God. Faith comes in degrees. Until we gain faith to heal the sick, how can we ever expect to move mountains and divide seas?

We have yet to receive such an outpouring of the Spirit of the Lord in our lives that we shall all see eye to eye in all things, that every man will esteem his brother as himself, that there will be no poor among us, and that all men seeing our good works will be led to glorify our Father who is in heaven. Until we live the law of tithing how can we expect to live the law of consecration? As long as we disagree as to the simple and easy doctrines of salvation, how can we ever have unity on the complex and endless truth yet to be revealed?

We have yet to perfect our souls, by obedience to the laws and ordinances of the gospel, and to walk in the light as God is in the light, so that if this were a day of translation we would be prepared to join Enoch and his city in heavenly realms. How many among us are now prepared to entertain angels, to see the face of the Lord, to go where God and Christ are and be like them?

We have yet to preach the gospel in every nation and to every creature. This must be done before the Second Coming. Ours is a missionary dispensation. In the waters of baptism every member of the

Church covenants to stand as a witness of Christ at all times and in all places and under all circumstances, even unto death. So far we have scarcely scratched the surface where this great commission is involved. Billions of the earth's inhabitants yet walk in darkness and have little present hope of hearing the warning voice of a legal administrator, one sent of God to herald the glad tidings of salvation. We need more missionaries, many more valiant souls who will use their time and their means to bring joy and hope to the honest in heart in all nations.

We have yet to search out our ancestors and perform the ordinances of salvation and exaltation for them in the temples of the Lord. Ours is the great dispensation of vicarious ordinances; it is the era in which all who are worthy, and who believe and obey in the spirit world, shall be inheritors of all the blessings of that God who loves all his children and desires all to gain salvation in his eternal kingdom. We need more temples, an expansion of the name extraction program, more vicarious ordinances performed for and on behalf of our brethren and sisters beyond the veil. In due course we shall build a temple in Jackson County and yet another in Old Jerusalem, to say nothing of great numbers of such holy houses in many nations.

We have yet to gather Israel into the stakes of Zion, to be established in all nations. We have yet to build up Zion and to establish her stakes as places of refuge among all people and in all nations. Ours is a message for all men; the gospel of Christ—and none other—has the power to save and exalt.

We have yet to prepare a people for the Second Coming of him whose we are, whose gospel we have received, and on whose errand we labor. Our time, talents, and wealth must be made available for the building up of his kingdom. Should we be called upon to sacrifice all things, even our lives, it would be of slight moment when weighed against the eternal riches reserved for those who are true and faithful in all things.

This is the dispensation in which saviors shall come up upon Mount Zion and the kingdom shall be the Lord's as the prophets foretold. The glorious gospel is and shall prosper forever. ("This Final Glorious Gospel Dispensation," *Ensign*, April 1980, pp. 24-25.)

NOR ARE THE DAYS of our greatest sorrows and our deepest sufferings all behind us. They too lie ahead. We shall yet face greater perils, we shall yet be tested with more severe trials, and we shall yet weep more tears of sorrow than we have ever known before....

Looking ahead, we see the gospel preached in all nations and to every people with success attending.

We see the Lord break down the barriers so that the world of Islam and the world of Communism can hear the message of the restoration; and we glory in the fact that Ishmael—as well as Isaac—and Esau—as well as Jacob—shall have an inheritance in the eternal kingdom.

We see congregations of the covenant people worshipping the Lord in Moscow and Peking and Saigon. We see Saints of the Most High raising their voices in Egypt and India and Africa.

We see stakes of Zion in all parts of the earth; and Israel, the chosen people, gathering into these cities of holiness, as it were, to await the coming of their King.

We see temples in great numbers dotting the earth, so that those of every nation and kindred and tongue and people can receive the fulness of the ordinances of the house of the Lord and can qualify to live and reign as kings and priests on earth a thousand years.

We see the seed of Cain—long denied the priestly power which makes men rulers over many kingdoms—rise up and bless Abraham as their father. We see the Saints of God, who are scattered upon all the face of the earth, rise in power and glory and stand as lights and guides to the people of their own nations.

We see our children and our children's children stand firm in defense of truth and virtue, crowned with the power of God, carrying off the kingdom triumphantly.

We see the faithful Saints perfecting their lives and preparing for the coming of him whose children they are, preparing for the glorious mansion he has promised them in the kingdom of his Father.

But the vision of the future is not all sweetness and light and peace. All that is yet to be shall go forward in the midst of greater evils and perils and desolations than have been known on earth at any time.

As the Saints prepare to meet their God, so those who are carnal and sensual and devilish prepare to face their doom.

As the meek among men make their calling and election sure, so those who worship the God of this world sink ever lower and lower into the depths of depravity and despair.

Amid tears of sorrow—our hearts heavy with forebodings—we see evil and crime and carnality covering the earth. Liars and thieves and adulterers and homosexuals and murderers scarcely seek to hide their abominations from our view. Iniquity abounds. There is no peace on earth.

We see evil forces everywhere uniting to destroy the family, to ridicule morality and decency, to glorify all that is lewd and base. We see wars and plagues and pestilence. Nations rise and fall. Blood and carnage and death are everywhere. Gadianton robbers fill the judgment seats in many nations. An evil power seeks to overthrow the freedom of all nations and countries. Satan reigns in the hearts of men; it is the great day of his power.

But amid it all, the work of the Lord rolls on. The gospel is preached and the witness is born. The elect of God forsake the traditions of their fathers and the ways of the world. The kingdom grows and prospers, for the Lord is with his people.

Amid it all, there are revelations and visions and prophecies. There are gifts and signs and miracles. There is a rich outpouring of the Holy Spirit of God.

Amid it all believing souls are born again, their souls are sanctified by the power of the Spirit, and they prepare themselves to dwell with God and Christ and holy beings in the eternal kingdom.

Is it any wonder that we both rejoice and tremble at what lies ahead?

Truly the world is and will be in commotion, but the Zion of God will be unmoved. The wicked and ungodly shall be swept from the Church, and the little stone will continue to grow until it fills the whole earth.

The way ahead is dark and dreary and dreadful. There will yet be martyrs; the doors in Carthage shall again enclose the innocent. We have not been promised that the trials and evils of the world will entirely pass us by.

If we, as a people, keep the commandments of God; if we take the side of the Church on all issues, both religious and political; if we take the Holy Spirit for our guide; if we give heed to the words of the apostles and prophets who minister among us—then, from an eternal standpoint, all things will work together for our good.

Our view of the future shall be undimmed, and, whether in life or in death, we shall see our blessed Lord return to reign on earth. We shall see the New Jerusalem coming down from God in heaven to join with the Holy City we have built. We shall mingle with those of Enoch's city while together we worship and serve the Lord forever. ("The Coming Tests and Trials and Glory," *Ensign*, May 1980, pp. 71-73.)

WE LIVE IN a day of evil and wickedness. The generality of men are carnal, sensual, and devilish. They have forgotten God and are reveling in the lusts of the flesh. Crime, immorality, abortions, and homosexual abominations are fast becoming the norm of life among the wicked and ungodly. The world will soon be as corrupt as it was in the days of Noah. ("The Lord God of the Restoration," *Ensign*, Nov. 1980, p. 50.)

WE KNOW WHAT the future holds and of the wars and plagues and desolations that will soon sweep the earth as a devouring fire.

This is a gloomy day of sorrow and sadness. The heavens gather blackness; men's hearts are failing them for fear...; nations are perplexed and know not where to turn to find peace and security.

This is a day in which mad men in high places can, in an instant, suddenly, unleash such fearful weapons that millions can be slain between the rising and the setting of the sun.

There has never been such a dire day as this. Iniquity abounds; all the perversions and evils of Sodom have their devotees. And the revealed word assures us that conditions will get worse, not better, until the coming of the Son of Man.

It is because of the evils and ills which cover the earth, because men have strayed from the Lord's ordinances and broken his everlasting covenant, because many walk in the ways of the world and are carnal, sensual, and devilish that the Lord has given us a message to deliver to our fellowmen. ("'Who Hath Believed Our Report?'" *Ensign*, Nov. 1981, p. 46.)

WE DO NOT say that everyone who accepts the restored gospel will escape the wars and plagues and desolations of the last days. But we do say that all their sorrows and sufferings will be swallowed up in the joy of the gospel.

Some who are true and faithful will perish along with the wicked and ungodly in the days ahead. But what does it matter whether we live or die once we have found Christ and he has sealed us his? ("'Who Hath Believed Our Report?'" *Ensign*, Nov. 1981, p. 48.)

SOMEDAY THE LORD will raise up a prophet, who will also be a seer and a translator, to whom he will give the brass plates that they may be translated for the benefit and blessing of those in all nations.

Would God that the work might commence at least in our day, though in fact we have no such hope. Why should the Lord give us what is on the brass plates or in the sealed portion of the Book of Mormon when we do not even treasure up and live by what he has already given us? ("The Doctrinal Restoration," *The Joseph Smith Translation: The Restoration of Plain and Precious Things,* Monte S. Nyman and Robert L. Millet, eds. [Provo, Utah: Religious Studies Center, 1985], p. 16.)

Chapter Thirty-Eight

Sexual Immorality

THERE IS...a difference between the earth and the world. The earth is this sphere, this planet upon which we reside. It is composed of natural elements—the things that make up the dust and the rocks and the trees. The world, on the other hand, is the society of men living on the face of the earth, a society that is carnal and sensuous and evil, a society which is living, in effect, a telestial law; and there will be a not distant day when the end of the world will come, which means by definition, the destruction of the wicked. This will take place in the day of millennial cleansing....

I suppose that in our day—in this age, with all the pressures of advertising, made possible by the use of all the modern inventions—that the enticement and pressures of the world exceed anything that has existed or prevailed in any age past. ("Love Not the World," *Improvement Era*, June 1958, pp. 438-39.)

THERE IS AN eternal law, ordained by God himself before the foundations of the world, that every man shall reap as he sows. If we think evil thoughts, our tongues will utter unclean sayings. If we speak words of wickedness, we shall end up doing the works of wickedness. If our minds are centered on the carnality and evil of the world, then worldliness and unrighteousness will seem to us to be the normal way of life. If we ponder things related to sex immorality in our minds, we will soon think everybody is immoral and unclean and it will break down the barrier between us and the world. And so with every other unwholesome, unclean, impure, and ungodly course....

To enable us to keep our minds centered on righteousness, we should consciously elect to ponder the truths of salvation in our hearts. Brother Packer yesterday pleaded with eloquence that we sing the songs of Zion in order to center our thoughts on wholesome things. I would like to add that we can also—after we have had the opening song—call on ourselves to preach a sermon. I have preached many sermons walking along...desert trails, or in lonely places, thus centering my mind on the Lord's affairs and the things of righteousness; and I might say they have been better sermons than I have ever preached to congregations. ("'Think on These Things'," *Ensign*, Jan. 1974, p. 48.)

I LEFT THE Missionary Executive Committee meeting this morning to come here, and the last item approved was a document to go to mission presidents, stake presidents, and bishops instructing each to counsel all returned missionaries to conform to the dress and grooming standards that had prevailed in their missions....

Conformity to dress and grooming standards is one of the tests the Lord imposes upon us to see if we will take counsel and to see if we can stand up against the pressures of the world. There is, of course, an underlying reason for all the counsels and commands relayed from the Lord by the Brethren to the Saints. Immodesty, for instance, leads toward immorality. Long hair and grubby grooming open the door to rebellion against the established order and to associations which lead away from the Church. Surely those who are so adorned are not living soberly, righteously, and godly in this present world. But even if we are not sufficiently in tune to recognize the valid reasons behind the dress and grooming standards, we are still expected to abide by them. ("The Ten Commandments of a Peculiar People," in *Speeches of the Year 1975* [1976], pp. 33-34.)

I RECEIVED A LETTER from a returned missionary whom I shall call Elder Carnalus Luciferno, for no one in his right mind would have such a name, and my correspondent was certainly out of his mind.

His letter told me of his own conversion, of his service as a zone leader in the mission field, and of making many converts. But after returning home, as he expressed it, "I returned to my old Gentile ways."

After thus ceasing to be a true Saint, and becoming a genuine Gentile, he met some representatives of another church who taught him that we are saved by grace, without works, simply by believing in the Lord Jesus.

Thereupon he was saved, and his letter, which he sent to many people, was an invitation to these others to believe in Christ and be saved as he was saved.

Later I said to his mission president, "Tell me about Elder Carnalus Luciferno."

"Oh," he said, "Elder Carnalus Luciferno was a good missionary who made many converts.   But since returning home he has been excommunicated."

"Oh," I said. "What was his problem?"

The mission president replied, "Before he joined the Church, he was a homosexual, and we understand that since his release he has reverted to his old ways." ("What Think Ye of Salvation by Grace," in *Brigham Young University 1983-84 Fireside and Devotional Speeches* [1984], p. 46.)

Chapter Thirty-Nine

Judgment

ALL OF US KNOW that we can deceive men. We can deceive our bishops or the other Church agents, unless at the moment their minds are lighted by the spirit of revelation; but we cannot deceive the Lord. We cannot get from him an unearned blessing. There will be an eventual day when all men will get exactly and precisely what they have merited and earned, neither adding to nor subtracting from. You cannot with success lie to the Holy Ghost. ("The Law of Justification," *Improvement Era*, June 1956, p. 421.)

ARE WE GUILTY of something akin to murder?

We instinctively recoil at the very thought of killing another person. To commit murder is the farthest thing from the mind of every honorable man. But how many of us fraternize with the two sins which are next of kin to murder, the two offenses which open the door to the shedding of innocent blood?

Murder, the unlawful killing of another with malice, is so heinous and reprehensible that our language cannot convey a full realization of the wickedness, the moral degeneracy, the depravity that attend its commission.

To take the life of a fellow being; to deny him his God-given right to the experience of mortality; to impose consequent suffering on others (the widow and the fatherless, perchance)—this is a crime against man, against society, against God, a crime for which a dreadful and awesome penalty must be paid; for God hath said, "Whoso sheddeth man's blood, by man shall his blood be shed." (Genesis 9:6.)

And this death penalty is but the beginning of the just retribution to be heaped upon the heads of those guilty of murder. All murderers are thrust down to hell, where they suffer the torments of the damned for eternity, where they welter in the vengeance of eternal fire.

But what of the common sins, the sins against God and man which do not cause us to shudder and tremble, the sins which invariably serve as the foundation upon which murder rests?...

Hate and *anger* precede murder.   These are the two sins of preparation.   No man will ever be guilty of the grossest of all crimes unless he first accepts the promptings of Satan to hate his brother and then in anger rises against him. ("The Sixth Commandment for Us," *Instructor*, Aug. 1957, p. 227.)

WE'RE UNDERGOING a test. We're going to be tested for everything in mortality. You don't get tested in just one field and let the rest of life's experiences go by the board. You get tested where the whole man, the whole personality, is concerned. We read a lot of things that, seemingly, are strange in the scriptures. Jesus says, "For every idle word that men shall speak they will give account in the day of judgment." We're going to be judged by the words that we speak.

The Book of Mormon designations and scriptures talk about the fact that we will be judged by our thoughts, by our words, and by our acts. What I'm saying is that in this mortal probation we're going to be judged by everything that we do. Now, some things have far greater import than others.   There isn't any question in any Latter-day Saint mind that the most important field of judgment is the spiritual. We're going to have to answer some questions where the spiritual is concerned. I don't know what questions we'll be asked and what we'll have to answer, but I do know the general fields.   When we're judged in the realm of spiritual things, we're going to be judged by what we thought of the Lord Jesus Christ,–that above all else–whether we accepted Him as the Savior and Redeemer, whether we took the counsel that He gave–"learn of me," "take my yoke upon you," and so on.

We're going to be judged by whether we walk by faith. We're going to be judged by the truths we believe, and if we don't believe all the gospel truths that we should, there's a deficiency.   If we believe something and accept it as truth, which is not, that's going to be taken into consideration in our judgment.

Now, I'm perfectly well aware of the theoretical postulates that go around about creation and evolution, and all the rest, and I know that the theories have changed radically from when I studied them here at the University of Utah to the day when you are now studying them. When your children and grandchildren study them they'll be changed again, and every generation of teachers will think that they're setting forth eternal, absolute, and ultimate truth. But nonetheless, these are the theories of men and they don't accord in many respects with the revelations. They assume, for instance, that death has always been in the world, and so on.

Well, we're going to be judged by what we believe, and we're going to be judged by what we think about Joseph Smith. We're going to be judged by whether we receive the Priesthood and magnify our callings. We're going to be judged by our attitude towards the Church. The Church happens to be the agency that God has established on earth to administer the gospel and to raise a standard of truth and light to the world. If the Church says this or that on a moral issue—such as the ERA—and we take a different stand, we're going to be judged by that when the day comes that we stand before the bar of Jehovah. We're going to be judged in the spiritual realm by how many of the gifts of the spirit we manage to get into our lives.

...We're going to be judged about moral things. That well could include under that heading all of the standards of the gospel—every principle of decency and sexual morality, every principle of honesty and integrity.

We've had a little fad sweeping Utah. I read in the paper—people who pretend to know—that Utahns were subject to more scam arrangements and financially abusive schemes than anybody else. Well, if we get involved in some of these pyramiding things, we're going to be judged for the lack of sense and understanding and wisdom that we had in that field aside from the fact that we'll probably lose everything that we put into it.

We're going to be judged by social matters. I suppose that could include marriage relationships that we form, the fellowship that we have in this organization or that among our fellowmen, the service that we perform for others, how we operate in the programs of the Church, the institutes and the seminaries, the Relief Society and Priesthood quorums. We're going to be judged by the power that we seek to get in political ventures and the wealth that we desire to acquire.

We're going to be judged in an intellectual field, and certainly, that's going to involve the seeking of truth and study. It's going to involve false doctrine....

There are moral issues all over, and we're going to be judged by them; there are intellectual pursuits, and we're going to be judged by them. We're going to be judged by physical things. We're expected to do things in the physical field that are right. We have a revelation in which the Lord says all things unto Him are spiritual, and He's never given a temporal commandment unto the children of men. Then, He says a very interesting thing, "...neither to Adam your father." All you have to do is go back and look at the list of commands that He gave to Adam. Almost every one of them that's in Genesis or in the Book of Moses is temporal, but the Lord calls them spiritual. What this means is that we're going to be judged by the way we plow our ground, plant our crops and harvest them, and everything we do in our business affairs as well as our spiritual affairs. ("The Probationary Test of Mortality," Salt Lake Institute of Religion Devotional Address, 10 Jan. 1982, pp. 9-11.)

Chapter Forty

Valiance

WHAT WE ARE striving to do is to be converted. It is not enough to have a testimony. You want to know what happens to people who have a testimony, who do not work at it? Read it in the vision of the degrees of glory (Doctrine & Covenants 76); it is talking about the terrestrial kingdom. And it says that those who are not valiant in the testimony of Jesus, obtain not the crown over the kingdom of our God. That means members of the Church who are lukewarm. They are members of the Church who manage to get in tune on occasions, so that a flash of lightning comes to them, and they know in their hearts that the work is true. Maybe they work at it for a while. Maybe they go on a mission for a couple of years and then they fall away. They get into the state where they know the work is true, but they are not valiant. They do not endure in righteousness to the end.

There are lots of people in the Church who know this work is true who do not do very much about it. But if you backed them into a corner and began to condemn the Church, they would stand up in wrath and ire and defend the kingdom. This is all to their credit and all to their advantage. But they go fishing; that is, they go off after the things of the world instead of putting first in their lives the things of God's kingdom, the things of righteousness. And hence they are lukewarm, they are not valiant. (*Be Ye Converted*, Brigham Young University Speeches of the Year [11 Feb. 1968], pp. 12-13.)

MAY I NOW illustrate some of the specifics of that divine worship which is pleasing to him whose we are?

To worship the Lord is to follow after him, to seek his face, to believe his doctrine, and to think his thoughts.

It is to walk in his paths, to be baptized as Christ was, to preach that gospel of the kingdom which fell from his lips, and to heal the sick and raise the dead as he did.

To worship the Lord is to put first in our lives the things of his kingdom, to live by every word that proceedeth forth from the mouth of God, to center our whole hearts upon Christ and that salvation which comes because of him. It is to walk in the light as he is in the light, to do the things that he wants done, to do what he would do under similar circumstances, to be as he is.

To worship the Lord is to walk in the Spirit, to rise above carnal things, to bridle our passions, and to overcome the world.

It is to pay our tithes and offerings, to act as wise stewards in caring for those things which have been entrusted to our care, and to use our talents and means for the spreading of truth and the building up of his kingdom.

To worship the Lord is to be married in the temple, to have children, to teach them the gospel, and to bring them up in light and truth.

It is to perfect the family unit, to honor our father and our mother; it is for a man to love his wife with all his heart and to cleave unto her and none else.

To worship the Lord is to visit the fatherless and the widows in their affliction and to keep ourselves unspotted from the world.

It is to work on a welfare project, to administer to the sick, to go on a mission, to go home teaching, and to hold family home evening.

To worship the Lord is to study the gospel, to treasure up light and truth, to ponder in our hearts the things of his kingdom, and to make them part of our lives.

It is to pray with all the energy of our souls, to preach by the power of the Spirit, to sing songs of praise and thanksgiving.

To worship is to work, to be actively engaged in a good cause, to be about our Father's business, to love and serve our fellowmen.

It is to feed the hungry, to clothe the naked, to comfort those that mourn, and to hold up the hands that hang down and to strengthen the feeble knees.

To worship the Lord is to stand valiantly in the cause of truth and righteousness, to let our influence for good be felt in civic, cultural, educational, and governmental fields, and to support those laws and principles which further the Lord's interests on earth.

To worship the Lord is to be of good cheer, to be courageous, to be valiant, to have the courage of our God-given convictions, and to keep the faith.

It is ten thousand times ten thousand things. It is keeping the commandments of God. It is living the whole law of the whole gospel.

To worship the Lord is to be like Christ until we receive from him the blessed assurance: "Ye shall be even as I am."

These are sound principles. As we ponder them in our hearts, I am sure we shall know increasingly of their verity.

True and perfect worship is in fact the supreme labor and purpose of man. ("How to Worship," *Ensign*, Dec. 1971, p. 130.)

WE ARE EITHER for the Church or we are against it. We either take its part or we take the consequences. We cannot survive spiritually with one foot in the Church and the other in the world. We must make the choice. It is either the Church or the world. There is no middle ground. And the Lord loves a courageous man who fights openly and boldly in his army....

Members of the Church who have testimonies and who live clean and upright lives, but who are not courageous and valiant, do not gain the celestial kingdom. Theirs is a terrestrial inheritance....(D&C 76:79.)...

What does it mean to be valiant in the testimony of Jesus?

It is to be courageous and bold; to use all our strength, energy, and ability in the warfare with the world; to fight the good fight of faith....The great cornerstone of valiance in the cause of righteousness is obedience to the whole law of the whole gospel....

To be valiant in the testimony of Jesus is to believe in Christ and his gospel with unshakable conviction. It is to know of the verity and divinity of the Lord's work on earth.

But this is not all. It is more than believing and knowing. We must be doers of the word and not hearers only. It is more than lip service; it is not simply confessing with the mouth the divine Sonship of the Savior. It is obedience and conformity and personal righteousness....

To be valiant in the testimony of Jesus is to bridle our passions, control our appetites, and rise above carnal and evil things. It is to overcome the world as did he who is our prototype and who himself was the most valiant of all our Father's children. It is to be morally clean, to pay our tithes and offerings, to honor the Sabbath day, to pray with full purpose of heart, to lay our all upon the altar if called upon to do so.

To be valiant in the testimony of Jesus is to take the Lord's side on every issue. It is to vote as he would vote. It is to think what he thinks, to believe what he believes, to say what he would say and do what he would do in the same situation. It is to have the mind of Christ and be one with him as he is one with his father.

Our doctrine is clear; its application sometimes seems to be more difficult. Perhaps some personal introspection might be helpful. For instance:

Am I valiant in the testimony of Jesus if my chief interest and concern in life is laying up in store the treasures of the earth, rather than the building up of the kingdom?

Am I valiant if I have more of this world's goods than my just needs and wants require and I do not draw from my surplus to support missionary work, build temples, and care for the needy?

Am I valiant if my approach to the Church and its doctrines is intellectual only, if I am more concerned with having a religious dialogue on this or that point than I am on gaining a personal spiritual experience?

Am I valiant if I am deeply concerned about the Church's stand on who can or who cannot receive the priesthood and think it is time for a new revelation on this doctrine?

Am I valiant if I use a boat, live in a country home, or engage in some other recreational pursuit on weekends that takes me away from my spiritual responsibilities?

Am I valiant if I engage in gambling, play cards, go to pornographic movies, shop on Sunday, wear immodest clothes, or do any of the things that are the accepted way of life among worldly people?

If we are to gain salvation, we must put first in our lives the things of God's kingdom. With us it must be the kingdom of God or nothing. We have come out of darkness; ours is the marvelous light of Christ. We must walk in the light. ("Be Valiant in the Fight of Faith," *Ensign*, Nov. 1974, pp. 34-35.)

Chapter Forty-One

Missionary Work and the Gathering of Israel

YOU AND I ARE in this kingdom at its beginning. The groundwork is being laid. Out of small beginnings come great things. We have had tremendous progression and growth; we are established and recognized in the world already; but there will be an eventual day when the whole earth will be converted to the truth, when every living soul will come into the Church of Jesus Christ of Latter-day Saints.

We are in the kingdom of God now which is exclusively an ecclesiastical kingdom. This kingdom is going to grow and increase, multiply and abound, and nothing can stop it, until the day comes that it will be both an ecclesiastical kingdom and a political kingdom, and it will govern in all things—spiritual, civil, temporal, and political. The kingdoms of this world are going to become the kingdom of our God and of his Christ. ("God's Kingdom on Earth," *Improvement Era*, Dec. 1958, pp. 966, 968.)

IF I HAD TO choose between the two, I would rather have my sons go on missions than have a college education. It will do more for them temporally and educationally to say nothing of the spiritual benefits that are involved. ("How to Prepare for Missions," *Improvement Era*, Dec. 1960, p. 931.)

EVERY LIVING BEING is a descendant of Adam. Now we of the Church are also the children of Abraham; we are his seed. We are natural inheritors by blood lineage or by adoption of all the blessings that God gave Abraham—the blessings of glory and immortality and eternal life. We are the children of the prophets. We are a select and favored group known as the house of Israel. We have been gathered in from the ends of the earth so that God can fulfill the covenants made with our fathers and offer to us again, as he offered to them, the fullness of every great, glorious gospel principle. And the summation of these is to have the family unit continue eternally. ("Households of Faith," *Ensign*, Apr. 1971, p. 5.)

THERE IS SOMETHING missing from our proselyting program. We are not getting the results that we ought to get. We are not getting the number of baptisms that in my judgment the Lord expects us to get. To a degree, at least, we are grinding our wheels without going forward....

How many converts should we make each year? How many people should come into the Church?

In principle—we should baptize as many people as the Church can assimilate and fellowship without causing the wild olive branches which are grafted in to overpower the tame branches and thus cause the apostasy of the whole Church as was the case in the Meridian of time.

I think this statement summarizes what ought to be: If you will ponder it in your mind, you will come up, in my judgment, with the conclusion that we could bring immeasurably more people into the Church than we are doing. We could fellowship more than we are fellowshipping.... Perhaps in due course it should be 24 times or 100 times as many as at present....

The Lord wants people to be baptized. Our objective is to get people into the Church. Very frankly, brethren, you will be judged by the number of people that are baptized in your missions. That will be the first column we look at always when we examine the reports that you send. ("Seven Steps to More and Better Converts," unpublished address given at mission presidents' seminar, 21 June 1975, pp. 3-4.)

TWO THINGS ARE accomplished by the gathering of Israel: First, those who have thus chosen Christ as their Shepherd; those who have taken upon themselves his name in the waters of baptism; those who are seeking to enjoy his Spirit here and now and to be inheritors of eternal life hereafter—such people need to be gathered together to strengthen each other and to help one another perfect their lives.

And second, those who are seeking the highest rewards in eternity need to be where they can receive the blessings of the house of the Lord, both for themselves and for their ancestors in Israel who died without a knowledge of the gospel, but who would have received it with all their heart had opportunity afforded.

Manifestly in the early days of this dispensation, this meant gathering to the mountain of the Lord's house in the tops of the mountains of North America. There alone were congregations strong enough for the Saints to strengthen each other. There alone were the temples of the Most High where the fulness of the ordinances of exaltation are performed.

However, in the providences of Him who knoweth all things, in the providences of Him who scattered Israel and who is now gathering that favored people again, the day has now come when the fold of Christ is reaching out to the ends of the earth. We are not established in all nations, but we surely shall be before the second coming of the Son of Man. ("Come: Let Israel Build Zion," *Ensign*, May 1977, p. 117.)[11]

CHURCH MEMBERS ARE prone to ask: Where shall I begin my personal missionary work? The scriptural answer is: With your nonmember kinsmen, the members of your family who have not yet come into the Church, and with your nonmember neighbors....

As to your nonmember neighbors—they are yet of the world; they are the ones who will be damned unless they believe, are baptized, and keep the commandments after baptism.

Our obvious course is this:...We invite them into our homes; we break bread with them. They are our Father's children and one day may be stalwarts in his kingdom. We invite them to church meetings, especially sacrament meetings and conferences. These are the occasions when the gospel is taught....

There are two words that summarize what we must do. They are: *Teach* and *Testify*. We are to teach the doctrines of salvation and then bear testimony of the truth and divinity of our words.

We are bound to take every opportunity to tell others of the restoration of the gospel, of the salvation that is in Christ and his atoning blood, of the appearance of the Father and the Son to Joseph Smith, of the coming forth of the Book of Mormon, and of all the glories and wonders that are ours. ("Let the Word Go Forth," *Ensign*, Feb. 1985, p. 74.)

---

11. President Spencer W. Kimball personally directed that the sermon from which this excerpt comes be printed in the *Ensign* so it would be accessible to the general membership of the Church.

Chapter Forty-Two

Salvation

LET US REASON together on this matter of being saved without the need to do the works of righteousness. Did you ever wonder why our missionaries convert one of a city and two of a family while the preachers of this doctrine of salvation by grace alone gain millions of converts?

Does it seem strange to you that we wear out our lives in bringing one soul unto Christ, that we may have joy with him in the kingdom of the Father, while our evangelist colleagues cannot even count their converts so great is their number?

Why are those who come to hear the message of the Restoration numbered in the hundreds *and* thousands, rather than in the hundreds *of* thousands?

May I suggest that the difference is between the strait and narrow way, which few find, and the broad way, "that leadeth to destruction, and many there be which go in thereat" (Matthew 7:13-14).

All men must have and do have some way of worship—call it what you will—be it Christianity or Communism or Buddhism or atheism, or the wandering ways of Islam. I repeat: All men must and do worship; this inclination is given them by their Creator as a natural gift and endowment. The Light of Christ is shed forth upon all mankind; all men have a conscience and know by instinct the difference between good and evil; it is inherent in the human personality to seek and worship a divine being of some sort.

As we are aware, since the Fall all men have become carnal, sensual, and devilish by nature; they have become worldly; and their inclination is to live after the manner of the flesh and satisfy their lusts and appetites.

Accordingly, anytime men can devise a system of worship that will let them continue to live after the manner of the world, to live in their carnal and fallen state, and at the same time one which will satisfy their innate and instinctive desires to worship, such, to them, is a marvelous achievement.

There is a true doctrine of salvation by grace—a salvation by grace alone and without works, as the scriptures say. To understand this doctrine we must define our terms as they are defined in holy writ.

1. *What is salvation?* It is both immortality and eternal life. It is an inheritance in the highest heaven of the celestial world. It consists of the fullness of the glory of the Father and is reserved for those for whom the family unit continues in eternity. Those who are saved become as God is and live as he lives.

2. *What is the plan of salvation?* It is the system ordained by the Father to enable his spirit children to advance and progress and become like him. It consists of three great and eternal verities—the Creation, the Fall, and the Atonement—without any of which there could be no salvation.

3. *What is the grace of God?* It is his mercy, his love, and his condescension—all manifest for the benefit and blessing of his children, all operating to bring to pass the immortality and eternal life of man....

4. *Does salvation come by grace, by grace alone, by grace without works?* It surely does, without any question, in all its parts, types, kinds, and degrees.

We are saved by grace, without works; it is a gift of God. How else could it come?...

In his goodness and grace he created this earth and all that is on it, with man as the crowning creature of his creating—without which creation his spirit children could not obtain immortality and eternal life. No works on our part were required.

In his goodness and grace he provided for the Fall of man, thus bringing mortality and death and a probationary estate into being—without all of which there would be no immortality and eternal life. And again no works on our part were required.

In his goodness and grace—and this above all—he gave his Only Begotten Son to ransom man and all life from the temporal and spiritual death brought into the world by the Fall of Adam.

He sent his Son to redeem mankind, to atone for the sins of the world, "to bring to pass the immortality and eternal life of man" (Moses 1:39). And again all this comes to us as a free gift and without works.

There is nothing any man could do to create himself. This was the work of the Lord God.

Nor did we have any part in the Fall of man, without which there could be no salvation. The Lord provided the way, and Adam and Eve put the system into operation.

And finally, there neither has been, nor is, nor ever can be any way nor means by which man alone can, by any power he possesses, redeem himself.

We cannot resurrect ourselves anymore than we can create ourselves. We cannot create a heavenly abode for the Saints, nor make provision for the continuation of the family unit in eternity, nor bring salvation and exaltation into being. All these things are ordained and established by that God who is the Father of us all. And they all came into being and are made available to us, as free gifts, without works, because of the infinite goodness and grace of Him whose children we are.

Truly, there is no way to overstate the goodness and grandeurs and glories of the grace of God which bringeth salvation. Such wondrous love, such unending mercy, such infinite compassion and condescension—all these can come only from the Eternal God who lives in eternal life and who desires all of his children to live as he lives and be inheritors of eternal life.

Knowing these things, as did Paul and our fellow apostles of old, let us put ourselves in their position. What words shall we choose, to offer to the world the blessings of a freely given atoning sacrifice?

On the one hand, we are preaching to Jews who, in their lost and fallen state, have rejected their Messiah and who believe they are saved by the works and performances of the Mosaic law.

On the other hand, we are preaching to pagans—Romans, Greeks, those in every nation—who know nothing whatever about the Messianic word, or of the need for a Redeemer, or of the working out of the infinite and eternal atonement. They worship idols, the forces of nature, the heavenly bodies, or whatever suits their fancy. As with the Jews, they assume that this or that sacrifice or appeasing act will please the Deity of their choice and some vague and unspecified blessings will result.

Can either the Jews or the pagans be left to assume that the works they do will save them? Or must they forget their little groveling acts of petty worship, gain faith in Christ, and rely on the cleansing power of his blood for salvation?

They must be taught faith in the Lord Jesus Christ and to forsake their traditions and performances. Surely we must tell them they cannot be saved by the works they are doing, for man cannot save himself. Instead they must turn to Christ and rely on his merits and mercy and grace....

Now let us suppose a modern-day case. Suppose we have the scriptures, the gospel, the priesthood, the Church, the ordinances, the organization, even the keys of the kingdom—everything that now is down to the last jot and tittle—and yet there is no atonement of Christ. What then? Can we be saved? Will all our good works save us? Will we be rewarded for all our righteousness?

Most assuredly we will not. We are not saved by works alone, no matter how good; we are saved because God sent his Son to shed his blood in Gethsemane and on Calvary that all through him might ransomed be. We are saved by the blood of Christ.

To paraphrase Abinadi: "Salvation doth not come by the Church alone: and were it not for the atonement, given by the grace of God as a free gift, all men must unavoidably perish, and this notwithstanding the Church and all that appertains to it."

Let us now come to the matter of whether we must do something to gain the blessings of the atonement in our lives. And we find the answer written in words of fire and emblazoned across the whole heavens; we hear a voice speaking with the sound of ten thousand trumpets; the very heavens and the earth are moved out of their place so powerful is the word that goes forth. It is a message that neither men, nor angels, nor the Gods themselves can proclaim with an undue emphasis.

This is the word: Man cannot be saved by grace alone; as the Lord lives, he must keep the commandments; he must work the works of righteousness; he must work out his salvation with fear and trembling before the Lord; he must have faith like the ancients—the faith that brings with it gifts and signs and miracles....

The blood of Christ was shed as a free gift of wondrous grace, but the Saints are cleansed by the blood after they keep the commandments....

Men must be doers of the word, not hearers only; they must do the very works that Christ did; and those who have true and saving faith in him accomplish this very end.

In our day, among other Christians at least, we are not faced with the problem of our predecessors. They had to show that any works then being performed were of no avail without the atonement, that salvation was in Christ and his spilt blood, and that all men must come unto him to be saved.

Our need in today's world, in which Christians assume there was an atonement, is to interpret the scriptures properly and to call upon men to keep the commandments so as to become worthy of the cleansing power of the blood of the Lamb....

And it is the will of the Father—as a thousand scriptures attest—that all men everywhere must endure to the end, must keep the commandments, must work out their salvation with fear and trembling before the Lord, or they can in no wise enter into the kingdom of heaven....

Salvation by grace alone and without works, as it is taught in large segments of Christendom today, is akin to what Lucifer proposed in preexistence—that he would save all mankind and one soul should not be lost. He would save them without agency, without works, without any act on their part.

As with the proposal of Lucifer in the preexistence to save all mankind, so with the doctrine of salvation by grace alone, without works, as it is taught in modern Christendom—both concepts are false. There is no salvation in either of them. They both come from the same source; they are not of God.

We believe and proclaim that it is life eternal to know the only wise and true God and Jesus Christ whom he has sent. Let men worship whomsoever they will, but there is no salvation in worshipping any God but the true God.

We believe and proclaim that salvation is in Christ, in his gospel, in his atoning sacrifice. We are bold to say it comes by the goodness and grace of the Father and the Son. No people on earth praise the Lord with greater faith and fervor than we do because of this goodness and grace.

As the Lord's agents, as his servants, as ambassadors of Christ—sent by him, sent to speak in his place and stead, sent to say what he would say if he personally were here—we testify that no man, as long as the earth shall stand, or the heavens endure, or God continues as God, no man shall ever be saved in the kingdom of God, in the celestial kingdom of heaven, without doing the works of righteousness. ("What Think Ye of Salvation by Grace?" *Brigham Young University 1983-84 Fireside and Devotional Speeches* [1984]. pp. 46-49.)

Chapter Forty-Three

Women

THE TRUE GOSPEL is family centered. Full salvation consists of the continuation of the family unit in celestial glory. Those for whom the family unit continues have eternal life; those for whom it does not continue do not have eternal life, for heaven itself is but the projection of a Latter-day Saint family into eternity.

That power by which salvation comes is so great that it can make of earth a heaven, and of man, a god.

The noblest concept that can enter the heart of man is the concept that the family unit continues in eternity, and that salvation is a family affair. ("Salvation Is a Family Affair," *Improvement Era*, June 1970, p. 44.)

WHERE SPIRITUAL THINGS are concerned, as pertaining to all of the gifts of the Spirit, with reference to the receipt of revelation, the gaining of testimonies, and the seeing of visions, in all matters that pertain to godliness and holiness and which are brought to pass as a result of personal righteousness—in all these things men and women stand in a position of absolute equality before the Lord. He is no respecter of persons nor of sexes, and he blesses those men and those women who seek him and serve him and keep his commandments.

The Lord is merciful and gracious unto all those who fear him, and he delights to honor those who serve him in righteousness unto the end—both male and female. It is to them that he promises to reveal all the hidden mysteries of his kingdom; they are the ones whose understanding shall reach to heaven and to whom he will reveal those things which eye has not seen, nor ear heard, and which have not entered into the heart of man....I have no hesitancy in stating that women from the beginning have acquired great spiritual talents.

Now, the Lord in his infinite goodness and wisdom has highly esteemed women from the beginning; he has honored and dignified them in his earthly kingdom, and in his dealings with mankind on earth, in a way that perhaps many of us have never supposed....

The sisters in the kingdom are great pillars of spiritual strength, of compassionate service, of devotion to the truth, of personal righteousness. As with their ancient counterparts they provide bodies for the spirit children of the Father; and as did the faithful sisters of old, they bring up their children in light and truth and teach them to have faith in the Lord and to keep his commandments. Nor does their service to mankind stop at the hearth. Their influence reaches forth in the Church, in the government, in uplifting organizations everywhere....

A married woman's place is in the home, where she sustains and supports her husband; a woman's place is in the Church, where she expounds scripture, writes wise documents, and learns much; a woman's place is out rendering compassionate service to her fellow beings, in and out of the Church; a woman's place is in preaching the gospel and doing missionary work; her calling is to do good and work righteousness in every place and under all circumstances.

It is thus that we see the mothers in Israel and the daughters of Zion today. We see them weeping at Haun's Mill; we see them standing beside burning houses in Missouri; we see them bowing before open graves at Winter Quarters. Our sisters are like those of old. They fight the family-destroying influence of unfortunate legislative proposals. They lobby in legislative halls and rally the forces of good around the ballot box. They importune the Lord for the preservation of their families and for his guiding hand over the destinies of nations.

The brethren do not stand alone in building up the Lord's latter-day kingdom. And when our faithful sisters depart this life, they will continue to labor with the downtrodden and spiritually depressed until the work of the great Jehovah shall reach its glorious consummation. ("Our Sisters from the Beginning," *Ensign,* Jan. 1979, p. 63.)

Chapter Forty-Four

Politics

IS POLITICS REALLY a sordid, sorry mess which decent people should avoid? Or does the Gospel standard call for participation in civic and governmental matters, and therefore in politics?

Some people say: "Two subjects are taboo: never discuss politics nor religion."

Would it not be wiser to say of politics and religion: "No two subjects are of greater concern; none are more deserving of intense attention and thoughtful and prayerful study; none should be discussed and weighed more carefully—politics because freedom itself depends upon our political structure, and religion because eternal salvation is at stake"?

Some citizens are cautious of political entanglements, feeling that such, at best, are only a necessary evil.

Would it not be better if all good citizens united to raise the standard of political and governmental operation?

Bitterness, inordinate and unbalanced partisanship, whispering campaigns of half truths and innuendo, special privileges for a select few—no decent Christian countenances these in friend or foe. But these are the type of things which arise because the "best people" often do not participate in politics and thereby exert their influence for goodness in government.

In the Gospel we have a complete way of life—one that covers every phase of earthly existence. True religion is not confined to ethics, to ordinances, to so-called spiritual matters only. The Gospel offers a solution to every problem; it gives direction in every field of human endeavor. Whether man's problems are political, educational, physical, cultural, economic, temporal, spiritual, or what have you, an answer to them is found or a course is charted in the restored Gospel.

Joseph Smith, crying out against the political oppression and religious bigotry of this day, gave to the Church a political motto. In his language, these are the things for which we stand:

1. The Constitution of our country, formed by the Fathers of liberty.
2. Peace and good order in society.
3. Love of God and good will to man.
4. All good and wholesome laws, virtue and truth above all things, and aristarchy, live forever!
5. But woe to tyrants, mobs, aristocracy, anarchy, and toryism, and all those who invent or seek out unrighteous and vexatious law suits, under the pretext and color of law, or office, either religious or political.
6. Exalt the standard of democracy!
7. Down with that of priestcraft, and let all the people say "Amen!" that the blood of our fathers may not cry from the ground against us. Sacred is the memory of that blood which bought for us our liberty.

Now, read the following scriptural passages: Doctrine & Covenants 58:21, 22; 98:4-10, 16; 101:76-80; 109:54; 134:1-12; Mosiah 29; Romans 13:1-7; I Peter 2:13-17.

From these scriptures we learn: 1. the principles upon which proper governments rest, and 2. the responsibilities of good citizenship. These, as taught in the cited passages, are summarized as follows:

Ten Revealed Laws of Government

1. Some governments are instituted of God for the benefit of man.
2. The Lord established the United States Constitution by the hands of wise men.
3. He raises up wise men to act in governmental capacities.
4. All mankind—people of every nation and kindred, not just those living in America—are endowed with natural and inalienable rights.
5. Deity expects that governments shall protect and preserve men in the full exercise of their inherent and inalienable rights.
6. Government officers are accountable before God for their acts "both in making laws and administering them, for the good and safety of society."
7. Unconstitutional laws are not of God, but "cometh of evil."
8. Just and righteous laws make men free.

9. "No government can exist in peace, except such laws are framed and held inviolate as will secure to each individual the free exercise of conscience, the right and control of property, and the protection of life."

10. The Lord approves of governments which guarantee freedom, thereby allowing men the free exercise of agency and consequent personal responsibility for their acts in the day of judgment.

Ten Commandments for Good Citizenship

1. Sustain and uphold the constitution of the land.
2. Obey the laws of the land.
3. Befriend and support laws which are constitutional.
4. Be subject to governmental control and regulation.
5. Seek for honest and wise men to hold public office.
6. Support and uphold good and wise men in their public acts.
7. Remember that when the wicked rule, laws are administered in unrighteousness.
8. Follow democratic electoral processes and select government officers by a majority vote, for this has divine approval.
9. Importune government officers for redress of grievances and redemption from imposition.
10. Renounce war and proclaim peace.

In our American democracy sovereignty rests with the people; political parties are the means by which governments are selected and controlled; and thus through them the people use their supreme governmental powers. ("Exalt the Standard of Democracy," *Instructor*, Sept. 1964, pp. 344-45.)

Chapter Forty-Five

God and History

HOW DOES GOD govern in the affairs of men and nations? What means does He use to direct the course of kingdoms and peoples? What means are employed to regulate the events of history so that His purposes will prevail on earth?

That Deity's hand is over and in all things—thus regulating for His own purposes the kingdoms and peoples of the earth—is known to thoughtful men everywhere. One nation rises, another falls; one people settles this land, another inhabits that; migrations occur; civilizations come and go; the surface and arrangement of the earth itself is changed—all as part of the divine plan, all to provide the type of probationary estate which the Lord's children need.

Our purpose now is to note some of the means used by the Lord to govern events of history. Among others there are the following:

1. Prophets Reveal God's Will

Prophets speak as moved upon by the Holy Ghost. Their voice is the voice of God; they reveal His mind and His will....

Ancient Israel drove out the inhabitants of Palestine; the Nephites and Jaredites came to America; the Latter-day Saints colonized Western America—all because prophets received revelation by the power of the Holy Ghost. Moses received the Ten Commandments and a host of other revelations, which have formed the pattern for the laws of many nations—all to the end that the Lord's power might be manifest in historical events.

2. National Leaders Aid the Lord's Cause

To a greater or lesser extent the Lord uses the leaders and wise men of nations to further His purposes. An Egyptian Pharaoh provided refuge for the budding nation of Israel. Inventors and scientists have brought forth the devices, medicines, and marvelous achievements reserved for this day in the earth's history. Selected wise men were sent to earth to lay the foundations of the American system of freedom. "I established the Constitution of this land, by the hands of wise men whom I raised up unto this very purpose," the Lord says. (Doctrine & Covenants 101:80.) Implicit in this pronouncement is the fact that He not only directed these "wise men" in their governmental deliberations, but He sent the appointed spirits to earth under those circumstances which would allow them to achieve that which was expected of them.

3. The Earth Itself Acts for Man's Benefit

The Lord regulates the elements and all that He has created so that His purposes will prevail among men. He created the earth as a habitation for man. He sent the flood to alter the course of history. A famine forced Abraham to find a new residence, and a similar dearth sent Jacob and his family into Egypt. Earthquakes, fires, plagues, and other disasters have changed the destinies of nations.

4. Man's Desires and Appetites Are Used by Deity

Men from Europe desired religious and political freedom, and as a result the American colonies were settled. Men from Spain, with an unquenchable thirst for gold and power, overran Mexico and parts of South America, thus laying the foundation for the modern nations which have custody of those portions of the earth's surface. Gold was discovered in California, causing thousands of wealth-seekers to forsake their eastern inheritances and cross a continent of wilderness, thus colonizing and opening up a new land. Lust for power and empire has caused the armies of the earth to go from one end of its surface to the other, age after age. All these and uncounted similar things have set the stage, in each age and dispensation, for the things the Lord wanted done among men.

5. Men Are Guided by the Light of Christ

Though many ways and means are used by Deity to cause men to do what must be done to further His purposes, in the final analysis they all tie into the Light of Christ. This Light is the agency of God's power. It is the Light, Influence, or Spirit which goes forth from His presence to fill the immensity of space. It is the power and means He uses to govern this earth and all things on it, as also the universe and all that is therein involved. ("How God Directs Events in History," *Instructor*, Nov. 1966, pp. 424-25.)

Chapter Forty-Six

Riches and Wealth

THE FULL ACCOUNT of these events [the story of the prophet Balaam] is found in Numbers 22:23-25; 31:8; 2 Peter 2:15-16; Jude 11; and Revelation 2:14.

What a story this is! Here is a prophet of God who is firmly committed to declare only what the Lord of heaven directs. There does not seem to be the slightest doubt in his mind about the course he should pursue. He represents the Lord, and neither a house full of gold and silver nor high honors offered by the king can sway him from his determined course, which has been charted for him by that God whom he serves.

But greed for wealth and lust for honor beckon him. How marvelous it would be to be rich and powerful—as well as having the prophetic powers that already are his.

Perhaps the Lord would let him compromise his standards and have some worldly prosperity and power as well as a testimony of the gospel. Of course he knew the gospel was true, as it were, but why should he be denied the things his political file leader could confer?

I wonder how often some of us get our direction from the Church and then, Balaam-like, plead for some worldly rewards and finally receive an answer which says, in effect, If you are determined to be a millionaire or to gain this or that worldly honor, go ahead, with the understanding that you will continue to serve the Lord. Then we wonder why things don't work out for us as well as they would have done if we had put first in our lives the things of God's kingdom?

What are the rewards of unrighteousness? Do they not include seeking for worldly things when these run counter to the interests of the Church?

And don't we all know people who though they were once firm and steadfast in testimony, are now opposing the Lord's purposes and interests on earth because money and power have twisted their judgment of what should or should not be?

Balaam, the prophet, inspired and mighty as he once was, lost his soul in the end because he set his heart on the things of this world rather than the riches of eternity. ("The Story of a Prophet's Madness," *New Era*, Apr. 1972, p. 7.)

As a young man, serving at the direction of my bishop, I called upon a rich man and invited him to contribute a thousand dollars to a building fund. He declined. But he did say he wanted to help, and if we would have a ward dinner and charge $5 per plate, he would take two tickets. About ten days later this man died unexpectedly of a heart attack, and I have wondered ever since about the fate of his eternal soul. ("Obedience, Consecration, and Sacrifice," *Ensign*, May 1975, p. 50.)

Bibliography

Allen, James B. "The Story of the Truth, the Way, the Life." *BYU Studies*, 1993. vol.33, no.4.

Ballard, Melvin J. *Melvin J. Ballard: Crusader for Righteousness*. Salt Lake City: Bookcraft, 1966.

Barton, Peggy Petersen. *Mark E. Petersen: A Biography*. Salt Lake City: Deseret Book, 1985.

Benson, Ezra Taft. Unpublished remarks at funeral of Bruce R. McConkie.

Carmack, John K. "The Testament of Bruce R. McConkie." BYU Fireside Address, 5 May 1985.

Carmack, John K. Typescript of taped interview, Mar. 19, 1997.

Church News. 12 Oct. 1946; 4 Apr. 1964; 29 Aug. 1964; 31 July 1965; Nov. 1966; 10 Jan. 1970; Oct. 1971; 21 Oct. 1972; 24 Jan. 1976; 20 May 1984; 28 Apr. 1985

Church of Jesus Christ of Latter-day Saints. Typescript of video biography of Elder Bruce R. McConkie. 1987.

Clark, James R. comp. *Messages of the First Presidency*, Vol. 4. Salt Lake City: Bookcraft, 1970.

Conference Reports: April 1947; Oct. 1947; April 1948; Oct. 48; Apr. 1949; Oct. 1950; Oct. 1951; Oct. 1952; Oct. 1953; Oct. 1955; Oct. 1976

Cope, Lloyd J. Unpublished notes. Paradise Stake, California.

Croft, David. *Church News* interview. 24 Jan. 1976.

Dew, Sheri L. "Bruce R. McConkie: A Family Portrait." *This People*, Dec. 1985/Jan. 1986.

Dew, Sheri L. *Ezra Taft Benson: A Biography*. Salt Lake City: Deseret Book, 1987.

Dew, Sheri L. *Go Forward with Faith: The Biography of Gordon B. Hinckley*. Salt Lake City: Deseret Book, 1996.

Flake, Lawrence R. *Mighty Men of Zion*. Salt Lake City: Butler, 1974.

Gibbons, Francis M. *George Albert Smith: Kind and Caring Christian, Prophet of God*. Salt Lake City: Deseret Book, 1990.

Gibbons, Francis M. *Harold B. Lee: Man of Vision, Prophet of God*. Salt Lake City, Bookcraft, 1993.

Gibbons, Francis M. *Heber J. Grant: Man of Steel, Prophet of God*. Salt Lake City: Deseret Book, 1979.

Gibbons, Francis M. *Joseph Fielding Smith: Gospel Scholar, Prophet of God*. Salt Lake City, Deseret Book, 1992.

Gibbons, Francis M. *Spencer W. Kimball: Resolute Disciple, Prophet of God*. Salt Lake City: Deseret Book, 1995.

Goates, L. Brent. *Harold B. Lee: Prophet and Seer*. Salt Lake City, Bookcraft, 1985.

Goates, L. Brent. *He Changed My Life*. Salt Lake City: Bookcraft, 1988.

Haight, David B. "The Sacrament–And the Sacrifice." *Ensign,* Nov. 1989.

Hale, Van. "What About the Adam-God Theory." Mormon Miscellaneous.

Hinckley, Gordon B. Unpublished remarks at funeral of Bruce R. McConkie.

Horne, Dennis B. *Proud That My Name Is Horne: A History of Walter and Marie Horne and Some of Their Ancestors.* [Privately Published], 1992.

Howard, F. Burton. *Marion G. Romney: His Life and Faith.* Salt Lake City: Bookcraft, 1988.

Journal of Discourses. Vols 1 & 4.

Kimball, Edward L. & Andrew E. Kimball. *Spencer W. Kimball.* Salt Lake City: Bookcraft, 1977.

Kimball, Edward L., ed. *The Teachings of Spencer W. Kimball.* Salt Lake City: Bookcraft, 1982.

Lee, Harold B. "Viewpoint of a Giant." Summer School Devotional Address, 18 July 1968.

Ludlow, Daniel H. ed. *The Encyclopedia of Mormonism.* New York: MacMillan, 1992.

Lundwall, N. B. comp. *Discourses on the Holy Ghost.* Salt Lake City: Bookcraft, 1959.

McConkie, Amelia S. "Aim for the Sun." Salt Lake City: Institute of Religion Devotional Address, Jan. 17, 1986.

McConkie, Bruce R. Address at Santiago Chile Area Conference, 1977.

McConkie, Bruce R. "Agency or Inspiration–Which?" *Speeches of the Year 1973.* Provo, Utah: Brigham Young University, 1974.

McConkie, Bruce R. "Are the General Authorities Human?" Salt Lake City: LDS Student Association Devotional, 28 Oct. 1966.

McConkie, Bruce R. "The Atonement." Unpublished talk given at Chico California Stake Conference, 15 March 1981.

McConkie, Bruce R. "Be Valiant in the Fight of Faith." *Ensign*, Nov. 1974.

McConkie, Bruce R. *Be Ye Converted.* Brigham Young University Speeches of the Year, 11 Feb. 1968.

McConkie, Bruce R. "The Bible: A Sealed Book." BYU: Church Educational System Symposium, 17 Aug. 1984.

McConkie, Bruce R. "The Caravan Moves On." *Ensign*, Nov. 1984.

McConkie, Bruce R. "Celestial Marriage." BYU Fireside Address, 6 Nov. 1977.

McConkie, Bruce R. "Charity Which Never Faileth." *Relief Society Magazine*, March 1970.

McConkie, Bruce R. "Christ and the Creation." *Ensign*, June 1982.

McConkie, Bruce R. "Choose an Eternal Companion." BYU Devotional Address, 3 May 1966.

McConkie, Bruce R. "Come: Let Israel Build Zion." *Ensign*, May 1977.

McConkie, Bruce R. "Come Unto Christ." *Improvement Era*, Dec. 1964.

McConkie, Bruce R. "The Coming Tests and Trials and Glory." *Ensign,* May 1980.

McConkie, Bruce R. Correspondence to Walter M. Horne, 13 Sept 1972 & 2 Oct. 1974.

McConkie, Bruce R. "The Dead Who Die in the Lord." *Ensign*, Nov. 1976.

McConkie, Bruce R. "The Divine Mission of Joseph Smith." *Improvement Era*, Dec. 1962.

McConkie, Bruce R. "The Doctrine of the Priesthood." *Ensign*, May 1982.

McConkie, Bruce R. "Drink from the Fountain." *Ensign*, Apr. 1975.

McConkie, Bruce R. "Eve and the Fall." *Woman*. Salt Lake City: Deseret Book, 1979.

McConkie, Bruce R. "Exalt the Standard of Democracy." *Instructor*, Sept. 1964.

McConkie, Bruce R. "The Foolishness of Teaching." Address to Seminary and Institute Personnel, 1981.

McConkie, Bruce R. "A God Is Born." Salt Lake City Tabernacle: Christmas Devotional, 11 Dec. 1980. Unpublished address. LDS Historical Dept. Archives.

McConkie, Bruce R. "God Foreordains His Prophets and His People." *Ensign*, May 1974.

McConkie, Bruce R. "God's Kingdom on Earth." *Improvement Era*. Dec. 1958.

McConkie, Bruce R. "Households of Faith." Brigham Young University Speeches of the Year, 1 Dec. 1970.

McConkie, Bruce R. "The How and Why of Faith-promoting Stories." *New Era*, July 1978.

McConkie, Bruce R. "How God Directs Events in History." *Instructor*, Nov. 1966.

McConkie, Bruce R. *How to Get Personal Revelation*. BYU Speeches of the Year, 1966.

McConkie, Bruce R. "How to Prepare for Missions." *Improvement Era*, Dec. 1960.

McConkie, Bruce R. "How to Worship." *Ensign*, Dec. 1971.

McConkie, Bruce R. "Jesus Christ and Him Crucified." *1976 Devotional Speeches of the Year*. Provo, Utah: BYU, 1977.

McConkie, Bruce R. "Joseph Smith: A Revealer of Christ." *1978 Devotional Speeches of the Year*. Provo, Utah: BYU, 1979.

McConkie, Bruce R. "Joseph Smith–The Mighty Prophet of the Restoration." *Ensign*, May 1976.

McConkie, Bruce R. "The Keys of the Kingdom." *Ensign*, May 1983.

McConkie, Bruce R. *The Keys of the Kingdom*. Brigham Young Speeches of the Year, 23 Apr. 1957.

McConkie, Bruce R. "The Keys of the Kingdom." Wilford Priesthood Meeting, 12 Feb. 1955. Unpublished address.

McConkie, Bruce R. "Knowest Thou the Condescension of God." *Speeches*, 1969.

McConkie, Bruce R. "The Law of Justification." *Improvement Era*, June 1956.

McConkie, Bruce R. "Lectures in Theology: Last Message Series." Salt Lake City: Institute of Religion Devotional Address, 22 Jan. 1971.

McConkie, Bruce R. "Let the Word Go Forth." *Ensign*, Feb 1985.

McConkie, Bruce R. *The Lord God of Joseph Smith*. Brigham Young University Speeches of the Year [4 Jan. 1972].

McConkie, Bruce R. "The Lord God of the Restoration." *Ensign*, Oct. 1980.

McConkie, Bruce R. "Lord, Increase our Faith." BYU Speeches of the Year, 31 Oct. 1973.

McConkie, Bruce R. "The Lord's People Receive Revelation." *Ensign,* June 1971.

McConkie, Bruce R. "Love Not the World." *Improvement Era*, June 1958.

McConkie, Bruce R. "Making Our Calling and Election Sure." BYU Fireside Address, 25 Mar. 1969.

McConkie, Bruce R. "A Man Called John." *New Era*, May 1984.

McConkie, Bruce R. "The Message of the Restoration." *Improvement Era*, Nov. 1949.

McConkie, Bruce R. *The Millennial Messiah*. Salt Lake City: Deseret Book, 1982.

McConkie, Bruce R. *Mormon Doctrine*. Salt Lake City: Bookcraft, various editions.

McConkie, Bruce R. *The Mortal Messiah*. Books 1-4. Salt Lake City City, Deseret Book, 1979-81.

McConkie, Bruce R. "The Mystery of Godliness." *Brigham Young University 1984-85 Devotional and Fireside Speeches*. Provo, Utah: BYU, 1985.

McConkie, Bruce R. "The Mystery of Mormonism." *Ensign,* Nov. 1979.

McConkie, Bruce R. *The New and Everlasting Covenant of Marriage*. BYU Speeches of the Year, 20 Apr. 1960.

McConkie, Bruce R. "A New Commandment–Save Thyself and Thy Kindred!" *Ensign*, Aug. 1976.

McConkie, Bruce R. *A New Witness for the Articles of Faith*. Salt Lake City: Deseret Book, 1985.

McConkie, Bruce R. "Obedience, Consecration, and Sacrifice." *Ensign*, May 1975.

McConkie, Bruce R. "On Reading the Standard Works." *Improvement Era*, Dec. 1959.

McConkie, Bruce R. Open letter to Honest Truth Seekers, 1 July 1980.

McConkie, Bruce R. "Our Belief in Christ." *Improvement Era*, Dec. 1970.

McConkie, Bruce R. "Our Gospel Came Not Unto You in Word Only..." *Improvement Era*, Dec. 1968.

McConkie, Bruce R. "Our Relationship with the Lord." BYU Devotional Address, 2 March 1982.

McConkie, Bruce R. "Our Sisters from the Beginning." *Ensign*, Jan. 1979.

McConkie, Bruce R. "Patterns of Prayer." *Ensign*, May 1984.

McConkie, Bruce R. "The Preexistence of Man." Typescript of summer 1967 lecture at BYU. BYU Religious Instruction Audiovisual Materials.

McConkie, Bruce R. "The Probationary Test of Mortality." Salt Lake City: Institute of Religion Devotional, 10 Jan. 1982.

McConkie, Bruce R. *The Promised Messiah*. Salt Lake City: Deseret Book, 1978.

McConkie, Bruce R. The Promises Made to the Fathers." *Studies in Scripture, The Old Testament*, Vol.3. Kent P. Jackson and Robert L. Millet, eds. Salt Lake City: Randall Book, 1985.

McConkie, Bruce R. "Remarks Given at Area Conference." Santiago, Chile: March 1977.

McConkie, Bruce R. "Report of Mexico City Area Conference."

McConkie, Bruce R. "The Rock of Salvation." *Improvement Era*, Dec. 1969.

McConkie, Bruce R. "Salvation: A Family Affair." *Improvement Era*, Apr. 1959.

McConkie, Bruce R. "Salvation Is A Family Affair." *Improvement Era*, June 1970.

McConkie, Bruce R. "The Seven Christs." *Ensign*, Nov. 1982.

McConkie, Bruce R. "The Seven Deadly Heresies." BYU Fireside Address, 1 June 1980.

McConkie, Bruce R. "Seven Steps to More and Better Converts." Unpublished address give at mission president's seminar, 21 June 1975.

McConkie, Bruce R. "The Sixth Commandment for Us." *Instructor*, Aug. 1957.

McConkie, Bruce R. "Stand Independent above All Other Creatures." *Ensign*, May 1979.

McConkie, Bruce R. "The Story of a Prophet's Madness." *New Era*, Apr. 1972.

McConkie, Bruce R. "Succession in the Presidency." *Speeches of the Year 1974*. [1975].

McConkie, Bruce R. "The Teacher's Divine Commission." *Ensign*, Apr. 1979.

McConkie, Bruce R. "The Ten Blessings of the Priesthood." *Ensign*, Nov. 1977.

McConkie, Bruce R. "The Ten Commandments of a Peculiar People." BYU Devotional Address, 28 Jan. 1975.

McConkie, Bruce R. "Testimony of the Restoration." *Improvement Era*, Dec. 1956.

McConkie, Bruce R. "Think on These Things." *Ensign*, Jan. 1974.

McConkie, Bruce R. "This Final Glorious Gospel Dispensation." *Ensign*, April 1980.

McConkie, Bruce R. "This Generation Shall Have My Word Through You." *Hearken O Ye People: Discourses on the Doctrine and Covenants*. Sandy, Utah: Randall Book, 1984.

McConkie, Bruce R. "Thou Shalt Receive Revelation." *Ensign*, Nov. 1978.

McConkie, Bruce R. "The Three Pillars of Eternity." *BYU Fireside and Devotional Speeches*. Provo, Utah: BYU, 1981.

McConkie, Bruce R. Transcript of unpublished remarks at funeral of S. Dilworth Young.

McConkie, Bruce R. Unpublished talk given at the Salt Lake City Emigration Stake Conference, 31 Aug. 1958.

McConkie, Bruce R. "What Is Meant by 'The Holy Spirit.'" *Instructor*, Feb. 1965.

McConkie, Bruce R. "What Think Ye of Salvation by Grace." *Brigham Young University 1983-84 Fireside and Devotional Speeches*. Provo, Utah: BYU, 1984.

McConkie, Bruce R. "What Think Ye of the Book of Mormon?" *Ensign*, Nov. 1983.

McConkie, Bruce R. "Who Hath Believed Our Report?" *Ensign*, Nov. 1981.

McConkie, Bruce R. "Who Shall Declare His Generation." BYU Devotional Address, 2 Dec. 1975.

McConkie, Bruce R. "Why the Lord Ordained Prayer." *Ensign*, Jan. 1976.

McConkie, Bruce R. *Ye Are My Witnesses*. BYU: Speeches of the Year, 14 Mar. 1967.

McConkie, Joseph Fielding. *Here We Stand*. Salt Lake City: Deseret Book, 1995.

McConkie, Joseph Fielding. Interview with author, Summer 1988.

McConkie, Joseph Fielding. *The Man Adam*. Salt Lake City: Bookcraft, 1990.

McConkie, Joseph Fielding. *Sons and Daughters of God*. Salt Lake City: Bookcraft, 1994.

McConkie, Joseph Fielding. and Robert L. Millet. *Sustaining and Defending the Faith*. Salt Lake City: Deseret Book, 1985.

McConkie, Joseph Fielding. Telephone interviews with author. 11 Jan. & 26 July, 1997.

McConkie, Joseph Fielding. Unpublished biography of Oscar W. McConkie. LDS Church Historical Library.

McConkie, Mark. *Doctrines of the Restoration*. Salt Lake City City, Bookcraft, 1989.

McConkie, Oscar W. Jr. "Ye Are My Witness...That I Am God." Salt Lake City: Institute of Religion Devotional, Oct. 29, 1971.

McKay, David O. "Items from David O. McKay's Office Journal Relating to the Publication of Bruce R. McConkie's '*Mormon Doctrine*.'"

McKay, David O. Unpublished letter to a BYU student, 3 Nov. 1947.

Millet, Robert L. and Joseph Fielding McConkie. *The Life Beyond*. Salt Lake City, Bookcraft, 1986.

Millet, Robert L. *The Power of the Word*. Salt Lake City: Deseret Book, 1994.

Nyman, Monte S. and Robert L Millet, eds. *The Joseph Smith Translation: The Restoration of Plain and Precious Things*. Provo, Utah: BYU Religious Studies Center, 1985.

Oaks, Dallin H. *The Lord's Way*. Salt Lake City: Deseret Book, 1991.

Packer, Boyd K. Correspondence to Dennis B. Horne, 24 Apr. 1990.

Packer, Boyd K. "Insights from My Life." *BYU Devotional Speeches of the Year*, Provo, Utah: 1976.

Packer, Boyd K. *Let Not Your Heart Be Troubled*. Salt Lake City, Bookcraft, 1991.

Packer, Boyd K. Unpublished address given at funeral of Bruce R. McConkie. 23 Apr. 1985.

Petersen, Mark E. *As Translated Correctly*. Salt Lake City: Deseret Book, 1966.

Petersen, Mark E. Unpublished talk given in Paris, France at a missionary meeting. 24 Jan. 1963.

Provo Daily Herald. 21 Apr. 1985.

Richards, LeGrand. *A Marvelous Work and a Wonder*. Salt Lake City: Deseret Book, 1950.

Romney, Marion G. Correspondence to President David O. McKay. 28 Jan. 1959.

Sharp, Marian C. "Bruce R. McConkie Sustained a Member of the First Council of the Seventy." *Relief Society Magazine*, vol. 33, no. 12. Dec. 1946.

Sherry, Thomas E. *Attitudes, Practices, and Positions toward Joseph Smith's Translation of the Bible: A Historical Analysis of Publications, 1849-1987.* LDS Church Historical Dept., unpublished thesis.

Smith, Joseph Fielding. *Doctrines of Salvation.* Vol. 1. Salt Lake City, Bookcraft.

Smith, Joseph Fielding. and John J. Stewart. *Life of Joseph Fielding Smith.* Salt Lake City: Deseret Book, 1972.

Smith, Joseph Fielding. *The Progress of Man.* Salt Lake City: Genealogical Society of Utah, 1936.

Smith, Joseph Fielding. "Status of the Negro." Unpublished talk given 11 Oct. 1958. LDS Church Historical Dept.

"Southern Australia Mission History, 1961-1964: They came, they saw, they conquered." LDS Historical Dept., Archives Division. Unpublished manuscript.

Swinton, Heidi S. *In the Company of Prophets.* Salt Lake City: Deseret Book, 1993.

Talmage, James E. *The Articles of Faith.* Salt Lake City: LDS Church, 1982.

Tate, Lucile C. *Boyd K. Packer: A Watchman on the Tower.* Salt Lake City: Bookcraft, 1982.

Tate, Lucile C. *LeGrand Richards: Beloved Apostle.* Salt Lake City: Bookcraft, 1982.

Turner, Rodney. "The Position of Adam in Latter-day Saint Scripture and Theology." Provo, BYU, Unpublished master's thesis. 1953.

Young, S. Dilworth. "Elder Bruce R. McConkie of the Council of the Twelve." *Ensign*, Jan. 1971.

INDEX

The biographical first half of the book has been thoroughly indexed. It was not as necessary to fully index the second half, as it is arranged by subject, somewhat like *Mormon Doctrine*. The abbreviation BRM has been used for Bruce R. McConkie.

A

left, 184; words spoken by, 205
Apostleship, BRM foreordained to, 121
Apostolic ministry, of BRM, 122
April Fool's joke, 76
Argue, not BRM's pattern, 141
Arimathaea, Joseph of, 208
Arimathaean's tomb, 208
Arizona, parts of in President
McConkie's mission, 28; Oscar
McConkie boards train for, 28
Articles of Faith, New Witness for, 86;
truths taught in the, 99
Ascension of Christ, 208
Ashton, Marvin J., sustained as eleventh
apostle, 120; on Bible Aids
committee, 189
Asia, great harvest in, 57
Athens, marble from, collected by BRM,
112
Atonement, virtue of, 56; organic
evolution rules out, 142; rejoice in
the, 171; for inhabitants of many
worlds, 174; reality of the, 178;
BRM's testimony of the, 204-5;
BRM narrates events of the, 206-
210; set forth in the most profound
of terms, 206; his rising from the
dead crowned the, 208; sure
knowledge of the, 209; was perfect,
210; of Jesus Christ, 221-233
Australia, BRM called as mission
president of, 73; freedom to worship
in, 74; missionaries love the people
in, 75; BRM breaks ground for first
temple in, 125; temple a crowning
event for the Church, 126
Australian mission, 190 missionaries in,
75
Australian saints, 125
Australian stakes, conference visitors to,
75
Australian states, missionaries called
from, 74
Australian temple, ground-breaking, 80
Australian Zion, 80
Authoritative credibility, of BRM, 72

Authoritative exposition, *Mormon
Doctrine* not an, 64
Authority, of priesthood, 54; in the
Lord's eternal kingdoms, 68; BRM
spoke as one having, 186

B

Ballard, M. Russell, filled BRM's place
on Council of Twelve, 215
Ballard, Melvin J., teachings about
blacks and the priesthood, 165
Bank, first in town, 26
Banner of civil rights, to stir up emotions,
153
Baptism, waters of, 179; essential for
salvation, 130
Baptisms, more per missionary, 29; after
powerful sermon, 79; people must be
touched, 80
Barabbas, 226
Barton, Peggy Petersen, biographer of
father, 71
Beguiled students, 139
Believing blood, 95
Benson, Ezra Taft, BRM assistant to, 57;
toured mission with Bruce, 80;
comments on Bruce's scholarly
writings, 100; BRM quoted him,
118; comments on BRM, 146; senior
and most spiritually experienced,
161; great-grandson of Ezra T.
Benson, 177; spoke at funeral of
BRM, 213
Bible, BRM & Amelia studied, 44;
Joseph Smith translation of, 89;
Book of Mormon contains Lord's
word to prepare the way to
understand the, 143; answers are in,
145; BRM calls it a sealed book,
170-71; LDS King James edition,
189; King James edition official
Bible of the LDS Church, 190;
understanding of the history, 191;
topical guide for the, 193; JST used
in footnotes of new LDS, 195

Bible Aids advisory committee, 189; renamed Scriptures Publications Committee, 193

Bible Dictionary, doctrine in closely mirrors *Mormon Doctrine*, 69; prepared for LDS edition of scriptures, 189; added to LDS scriptures, 190; Cambridge edition used as basis for LDS edition, 191; on solid ground, 191

Biblical commentaries, non-LDS, 90; most are far from faith promoting, 181

Biblical passages, explained by BRM, 93

Biblical prophets, 85

Blacks and the Priesthood, notable entry on in *Mormon Doctrine*, 67; denied the privilege of bearing, 151; would never receive priesthood in this life, 152; church clarifies position on, 153

Blessed virgin, 175

Blessing given to Harold B. Lee, 27

Blessings, of heaven, 29; of the priesthood, 159-60

Book of Mormon, 23; at age eleven BRM read from, 35; BRM had read 3 times before his mission, 38; BRM's study of, 53-54; BRM read more times than he has fingers, 54; a true witness of Christ, 54; at age 19 BRM cross-referenced every verse in the, 61; sealed part of the, 68; copies sold in Australia, 74-75; one of first things investigator is taught, 76; BRM taught and explained to his family, 106; pray about the, 143; Boyd K. Packer read from, 156; original printer's manuscript studied, 190; heading clarified by BRM, 192; changes in by Joseph Smith are true, 195; the sealed portion of the, 285; 345-348

Bookcraft, *Mormon Doctrine* published through, 61; Marvin Wallen manager, 88

Born again, a process, 174

Brandt, Edward J., on Bible Aids committee, 189; comments on BRM, 192

Brazil, rose quartz, BRM collected, 112; gathering place for, 119

Brigham Young University, attended by Oscar, 25; attended by Margaret McConkie, 31; BRM at devotional, 132; doctrinal difficulties arose at, 138

British Empire, strong feelings for, 75

Brother of Jared, 68, climbed mountain, 77; a good illustration of how knowledge of God is gained, 96; moved Mt. Zerin, 273

Brother Smith, BRM joked about being, 132

BYU, 53; BRM at devotional, 132; BRM spoke on problem at, 138; messages of BRM to, 141; fireside on Seven Deadly Heresies, 146; sports boycotted over black issue, 152; went to locate men for committee, 189; contracted with MacMillan Publishing, 195; BRM's last assignment at Motion Picture Studio, 202

C

Caesar's power, Romans wielded, 206

Caiaphas, 206

Cain, lineage of, 151; Lord denied the priesthood to the seed of, 159

California, Gridley Stake, 55

California Mission, Oscar President of, 26; private home in, 27, without purse or scrip, 29; tour of by Harold B. Lee, 55

Calling and Election, 93; to die in the faith is the same thing as receiving, 126

Calvary, hill called, 207

Cambridge University Bible publishers,

typeset LDS Bible, 190-91

Cannon, George Q., statements on negroes, 164

Canon of holy writ, 143

Carmack, John K., 28; BRM had great impact on, 56; called on by BRM, 57; with BRM in Idaho Falls, 126; tells story of BRM and an Elder, 186; comments on the death of BRM, 213, 216

Catholic Church, California heavily, 29; changed in *Mormon Doctrine*, 67

Celestial couple, BRM and Amelia were a, 106

Celestial Kingdom, inheritance in, 267; view of the, 277

Celestial marriage, essential for salvation, 130; time to extend to blacks, 159

Celestial world, 54; highest heaven of the, 93, 97

CES, organizations like, 146

Chapels, built in Australia, 74-75 construction a high priority, 80

Chief apostle, Joseph Smith, 124

Children of the devil, 178

Chile, conference in, 108; vision of people in, 125

Chilean missionaries, 125

Chores, Oscar's, 25; BRM tending animals, 35

Christ Child, 24

Christ, light of, 38; Book of Mormon a true witness of, 54; need for all men to come unto, 76; bring souls to, 81; books dealing with the life of, 85; sit with, 93; light of, 96; six large volumes on, 100; BRM writes hymn about, 132; evolution rules out atonement of, 142; two thirds followed, 151; Redeemer of mankind, 169; BRM's purpose in writing was to get people to believe in, 171; universe created by, 173; manner of his birth, 174-75; his youth, 176; walked on water, 177;

time of second coming is fixed, 181; standeth in the center of all things, 184; BRM taught of the final days of his mortal ministry, 204; full import of Gethsemane, 206; laid on the cross, 207; father of immortality, 208; atonement of was perfect, 210; Atonement of, 221-233

Christendom, 90; where among is the ordinance of washing of feet, 180

Christmas, doctrine of, 126

Church Administration building, BRM sliding down banister of, 128

Church building supervisors, 75

Church Educational System, President Lee spoke to teachers in, 68; to look for men for committee, 189

Church headquarters, in Salt Lake City, 75; stake president visits BRM in, 111; saints used to gather to, 119

Church history, 40; BRM reviewed main events of, 76

Church leaders, integrity of teachings of, 138

Church manuals, use of *Mormon Doctrine* in, 72

Church membership, does not save, 273

Church News, ran story on McConkie family, 31; BRM wrote front page articles for, 45 ; article introducing new General Authority, 52; article on *Mormon Doctrine*, 70; information in, regarding BRM's service in Australia, 73-74

Church of England, Farrar our British friend from, 180

Church of Jesus Christ of Latter-day Saints, 63; revelation for, 88; BRM forsees future of in Chile, 125; growth of in Australia, 126; became a victim of the times, 153; the Lord is not far distant from, 162; revelation changed the whole direction of, 163; thanksgiving in the hearts of members of, 164; enter through initiatory principles and

them to rush to their anvils, 137

Criticism, *Mormon Doctrine* brought BRM, 61

Crucifixion, of Christ, 207; for the sins of the world, 210

Crystalina, Brazil, 132

Cult group, Church graduated from, in Australia, 75

Cultism as Practiced by the so-called Church of the Firstborn of the Fullness of Times, treatise, 88

Cultivated mind, of BRM, 148

Cults, leave alone, 145; they are the gate to hell, 146; false church, 182

Cultists, 142

D

Damned, by false doctrine we believe, 142

Dangers in work of the Lord, 182

Dark ages, apostate church in the, 67

Darkness, among Nephites, 207

Darn fool, 29

Day of judgment, 93

Day of Pentecost, felt something akin to what happened on the, 159; no cloven tongues like on day of, 161

Deacon, BRM becomes a, 35, 37

Dead prophets, pit against living, 146

Deadly heresies, 146

Death, in Bible dictionary and *Mormon Doctrine*, 69; of Moses, 93; probation is ended in, 127; Three Nephites given power over, 192; of Christ, 208; Jesus broke bands of, 209; BRM sealed up unto, 211; Carmack's comments on BRM, 216

Debate, BRM doesn't, 141; devil champions divisions and, 144; anti-Mormons are dens of, 145

Deity, dealings with man, 175

Delta Phi, BRM a member of, 44

Delusions, absurd sectarian, 90

Denunciation, of views which deviated, 138

Derrick horses, 25

Deseret News, BRM worked at, 45; worked at for a year, 51; BRM at reporters' table covering conference, 51

Desolation, shall cover the earth, 182

Destiny, of the LDS Church, 89

Devil, not dead, 139; Spirit of champions division and debate, 144; not had a new idea in a hundred years, 145; cast out of heaven with his angels, 151; children of the, 178; attitude about JST part of his plan, 195; through the atonement we are saved from the, 205

Devotion, of Amelia, 106

Diary of Joseph Fielding Smith, 40

Dignity, negroes should be treated with, 152

Diplomacy, BRM more concerned with false doctrine than, 138

Direct Revelation, evidence of, 52

Disciples, perfectly united, 158

Disciplinarian, BRM not a strict, 107

Disclaimer in *Mormon Doctrine*, 62

Discrimination, we know something of, 153; by the church toward the negro, 154

Dissident groups, false theories of, 142

Disunity, the devil champions, 144

Divergences of views, 144

Divine, approbation, 33; timetable, 155

Divine Householder, 179

Divine Sonship, 178; authors who believe in, 181

Divine Voice, 181

Doctrinal authorities, BRM among the elite of, 148

Doctrinal information, 30; doctrinal subject, 36; doctrinal authority, 61; BRM alone responsible for doctrinal and scriptural interpretations, 62; recognized authorities on, 62; errors, 67; JST revisions changed doctrinal meaning, 72; reaches level few have equaled, 86; doctrinal traps and false conclusions, 90; doctrinal understanding, 130; doctrinal teachings of BRM, 136

Doctrinal New Testament Commentary, three volumes of, 89; designed as a tool to aid saints gain knowledge, 90; third volume published, 94; Messiah Series not long after the, 168; 169

Doctrine, extraordinary understanding of, 61; of the kingdom, 85; of Christmas, 126; every wind of, 152; of Christ, 182; of Second Coming, 184; of revelation, 205; atonement is the most basic and fundamental, 209; of Preexistence, 326

Doctrine & Covenants, BRM's study of, 53; quoted extensively from, 89; resurrection in Section 76, 144; Boyd K. Packer read from, 156; official declaration now appears in, 165; errors and the comma in section 89, 190; BRM wrote headings, 191; BRM recommendation on D&C 137 & 138, 193; changes in by Joseph Smith are true, 195; BRM owned an old edition, 197; Elder Packer quotes from in blessing, 211

Doctrines of Salvation, sermons of Joseph Fielding Smith, 86; among the most popular LDS books ever published, 88; *Doctrines of the Restoration* patterned after, 101

Doctrines, of the kingdom, *Mormon Doctrine* first major attempt to explain the, 62; studying the, 89; of salvation, 100; understanding of the, 139; balanced approach to, 145; if ye cannot believe, 145; each must learn for himself, 146

Doctrines of the Restoration, book compiled by Mark McConkie, 101

Dove, Holy Ghost descended like a, 68

Dream of Christ Child, 24

Dreams, 25; opinion of Oscar's by

Harold B. Lee, 26; of the coming of Elders, 27

Dummelow, J. R., 102

E

Earth, Jesus to transform into celestial home, 172; Father visiting his Son on, 178; geologic changes in, 183-84; different states of the, 185; will be burned, become celestial sphere, 185; three great realities in the history of, 209

Earthly kingdom, 98; affairs of the, 159

Earthquake, time of crucifixion, 183

East High School, 42

Eastern States Mission, BRM called to, 38; mission to, 42

Eden, earth will again be, 184; deserts become gardens, 185; symbolism in the garden of, 236-239

Edenic paradise, 209

Edersheim, author, 180

Educational world, 142

Elder Lee's tour, 26

Elder Smith, BRM mistakenly introduced as, 130

Election, see Calling and election

Elements, controlled by properly gifted persons, 98

Elijah, Oscar had faith like unto, 26; taken up without tasting death, 93; Jews to know that he came, 183; faith like, 209

Elohim, at the transfiguration, 178

Emigration Canyon, BRM and Amelia in, 121

Encyclopedia of Mormonism, Daniel Ludlow was chief editor, 195

Encyclopedic commentary, *Mormon Doctrine* was first attempt, 62

Endowment House, 23

Endowments, purpose of, 175

Enemies of the Church, 152; prejudice of, 154

Enoch, Oscar had faith like unto, 26, 34;

Father dealt directly with him after he was translated, 175; faith like, 209; Enoch's city, 272

Enos, 56; like with, 161

Ensign Peak, BRM and Amelia hike, 73

Ensign Stake high council, 30

Ephraim, two thousands of, 125; temple to be built particularly by, 183

Equal opportunities, each citizen must have, 153

Erring teachers, 139

Eternal inheritance, 98

Eternal law, 178

Eternal life, 56; sealed up unto, 91, 93; greatest of all the gifts of God, 99; faithful members chart a course to, 126; what we must believe to gain, 138; it is our aim and our objective, 280; inheritors of, 282

Eternal lives, 54

Eternal marriage, BRM changed his talk to, 141; 305-313

Eternal power, throne of, 96

Eternal Presence, 333, Christ dwelt in the, 335

Eternal progression, 247-52

Eternal salvation, 96

Eternal worlds, 175

Evangelists, in true church, 98

Eve, 69; 153; do not pray to, 175

Everlasting glory, 205

Evil spirit, 27

Evolution, 142; 258-60; 1913 First Presidency doctrinal exposition on, 334

Evolutionists, 142

Exaltation, 54

Exalted beings, 97

Experienced, Presidents Kimball and Benson most spiritually, 161

F

Fad, spiritually dangerous, 138

Faddist interpretation, 145

Faith, like unto Enoch, 26, 34; Oscar W. McConkie Sr., a man of great, 33; power of, 38; BRM's study of, 53; fruits of, 96; power of God, 96; and priesthood, 97; unity of the, 98; increase through study of scriptures, 100; President Smith's life of, 118; if we die in the, 127; views of Paul and James, 144; church position on blacks a matter of, 151; matters of not within the purview of civil law, 153; President Kimball sought the Lord in, 155; leads us on with safety, 165; runs in families, 177; BRM had absolute, 202; like Enoch and Elijah, 209; all things can be done by, 267

Faith promoting experiences, 27

Faithful members, greeted revelation with joy, 164; view of the Second Coming for the, 184; reward of, 314-22

Fall of Adam, 69; Father dealt directly with Adam before the, 175; earth became telestial after, 185; if there had been no, 209

Fall of man, organic evolution rules out, 142; Creation and the fall, 234-235

False Christs, definition of, 182

False doctrinal conclusions, 90

False doctrines, all churches that teach, 67; theories of men are, 88; willingness to expose, 137; BRM concerned with, 138; no end to, 139; need to learn difference, 141; of anti-Mormons, 145; our espousal will not make it true, 146; sermon on seven heresies, 146

False theory, of organic evolution, 142

Family, BRM's talk on, 56; unit in eternity, 97

Farm skills, BRM learned, 37

Farrar, Conan, wrote about Christ, 180

Fasting, excessive length of, 148

Father in heaven, promise of, 92; true fellowship with, 138; all are spirit children of, 153; created man, 173; knowledge of the, 175; proper prayers addressed to, 175; eternal plan of, 204; his plan, 210; we dwelt in his presence, 281; the Firstborn was with him in the beginning, 328

Father's kingdom, 54; glory and honor of, 93; inheritors of, 180

Faust, Elder James E., BRM gave rock gifts to, 112; spoke at BRM's funeral, 213

Feminists, 142

Fiery darts of adversary, against BRM, 137

Firmament, entry in *Mormon Doctrine*, 67

First coming, of Messiah, 168

First Council (Quorum) of Seventy, BRM called to, 51; BRM youngest member since 1888, 52; privilege of being a member of, 54; BRM a member for 26 years, 55; after fifteen years in BRM called as mission president, 73; BRM's last conference talk as a member of, 117; as member of reinterpreted a gospel principle, 119; BRM served in with S. Dilworth Young, 127

First Presidency, 26, 51, 56; declarations by, 62; considered the matter of *Mormon Doctrine*, 64; consideration of for the welfare of BRM, 65; deliberations of the, 71; notified BRM of his call to be a mission president, 73; direction of stake responsibilities, 75; sermons of, 88; Romney a member of, 102; invited BRM to accompany them to Mexico, 119; hold keys of the kingdom, 122; BRM had meetings with every Thursday, 126; privilege to sit at feet of, 128; acknowledgment of BRM's doctrinal and scriptural acumen from, 146; meeting of to discuss clarifying church position on blacks and the priesthood, 153; counselors

in the, 158; Holy Ghost poured out upon, 160; statement on the revelation on priesthood prepared by, 162; Francis M. Gibbons was secretary to, 166; appointed Bible Aids advisory committee, 189; discussed comma in D&C 89:13, 190; BRM makes recommendation to, 193; broadcast fireside to promote new LDS scriptures, 198; met every Thursday, 211; 1916 Doctrinal Exposition on the Father and the Son, 334

Firstborn, Son, 91; Church of the, 97; Jesus was the, 327

First Born Spirit, Jesus is the, 337

Flesh, in Bible dictionary and *Mormon Doctrine*, 69

Flood, in days of Noah, 183; no seasons before, 184

Forceful sermons, Oscar gave, 26

Forgery and murder, 125

Forgiveness, an added entry in *Mormon Doctrine*, 67

Fort Douglas, BRM served at, 45

Fort Henry, 40

Four gospels, doctrinal commentary on, 168

Frontier town, 25

Fruitless contention, 145

Fruits of faith, 96

Fulness of the everlasting gospel, 159

Fundamental doctrines of the kingdom, 139

Fundamentalists, 88; polygamists and, 142

Funeral of Mark Vest, 28

Funerals, BRM spoke at, 127

G

Gabriel, 90

Garden of Eden, symbolism in the, 236-239

Gathering, places, 119; of Israel, 381-83

Gazalem, 67

Genealogy class, BRM taught, 44
General Authority, John K. Carmack,
28; Oscar McConkie could have
been but was never called as, 33;
BRM as a new, 35; experience for
BRM to become, 40; work load of a,
44; lifestyle and public perception
of, 51; introduction of BRM as new,
52; few called before age 31, 53;
most important duty of a, 56;
Mormon Doctrine story began when
BRM called to be a, 61; proper
place of a book by a, 62; not publish
books until approved, 65; members
look forward to visits by, 75; BRM
toured mission with, 80; nearly forty
years of service as a, 85; duties of,
86; have written fine works, 90;
arduous schedule of, 99; Amelia
daughter of a, 105; BRM spoke as
at funeral, 118; rare times they are
perfectly united, 158; Russel Taylor
now-deceased, 186; members of
were to oversee committee, 189;
committee brought together, 193
General Conference, 27; Oscar
McConkie reported in, 29; BRM
called to First Council of Seventy in,
51; BRM attended in 1962, 73;
third trip from Australia to General
Conference, 74-75; new apostle
named in, 118; President Lee's
instruction, 119; BRM struggling to
get inspiration on what to say in,
139; BRM shares his last address
with his wife, 203; BRM's last talk
in, 204-210; captured
congregation's attention, 205;
BRM's last sermon in, 210; BRM
at, 211; Elder Ballard spoke at the
one after BRM's death, 215
Genius of BRM, 44; his gift to write and
speak concisely, 60; fellow Brethren
recognized, 100
Gentiles, compared to when the Lord
told Israel to take the gospel to, 165;

bring wealth to adorn temple, 183
Geologic changes in earth, 183
Gethsemane, purifying power of, taught
by BRM, 204; holy ground, 206;
price of, 209; at Golgotha, 210;
Garden of the Oil Press, 221
Gibbons, Francis M., comments on 1978
revelation on priesthood, 156;
explains the announcement for the
revelation on the priesthood, 162;
secretary to the First Presidency, 166
Gift of prophecy, 286
Gifts of God, 96; of testimony, 121
Gifts of the Spirit, 98; as members we
enjoy, 121; 267-87
Gleaner class, BRM taught, 44
Glimpse within the veil, 24
God, of miracles, 98; eternally
progressing, 132; of nature, 207; and
history, 394-96
God the Father, 30; Christ the literal
offspring of, 91
Godhead, pamphlets on the, 86; doctrine
on our relationship with, 138; Holy
Ghost is member of the, 276; 240-
243
Godhood, assurance of, 93; becoming a
god, 96
Godly conduct, 179
Gods, exalted to highest state, 96
Golgotha, Gethsemane in, 210
Golgotha, Dialogue at, book by Oscar
McConkie Sr., 30
Good parentage of Oscar McConkie Sr.,
29
Good Works, added entries in *Mormon
Doctrine*, 67
Gospel, blessings of, 29; taught in
seventeen different languages, 119;
of Jesus Christ may in due time
become available everywhere, 154
Gospel-centered writings, 85
Gospel doctrine, caution in labeling a
book, 68; students of greatly blessed,
100
Gospel doctrine classes, BRM taught, 44

416

same thing, by the power of the, 161; revelation by the power of the, 163; came by the power of, 164; scripture comes from God by the power of the, 173; Mary with child by the power of, 176; BRM spoke by the power of the Holy Ghost, 204; revelation by the power of the, 205-6; sure witness borne by the, 210; is a sanctifier, 267; constant companionship of, 276; a revelator, 277

Holy Ghost, book by Oscar McConkie Sr., 30

Holy of Holies, 133

Holy Scriptures, RLDS publication, 194

Holy Spirit, influence of, 38; companionship of, 54; personal revelation from, 117; seek to get in tune with, 130; told BRM of his call to the Quorum of Twelve, 133; those who understand the scriptures are in tune with, 138; everyone who is sound spiritually has the guidance of the, 139; companionship and guidance of the, 169

Holy writ, fountain of, 143

Home of Satan, 26

Honest truth seekers, letter, 142

Hong Kong, McConkies and Bensons visit, 57; BRM collected jasper and bloodstone from, 112

Horses, 25; BRM's account of riding, 37

Hosts of heaven, one third of, 151

House of Israel, members of the, 98; statements that limited the gospel to the, 165; rule forever in the, 186

Human personality, the spirit is the intelligent part of the, 278

Humility of Oscar W. McConkie Sr., 26

Humor, Brethren have a very rich sense of, 128

Hunter, Howard W., visited BRM's mission, 80

Hygeia Ice Company, BRM worked at, 43

Hysterical emotions, over blacks issue, 153

I

I Believe in Christ, hymn, 132

Idaho Falls, Idaho, BRM in, 126

Ignorance, keeps people from reading and understanding, 171; reject message of salvation through, 179

Immorality, sexual, 370-72

Immortality, all men will be raised in, 56; state of, 186; Christ is the father of, 208

Improper intellectualism, 138

Improper prayer patterns, 139

Improvement Era, advertisement for BRM book, 88

Incarnate devils, 206

India, McConkies and Bensons visit, 57

Indian Branch, 28

Indians, Oscar sees in vision, 28

Infinite universe, 173

Inspiration, in missionary work, 78; BRM always struggling to get, 139; Spirit of, 144; revelation on priesthood reaffirmed by the spirit of, 162; BRM wrote treatise by, 169; spirit of frequently influenced committee, 193; fine balance between agency and, 281

Inspired interpreter, we often need, 143

Inspired Version of the Bible, 63; Mark E. Petersen's misgivings about, 71; BRM made special use of, 89; BRM's heavy use of, 93-94; excerpts from put in Bible, 190; distrust of LDS leaders for, 194; nagging uncertainty about, 195; changes found in footnotes of new Bible, 196

Instant healings, 27

Integrity, of teachings of church leaders, 138

Intellectual closeness, of BRM and Amelia, 107

Intellectual dissidents, 142; presumed to

take credit for pressuring the Church into announcing a policy change, 164

Intellectuality, men worship at the shrine of, 142; keeps people from reading and understanding, 171

Intellectualism, avoiding improper, 138; 253-257

Intellectuals, BRM said something that offended, 124

Intelligence, BRM served in army, 45; preexistence and, 326-38

Intercession, principle of, 68

Investigators, would they be driven away, 137

Isaiah, his prophecy, 126; BRM writes a bit like, 171

Israel, house of, 67; members of the, 98; restoration of scattered, 119; gathering of, 119; temple built by gathered, 183; rule forever in the house of, 186; missionary work and the gathering of, 381-83

Israel's lawgiver, 93

Ivins, Antoine R., called to Seventy, 51

J

Jacobean English, 85

Jackson County, New Jerusalem to be built in, 183

James, apostle, 91; confer priesthood, 93; did not have differing views than Paul, 144

Jamieson, Fausset and Brown, 102

Janitorial work, Oscar did, 25

Japan, McConkies and Bensons visit, 57; the way BRM kissed his wife you'd think he was off to, 106

Jehovah, Spirit of came forth, tabernacled in clay, 175

Jehovah-Christ, created the earth, 173

Jerusalem, building temple in, 183; walls of, 207

Jesus Christ, testimony of, 30, BRM's, 54; witness of, 56; commentary on the teachings of, 89; birth of, 90-91; literally the son of Mary, 91; on resurrection and marriage, 92; Son of the Living God, 117; perfect knowledge of, 121; crucified for the sins of the world, 122; in the clouds of heaven to reign personally upon the earth, 124; controversy of trying to gain an extreme close relationship with, 138; improper practice of praying to, 148; gospel of to become available everywhere, 154; ministry of, 168; literal son of God, 169; second coming of, 172; his youth, 176; walked on water, 177; his coming death and resurrection, 178; as the Second Comforter, 178; sends apostles and prophets among the Jews, 179; burial clothes of, 181; BRM's testimony of the atonement and, 204-210; suffering of, 206; hung on the cross, 207; broke bands of death, 209; son of the Living God, 210; BRM passed to mansion of, 213; Atonement of, 221-233; he is an high priest forever, 283

Jesus the Christ, scholarly work of Elder James E. Talmage, 168; qualifications of Talmage to write, 169

Jews, wickedness of, 179; will not build temple in Jerusalem, 183; sat in Aaron's seat, 206; measured time, 208

Jogging, BRM's hobby, 109

John, book of, revealed truth, 175

John, saw the Holy Ghost, 68

John the Baptist, not Elias who appeared with Moses, 91; gospel and writings of, 176; immersed the Lord Jesus in the murky waters of the Jordan, 286

Jokes and stories, BRM didn't tell many, 136

Joseph and Mary, 90-91

Joseph of Arimathaea, 208

Joseph Smith III blessing, 122-124

Joseph Smith Translation, 63-64, BRM
made special use of, 89; more
accepted as a resource for members,
94; excerpts from put in LDS Bible,
190; inclusion in the new LDS
scriptures, 194-98; integrity of
established, 194; brethren crossed
the bridge in using, 195; not been
completed, 196

Journal of Discourses Series, 88

Journal, of Oscar W. McConkie Sr., 24;
of George Albert Smith, 52

Journals, BRM invites members to
record his prophecy in, 125

JST, Inspired Version known as, 190;
references to cropped up in study
guides, 194; Ludlow writes
Maxwell regarding, 195; BRM
frustrated over reluctance to
embrace, 196

Judas, Jesus confronts, 206

Judge, Oscar elected, 26

Judgment, 373-76

Juris Doctorate degree, BRM's, 45

K

Kangaroos, 80

Key of the knowledge of God, 284

Keys of the kingdom, 88; brethren who
hold, 122; use of the, 178;
priesthood and, 291-295

Kimball, Spencer W., assigned to work
with BRM on revising *Mormon
Doctrine*, 65-67; his slogan, 109-
111; BRM accompanied to Tahiti,
122; 124; announces temple in
Santiago, 125; traded coats with
BRM, 128; faced priesthood issue
like Wilford Woodruff faced plural
marriage issue, 155; advised his
counselors that they would discuss
the blacks getting the priesthood,
156; comments on 1978 revelation,
156; in the temple, 157; brought up
matter of possible conferral of the

priesthood upon those of all races,
159; senior and most spiritually
experienced, 161; man of almost
infinite spiritual capacity, 161;
altered the course of the past, 162; a
grandson of Heber C. Kimball, 177;
set up Bible Aids committee, 189;
his proposal 193; presided over
BRM's funeral but did not speak,
213

Kindliness of Oscar McConkie, 26

King Benjamin, 223

King James edition of the Bible, Church
edition, 189; official Bible of the
LDS Church, 190; changes made by
Joseph Smith, 196

King of Kings, 67

Kingdom of God on earth, 67; keys of
the, 88; members of the church, 121;
keys of, 122

Kingdom of the devil, 178

Kirkham, Oscar A., sustained to Seventy,
51

Kirtland temple, at the dedication of,
159; Elijah came to, 183

Knowledge of God, how gained, 96

Knowles, Eleanor, comments on BRM,
99

Korea, McConkies and Bensons visit, 57

L

Lamanites, Vision of Mark Vest before,
28; the mark on the, 182; were
wicked, 183

Lamb of God, 68

Land Down Under, 73-74

Land of the north, ten tribes in, 99

Lapidary Journal, 111

Lapidary work, hobby of BRM, 111

Latter-day gathering, 119

Latter-day Saints, have a complex, 163

Law, Oscar practiced, 25; BRM opened
practice with three friends, 44; of
common consent, 88

LDS Bible students, 93

LDS Church, destiny of, 89

LDS publishing, one of the most popular books in, 69

LDS University, BRM went to high school at, 37

Lee, Harold B., 26; cast out evil spirit, 27; administers to Mark Vest, 28; BRM accompanied, 55; clarifies position of Brethren on books, 68; major player in BRM's life, 117; mantle of prophet fell on, 118; instruction at general conference, 119; BRMs account to, 120; in most sacred room of temple, 121; 124; BRM almost ran into, 128; tells of BRM's experience being called to the Quorum of the Twelve, 133; suggestion on Inspired Version presented to, 194

Lehi, his seed divided into two nations, 182; talking to Jacob, 330; makes some marvelous arguments, 331

Lengthening my stride, t-shirt, 109-111

Letter to erring university professor, 138

Letters, flood of, 142; about negroes receiving the priesthood, 164

Lieutenant colonel, BRM retired a, 46

Life of Jesus Christ, 168

Light of Christ, 96-97

Light of truth, 96

Literary miracle, *Mormon Doctrine* was, 69

Living and dead, priesthood revelation affects, 163

Living Oracle, 54

Living prophet, strong counsel to follow, 138

Lord's Supper, Brethren partook of, 158

Lord's word, Book of Mormon contains, 143

Los Angeles mission president, 31

Lost tribes, location of, 99

Love, Oscar McConkie's, for the Brethren, 29

Lucifer, 27; and his followers, 221

Ludlow, Daniel H., chief editor of Encyclopedia, 195

Luke, book of, revealed truth, 175

Lukewarm members, 96

M

Mainstream of the church, 139

Man, created by the Father, 173

Manasseh, thousands of, 125

Manifesto, revelation on priesthood similar to, 163

Mark, book of, revealed truth, 175; account of Jesus' body and burial clothes, 181

Mark on the Lamanites, 182

Marriage, BRM's thoughts on, 43, in the church, 80; in heaven, 92; BRM and Amelia, 105; BRM speaks on at BYU, 141; eternal, 305-11

Mary Magdalene, 208; Christ appearing to, 209

Mary, mother of Jesus, 90; a virgin, 91; provided the womb for the Spirit Jehovah, 175; greatest mortal of her sex, 175; about fifteen years of age and inexperienced in meeting the trials of life, 176; virgin birth, 339-44

Master Weaver, 184

Matthew, book of, revealed truth, 175

Matthews, Robert J., on Bible Aids committee, 189; comments on BRM, 192; interview with, 200

Maxwell, Neal A., advisor to BYU Encyclopedia project, 195

McConkie, Amelia Smith, becoming a McConkie, 38; met Bruce, 42; marriage, 43; first baby born, 44; her family, 53; trip with BRM and the Bensons, 57; BRM took her on a hike up Ensign peak, 73; took boat to Australia, 73; her comments on BRM as a mission president, 76; anxious about pregnant daughter, 78; budgeting, 78-79; threw out BRM's old tie, 79; joked, 86; and family life,

105-115; a true helpmeet, 105; taught lessons in Relief Society, 106; BRM claimed she was perfect, 106; life perfectly normal with BRM, 107; fainted, 108; joked that Bruce was not very bright, 109; joked about BRM's jogging, 109; one of his two great loves, 112; further information on, 115; helped give oxygen to her father; 118; learned of BRM's call to the Twelve, 121; as Sister Smith, 132; notices BRM's change of appetite and feeling of tiredness, 201; her account of BRM believing he would be healed, 202; only she knew the pain BRM felt, 203; doctor tells her BRM is dying, 204; her account of BRM after his final blessing, 211

McConkie, Bruce Redd, knew scriptures chapter and verse, 29; eldest child, 31; difficult and miraculous birth of, 35; avidly read books, 36; childhood recollection of, 37; called on a mission, 38; most excellent elder, 40; regarded highly by Amelia's parents, 42; how he used his time, 43; received bachelor of laws degree, 44; joined ROTC, 45; memorized a scripture a day, 47; called to Seventy, 51; set apart in Quorum of Seventy, 52; physical description of, 52; member of First Quorum of Seventy for 26 years, 55; his duty as a General Authority, 56; questions missionaries, 57; established as a doctrinal authority, 61; extraordinary understanding of gospel doctrines, 62; use of forceful language, 63; extraordinary man, 63; made corrections to *Mormon Doctrine*, 64; his character is revealed, 65; commented on controversy about *Mormon Doctrine*, 68; doctrines clarified by, 69; called to head Southern

Australia Mission, 73; third trip from his mission, 74; 250,000 miles of air travel, 75; invited missionaries to top of mountain, 76; vintage McConkie style, 77; Jacobean English phraseology, 85; felt there were few scriptorians in the church, 89; opinion of non-LDS biblical commentaries, 90; expressed himself plainly, 99; comments on time to write, 99-100; best known sermons of, 101; had fine library of well-read books, 102; the way he kissed his wife, 106; did not force feed gospel to his family, 108; hobby of walking and jogging, 109-111; rock hunting of, 111-112; the gospel his second great love, 112; poem by, 113; call to the Twelve, 117-135; spoke at Mexico City conference, 119; heard his own name announced as twelfth apostle, 120; testimony of, 121; his chief duty and obligation was to testify of Jesus Christ, 122; teaching doctrines he didn't know, 122; what the Lord would say, 124; directed by inspiration, 125; in Idaho Falls, 126; blessed S. Dilworth Young, 127; commented on his sense of humor, 132; his greatest desire, 136; attracted doctrinal critics, 136; willingness to expose false doctrine, 137; bold, direct, uncompromising in views, 138; preached and wrote more on Jesus Christ than any other member living, 139; messages at BYU, 141; not one that could be misunderstood, 142; on gospel hobbies, 145; his strengths and gifts, 148; comments on blacks and the priesthood, 151-52; present when Spencer Kimball received revealtion, 158; his account of Kimball's prayer, 159-60; his account of President Kimball and the revelation on the priesthood, 161; support for

President Kimball, 163; forget his statements on negroes and the priesthood, 165; starts his Messiah series, 168; qualified to write, 169; wrote around 3,200 pages of commentary on the Son of God, 170; trusted in his own inspiration, 186; BRM made greatest contribution to new editions of scriptures, 188; appointed to Bible Aids committee, 189; obtained approval of footnotes, 193; impact on use of JST, 195; raised up for a specific purpose, 198; goes to the doctor and begins chemotherapy, 201; health began to fail rapidly, 202; outlived doctor's time estimate, 203; doctor warns about going on television, 204; powerful testimony of Christ and the atonement, 204-210; unshakeably firm testimony, 205; his promise about scripture study, 209; testifies he is a witness of Christ, 210; his last sermon, 210-11; blessing by Elder Boyd K. Packer, 211; passed away, 213; funeral remarks, 213-14; some of his most intriguing doctrinal teachings, 326

McConkie, Bruce Redd, author, 55; 85-103; repetition and prayerlike prose, 85; scriptural language became second nature, 86; authored many articles for Church magazines, 86; *Sound Doctrine*, 88; treatise on cultism, 88-89; unable to review *A New Witness*, 94; knew how to write, 99; inspired in his understanding of the sacred records, 169; he explains why he wrote, 170; often rather formal, wordy, and poetic, 171

McConkie, Bruce Redd, gospel knowledge of, 53-54; reputation as a scholar, 142; similarity with Talmage, 170; a profound and deep

knowledge of gospel truths, 172

McConkie, Bruce Redd, humor of, 39; missionaries getting biggest wallop out of him, 78; note to Amelia, 78-79; practical joke streak, 79; story about choosing his wife, 107; stepped over his fainted wife, 108; broken foot, 111; sliding down the banister, 128; trading jackets with Spencer W. Kimball, 128; injected humor into some of his talks, 130; rock hunting instead of touring missions, 132; joked about graduating from the Univerisity of Utah, 132; joke edited from his talk, 132; tells Elder he can quote him, 186; delightful sense of, 197; dying, but not losing his sense of, 201; jokes with his doctor about dying, 202

McConkie, Bruce Redd, law practice of, 44; legal training, 85

McConkie, Bruce Redd, military service of, 45; veteran of WWII, 53; military background, 55

McConkie, Bruce Redd, mission president, 73-82; visited Salt Lake City 3 times while a, 75; talked about basic subjects, 76; loved by his missionaries, 76; shows up late to missionary meeting, 77; elder's impressions of, 81

McConkie, Bruce Redd, newspaperman, wrote articles for *Church News*, 45; newspaper reporting of, 85

McConkie, Bruce Redd, rock hunting, 132

McConkie, Bruce R. Jr., died as infant, 105

McConkie, France Briton, war hero, 31

McConkie, George Wilson, father of Oscar, 23

McConkie, George, risked his life, 25

McConkie, James Wilson, 26; musical genius, 31

McConkie, Joseph Fielding, son of

BRM, 53; on mission to Scotland, 73; assembled book *Journal of Discourses Digest*, 88; story and commentary about his father, 102; 105; loved sports, 107; says McConkie family is peculiar, 108; comments on when his mother passed out, 108; Amelia calls him, 204; comments on BRM's last conference talk, 210; gave family prayer before BRM departed, 213

McConkie, Margaret, sixth child of Oscar W. McConkie Sr., 31

McConkie, Mark Lewis., son of BRM, 101; 105; tells of his parents being a perfect team, 106

McConkie, Mary Ethel, daughter of BRM, 53; 105

McConkie, Oscar W. Jr., 24; serving mission in New England, 29, fourth son of Oscar W. McConkie, 31

McConkie, Oscar W. Sr., 23-34; bid for governor, 25; prediction about Harold B. Lee; 27; administers to Mark Vest, 28; could quote scriptures, 29; testimony of, 30; deep powerful speaking voice of, 30; passed away, 31; man of great faith, 33; moved family to Monticello, 35; spiritual sensitivities of, 37; highly spiritual and doctrinally knowledgeable man, 53; Harold B. Lee tours California Mission with, 55; in council in spirit world, 121; faith exemplified in the life of, 209

McConkie, Rebecca, daughter of BRM and Amelia, 105

McConkie, Sarah Jill, daughter of BRM and Amelia, 105; tells of her parents' marriage, 106

McConkie, Standford Smith, son of BRM and Ameilia, 53; served as missionary under his father, 79; 105; told story of his father, 136; commented on criticism of Messiah

series, 186; comments on BRM's last testimony, 210

McConkie, Stephen Lowell, son of BRM and Amelia, 105

McConkie, Vivian, wife of Oscar, 31

McConkie, Vivian, daughter of BRM, 53; tells how BRM threw out some of his papers, 61; pregnant, 78; 105; she remembers story of her father, 107

McConkie, William Robert, fifth son of Oscar W. McConkie Sr., 31

McConkies, wives joke that they are the only ones in church that understand anything, 108

McKay, David O., 51; assigned Marion G. Romney to read *Mormon Doctrine*, 63; informed the Twelve of decision regarding *Mormon Doctrine*, 64; reported conversation with President Smith to his Counselors, 65; journal entry, 77; comments on Joseph Fielding Smith's *Man, His Origin & Destiny*, 71; BRM's interview with, 106; 124; comments on blacks and the priesthood, 154; taught of priesthood restriction and preexistence, 165

McKonkie, BRM.'s name misspelled, 52

Mediation, principle of, 68

Melchizedek Priesthood, keys and authority, 91

Melbourne, Australia, 78

Melbourne Stake, Australia, 74; mission headquarters in, 75; stake conference, 78

Memory Grove, 42

Menace of Mormonism, 95

Mercy of God, 154

Meridian Israel, 165

Meridian of time, 90; priesthood offices had in the, 98

Merril, Joseph F., son of Marriner W. Merril, 177

Merril, Marriner W., 177

Messiah, ministry of, 168

Messiah Series, six volumes, 94; time to write them, 100; 168-87; near-biography, 170; some minor seals, 171; short excerpts from, 172-186; most of it is original with BRM, 186

Method of speaking, BRM's, 56

Mexico area conference, 119-120

Mexico City, 119; BRM and Spencer W. Kimball on assignment in, 128

Michael, is but the illustration, 173; an angel from the courts of glory, 206

Military intelligence, BRM in, 45

Milk, spilled, 25

Millennial day, 98

Millennial Messiah, how written, 170; short excerpts from, 181-186

Millennium, 68; the church in the, 97-98; will not be ushered in prematurely, 181; earth receives paradisiacal state, 184; prophetic accounts of, 184-85; people changed during, 185; two kinds of people during, 185-86

Michigan, University of, 35

Minnesota, University of, 31

Miracles, healings only the beginning of, 98; wonders and glories, 121; a gift of the Spirit, 283

Miraculous, 26

Misguided students, BRM addresses at BYU, 138

Mission home, 38

Mission President, Oscar McConkie Sr., serving as, 53; BRM in Australia, 125; John K. Carmack as a, 126

Missionaries, wives of, 25; BRM questions, 57; success of in Australia, 74; aided by modern methods, 75; learned to love new mission president, 76; waited an hour for BRM, 77; problems with, 79-80; BRM assigning, 126; raced for their cameras, 128; how called, 134

Missionary tracts, BRM wrote, 86

Missionary work, difficult method of, 29; BRM responsive to suggestions on, 55; BRM actively involved in worldwide, 73; new chapels aid in, 74; modern methods of, 75; teach basics, 76; inspiration in, 78; certain things other than, 79; BRM worked with Elder M. Russell Ballard, 215; and the gathering of Israel, 381-83

M-Men, Bruce McConkie taught, 44

Moab Relief Society, 24

Moab, Utah, 23; frontier town, 25; BRM spoke in, 56

Mob violence, we as a people have experienced, 153

Modern, word used in 2nd edition of *Mormon Doctrine*, 67

Modern prophet, get in line with, 164

Modern revelation, 89; those who do not accept the principle of, 154; phrase used in Bible dictionary, 191

Modernistic views, 90

Monson, Elder Thomas S., on scriptures publications committee, 188; chairman of Bible Aids committee, 189; concurred with decision on the comma in D&C 89, 190

Monticello, Utah, 25; Oscar McConkie Sr., bishop in, 30, BRM moves from, 35; every summer Bruce went back to, 37

Mormon Doctrine, book by BRM, 54, 61-72; brought him notice, 61; one of the most used, studied and quoted books, 61; first book of its kind, 61; disclaimer in, 62; report of committee on, 63; First Presidency decided it should not be republished, 64; caused considerable comment throughout the Church, 65; second edition published, 67; BRM felt free to quote from in his talks, 68; increased in favor among members, 69; Bible dictionary closely mirrors, 69; advertisement for, 70; collector value of 1ˢᵗ editions, 70; not an official publication of the Church, 71; frequent use of the book, 72; encyclopedic in format, 85; BRM worked on, 88; organized by subject, 89; BRM relied heavily upon, 93; entry on negroes in first edition of, 151; printings after 1978 have old entry on negroes and priesthood removed, 165; 169; entry on the Covenant of Abraham in Bible dictionary the same, 191

Mormon story, told by missionaries, 75

Mormonism, menace of, 95; marvelous defense of, 102

Mortal man, sees Holy Ghost, 69

Mortal Messiah, 4 volumes, 170; short excerpts from vol. 1., 176; from vol. 2., 177; vol. 3., 178-179; vol. 4., 179-181

Mortimer, William James, of the Church's printing services, 189; took footnote proofs to BRM's home, 193

Moses, climbed mountain, 77; appeared with Elias, 91; translation of, 93; in the similitude of Christ, 174

Motion Picture Studio, BRM at BYU, 202

Mount Hermon, on the slopes of, 178

Mount of transfiguration, 91; Elohim in the cloud, 178

Mount Wellington, 77

Mountain, meeting on top of, 77; ability to move, 98; of the Lord's house, 126

Music, worship through, 133

Mutual Improvement Association general board, 80

Mysteries, are not to BRM, 99; BRM said to leave them alone, 145; 261-66

N

Nature, God of, 207

Negro, statement regarding church position on the, 153; time had arrived for them to get all priesthood blessings, 155; doesn't make a particle of difference what anybody ever said about before revelation, 165

Negroes, in this life denied the priesthood, 151; are children of God, 152; statements in our literature about, 164

Nelson, Elder Russell M., witnessed the Spirit inspiring BRM, 122

Nephi, appearance of the Spirit of the Lord to, 68; climbed mountain, 77

Nephite, Vision of Mark Vest, 28

Nephites, who maintained membership, 182; were righteous, 183; darkness among, 207

Nepotism in councils of the Church, 52

Neutrals in preexistence, 151

New England, Oscar McConkie Jr., serving mission in, 29

New Era, article by BRM, 68

New Jerusalem, to be built in Jackson County, 183

New LDS scriptures, 188-200; vast amount of work on, 188; needed to be correct, 189; story behind is fascinating, 189-90; published in 1979, 189

New Testament Commentary, See *Doctrinal New Testament Commentary*

New Testament, works on and study of, 89; commentaries prepared by scholars, 90; accounts of transfiguration, 91; contains more revealed truth about Son of God than all other scriptures, 175; four Gospels contain more revealed truth, 175

New Witness for the Articles of Faith, a masterwork, 86; delivered to publisher shortly after his passing, 94; precious content, 215

with BRM, 112

Pearl Harbor, 45

Pearl of Great Price, Boyd K. Packer read from the, 156; textual changes in, 190; all JST changes are scripture and true as if they were in the, 196

Peleg, continents divided in days of, 183

Pentecost, Day of, 159; Pentecostal spirit, 161

Perfect knowledge, gained by faith, 96; BRM has that Jesus Christ is the Son of the living God, 121

Perfection and righteousness, 278

Perry, Elder L. Tom, told humorous story about BRM, 128

Personal revelation, 117; President Kimball and each of the brethren had, 160

Perth, Australia, mission conferences in, 75; district conference in, 79; BRM flew to monthly, 80

Pestilence, shall cover the earth, 182

Peter, 124; walked on water, 177

Peter, James and John, 91; confer priesthood, 93; conferred the keys of the kingdom with sealing powers, 178; ordained Joseph Smith and Oliver Cowdery before Church was organized, 186

Petersen, Mark E., BRM worked with, 45; studied his own copy of *Mormon Doctrine*, 63; extraordinary man, 64; pointed out errors in doctrine not in harmony, 71; in South America on assignment, 163; cuts off ear of Malchus, 224

Petty wrangling about semantics, 138

Pharisees, 179

Phelps, W. W., epistle of, 336

Philippines, McConkies and Bensons visit, 57

Philosophical reasoning and syllogisms, 330

Philosophies of men, hook of the, 136;

cast aside the, 209; some in the Book of Mormon are quite deep, 330

Piano, playing by James McConkie, 27; concert pianist, 31

Pilate, 206, 225

Plan of Salvation, without knowledge of, 90; some try to make it revolve around some field or particular interest, 145; the true plan, 146-47; those who seek Christ first need knowledge of, 172

Plural Marriage, George entered into, 23; 89; cultist practice, 145; are adulterers, 146; Wilford Woodruff wrestled with, 155

Poetry, of BRM, 113, 115

Polio, James Wilson McConkie died of, 31

Politics, Oscar practiced, 25; 391-93

Polygamists, 142

Polygamy, test case, 105

Popular will, simple to act according to, 154

Population growth, curtailing of, 142

Porter, Aldin, called on by BRM, 57

Position on blacks, church pressured to change, 152

Possessed by evil spirit, member of stake, 27

Power of the spirit, General Authorities witness by the, 162; we must be enlightened by, 173

Powerful outpouring of the spirit, 161

Practical religion, BRM lived, 136

Pratt, Orson, recognized doctrinal authority, 62

Pray, to get testimony, 76; Julina Smith prayed and vowed a vow, 118; for further light and knowledge, 145; when dying BRM didn't want anyone to, 211

Prayer, BRM in temple, 120; improper patterns in, 138, 148; proper prayers, 175; given before BRM's death, 213; 288-290

Preaching the gospel, privilege of, 54

Pre-Adamites, 69; there were no, 173

Preexistence, developed talent in, 95; priesthood holders in, 97; spirits in the divine presence, 98; various degrees of valiance, 151; status of negro rests on the foundation of, 151-152; we can only suppose it is on the basis of, 164; and intelligence, 326-38

Pre-mortal, probation, 152; devotion, 164

Presidency, Succession in the, 296-300

President of the Church, declarations by, 62; difference of a book coming from, 68; Harold B. Lee set apart as, 118; BRM received total support of, 119; controls access to Holy of Holies, 133; calls new missionaries, 134; personal revelation came to, 160

Priesthood, power of, 38; authority of, 54; 1978 revelation on, 67; conferral of authority and offices, 88; keys and authority, 91; maybe light of Christ is, 97; keys of the, 98, 124; 1978 revelation on the, 151-167; some of those who fought for blacks to hold did not even believe in, 153; comes as a blessing from God, 154; the time had come, 158; time to extend to blacks, 159; miraculous and marvelous revelation on, 160; blessings of should be extended to worthy men everywhere regardless of lineage, 160; announcement to church of revelation on, 162; changes made in *Mormon Doctrine*, 165; and all its saving ordinances, 169; revelation on the, 178-80, 193, 200; 291-95

Primary, Amelia taught, 105

Prime Minister, Elder Benson and BRM with, 80

Primitive church, 98

Primordial swamp, BRM joked about, 132

Prince Philip of Great Britain, Elders Benson and McConkie with, 80

Private doctrines, there are no, 146

Private letter, in unscrupulous hands, 138

Probationary estate, 127; earth life is, 185

Procreation, began with Adam, 173

Professional anti-Mormons, 145

Progression, eternal, 247-52

Promised Messiah, came off the press in 1978, 170; in the preface, 171; short excerpts from, 172-175

Prophecy, more sure word of, 91; spirit of, 125; BRM's on a temple in Chile, 125; spirit of, 172; 360-69

Prophetic mantle, 117; men who wear are still men, 144

Prophetic utterances, not every word of a prophet is, 144

Prophetic writers, 143

Prophets, authority of priesthood resides with, 54; of the meridian day, 89; in true church, 98; compared, 100; geographical gathering spoken of by, 119; time vindicated, 125; view of old, 138; need interpreter to help us understand, 143; harmonizing the scriptures with the statements of the, 144; doctrines contrary to, 145; Jesus sends among the Jews, 179; philosophy not set forth by, 182; on his right hand and on his left, 184; words spoken by, 205; faithful saints and, 208; 356-9

Protestant scholars, foundation of Bible dictionary prepared by, 190

Public speaker, BRM as, 44

Q

Questions, several thousand, 142

Quickening, spirit enters body at time of, 336

Quorums of seventies, BRM was instructor to, 44; BRM member of the 261st, 45; BRM set apart in, 52; organization of into proper quorums,

200

Quorum of the Twelve, see Council of
Twelve

R

Racial equity, 152

Racist, enemies label church leaders as,
152

Raising the dead, gift of the Spirit, 98

Rallies and demonstrations, on black
issue, 152

Rasmussen, Ellis, on Bible Aids
committee, 189; praises BRM, 197

Realm of spiritual things, 141

Rebellion, in heaven, 151

Recognized doctrinal authorities, those
BRM considered to be, 62

Redd, Lemuel Hardison, granddad to
BRM and Marion G. Romney, 121

Redd, Margaret Vivian, 25; see also
McConkie, Vivian

Redeemer of mankind, 169; Savior and,
210

Redemption, false concept of, 182;
preaching gospel of, 211

Refiner's fire, 152

Regional Representatives, BRM worked
with, 55

Relief Society President, 24; Vivian
McConkie served in, 31; Amelia
was president of, 105; Amelia
taught lessons, 106

Religion, a thing of the Spirit, 142;
position of church on blacks falls
wholly within the category of, 153;
personal participation in, 269

Religious dictatorship, 171

Repent, up to the individuals involved
to, 138

Repentance, condition of, 206;
preaching gospel of, 211

Repetition in teaching, 85; in the
Messiah Series, 171

Replenish, in Bible dictionary and
Mormon Doctrine, 69

Responsibility, to find own answers, 143

Restoration, Oscar McConkie's
testimony of the, 29-30; BRM's
testimony of, 54; one of first things
an investigator is taught, 76; of
scattered Israel, 119; one of BRM's
best talks on, 122; Joseph Smith the
mighty Prophet of the, 196; messag
of the, 197

Resurrection, and marriage, 91;
resurrected persons, 96; Alma on,
144; Jesus' and the burial clothing,
181; living in a resurrected state,
186; made him like his resurrected
Father, 208; truth of the, 208;
Alma's personal views on, 270

Revealed gospel, always the standard of
measure, 102

Revealed religion, foundation of, 138

Revelation, evidence of direct, 52, of
eternity, 77; for the church, 88; in the
church, 122; on blacks holding the
priesthood, 151-167; conferring the
priesthood on blacks must await a,
154; came to President Kimball,
160; truly a revelation from God,
161; of tremendous significance,
163; some would like to think that
Joseph Smith delivered the, 164; on
the priesthood, 193, 200; BRM
defines doctrine of, 205; by the
power of the Holy Ghost, 205-6; and
gifts of the spirit, 267-87

Reverence, demonstrated by obedience,
169

Revolutionary War, 23

Reward, of the faithful, 314-22

Reynolds, Amelia Jane, wife of George
Reynolds, 105

Richards, LeGrand, spiritual experience
of, 154

Riches, and wealth, 397-98

Rigdon, Sidney, 271

Righteous living, 89

Righteousness, faith obtained through,
26

RLDS Bible, 63
RLDS Church, disagreements with, 194
Robbers, in Moab, 25
Roberts, B. H., 334
Rock hunting, hobby of BRM, 111
Romans, wielded Caesar's power, 206; soldiers, 207
Romney, Marion G., assigned to read *Mormon Doctrine*, 63; had a high regard for *Mormon Doctrine*, 63; extraordinary man, 64; experience from his life, 70-71; his report, 71-72; BRM relates story to, 102; chosen to be second counselor in First Presidency, 118; discussion with BRM, 121
ROTC, BRM joined, 45
Rough frontier life, Oscar wintessed, 25

S

Sadducees, and other worldly and ungodly people, 92
Sahara, this planet like one speck of dust over the, 173
Saints, finest people in the world, 59
Salina canyon, BRM rock hunting in, 111
Salt Lake City, BRM moves to, 35; BRM assistant attorney at, 44; Fort Douglas at, 45; BRM visits for conference, from Australian mission, 73; telegram from, 78; McConkies return to, 81; servants who preside over his kingdom from, 183
Salt Lake City Mission Home, 38
Salt Lake City prosecutor, BRM was, 44
Salt Lake Endowment House, 23
Salt Lake Tabernacle, BRM's funeral held in, 213
Salt Lake Temple, BRM & Amelia married in, 43; George Albert Smith sets BRM apart in, 52; BRM and Amelia overlook, 73; dagte BRM married Amelia in, 107; meeting in

upper room of, 154; dedicated by Wilford Woodruff, 155; together in an upper room of the, 158; First Presidency and Council of Twelve meet in every Thursday, 211
Salvation, truths of, 89; plan of, 90; truth can lead a soul to, 136; basic truths of, 145; doesn't come by simply confessing the Lord, 145-46; priesthood revelation helps make those in spirit world heirs of, 163; need knowledge of plan of, 172; false concept of, 182; eternal plan of, 204; through his atoning blood, 210; is for the whole world, 272; 384-88
San Francisco, BRM and Amelia flew to, 73
San Juan Record, 26
Sanctification, born again, 174; of saints, 175; false concept of, 182
Sanhedrin, incarnate devils of the, 206 Judas connives with, 224
Santiago, Chile, conference in, 108; area conference in, 125
Sarah, sits at her husband's side, 175
Satan, 27, home of, 26; anxious to thwart the purposes of God, 93
Savior, impossible to write true biography of, 170; God's Almighty Son is the, 210
Scholars, of the world, 90
Scholarship, gospel, 261-66
Schooling, in preexistence, 338
Schools, teach principles of socialism, 142
Scotland, ancestors from, 23
Scribes and pharisees, 179
Scriptorian, BRM looks for a, 57; there are few in the church, 89
Scriptural commentaries, BRM not rejecting, 143
Scriptural interpretations, BRM alone responsible for, 62
Scripture, anything his servants say when moved upon by the Holy Ghost, 144; understanding, 172; comes from God

by the power of the Holy Ghost,
173; BRM's last conference address
falls under the definition of, 204;
words of BRM, 205

Scriptures, BRM's unusual knowledge
of, 35; Amelia & BRM studied the,
44; study of, 78; BRM's love for,
85; study of the, 100; were
everything to BRM, 136;
commanded to search the, 143;
something sacred in studying, 144;
BRM understood the, 172; new
edition was one of the three things
that will most help spread gospel,
198; truth of the, 205; we must
search the, 209

Scriptures Publications Committee,
BRM's role with, 69; participating
as a member of, 127; and the Joseph
Smith Transaltion, 188-200; did not
take any action on comma in D&C
89, 190; discussed headings to
scriptures, 192; Bible Aids
committee renamed, 193; footnoting
began, 194; BRM served on for
nearly his entire length of service as
an Apostle, 198; BRM at Motion
Picture Studio to promote project,
202

Sea of Galilee, walking on water, 177

Second Chance theory, 323-25

Second Comforter, 178

Second Coming, ideas of faddists, 145;
revelation on priesthood had to
happen before, 164 revealed
realities relative to his, 168; BRM
searched for and wrote on the, 170;
Jesus shall come again, 172; time
fixed, 181; watch and be ready, 182;
New Jerusalem to be built before
the, 183; view of the, 184; we may
have received all the revelation
needed before the, 284

Sectarian, word used in 2nd edition of
Mormon Doctrine, 67; delusions,
90; commentaries, 93; scholar, 102;

foolish things taught in, 139; biblical
commentaries, 181

Seed of Abraham, 95

Seek the Spirit, mission motto, 78

Sendal, BRM spoke in, 57

Seneca and Albany Districts, 40

Sermons, BRM's in conference, 54;
doctrinal in nature, 64; powerful
baptismal sermon, 79; distinctive
style of BRM, 85; by Joseph
Fielding Smith, 86; delivered by men
who knew the Prophet Joseph, 88;
BRM's deeply spiritual sermon at
funeral, 118; BRM on Christmas,
126; on faith, 127; always instructive
and rewarding, 128; of BRM, 136;
leave anyone uncomfortable?, 137;
on need for members to discern true
doctrines, 141; of Joseph Smith, 143;
on Seven Deadly Heresies, 146;
Wilford Woodruff's last, 155;
BRM's last, 210

Service, value of, 23; Oscar labored in
26; President Smith's life of, 118

Servicemen, Church's program for, 55

Seton, Ernest Thompson, BRM liked to
read, 36

Seven Deadly Heresies, 146

Seventy, see Quorum of Seventy

Sexual immorality, 370-72

Short hair, essential to salvation, 130

Shrine of intellectuality, men worship at
the, 142

Sidereal heavens, 97

Signs of the times, set by individuals,
145; something that had to occur
before the Second Coming, 164

Sin, penalties of, 206; bondage of, 211

Sincere heart, of BRM, 148

Singapore, McConkies and Bensons
visit, 57

Smith, all had the name in the beginning,
38

Smith, Amelia, see McConkie, Amelia

Smith, Ethel, second wife of Joseph
Fielding Smith, 105

Smith, George A., father of John Henry Smith, 177

Smith, George Albert, seriously ill, 27; 124

Smith, Jessie, Joseph Fielding's third wife, 78

Smith, Joseph Jr., birthplace, 38; great ministry, 40; recognized doctrinal authority, 62; you can't argue with a testimony of, 75; restored the gospel, 76; revelation on transfiguration, 91; teachings of, 94; born with scriptural talents, 95; council with the Savior and Heber J. Grant's father, 120; latter-day prophet, 124; BRM preached doctrines from the writings of, 128; sermons and writings of, 143; taught that not every word a prophet speaks is a prophetic utterance, 144; blacks denied the priesthood upheld from the days of, 151; and all succeeding presidents have taught that negroes cannot hold priesthood, 153; some would like to think he came to deliver the revelation, 164; Lord revealed eleven verses of John the Baptist's writings, 176; Elijah appeared to, 183; most quoted by BRM, 186; early editions of Book of Mormon edited by, 190; dictated many corrections of the Bible, 194; his changes in the Bible are true, 195; mighty Prophet of the Restoration, 196; his revelations make salvation available, 275; taught school in preexistence, 338; BRM's teachings about, 349-55

Smith, Joseph Sr., first patriarch of the Church, 177

Smith, Joseph F., visited funeral of his son, 118; 124; BRM owned his wife's old Doctrine & Covenants, 197

Smith, Joseph Fielding, visited BRM's mission, 38-39; recorded in diary he met BRM on mission, 40; lectures Amelia, 42; BRM married the daughter of, 52; recognized doctrinal authority, 62; didn't know about *Mormon Doctrine*, 63; called on phone by President David O. McKay, 64; conversation with David O. McKay reported to Counselors, 65; his *Man, His Origin & Destiny* not an official church publication, 71; visited McConkies in Australia, 78; sermons compiled by BRM, 86; his doctrinal analysis, 86-88; father of Amelia, 105; major influence in BRM's life, 117; his death in the McConkie home, 117-118; BRM read from his patriarchal blessing, 118; 124; son of Joseph F. Smith, 177

Smith, Julina, daughter of Joseph Fielding Smith, 42; BRM spoke of her, 118; BRM owned her copy of the Doctrine & Covenants, 197

Smith, Lewis, son of Joseph Fielding Smith, 42

Smith, Mary Fielding, Amelia reminds of, 106

Smith, Susan, first wife of Oscar McConkie Sr., 23

Snow, Lorenzo, 124

Socialism, schools teach principles of, 142

Solemn Assembly, BRM hears voice of the Lord in, 56; 157

Sommerville, Emma, 23-24

Son of God, BRM wrote more pages on than any other, 170; perfections of the, 175

Son of Man, 81

Son of the living God, 121

Sound Doctrine, book by BRM, 88

Sound doctrine, never so much put together before, 69; gospel study, 148; from scriptures, Joseph Smith and BRM, 187

Sound of rushing wind, not a, 161

South America, BRM traveled through, 59; one apostle in, 158; Mark E. Petersen on assignment in, 163

South Australia, 75

Southern Australian Mission, BRM called to be president of, 73; one of the largest in the church, 74; 260 missionaries laboring in, 75; BRM president of, 78

Southern Baptist preacher, Oscar McConkie sounded like, 28-29

Spare time, BRM had little, 44

Special Witness, 64; BRM and James Talmage called as, 169

Spirit birth, 331

Spirit children of God, 333; we were begotten as, 336

Spirit Christ, 68, 336

Spirit, gifts of the, 267-87

Spirit, male and female, 332

Spirit matter, 329

Spirit of Christ, 96-97

Spirit of God, 142

Spirit of Inspiration, 144; revelation reaffirmed by, 162; frequently influenced progress of committee, 193

Spirit of prophecy, 121; BRM spoke by, 125; only way to understand any Messianic prophecy, 172

Spirit of Revelation, importance of, 78; seemed to be brooding upon the prophet, 156

Spirit of the Lord, identity of, 68; light of Christ, 96; outpouring of the, 125

Spirit of true worship, 158

Spirit offspring, 151

Spirit, pattern of the, 125; BRM never hesitated to speak, when motivated by the, 137

Spirit, voice of, whispered into our minds, 161

Spirit paradise, 208

Spirit, power of the, 158

Spirit prison, 208

Spirit World, Oscar W. McConkie Sr.,

in the, 33; those who reject gospel in mortality but accept in, 96; council in, 120; priesthood revelation changes what goes on in the, 163; Brethren in the Church in the spirit world, 163; Christ departed to, 207; sons and daughters assembled in, 208; of the dead, 211

Spirits, from paradise, 91

Spiritual events in Church history, 41

Spiritual experience, 92-93; must get revelation from the Holy Spirit to have a, 279

Spiritual giant, Oscar W. McConkie Sr., was, 31

Spiritual gifts, 267-287

Spiritual law, 77

Spiritual maturity, BRM's mission added, 40

Spiritual rebirth, happens gradually, 174

Spirituality of women, 181

Spiritually dangerous fad, 138

Spiritually experienced, Presidents Kimball and Benson were most among the Twelve, 161

Spiritually immature, 145

Spiritually unstable, 145

Spirituality, high degree among missionaries, 27; talent of, 98

Spontaneous inspiration, the Lord had given his apostle, 125

Stake Mission, managing director of, 55

Stake Conference, visits by BRM to, 54

Stake M-Men presidency, BRM in, 45

Stake organizations, 75

Standard works, subject study of, 53; BRM undertook a subject study of, 61; studying the, 100; answers to important doctrinal questions found in, 143; are scripture, 144; new editions of LDS, 188-200; new editions one of the great miracles of our time, 188; BRM had to reread to make headings, 191; personal understanding of the, 192; cross-referenced, 193; near-ten-year project to revise, 196; BRM grateful to be part of the work, 198

Strong counsel, in letter, 138

Study, deficiencies in, 89; to achieve high state of gospel scholarship, 143; for further light and knowledge, 145; responsibility to, 146

Stories, BRM told few, 128; BRM didn't tell many, 136

Succession in the Church, 124

Succession in the Presidency, 124; 296-300

Suffer, BRM permitted to, 202

Sunday School, McConkie family discussed at dinner, 38; BRM in superintendency, 44; Amelia taught, 105

Supreme Court, test case, 105

Sure foundation, 136

Sydney Hebersham Stake, 125

Symbolism, in the Garden of Eden, 236-239

T

Tabernacle, Wilford Woodruff gave his last sermon in, 155

Tabernacle choir, 74; BRM read lyrics with, 132

Tahiti, President Kimball wins over governor of, 122

Taiwan, McConkies and Bensons visit, 57

Talent of Spirituality, 98

Talents, men are not born equal in, 95

Talmage, James E., Elder Packer compared BRM to him, 101; one of BRM's most prominent predecessors, 168; BRM not less than, 169; similarity with BRM, 170

Taylor, Elder John H., member of Seventy, 51

Taylor, John, recognized doctrinal authority, 62; 124

Taylor, Russel, asked BRM a question, 186

Teachers, in true church, 98

Teaching, method of repetition, 85; Lord's system of, 144; if ye receive not the Spirit, 169; 261-66

Teachings of the Prophet Joseph Smith, McConkie quoted from, 93

Telestial, earth became, 185

Television relay stations, 77

Temple, Vivian McConkie in, 31; ordinance of washing of feet in, 92; BRM wrestled in spirit in, 120; President lee in most sacred room in, 121; in Santiago, 125; figurative language where they will be built, 126; Spencer Kimball in, 157; time to extend blessings of to blacks, 159; all of the General Authorities present in the, 162; blessing of to every race and color, 178-79; building in Jerusalem, 183; ordinances, 301-4

Temple president, Briton McConkie, 31

Temple work, twisted emphasis on, 145

Ten tribes, location of, 99

Tenth President of the Church, 27

Terrestrial, beings, 95-96; earth changed from to telestial, 185

Terrible tussle, 25

Testimony, 23; powerful testimony of Harold B. Lee, 27; powerful testimony of Oscar McConkie Sr., 29, 33; BRM's of Jesus Christ, 54; account by BRM on strengthening his, 55; bore early in his ministry, 56; of Joseph Smith, 75; must pray to get, 76; BRM's of the Savior, 117; BRM's tender feelings, 121; on revelation, 122; inspired testimony of BRM, 124; song bears powerful, 132; BRM's testimony of Jesus, 170; the bearing of, 178; BRM bears powerful testimony of Jesus Christ, 204; unshakeably firm, 205; one of the most powerful, 210; BRM's final testimony of Christ, 210-11; and allegiance to Jesus Christ, 211

Thailand, McConkies and Bensons visit, 57

Theologians, few in the church, 89

Theology, matters of not within the purview of civil law, 153

Theories of men, 88; doctrinal teachings less obscured by the, 136; Adam-God, 244-46; second chance, 323-25

This is the Place Monument, 121

Thomas, words spoken by, 213

Three Nephites, clarification on time of translation, 192

Time and geologic changes, 183

Tokyo, BRM spoke in, 57

Tone deaf, BRM was virtually, 132

Topical Guide, for the Bible, 193

Tour of California Mission, 26-27

Town marshal searched for by outlaws, 25

Traditions of Indians, 28

Transfiguration, 91; mount of, 178

Translated beings, 91; of Moses, 93; taken up into heaven, 98

True and faithful, President Joseph Fielding Smith was, 118

True believers, 287

True church, name of the, 89; one sign of the, 152; *Jesus the Christ* should be studied by every member of the, 168

True doctrine, 126-149; struggles faced by this teacher of, 136; BRM's commitment to, 137; BRM invited erring teachers and beguiled students to repent, 139; BRM focused on teaching only, 139; need for members to learn how to discern, 141; determined efforts of BRM made to cultivate learning and teaching of, 146

True fellowship, 138

True gospel, miracles a part of, 98

True prinicples, BRM taught, 60

True Religion, 274

Truth, pure, unmixed with error, 136; BRM's concern was declaring, 137; always in harmony with itself, 144

Truth seekers, 146

Truths of salvation, 89

Twelve Apostles, authority of, 88

Typhoid, Oscar had severe case of, 25

U

Unbelievers, of the revelation on the priesthood, 164

Understanding, of gospel truths, 144; scripture, 172

Uniform in opinions, Brethren not always, 63

Unimportant matters, 145

Uninformed outcries, about blacks and priesthood, 153

"Uninspired," word used in 2nd edition of *Mormon Doctrine*, 67; reason, 171

United in effort, the Brethren are, 63

Unity, of the faith, 98; together in the spirit of true worship and with, 158; outpouring of, 159; President Kimball prayed for, 160; among the brethren, 162

Universal flood, 183

Universe, light of Christ fills, 96

University of Michigan, Oscar studied law at, 25; 36

University of Minnesota, James McConkie taught music at, 31

University of Utah (Salt Lake City), Oscar studied at, 25; BRM attended, 37; BRM a freshman at, 42; attended law school at, 43; Bruce completed law degree at, 44

Unspeakable joy, 24

Unscrupulous individuals, letter in hands of, 138

Unstable views, 90

Urim and Thummim, 279

Utah, saints need not gather to, 119

Utah State Agricultural College (Logan)

Oscar studied at, 25
Utah Zion, 119

V

Vain and foolish things, 139
Valiance, 377-80
Value of Service, 23
Veil, Oscar McConkie receives glimpse
    through, 27; doesn't matter which
    side we serve on, 118; Wilford
    Woodruff appearing through, 155;
    gospel powers on both sides of, 178;
    the day it parts and the heavens roll
    together, 181
Vermont, Joseph Smith's birthplace, 38
Vest, Mark Johnson, 27; a Cochapa
    Indian, speaks in vision, 28
Vicarious ordinances, 163
Victoria, headquarters of Southern
    Australian Mission, 74; state of, 75
Vietnam, McConkies and Bensons visit,
    57
Views, prophets have their own, 144
Vineyard, prune the, 81
Violence of Fire, 98
Virgin birth, 339-44
Visions, of Christ Child, 21; of Mark
    Vest before Lamanites, 28;
    television wave band compared to,
    77
Voice, of the Spirit, Oscar has, 26; BRM
    hears voice of the Lord, 56; BRM
    hears voice of God, 122; scriptures
    are, 144; whispered with certainty
    into our minds, 161
Voice, strident and senatorial, Oscar
    had, 26

W

Walking on water, gift of the spirit, 98
Walking, hobby of BRM, 109; on water,
    177
War, shall cover the earth, 182
Wasatch Front, BRM in demand, 44

Washing of feet, 92; a sacred ordinance,
    179
Watch and be ready, 182
Watchman on the tower, 137
Water, Jesus walked on, 177, 327
Waters of baptism, 179
Wave band, radio, compared to visions,
    77
Wealth, and riches, 397-98
Wells, Robert E., present when Amelia
    fainted, 108
Western Australia, 75
Western Central States Mission, BRM
    toured, 56
Wife, Oscar McConkie's treatment of
    his, 29
Wisdom, Oscar prays for, 26; of God,
    154; of the wise, 209
Witness of Christ, Book of Mormon a
    true, 54; most important duty of
    General Authority is to, 56; of the
    Savior, 122
Witnesses, Romney, Petersen and BRM
    were, 64; 88; to the events of the
    1978 revelation on priesthood, 155
Womanhood, noble example of, 106
Women, spirituality of, 181; 389-90
Women's liberation, 142
Wonders of the millennium, 185
Wood, cut and hauled by Oscar, 25
Woodruff, Abraham O., 177
Woodruff, Wilford, 124; seated above the
    organ in the temple, 154; dedicated
    Salt Lake temple, 155; priesthood
    revelation similar to the Manifesto
    issued by, 163
Word of the Lord, is truth, 144
Word of Wisdom, faddist interpretation
    of, 145
Work, in the church, for further light and
    knowledge, 145
Works, views of Paul and James, 144;
    judged according to, 152
World, of Spirits and mortality, 155;
    Redeemer of mankind and of the,
    169

World War II, 46; BRM a veteran of, 53
Worldly men, uninspired nature of, 168
Worlds, created, 96; priesthood and faith
    are the power by which, 97; the
    Father is the Creator of, 337
Worlds without number, 97;
    innumerable unto man, 173
Worship of false gods, 182

Y

Yalecrest ward, 42
Young, Brigham, recognized doctrinal
    authority, 62; history of priesthood
    authority of, 89; 124; taught that
    negroes would eventually get
    priesthood, 152; statements made
    on negroes, 164; had ideas that were
    not the Lord's ideas, 271
Young, Levi Edgar, called to Seventy,
    51
Young, S. Dilworth, relates information
    on BRM, 47; sustained to Seventy,
    47; gives synopsis of Amelia, 105;
    BRM spoke at funeral of, 127;
    BRM blessed S. Dilworth Young
    and his wife, 127; pulled practical
    jokes on BRM, 132
Yuba City, new chapel dedicated in, 55
YWMIA, Amelia taught in, 105

Z

Zion, Australian, 80; around church
    headquarters, 119
Zone leader [president], BRM called as,
    41